CW01371419

Understanding and Helping an Addict
(and keeping your sanity)

Also by this author:

The Alcoholic / Addict Within:
Our Brain, Genetics, Psychology, and the Twelve Steps as Psychotherapy

A Trip Through the 12 Steps
With a Doctor and Therapist

Uplift Your Self-Esteem
A how-to guide to healthy, stable, unconditional self-esteem

These books are available in paperback and eBook versions from amazon.com

Understanding and Helping an Addict

(and keeping your sanity)

Andrew Proulx MD

Copyright © 2021 Dr. Andrew Proulx

and Recovery Folio Publishing

All rights reserved.

Print Edition

ISBN 9798598966839

Contact the author at alcoholism.addiction@gmail.com

or

visit the author's website at

www.alcoholism-addiction-psychology.com

Contents

Introduction ... 1

Section 1 – Understanding an Addict

Chapter 1 – Why Some People Become Addicted and Some Don't ... 11
Chapter 2 – Why Do They Call Addiction a Disease? ... 26
Chapter 3 – Addictive Substances 101 ... 33
Chapter 4 – The Core Symptoms and Behaviors of Addiction ... 69
Chapter 5 – The Addicted Brain ... 97
Chapter 6 – The Addicted Mind ... 120
Chapter 7 – The Link Between Addiction and Mental Illness ... 133

Section 2 – Helping an Addict

Chapter 8 – How to Talk to and Connect with a Loved One in Addiction ... 147
Chapter 9 – How to Help a Loved One Become Ready and Willing to Accept Help ... 165
Chapter 10 – What Happens in Addiction Treatment, and How You Can Help ... 185
Chapter 11 – Recovery and Relapse Prevention, and How You Can Help ... 209

Section 3 – Staying Healthy and Sane While Helping an Addict

Chapter 12 – Challenging and Changing Your Attitude ... 249
Chapter 13 – Boundaries ... 268
Chapter 14 – Recovering Your Peace of Mind and Happiness ... 290
Appendix – A Primer on Meditation ... 336

Works Cited and Consulted ... 353

Disclaimer: The information in this book is not intended to be medical advice. Anyone who thinks they may have substance use or any other mental health disorder should consult a licensed health practitioner.

Introduction

Have you ever seen one of those Chinese finger traps? The contraption is a little stretchy tube that slides over both index fingers like a sleeve, and the challenge is to remove it. Your inclination is to pull your fingers away from each other so it'll slide off, but instead... pulling just tightens it. Your natural instinct makes you pull harder, but the harder you pull, the harder the wretched device clenches. It even starts to hurt. However, if you just let go of your compulsion to pull harder, and instead relax your muscles and bring your fingertips back together, the tension releases and the device just pops off your fingers. I think the Chinese intended a life lesson in there somewhere, besides sharpening our swearword repertoire. Sometimes obeying our instinct to work harder and harder is the wrong way to solve a problem. Some problems are best solved by going against our instincts. Helping an addict is like that.

If asked what the greatest mistake that families and friends make when trying to help an addict loved one, I would unhesitatingly say this: *they go at the problem too hard, push too hard, and become too involved*. They definitely do it out of boundless love and caring, but they're doing it wrong. Our instinct is to try harder when the solution to a problem eludes us, and logic tells us that throwing ourselves harder at the problem and pushing harder will help us beat it. Well, addiction isn't a logical problem. When it comes to addiction, it's much better to act smart rather than act harder. This is one time that more brains are required, and less brawn.

The problem with using our brain to help an addict is that addiction doesn't make any sense. The human brain can't wrap itself around addiction because addiction defies logic and understanding. After all, why would anyone keep doing something that's clearly destroying everything that's important to them, *and* is making them miserable? *Why don't they just stop???*

Well, the truth is that addiction makes a lot of sense. Once you understand the specific effects of repeated substance use on the brain, all the bizarre thought processes and the maddening behaviors suddenly make perfect sense. Once we understand addiction, we can use that knowledge to take an approach to helping an addict that's a lot smarter and more effective, and requires much less effort, frustration, and personal sacrifice. Kind of like letting go of the tension and bringing our fingers together to escape from a Chinese finger trap.

*

I'm going to presume to make a couple of assumptions here... about you. Since you're reading my book, I'm guessing that someone else's substance use has created chaos in your life, and it has been affecting your physical, mental, and emotional health, as well as your overall well-being, finances, and ability to function properly. I'm going to further guess that someone else's substance use is robbing you of your happiness and peace of mind, causing you to be haunted by guilt, worry, fear, and maybe even depression and anxiety. I'll also venture that you've had a lot of sleepless nights and worry-filled days. Maybe you even blame yourself for someone else's substance use and all the problems it's causing, and maybe you feel guilt because you believe you somehow caused the problem or should've been able to stop it.

By the time you bought this book you've probably tried everything. You've probably argued, threatened, and given ultimatums. You've tried a soft approach and a hard approach. You've probably pleaded, reasoned, negotiated, and maybe even bribed. You've probably explained how dangerous, destructive, and hurtful the substance use has become, a thousand times over. But nothing seems to work. I'll bet there's tension, anger, and frustration in both directions that forms a palpable barrier between you and your addict loved one. I'll bet this tension is spilling over and affecting your relationships with other family members, people at work, and friends.

If my assumptions are correct, then you've probably discovered on your own one of the unfortunate truths about addiction: that it's a family disease. It almost never just affects one individual in isolation. Some estimates suggest that for every addict there are five non-addicts whose lives are deeply affected by the addict's substance use and related behaviors. That's why this book is *not* just about helping addicts to beat addiction, it's also about helping those affected by the addict to restore some sanity and order to their household, their relationships, and their life. Believe it or not, by separating yourself from the addict's circle of chaos, you're not only helping yourself, but you'll be much more effective at helping the addict.

I'll further guess that you're perplexed by how your normally loving, thoughtful, and intelligent loved one could have changed so much, and become so seemingly unthinking, selfish, angry, hateful, and uncaring. How can your loved one throw everything away for substance use? Of course, the big question: *if the addict is miserable and unhappy, and losing everything important in life, why don't they just stop???*

Well, our shared goal here as we set out together on this guided tour of addiction is to find the way to move someone who's important to you from problem substance use to an enduring recovery that includes healing and a return to good health and function. However, our goal is also to restore some order and sanity to you, your home, and anyone else whose life has been affected by someone else's substance use. We'll discuss how you can – and must – learn to find and protect your happiness and peace of mind, regardless of what the addict in your life is doing. We'll discuss how you can – and must – stop allowing the addict in your life to determine whether or not you're happy today and having a good day.

Surrendering power over your happiness and peace of mind to an addict is just a bad idea, yet in my work in addictions I see lots of good people do exactly that. It turns people into frustrated, nervous wrecks, and it does nothing to help the addict become ready and willing to accept help and get on with recovery. Ironically, most of the people I see who're giving every ounce of themselves to helping an addict are actually enabling the substance use, so they're worsening the problem. They're just like the person furiously trying to pull their finger out of the Chinese finger trap – their instincts tell them to go harder and harder, but they're only making the problem worse.

Releasing the pressure doesn't mean you stop caring, or loving, or that you stop wanting to do everything in your power to help your loved one. Rather, as we wind our way through our exploration of addiction together, you'll learn how to help your addict loved one in a way that's smart, disease-oriented, and supported by research. You'll learn how to use your newfound knowledge of addiction to target the specific barriers that hold addicts back from recovery, and how to help them along in the psychological process that addicts undergo as they finally become ready and willing to accept the help they need. You'll learn how to stop losing control of situations and getting sucked into pointless arguments, and how to communicate with a know-it-all addict. Finally, we'll talk about how to support your addict loved one's recovery in a way that isn't perceived as intrusive or nagging, and actually improves the recovering addict's chances of success.

Perhaps most importantly, we'll talk about how to extricate yourself from the circle of chaos that surrounds every addict. By removing yourself from the chaos, you stop participating in the addiction and enabling the substance use, and you can finally work on getting back your sanity. We'll talk about how you can find healing and recovery from the ravages of living through someone else's substance use. Just like addicts need healing and recovery from the effects of addiction, so too do the people whose life, health, and sanity have been ravaged by the effects of someone else's addiction. The time to stop the insanity in your life and begin healing is now, regardless of whether your loved one is still using and drinking, in recovery, or gone from your life.

You may have noticed that this book is divided into three sections; the first two are about understanding and helping an addict, and the last is about regaining your health and sanity. By putting the section about your recovery from someone else's addiction last, I'm not saying that the addict is more important than you, not at all. Quite the opposite; people who're happy, healthy, and at peace and who live outside the addict's circle of chaos are much better able to help the addict. So, if anything, the section about your health and happiness should've come first. However, I put it last because the most important aspects of regaining your sanity – changing your attitude (about addiction, addicts, and your role in helping an addict), putting in place boundaries, and asserting loving detachment – all require that you have a solid understanding of addiction. So, I had no choice but to put the section about you last. Of course, you can skip ahead and read the last section of the book first, but it'll make much more sense once you've read the rest of the book.

*

To find a solution to any problem you must first understand the problem. Nowhere is that more true than when the problem is that someone important to you is having the life sucked out of them by compulsive substance use. As anyone who has faced a loved one in addiction knows, it's a really tough thing to try to understand. But understanding the problem seems impossible: everything about addiction is so illogical and counterintuitive. Addiction is so irrational that even addicts don't understand it. I'm a doctor, and I certainly didn't understand what was happening to me when I was in active addiction. However, once you understand the how and why of addiction it all becomes clear, and a sound pathway to helping your loved one opens up.

It can be the hardest thing in the world to watch – a loved one self-destructing with substance use. Everything they once cared about no longer seems to matter: their kids, relationships, job, money, health… it's all being squandered as the substance use worsens and consumes more time, money and attention. *Why don't they care about anyone or anything anymore?*

Addiction is about getting high and feeling good, right? Everybody knows that. Well, while addiction may begin that way for some people (a minority of people with addiction, actually), it doesn't last long. Because of adjustments made by the brain to compensate for the substance use, tolerance develops and before too long there's little or no high. Addicts reach a point where the substance use ceases being fun, and in fact makes them miserable. Besides, if addiction was about enjoying being high, why doesn't everybody who tries drugs or alcohol become addicted to the high? Obviously, there's something else that keeps addicts going in their substance use despite all the costs… *but what is it?*

When a loved one gets dragged downward into addiction, their whole personality seems to change. Suddenly, you can't reason with them, and stuff that once really mattered to them doesn't seem to matter anymore. They begin doing things that they ordinarily would never do, like blowing off their kids, skipping work and other responsibilities, and maybe even stealing or committing other crimes. They lie all the time and sneak around. They're not like that, but here they are, doing it. *Why is their personality so different? Can we ever get our loved one back to their old self again?*

When a loved one caught in compulsive substance use needs help, it's usually pretty obvious. Addicts typically try over and over again to stop or control their substance use on their own, in their own way, but fail every time. Sometimes they'll make it for a few days or even a few weeks, but then end up right back at it. They keep promising they'll stop, and they really seem to mean it. But they fail every time. *Why do they keep promising to stop when it's obvious they can't? Why can't they see that they need help?* They seem to really want to stop the substance use – maybe even desperately – *so why do they keep refusing help?*

Addiction is a matter of choice, right? A matter of willpower, morality, and making the right choices. Well, if that's the case, why is it that so many people with lots of willpower, who've done incredible things in life, who're moral and upstanding members of society, and who usually make smart decisions become addicted? Is addiction really related to willpower, morality, and intellect? Will helping addicts to increase their willpower, morals, and ability to think help them beat addiction?

Addiction usually only happens to people who had a bad upbringing, or who were abused, or who live in bad neighborhoods, right? Or to people who're depressed, or whose life isn't going well? Well, sure, but at the same time many people who're doing very well in life, had a great upbringing and come from good families, and who don't suffer from any mental health problems also develop addiction. Lots of addicts had great jobs, a lovely family, a beautiful home, and no great problems in life. *How did they end up as addicts?*

It's well known that addiction is genetic, but why is it that many people who develop addiction have no family history of addiction? And, why is it that many people with lots of addiction in the family are able to go through life and use alcohol and even drugs without becoming addicted?

These are all great questions that I hear from families all the time, and these questions show that addiction doesn't make sense. They call addiction the disease of paradoxes, and with good reason. When I was in active addiction, I was a trained physician and psychotherapist, but I couldn't understand my own behaviors, why my mind was working (or not working) the way it was, and why I couldn't stop the insanity of my addiction. So don't worry if you don't understand your addict loved one's behaviors; you're in good company.

One of the most frustrating aspects of watching an addict loved one struggling as their life spirals downward is that it seems impossible to help them. They don't seem to want to be helped, and even get defensive and aggressive when we try to talk to them about their substance use. *How do we even help them?* Should we help them by giving them money to pay their rent and buy groceries, or should we cut them off unless they get help? Should they be coddled, or should they be given some tough love? Sadly, in my work with people in addiction, I see lots of family and friends who're doing their utmost to help the addict in their life, but they make big mistakes that cause more harm than good. They do so, not out of bad intentions – in fact they would do anything to help the addict – but because they really don't know what to do. They want to help, but they just don't know how. In most cases, they're trying too hard, pushing too hard. They're trying to use more and more muscle and force to get free from the Chinese finger trap.

Well, fortunately there's a lot we can do to help loved ones and move them toward a readiness to accept the help they need, all without enabling and worsening the substance use, and without driving ourselves crazy in the process. The first step is to understand addiction by answering all the questions that we just asked over the previous few pages. Once you understand the who, why, and how of addiction, you can understand the addict, what's making them think and behave the way they are, and how you can help get back the healthy loved one you once knew.

*

There are a couple of fundamental truths about addiction that'll become evident as you read this book, but I'd like to put them out there now, because they're important to know from the beginning. The first is that every person – I repeat, *every person* – is capable of life-long recovery from addiction. In fact, many are happier and better able to function in life after addiction than they were before. That's because during treatment they learn skills for coping with stress and adversity in a healthy and productive way, and they have a chance to confront and deal with issues that may have plagued them for a long time (such as mental health symptoms, or emotional pain from past traumas, for example). No matter how badly addicted individuals are, how many or what kinds of drugs they've been using, how long they've been using drugs or alcohol, how badly they've messed up their life, and how messed up they seem to be in the head, every single individual is capable of a lasting abstinent recovery.

Another truth is that addiction is a matter of biology, not an issue of morality, weakness of character, or lack of willpower. In fact, as we'll discuss in chapter 2, addiction is widely accepted to be a disease, with demonstrable brain pathology that occurs in susceptible individuals when exposed to addictive substances. The reasons for the disease model of addiction are compelling, and we'll see how addiction begins and behaves very much like other diseases, such as viral infections, diabetes, or even cancer. Although people in active addiction behave in a way that makes them appear like weak-willed, compulsive liars with no moral boundaries, these behaviors are effects of a brain disease, not a reflection of the person, and they all fall under the umbrella of typical symptoms of the disease of addiction. As Dr. Alan Leshner, the former director of the U.S. National Institutes of Health, once put it: *once addicted, the individual has moved into a different state of being*. This is why otherwise good, moral, and strong individuals appear completely transformed when they're struck down by addiction, and why they can return to their good old selves again after proper addiction treatment.

Another truth is that addiction treatment isn't about developing willpower to "say not to drugs," nor is recovery from addiction simply about the absence of using drugs or alcohol. Rather, recovery requires identifying and addressing the underlying causes of each individual's addiction, as well as healing from the effects of the addiction. Without that necessary part, people who're abstinent from substance use will still have the psychological dysfunction and pain that underpins obsessive substance use, and the risk of relapse is high.

When you finish reading this book, your knowledge about addiction and how to help people with addiction will be deeper than the vast majority of doctors and psychologists…. far deeper. I went to medical school in the 1990's, but I've been involved in medical education since, and I can tell you this: medical professionals have very little training in addiction. Indeed, before I went through addiction myself and began learning about addiction when I was in recovery, I didn't understand it myself. As a practicing doctor I had always seen people with addictions as bad people who wake up every day and make bad decisions. Too, although I had seen many patients who were engaged in regular substance use, I had no idea whatsoever what their lives were like. Addicts are experts at hiding their problems and putting on airs as if all's well, but the average individual would be shocked at how these people live. Experiencing it myself, and my work with addicts since then has been a real eye-opener. As we work through the root nature of addiction together, you'll not only get a behind-the-scenes look at the lives of addicts – including possibly the one living right under your nose – but you'll also get a look at what goes on inside their head and why they continue driving themselves to destruction with their obsessive substance use, even long after it's no longer enjoyable or fun.

I've found addiction to be such a fascinating area of discovery that I've focused my entire professional and academic career on addiction research, teaching, and writing. I think you, too, will find it interesting as we explore the bizarre and unique effects of addictive substances on the human brain and mind. Certainly, you'll find a new understanding of your addicted loved one and new ways to bond with them.

*

Before we get started, I need to take care of a couple of stylistic notes. The English language has a real problem right now with pronouns – the words we use to replace proper nouns. English language pronouns indicate the gender of the person being talked about, so we often must use "she/he" to ensure that no one is offended or left out when we talk about someone whose gender isn't identified. For example: *when your loved one goes to the store,* **she/he** *should bring money*. As awkward as it is to use the she/he combo throughout a manuscript, we've now arrived at the point in societal development where we also need a gender-neutral third person pronoun so as to include everyone and not offend, but – alas – the English language doesn't have such a word. After consulting with literary experts at two universities, I've decided to get around this problem by using the words "they" and "them" and "theirs." For example: *when your loved one goes to the store,* **they** *should bring money*. Although this use of plural pronouns to refer to a single person is traditionally grammatically incorrect, a number of key writing authorities (such as the Chicago Manual of Style, and the Associated Press) now consider "they" as a singular third-person pronoun for exactly the same reasons that I will use it.

Another stylistic note has to do with the term "addiction." The word "addiction" isn't a proper medical term. Until 2013, the accepted medical terminology for addiction was *substance dependence* and *substance abuse*. Since 2013 it has been *substance use disorder (SUD)*. However, I prefer to use the term "addiction." It's unequivocal, to the point, and understood by everybody. The medical community keeps changing their terminology, but we always understand the word addiction.

Different types of drugs have differing characteristics, but they all have the same end effect when it comes to addiction. This includes alcohol, which is just another type of addictive drug. Although people with alcoholism may be offended at being referred to as "addicts," they are, after all, addicted to the drug known as alcohol. I've decided to use the word "addiction" to refer to any kind of substance use disorder regardless of the substance, including alcohol. I hope that nobody is offended.

I also use the word "addict" to refer to people with addiction. I'm aware that some people may see that term as being derogatory, and that by referring to persons who suffer from addiction as addicts I may sound like I'm defining them by their disease. However, I'm more comfortable with that term than most people may be; it's been years since the last time I tasted alcohol or took a drug, but I still refer to myself as an addict. At the risk of offending some, I've decided to refer to persons with addiction as addicts in this book, if for nothing else than just for expediency. It's not intended to be derogatory or defining, so I hope people take it in the intended context.

*

I loathe long introductions, but before we get on with what we're here for, I thought it appropriate to give a quick bit of background about me and how I came to write this book. I've been on both sides of addiction. I grew up in a home under the dark cloud of a raging alcoholic father. I spent my entire childhood afraid, worried, and confused about my father's behaviors, and questioning what was wrong with me that my father would treat me the way he did. I watched helplessly as my mother suffered from my father's alcoholic behaviors. It took me years as an adult to overcome the psychological hang-ups that lived in my head after the experience. Then, I became *that* guy, as I became addicted to alcohol and opioids later in adulthood, and subjected my own loved ones to the same worry, turmoil, frustration, and unkind behaviors that my family had suffered under my father.

Despite having practiced as a medical doctor and psychotherapist for fifteen years, when I went through addiction I couldn't understand what was making me behave the way I was, like a totally different person I couldn't even recognize. I hated who I was and what I was doing, but I couldn't stop myself. I was miserable from my substance use and I was losing everything, but I couldn't understand why I couldn't just stop. I tried earnestly over and over again to stop my drinking and using, but I just couldn't seem to do it.

When I finally accepted the help I needed and came to recovery, I needed to know what happened to me, why I behaved the way I did, why I threw all my priorities out the window and chose substance use over everything else, and why I couldn't stop when I desperately wanted and needed to. I was taking time off work, so I embarked on a quest to find out what happened to me. So began my foray into understanding addiction.

Since then, I've re-oriented my career so that it's focused on addiction. I'm involved in addiction research, educating the lay public as well as health care professionals about addiction, and writing about addiction. This is my third book on the subject of addiction and recovery. I've been so taken by my interest in this odd but devastating disease that I even went back to school to do my PhD in Addiction Psychology. Nevertheless, I learn the most from the addicts and their families that I encounter in my work.

*

Lastly – before we get started – I want to make sure that it's understood that I'm not trying to sugar-coat the deadly seriousness of addiction, and that I'm not offering any kind of assurance that things will turn out well for your addict loved one. Addiction is a serious, lethal disease with many victims. Although everyone is capable of recovery with the right help and the right mindset, not everyone makes it before tragedy befalls them. The trajectory of addiction is sobering. Addicts may perish from an overdose or from substance use-related consequences, or they may be chronically impaired for the rest of their life, going in and out of treatment and recovery, or they may be immensely successful at sobriety and recovery and live out a healthy and happy life. My goal here is to help you and your loved one to triumph over addiction, as millions of people before you have done.

With that in mind, let's get to it.

Section One – Understanding an Addict

1

Why Some People Become Addicted and Some Don't

If you know someone who tries to drown their sorrows, you might tell them sorrows know how to swim.

– Ann Landers

Nobody grows up dreaming of one day becoming addicted to drugs or alcohol, and nobody ever wakes up one day and decides: *today my goal is to become an addict.* So, addiction isn't something that occurs by design. There appears to be a lot more to addiction than simply being drawn to the euphoric and relaxing effects of substance use. After all, many people find the "high" from drugs and alcohol enjoyable in some way, but not everyone becomes addicted. So, there's a bit of a mystery there: *why do some people become addicted when they take drugs or alcohol, while most do not?*

Most people can walk away from using drugs or alcohol once they realize that it's becoming a problem for them. But some don't, even when they begin losing things that are very important to them and they can see that they're going downhill. So, what's the difference between the individual who walks away from substance use when it becomes a problem and the one who doesn't... or can't?

Further confounding our ability to predict who will become addicted is the fact that not everyone fits the picture of the standard risk factors. Addiction to drugs or alcohol doesn't just affect people who're vulnerable or down on their luck. There are well-defined risk factors, but no one is immune; many victims of addiction have few or no risk factors. Thus, the questions: *why do some people become addicted when they use drugs or alcohol and some don't? Is there any way we can know who will become addicted when they're exposed to alcohol or drugs? Could I have foreseen my loved one's addiction?*

We're going to answer those questions in this chapter.

*

People develop addiction based on two overall factors: 1) genetics, and 2) environmental factors. Genetics are our DNA, the material within the nuclei of our cells that's the blueprint for many of our physical and mental characteristics, such as how tall we are, the color of our eyes, and so on. Environmental factors are all those things that we're exposed to after birth that shape who and what we are. Examples of environmental factors are the quality of our nutrition, the quality of the parenting we get as children, our education, and the influence of our friends.

Scientists sometimes refer to our genetics as our "nature" – because it's embedded within us and determines what we'll be like – and our environment as "nurture" – because it's how our experiences in the world and in society shape who we become. So, the question is: *how much of addiction is nature and how much is nurture?*

Well, we know the answer to that question quite well, thanks to research based on data collected from tens of thousands of people with addiction (specifically from the huge annual U.S. National Survey on Drug Use and Health, or NSDUH). It turns out that addiction is about half due to nature and half due to nurture. The data show that the influence of the two factors differs from person to person, but whether or not we'll become addicted when exposed to addictive substances is 40-60% genetic, and 40-60% environmentally determined. The reason that there's so much of a range in the statistics is because it varies from person to person, and every person's specific circumstances are different. For example, one person who has very little genetic predisposition to addiction may become addicted when exposed to addictive substances if they're going through a very stressful time in life and can't cope with the stress, so they turn to substance use to "help them through the stress." On the other hand, an individual who has a high genetic predisposition to addiction may never develop substance use problems if they're subjected to lower levels of stress, or learns early in life how to use effective healthy coping mechanisms for stress.

The genetic and environmental determinants of addiction are collectively referred to as the risk factors for addiction. Although there are well-defined risk factors for developing addiction, I've met many people with all the risk factors and a lot of troubles and tribulations in life, but who've never become addicted when they drank alcohol or tried drugs. Conversely, I've met many people who have few or no risk factors and who have a "perfect" life, but who fall hard into addiction. The lesson there: addiction can happen to anyone. Every person is an individual entity with their own genetic makeup, life situation, and life history; however, no one is immune to addiction.

Even though the risk factors for addiction don't definitively define who will or will not become addicted when they're exposed to addictive substances, they do serve a couple of practical purposes. First of all, they give us an idea of people who should be watched carefully for early signs of problem substance use, especially in times of stress. As well, knowing the risk factors for addiction helps us to try to reduce the addiction rate by addressing risk factors that are modifiable. Given how bad the addiction problem has become, we need every advantage we can get in preventing and treating problem substance use.

For example, if a certain individual is going through a particularly stressful time in their life, it may be wise to identify any other risk factors they may have for addiction. If they're talking to their doctor about their stress levels, the doctor may screen them for depression or anxiety symptoms, both of which are major modifiable risk factors for addiction. Likewise, family members who're knowledgeable about addiction may also be aware of the individual's risk factors for addiction and keep a watch out for symptoms of early addiction, such as social isolation, or secretiveness. The earlier problem substance use is detected the easier it is to intervene and prevent disaster.

Let's now talk about each of the major genetic and environmental risk factors for addiction, and look at how they play a role in determining an individual's reaction to addictive substances.

*

Family history of addiction. This risk factor plays out in two ways: 1) the genetics inherited from family members (i.e. "nature"), and 2) the influence of the family on the individual, especially during childhood and adolescent development (i.e. "nurture").

Our DNA is organized into functional units known as genes. Each gene is responsible for a very specific aspect of our makeup, and together all our genes represent the blueprint for much of who we are. In many cases a single "bad" gene can cause a disease, such as cystic fibrosis or sickle cell anemia. However, most diseases and disorders are more complex and involve many different genes that together determine a particular individual's level of risk of developing the disease. This is the case with addiction, where there's no single "addiction gene" that determines if someone will become addicted when exposed to addictive substances. Rather, there are many genes (probably in the hundreds) that have varying degrees of influence over an individual's likelihood of one day developing addiction.

Even if an individual has a parent with many "addiction genes," that doesn't necessarily mean that the individual also carries the same gene.

Human reproduction has built-in processes that ensure that there's a huge variety in the genetics between people and to make sure that we're not exactly like our parents. Our own genetic profile is a mixture between our two parents' genetic profiles, and even then there are other natural processes that are built into reproduction to ensure variability. So, when parents' DNA is mixed together during reproduction, the child's DNA will be a random mixture of both parents' DNA (through a process known as *homologous recombination*, for you science nerds). There are about 70,368,744,177,664 possible combinations that can result from the DNA of two parents, which is trillions of times more combinations than there are people who have ever lived. That's why no two people are exactly alike (except, of course, identical twins, who have the same DNA), and why brothers and sisters are not totally like each other, and why we're not exactly like our parents.

As if this wasn't enough possible combinations of DNA in parents' offspring, there's more biodiversity introduced through a process known as *genetic crossing-over*. When a copy of one parent's DNA is combined with a copy of the other parent's DNA, some sections of DNA stick together and cross over from one parent's copy to the other, further introducing billions of other genetic possibilities. Then, to top it off, genetic mutations also occur during reproduction and the formation of the baby, and these mutations can result in further changes to the offspring's genetic profile. The end result of these DNA processes that occur during reproduction is that none of us is a genetic copy of either of our parents, so just because one parent has a particular "addiction gene" doesn't necessarily mean the child will as well.

A lot of people in recovery from addiction carry a lot of guilt because they believe they have an "addiction gene" and that they've passed the gene on to their kids, thereby condemning them to a future of problem substance use. However, as we've just discussed, there are many different addiction-related genes, and these are not necessarily passed on to offspring due to the many mechanisms of genetic variability that are built into reproduction. Besides, there's no single "addiction gene" that's a home-run guarantee of developing problem substance use. As such, I always reassure people about their concerns. The truth is that there's no way to know for sure what – if any – addiction-related genes that an individual carries. Although we have lab tests that map out our genetic profile, these are expensive and not in routine use, and we're still woefully lacking in knowledge about the genetics of addiction.

I always explain to parents that their guilt about possibly passing "addiction genes" on to their kids is misplaced. Even if they did pass a few genes on, they can more than make up for it with their knowledge of addiction. They can make sure that they provide a safe and caring environment for their kids, and do their best to reduce or eliminate environmental risk factors for addiction. As well, their own experience with addiction will better equip them to talk to their kids about substance use, and to raise red flags when problems may be arising. As such, they can make good on any possible "nature" risks by optimizing the "nurture" part of addiction risk. By reading the information in this book, you too will have an enhanced ability to talk to your children and other loved ones about addiction, and recognize and address problems if they were to arise.

The other aspect of family history of addiction as a risk factor for developing substance use problems is the nurture aspect, the environmental influences on addiction risk. Many of these environmental factors occur within the family unit, thus the influence of family history of addiction. The family's influence on a particular individual is strongest during the first ten or twelve years of life, at which point the outside environment – such as friends and school – becomes increasingly more important.

A history of addiction in the parents can be protective, or a negative risk factor. If the parents are knowledgeable about addiction, have good parenting skills, and are attentive to their children's needs, they may exert a very positive influence over their children with regards to substance use. However, when children grow up in a neglectful, abusive, chaotic home, their risk for developing addiction (and other mental health problems) jumps significantly. Having parents who're in active addiction can be an absolute disaster for the children. I know one woman whose life-long struggle with addiction began when she was smoking crack cocaine with her mother in her home at age nine.

Data from the NSDUH show that about one in eight children in the U.S. live in a household with at least one parent with a substance use disorder. Certainly, not all children who live in a household with a substance-using parent will be subjected to neglect or abuse. However, they are at higher risk of maltreatment and involvement of child protective services than are other kids. As we'll see as we progress through our discussion about addiction, people in active addiction lose interest and even stop caring about their responsibilities and obligations, including childcare. As well, the addicted mind is usually ridden with anger, resentment, blamefulness of others, and frustration, a perfect recipe for abuse. Sometimes even previously excellent parents can become neglectful and even abusive when in active addiction.

Addiction is expensive, and drains resources. People in active addiction often lose their job, income, and health benefits before too long (if they had these to begin with), and quickly rip through their financial savings and other resources. Obtaining their drink or drug takes priority over everything else, and money intended for rent, groceries, and utilities gets diverted to substance use. The result can be raising a child in poverty, poor nutrition, and squalor.

As well, more than half of people with addiction also have a mental health disorder, which may further impair their parenting skills. Substance use worsens mental illness symptoms and prevents otherwise effective medications from working properly. This, too, may affect the home environment in which children and adolescents spend their formative years.

The overall result is that children with at least one substance-using parent are at higher risk of developing mental and behavioral disorders and addiction at some point in their life. Addiction is truly a family disease, as its effects extend well beyond the addict; this is most especially seen in its impact on the children who're caught up in the chaos of a parent's addiction. However, even in the absence of a substance-using parent, there are many risk factors in the home that predispose a child to later developing addiction. These risk factors often occur together in clusters and are cumulative. We'll talk about these childhood factors next.

Childhood factors. Besides family history, other childhood factors are known to predispose to the later development of problem substance use. These are:

- Early exposure to addictive substances – being around parents and family members, or peers who use drugs or alcohol or who break the law can increase children's risk of future substance use,
- Early use – the earlier in life that individuals first try drugs or alcohol, the more likely they are to develop addiction,
- Social exclusion, poor social skills, social anxiety – attempts to gain social acceptance, show independence, and succumb to peer pressure is a common pathway to substance use among young people. Many find that drugs or alcohol also help them to overcome shyness, social awkwardness, or social phobia, which can lead to repeated use. As well, adolescents are more likely to use alcohol or drugs if they hang out with deviant friends, or if they seek out friends who will facilitate substance use,
- Poor school performance,
- Availability of drugs at school, and
- Lack of parental supervision – a recent study out of Iowa State University showed that parents can reduce the risk of addiction in their adolescent children simply by becoming involved in their kids' lives. Getting to know what's going on with their kids and their friends helps to counteract negative social influences. You don't even have to be a "super-parent" to make a big difference; the researchers found that as long as parents are in the 71st percentile of parenting, they can counter-act negative peer effects. The important thing is to invest time – especially in pre-adolescence and adolescence – to build a relationship and rapport. Open, respectful, and non-judgmental communication is key; if kids don't think talking things over with their parents is safe, they will keep secrets.

Aggressive Behavior. While it may sound odd that aggressive behavior is a risk factor for addiction, many sources consider it to be one of the most significant risk factors. Indeed, the Twelve Step program regards anger and resentment – the underlying psychological elements of aggressive behavior – as the primary underlying driver of addiction. I tend to agree with them. Anyone who has been around people in active addiction may have noticed that addicts tend to be angry, resentful, and defensive people. They see themselves as victims of an unfriendly world and they blame everybody and everything (except themselves) for their life situation.

Aggressive behavior is an especially toxic risk factor for youth, because aggression is significantly related to early substance use, and early substance use initiation (prior to age 14) more than quadruples the odds of developing a substance use disorder by early adulthood.

One of the major focuses of addiction treatment programs is helping individuals to identify, confront, and find peace with the anger and resentments that underpin their aggressive behavior. By treating the emotional dysregulation that leads to aggression, the risk of subsequent relapse into substance use is significantly reduced.

Chronic stress. Becoming overwhelmed by stressors is a common pathway to addiction. It's very common to see people who have some or even many risk factors for addiction but are able to go through life using alcohol and even trying or "recreationally" using drugs without becoming addicted, but when they're exposed to overwhelming stress they suddenly develop a deep addiction.

At its core, addiction is a dysfunctional coping mechanism, what psychologists refer to as *escape/avoidance coping*. By numbing their mind with psychoactive (mind-altering) substances and withdrawing into social isolation people attempt to shut out the world and all its problems. It provides temporary relief from stress, if only for a short period of time. Unfortunately, it inevitably worsens the stress, because the effects of addictive substances on the brain lower stress tolerance, and avoiding problems never leads to a solution.

For many people, life stressors, conflict, and problems are their greatest trigger for substance use. However, it's impossible to avoid stress and difficulties in life; life will always have its ups and downs. Because of this, addiction treatment programs place heavy emphasis on learning new, healthy ways to handle life on life's terms and to cope with stress.

History of trauma and adverse experiences. Some people turn to substance use to cope with the ongoing psychological impact of traumatic events, either recent or in the distant past. Many survivors of trauma – especially deliberate trauma at the hands of others – live life with a deep sense of insecurity and mistrust. They don't view the world as a safe place, and they put up walls that prevent closeness with other people. Their pain and haunting memories are a source of deep anger and resentment, which is understandable, given that life has been so unfair. Some people experience invasive thoughts and memories of their trauma, including nightmares and flashbacks, which keeps the pain fresh. These haunting memories, and the assortment of negative feelings (such as anger, guilt, injustice, fear, anxiety, and shame) become a daily source of pain and unhappiness for them, and they may find temporary relief through substance use to be a welcome break from their tortured thoughts and feelings.

The condition known as post-traumatic stress disorder (PTSD) has become a household name because of its life-disrupting symptoms. Given the severity of the psychological symptoms of PTSD, it's not surprising that there's a very high association between PTSD and addiction. There's very little medical science can do to heal PTSD, so affected people are prone to seeking refuge in drugs or alcohol. However, true PTSD isn't nearly as common as people would believe by the amount that the term is bandied about; in fact, only about 20% of people who experience severe trauma will go on to develop PTSD. However, people don't have to develop full-out PTSD or even experience severe trauma to develop significant disruptive and painful symptoms related to past experiences that elevate their risk of developing addiction.

Significant trauma may not be from just from one horrible event, but may result from a pattern of events over time. For example, being bullied in school over a prolonged period of time, being subjected to repeated workplace harassment, living in poverty, or being neglected over an entire childhood can cause the same psychological trauma as can a single significant event. What matters is how it affects the individual's thoughts and feelings, not the specifics of the trauma.

Identifying and confronting past trauma is a significant part of addiction therapy, so that the individuals will no longer be attracted to "escape/avoidance" coping mechanisms – such as substance use – for dealing with the psychological pain. Too, we must recognize that living through addiction is, in itself, a deeply traumatic experience. It destroys self-esteem, self-confidence, and disrupts normal brain function. It's associated with great loss: material wealth, employment, family and friends, health, and happiness. It's a miserable and prolonged experience, a struggle of a lifetime. The traumatic effects of addiction are addressed during addiction therapy in order to give individuals the peace of mind they need for a return to good health and function and to prevent relapse.

Mental illness. Mental health disorders and addiction are very closely linked. In fact, addiction is itself classified as a mental health disorder by the medical community's standard diagnostic manual (the DSM 5 – the *Diagnostic and Statistical Manual of Mental Disorders*). Addiction and other mental illnesses share genetic causes, risk factors, and even many of the same symptoms.

Addiction and mental illness are so closely tied together that one can cause the other, and it can be difficult to tell which came first. Many people begin their substance use in efforts to "self-medicate," which means they use addictive substances to attempt to relieve their mental symptoms. Lots of them aren't even aware that they have a diagnosable and treatable mental disorder; they've been living with the symptoms for so long that they've come to believe that it's just normal for them. A little more than half of people with addiction also have a mental health disorder, most commonly depression or anxiety.

The link between mental illness and addiction underscores the huge importance of early recognition, diagnosis and treatment of these problems in anyone who struggles with mental health problems. This is especially so in children and adolescents, who tend to internalize their symptoms and may not recognize that something's wrong. They also fear social stigmatization if they're found to have mental issues, so they tend to be secretive and even evasive about discussing their symptoms. Most mental health disorders are easily treated, so it truly is a tragedy when anyone lives unnecessarily with such distressing symptoms, and doubly so if it results in addiction.

*

When we see an otherwise healthy and thriving person suddenly spiral downwards into life-consuming addiction, we always wonder: *how did this happen? How did they get to this point?* Well, most people who develop addiction – regardless of their starting point – get there through one or more of only a few pathways. Knowing these pathways to addiction helps us to recognize when someone may be starting down an ominous road, and understand how to intervene and help them before it's too late. It also allows us to help loved ones in recovery because we can watch out for these pathways back to substance use and help our loved one to avoid them.

It's tempting to believe that people get addicted because addictive substances make you feel good, and everybody likes feeling good. However, there has to be a lot more to it than that, because the U.S. National Institute of Health's huge National Survey of Drug Use and Health (NSDUH) tell us that by age 26 over 87% of Americans have used alcohol, and just over 50% have used illicit drugs. If addiction occurred because we like to feel good, then we'd expect a lot more people to become addicted. However – again according to statistics from the U.S. National Institute of Health – only about 10% of people develop a drug use disorder in their lifetime and up to 29% develop an alcohol use disorder (although this statistic may be a bit high, according to other data), so most people can experience the "feel-good" aspect of substance use and not become addicted.

It's also tempting to conclude that people develop addiction because of a lack of morals. However, if deciding to take a drink or drug makes a person immoral, then there are *a lot* of immoral people in America. In my work with people in addiction I've encountered many very good and upstanding people who've fallen to addiction, including – if you take that to be an indication of morality – members of the clergy. For anyone who believes that addiction is the result of a lack of willpower, or a lack of character, or just not caring about life and health, then science would disagree. Let's put that point on hold for now, and in the upcoming chapters where we discuss the effects of addictive substances on the brain and mind we'll see why addiction is a matter of biology, not a matter of morality, willpower, or character strength.

Addiction develops because of the effects of repeated substance use on the brain of susceptible individuals. As we've discussed, they may be susceptible due to a combination of genetic and environmental factors. The pathways to addiction are the reasons that individuals use psychoactive substances repeatedly, allowing addiction to develop from the repeated exposure.

Let's now look at each of the pathways to addiction. Virtually all people with addiction get there through one or more of these pathways. See if you can identify which pathway to problem substance use your addicted loved one fell to.

Becoming addicted to prescription medications. There are a number of prescription drugs that have a high addiction potential, and just because they're taken by prescription for a legitimate medical reason doesn't insulate people from becoming addicted. The transition from taking prescription medications for their intended medical purpose to using them improperly can be very subtle, and people are often unaware or in denial when this transition happens. For example, people who take prescription pain medications (opioids such as codeine or oxycodone) may continue using them for their euphoric effects as their pain decreases and their need for pain medication wanes. Even though their primary motivation is the euphoric effects, they can easily rationalize it by telling themselves that they still need the drugs for pain.

As people who misuse their prescription medications develop tolerance, they require more and more of the drug to get the same effects, and they begin taking more of the drug and more often than it was prescribed. The prescriber will flag on this when the individual comes in asking for higher doses, early refills, or reporting "lost or stolen" prescriptions, and will probably stop prescribing the drug. Difficulty in obtaining enough drug causes desperation: people may resort to drug-seeking behavior with healthcare providers ("doctor shopping" by going to multiple prescribers in one day, or faking illness to get prescriptions), dealing drugs, obtaining drugs on the street, resorting to harder drugs that are cheaper and easier to obtain (such as heroin), and crime.

This may sound extreme, but it happens. And it happens to good, regular people who may have never even thought of using drugs before. And it happens a lot. The U.S. is the highest consumer of prescription opioids in the world, with Canada being the second highest. In 2012, a total of 255 million opioid prescriptions were dispensed in the U.S., making opioids the most frequently prescribed medications in America. That comes out to 81.3 opioid prescriptions per 100 people. The opioid prescribing rate has been falling since then, with 168 million prescriptions in 2018 (51.4 prescriptions per 100 people). Even though the total number of opioid prescriptions has been falling since 2012, the dosages have been increasing, and the average daily dose is now about triple what it was in 1999. (These numbers have all been provided by the U.S. National Institutes on Drug Abuse (NIDA) and the Centers for Disease Control and Prevention (CDC) – see the list of references at the back of the book.)

Data from the 2018 U.S. National Survey on Drug Use and Health (NSDUH) show that eight out of ten heroin users in the U.S. began their addiction by using prescription opioids, and that people who become addicted to prescription opioids are 40 times more likely than the general population to end up as heroin addicts. About 21-29% of people who're prescribed opioids for legitimate medical reasons misuse them, and about 8-12% develop an opioid addiction. About 4-6% of people who misuse prescription opioids transition to heroin.

In 2018, about 9.9 million people in the U.S. misused prescription opioids. "Misuse" means taking them without a prescription, in doses above what was prescribed, for longer than prescribed, or for reasons other than what they were prescribed for. More than half (51.3%) of the people who misused prescription opioids obtained them from a friend or relative. More than a third (37.6%) obtained the opioids by prescription or by stealing from a clinic. A further 6.5% obtained their opioids by purchasing them from a dealer or other stranger.

There's a lot of medical and legal pressure on prescribers to stop putting prescription pain medications on the street, so many people who truly need them (such as people with severe cancer pain) have difficulty getting enough medications (or even any medications) to relieve their pain or to help them function. This rebound effect of the opioid crisis – where people who need pain medications can't get them prescribed – is sometimes referred to as the "other opioid crisis." Reduced access to prescribed opioids for those who truly need them has driven many to seek opioids from illicit sources, or to resort to using cheaper, more easily accessible illicit opioids, such as heroin.

So far, we've just been talking about opioid medications, but there are other types of prescription medications that are addictive: sedative/hypnotics (such as benzodiazepines), stimulants (such as medications used to treat ADHD), and hallucinogen/dissociatives (such as the anesthetic ketamine). All are associated with addiction potential, and a similar escalation as opioids. We'll talk more about the different types of addictive drugs in chapter 3.

Self-medicating symptoms of mental illness. Most mental illness symptoms are very uncomfortable and difficult to live with, and can even be excruciating. These symptoms often significantly disrupt people's ability to function properly in life, and cost people opportunities for jobs, education, relationships, and so on. Many don't even realize they have a treatable mental health problem; this is especially the case for young people, particularly adolescents. When people with mental symptoms try drugs or alcohol and experience relief from their symptoms, it makes them want to do it again. Thus can begin repeated substance use and addiction.

The ironic thing about self-medicating mental symptoms with addictive substances is that although there may be brief relief from the torment, the substance use actually worsens the symptoms afterwards. As we'll discuss in chapter 7, mental health disorders are largely caused by abnormal levels of certain brain chemicals (known as *neurotransmitters*), and the rebound effect from substance use further worsens the abnormal neurotransmitter levels, thereby worsening the symptoms. Because of this, a vicious cycle begins: mental health symptoms –> substance use to relieve the symptoms –> worsened symptoms –> more substance use –> and so on.

Self-medicating mental illness is a common pathway to addiction: just over half of people with addiction have a co-occurring mental health disorder.

Social Reasons. This is an especially prevalent pathway to addiction among adolescents and young adults. Many people begin their substance use because they feel socially awkward or phobic and the substance effects makes them feel at ease in a social setting. They usually discover this by accident when they try drugs or alcohol at a social gathering, and are surprised as the disinhibiting effects of the drugs makes them come out of their shell. They like their newfound substance-induced social skills, and repeated substance use begins.

As well, peer pressure to use drugs or alcohol is a significant factor, especially among adolescents, who wish to impress their friends, be a part of the group, and demonstrate their independence.

They like how it makes them feel. Addictive substances produce effects that many people enjoy, such as euphoria (an intense feeling of happiness and well-being), sedation (i.e. feeling calm and relaxed), a feeling of being detached from the world, or even hallucinations. Some people enjoy these effects of the substances so much that they repeatedly use them, and addiction develops.

The "high" that people get from substance use can be fleeting, however, and this often leads to an escalation in how much and how often they use the substance as tolerance develops and they "chase the high." This is why addiction tends to escalate as it progresses. After a while, because of tolerance, many people feel little or no effect from their substance use. This may result in dangerously high levels of drug use, or experimenting with stronger drugs (such as the ultra-high potency opioids, like fentanyl or carfentanil), and trying other types of drugs – and the risk of overdose elevates.

When tolerance develops, addicts usually find that they no longer experience a "high" from their substance use, and their substance use becomes about avoiding withdrawal symptoms rather than getting high. Addicts commonly report that they reached a point where the substance use was no longer "fun," and they now use just to "feel normal" rather than get to high.

Coping mechanism. Some people feel that they can handle stress better when they're using substances. Stress is a normal part of life – it helps us to maintain a level of alertness and ensures that we direct our efforts toward problems that require attention. However, some people find stress overwhelming, particularly if they have a negative outlook or are prone to other negative feelings such as depression. Sometimes people are facing more stress than usual because of problems that suddenly piled up. Individuals who have difficulty coping with stress or who lack healthy coping strategies may find the temporary stress relief brought on by the sedating effects of substance use to be desirable.

Individuals who've gone through life using alcohol or even drugs without becoming addicted may suddenly find that things change when they're hit with overwhelming stress from a life crisis, such as a difficult divorce or losing their job. As they repeatedly turn to drugs or alcohol to cope, their brain undergoes the changes that create addiction.

A lot of people resort to substance use in order to cope with negative feelings. There are many people among us who go through life with overwhelming guilt, sadness, remorse, anger, and other negative feelings. Many experience grief that they can't seem to come to terms with. While we all feel those emotions from time to time, for some people those emotions are ever-present, and represent a source of constant unhappiness and mental turmoil. This happens a lot with people who've experienced significant trauma, and those with mental illness. The brief relief they get from substance use may drive them to drink or use repeatedly. We'll talk much more about trauma, grief, and mental illness in upcoming chapters.

Using substances to cope with stress, grief, or negative feelings is referred to by psychologists as *escape/avoidance coping*, because individuals are resorting to psychoactive drugs or alcohol to numb their minds and get temporary escape from the reality of life. This is a dysfunctional coping mechanism, because escaping or avoiding problems does nothing to solve anything, and often makes problems worse because they go unaddressed. Substance use is often combined with another escape/avoidance coping mechanism: social avoidance. People shut themselves out from other people and the world in general by disappearing on a binge or isolating themselves at home to avoid life and its problems. Noticing a loved one beginning to socially isolate is often one of the very first red flags that they may be developing addiction.

Even people whose addiction didn't begin as a coping mechanism end up using their substance use to cope with the stress as their life crashes down around them. Addiction is characterized by negative and painful feelings and emotions – such as anger, guilt, shame, remorse, and self-loathing – and as addiction develops addicts will seek relief from these harsh emotions through more substance use.

Performance enhancement. This is an especially common reason for using stimulants, either prescription (such as medications used to treat narcolepsy or ADHD) or non-prescription (such as cocaine or crystal methamphetamine). These drugs make people feel more alert, energetic, and confident, so they feel they can perform better in life when they take these drugs. When they take the drugs repeatedly addiction may develop, which almost invariably ruins their life rather than enhancing their performance.

Besides stimulants, some people also feel that they can perform better in life with other drugs or alcohol, due to the relaxing, disinhibiting, and confidence-boosting effects of the high. They may find stressful tasks such as job interviews easier to face, and may believe that they perform better under the influence of substances. Eventually, they begin to rely on their substance use for everyday life and addiction develops.

Avoidance of withdrawal. Withdrawal from repeated substance use can cause very uncomfortable or even dangerous physical and psychological symptoms, as well as intense cravings that may last for days or weeks. As addiction progresses and tolerance develops, avoidance of withdrawal usually becomes the primary driver of continued substance use.

Stopping withdrawal symptoms may also propel some people to continue using their prescription medications even though they no longer have a medical need. This is why a tapering and detoxification plan should be an integral part of the treatment plan when medications that are associated with withdrawal symptoms are prescribed. Unfortunately, this often doesn't occur.

*

Even people with lots of genetic and environmental factors that favor addiction go through life without becoming addicted when they drink alcohol or try drugs. Often it takes a situation that becomes overwhelming, such as experiencing trauma (such as an assault or a sudden loss of a loved one) or a particularly distressing life event (such as a divorce or a bankruptcy) before they're triggered to seek refuge in drink or drug. Conversely, people with few genetic or environmental risk factors can easily become addicted to substances in the right circumstances.

This underscores the importance of seeking support when we're knocked down in life. People have a strange tendency to try to handle adversity all on their own, because they feel it's a weakness to reach out to others, or because they don't want to "bother" other people with their problems, or perhaps because they're embarrassed about their problems. Opening up, getting things of our chest, and sharing our worries and hardships has a remarkable therapeutic effect. In section three we'll discuss healthy coping strategies for handling stress. It's when people lack such healthy habits and practices that they seek escape/avoidance coping, often in the form of substance use and social isolation.

Likewise, when we see that a loved one is struggling with difficulties in life, we can do much to prevent addiction or other mental health problems from developing by reaching out and offering meaningful support. Adolescents are especially prone to internalizing their stress and trying to deal with their troubles on their own. Their lack of life experience makes them vulnerable to the adverse effects of real-world stress.

In the next chapter, we're going to look at a very important concept of addiction, one that some people may initially turn their nose up to: the concept that addiction is a disease. If you're one of those people who recoil at the suggestion that addiction is a disease, then I ask that you keep an open mind, and hear me out. I was once one of those people, too.

2

Why Do They Call Addiction a Disease?

Addiction is like the Trojan horse, welcomed under false pretenses only to usurp the power that first received it.

– David Batho

Some people get their back up and seem deeply offended when addiction is referred to as a disease. After all: *it's a choice, not a disease, right?* When I was in general practice, I didn't really buy into the disease idea of addiction, because I, too, believed that people with addiction were just bad people who woke up every day and made bad decisions. However, since being through addiction myself and becoming an addictions researcher, I've become convinced that the disease model of addiction is entirely correct. Who cares, though? Why does it matter if we call it a disease or not? Well, it does matter for a couple of important reasons.

When we classify addiction as a disease it helps break down the terrible stigma that burdens people with addiction and presents a barrier to recovery. It helps people understand that by the time someone has crossed the line into addiction, they've long ago lost freedom of choice over their substance use, and are now displaying the symptoms of a brain disease brought on by the toxic effects of repeated substance use. Although in the very beginning drinking alcohol or using drugs was a choice, the ability to choose is lost. Otherwise, people who develop addiction would do what everybody else does – stop the substance use when it begins tearing down their life.

In this chapter we'll discuss exactly why addiction qualifies as a disease. If you're skeptical, I ask only that you keep an open mind. I, too, was skeptical once, but developments in neuroscience over the past decade have provided irrefutable objective support for the "disease model of addiction."

*

The science world lacks consensus on a definition of what, exactly, constitutes a disease. Over time the concept of what defines a disease has wavered, and has undergone some very unfortunate and unscientific twists and turns. The disease definition has often been influenced by opportunity for profit by private industry, and by public stigma and beliefs rather than by science. Addiction has been caught up in this unfortunate process, often with some disastrous effects that have impacted our ability to handle the addiction crisis.

Addiction is not the only condition that has suffered from the lack of a consensus definition of what constitutes a disease. For example, osteoporosis (pathological thinning of the bones) was long considered to be nothing more than a normal, unavoidable part of aging, until it was officially recognized as a disease by the World Health Organization (WHO) in 1994. Using the same logic that was applied to osteoporosis, you could consider atherosclerotic heart disease (the process that causes heart attacks, the leading cause of death in the Western world) as a normal, unavoidable part of aging, but very few people would argue against classifying heart attacks as a disease.

Another unfortunate victim of the lack of a disease definition is homosexuality, which was long categorized as a pathological mental disease. Because of this, disastrous and humiliating unrelenting attempts were made to "cure" homosexuality, using hormone treatments, hypnosis followed by a trip to a brothel, electroshock therapy, testicle transplants, shocks to the genitals while looking at gay porn ("aversion therapy"), and even brain surgery. It was not until 1974 that homosexuality was officially declassified as a disease by the American Psychiatric Association. As you can see, the process of determining what qualifies as a disease often has little to do with science.

Unfortunately, government and private industry are often given undue influence over what's defined as a disease for reasons that have nothing to do with the best interests of the general public. Determining what constitutes a disease often boils down to deciding what will best manipulate insurance liabilities or promote pharmaceutical sales. This has very much been the case with addiction, where much of the opposition to the acceptance of addiction as a disease is motivated by political and profitability concerns, rather than medical science. Insurance companies try to dodge the billions of dollars in payments that would be required to cover addiction treatment and time off work to recover, and therefore oppose defining addiction as a disease. Likewise, government policy-makers have also often opposed the medicalization of addiction. Their opposition is based on various motivations, including the powerful lobbies of the health insurance industry and the privatized prison system. Politicians who become involved in advocacy for addiction may risk alienating much of their electorate, who may not be familiar with the nature of addiction. People in active addiction generally do not vote or make campaign contributions, and there's no well-heeled "behind the scenes" lobby that represents people with addiction.

Besides political and financial motivations, the social stigma of addiction and other mental disorders represents another significant barrier to acceptance of the disease model of addiction. Throughout the general public and even among healthcare professionals, addiction remains widely stigmatized as a failing of morality or just bad decision-making, rather than a pathological brain affliction. Even if that were so, it would not preclude the classification of addiction as a disease; lung cancer, for example, is uncommon outside of people who smoke, and few people would deprive lung cancer of disease status because it's based on a decision to use tobacco. However, addiction suffers from deep-seated stigma and bias that goes well beyond that of smoking.

The stigma of addiction that plays a role as a barrier to acceptance of the disease model of addiction arises largely from the behaviors associated with addiction. The most visible people with addiction often are unkempt, pathetic-looking individuals who may behave aggressively, be involved in criminal behavior, and act strangely and anti-socially. Frankly, they can be dirty, homeless, scary people. However, as we'll see as we review the effects of addictive substances on the brain, these are simply symptoms of the disease of addiction, and these very same scary and undesirable people were once normal, functioning people just like us, and will again be just like us if they succeed in finding their way into healthy recovery.

The stigma of addiction has been worsened by the so-called "War on Drugs." While the superhuman efforts of the men and women of the various agencies involved in efforts to eliminate sources of production, importation, and distribution of drugs is laudable, policy-makers also declared war on individual substance users by making possession of drugs for personal use a criminal offense.

The term "War on Drugs" has disappeared from official use, having been dropped by the U.S. Office of National Drug Control Policy (ONDCP) during the Obama administration. However, simple possession of drugs for personal use remains a crime in America and many other countries. This policy diverts people with addiction away from the medical system, instead channeling them into the criminal justice system. With addiction being criminalized, people who're already socially isolated and marginalized have been driven even further underground.

Many people who suffer from addiction refuse to admit their problem or even discuss it with their doctor for fear of being reported or arrested. Fear of arrest keeps many individuals from calling for help in overdose situations, and the criminalization of addiction has therefore almost certainly contributed to the huge overdose death rate. I recently conducted a survey among individuals at a safe injection site, and only one in five addicts said they would call for help if they or a friend were overdosing. In every case, they said it was because of fear of arrest. Many of the people I've interviewed who just survived an overdose said that all their drug-using friends ran away from the scene without calling for help when the overdose occurred.

Humans Rights Watch reported (in their 2016 report *Every 25 Seconds: The Human Toll of Criminalizing Drug Use in the United States*) that every 25 seconds someone in the U.S. is funneled into the criminal justice system accused of nothing more than possession of drugs for personal use. Many of these people are charged for "drug residue," where swabs of their belongings find "trace" amounts of drugs that are so small that they can only be detected by specialized laboratory equipment. A hollow victory, at best, that does nothing to contribute to solving the addiction crisis.

The criminalization of drug possession results in many people – especially young people – being burdened with a criminal record that deprives them of opportunities to succeed in life once they've overcome their addiction. They're alienated from opportunities for education and employment, and often even stripped of voting rights. Single mothers may be prevented from accessing social supports that they need to raise their children in a healthy environment.

Virtually every country has healthcare systems that are desperately lacking in funding for addiction treatment programs, yet they spend massive amounts of public funds on policing and incarcerating addicts for simple drug possession. In some countries, the privatization of prisons has resulted in incarceration becoming a lucrative private-sector business that can afford lobby activity to keep the prisons full. As such, there's often much pressure on governments and financial incentive for politicians to maintain the status quo of the criminalization of addiction.

The point here is that there are powerful forces at work that maintain the pernicious negative stigma against those who suffer from addiction, and this stigma plays a significant role in closing people's minds to the concept of addiction as a disease. People view addiction as a crime rather than an illness. Acceptance of the disease model of addiction represents a significant step toward reducing the stigma of substance addiction, and moving addiction from the criminal justice system to the medical system, where it belongs. However, speaking strictly from a medical perspective, addiction does indeed qualify as a disease. Let's discuss that now.

*

Although there's no widely accepted definition of a disease, a reasonable, all-encompassing definition may be: *a disorder of structure or function that produces specific signs or symptoms that affect a specific system, organ, or group of organs of the body*. A disease may be caused by various agents, such as infection (viruses or bacteria, for example), inflammation, genetic defects, toxins, or environmental factors, but usually does not include injury. Diseases disrupt the body's usual functions, and often usurp the body's natural processes in order to propagate themselves. For example, a virus causes disease by entering the body, then using the body's own physiological processes to invade cells and use the cells' DNA protein synthesis apparatus to reproduce itself, resulting in the production of "baby viruses" that then leave the cell and carry on the disease process. The virus thereby "hijacks" the body's own natural processes to propagate itself, disrupting normal body functions in the process. The result is specific signs and symptoms that are caused by the virus's effects on a body organ or system, and these signs and symptoms are what we call a disease. Some viruses act mainly on the liver (causing hepatitis), some act mainly on the lungs (causing pneumonia), and some act specifically on the brain (causing encephalitis).

Like viruses, addictive substances are foreign substances that enter the body and alter the body's natural functions and processes to propagate their continued use. The result is a specific syndrome of signs and symptoms that we know of as addiction. Like many diseases, addiction has a strong genetic component that makes some individuals more susceptible than others.

As with other diseases, addiction causes physiological and structural changes to the body. An overwhelming body of research evidence has shown that addiction involves physical changes in DNA expression and other molecular structures and functions in the body's brain cells, and changes in the connections and activities of brain circuits (if you're not sure what exactly that means, don't worry – you'll be an expert by the time you've finished this book). These are real changes that can be seen on MRI scans and under the microscope. As well, addictive substances cause an activation of the brain's immune system, resulting in harmful inflammation, which also happens with viral infections. As such, addiction is demonstrably a physical disease that causes physical changes in the body that serve to propagate itself, not at all unlike how viruses cause disease.

As we'll see in the chapters that follow, the brain changes brought on by repeated addictive substance use alter the structure and function of the brain in a significant way, producing the pathological thought processes and behaviors that make up the symptoms of addiction. The altered brain effects promote continued substance use, create barriers to seeking and accepting help, and favor relapse in those who attempt to stop. Non-addicted people will halt their drug or alcohol use once it begins causing them problems. However, once addiction develops, such self-control over substance use is no longer possible. Even when the substance use is destroying their relationships, health, livelihood, and happiness, and is no longer "fun," people with addiction are unable to stop without proper treatment, despite the earnest desire to stop and multiple attempts to do so. At that point, they're under the power of a disease, and they're no more able to make it go away than cancer victims can make their malignancy go away.

Another factor that favors the disease definition of addiction is that these patterns of symptoms are remarkably uniform between different people, regardless of race, culture, age, or gender. Whether an individual grew up in Japan or England, is young or old, is male or female, is educated or not, is rich or poor, the symptoms of addiction are remarkably uniform between individuals. The same can be said of other diseases, like cancer or diabetes.

*

The disease model of addiction is important for several reasons. First of all, it helps medical practitioners and researchers to frame addiction in the proper context and to give it the attention it deserves. It also opens the door for medical insurance organizations to provide coverage for treatment, and for employers to provide sick leave for treatment and recovery. As well, the disease model is an important step for reducing the stigma that's attached to addiction, so that people at all levels of society can realize that addiction is a matter of biology, not a failing of morality or a weakness of character.

Systemic biases can also be addressed better by using the disease model as a framework for understanding addiction. For example, employers who understand addiction as a disease are more likely to hire people who're in recovery from addiction when they realize that the person was afflicted with a disease and not possessed of weakness, or a flawed personality. Companies are more likely to view employees who develop addiction as treatable, rather than a lost cause suitable only for automatic firing. Policy-makers are more likely to make changes to keep people arrested for simple drug possession out of prisons and jail, and to make funds for treatment more widely available so that people have a way out when they're ready to accept help. The disease model is a major tool for helping to end the enduring effects of the destructive "War on Drugs" that channeled substance users into the criminal justice system.

The disease model also helps people who're suffering from active addiction to understand that there is treatment available, and that remission and recovery is possible. Many don't see that, and won't seek or accept help because they believe that they're not capable of recovery. When society sees them as simple criminals rather than as people with a treatable medical condition, they may see themselves the same way.

The disease model of addiction offers benefits that will help us fight the addiction epidemic, and help your loved one. However, viewing addiction as a disease boils down to a simple matter of science. When addiction is viewed through the lens of science and without the fog of societal stigma, it is fundamentally a disease process where susceptible individuals have their health altered by a foreign substance that uses the body's natural physiological processes to propagate itself. As we progress through our examination of addiction together, we'll discuss these biological effects of toxins (i.e. addictive substances) on the brain, and how these changes explain all the weird and illogical symptoms and behaviors associated with addiction. Suddenly, your loved one's baffling demeanor will make perfect sense. An understanding of this disease process is the fundamental basis to learning how to understand and help a loved one who suffers from addiction.

3

Addictive Substances 101

Cocaine habit-forming? Of course not. I ought to know. I've been using it for years.

– Tallulah Bankhead

In this chapter we review the various classes of addictive substances. An understanding of the particular substance or substances that your loved one is using is important because each has its own characteristics in terms of how addiction plays out, its health effects, and withdrawal effects when a person stops using it. A good understanding of the substance involved makes you better equipped to understand and help your loved one. You may wish to skip ahead to the particular substance that your loved one uses – their so-called "drug of choice." However, be careful, because the majority of people in active addiction are "polysubstance users," meaning that they're using more than one kind of substance. We'll discuss the specific concerns with polysubstance use at the end of the chapter.

Alcohol

Alcohol (known to science as *ethyl alcohol*, or *ethanol*) is one the most commonly used addictive substances, largely because it's widely available, cheap and easy to get, legalized, and considered to be a socially acceptable drug. Alcohol is classified as a *central nervous system (CNS) depressant* – the "central nervous system" is the brain and spinal cord – because it slows down brain function.

As a depressant, alcohol has relaxing and euphoric effects, which is why it's so widely used as a "recreational" drug. During acute intoxication (i.e. being drunk), it induces a sense of well-being, reduced anxiety, disinhibition, increased sociability, and sedation. During intoxication it impairs the main higher brain functions, including cognition (the ability to think, plan, use judgment, and make decisions), motor function (body movements, walking, coordination), and sensory function (the sense of touch, as well as smell, hearing, vision, taste, and so on). With repeated or chronic use, other brain impairments develop that favor addiction, and these impairments persist even when the individual isn't intoxicated.

Alcohol works by increasing the effects of the brain chemical that's responsible for slowing the brain down (the neurotransmitter known as "GABA"), which is why it's a CNS depressant. This is why the brain slows down during alcohol intoxication and people have slowed reaction time, slurred speech, slow thinking, and slow body movements. With repeated exposure to alcohol, the brain tries to compensate for the excessive slowing by speeding things up, which results in the brain becoming overactive after the alcohol wears off. Thus, people get jittery, nervous and anxious, shaky, and can even have seizures after a night of drinking.

Early in my medical career I worked on a trauma team in the ER of a big hospital. I got to see first-hand the effects of alcohol intoxication: more than half of all trauma patients are intoxicated with alcohol at the time of their injury. In addition, alcohol is often involved in suicide attempts due to the lowered inhibition, depressed mood, and impaired ability to reason that it induces. Alcohol use is the fourth leading cause of preventable death in the United States (after smoking, high blood pressure, and obesity). According to the Centers for Disease Control and Prevention (CDC), excessive alcohol use led to about 88,000 deaths (62,000 men and 26,000 women) and 2.5 million years of potential life lost each year in the United States from 2006 – 2010. The economic cost of excessive alcohol consumption in 2010 alone was $249 billion, or $2.05 a drink.

Based on the U.S. National Longitudinal Alcohol Epidemiologic Study, the following statistics apply to the U.S. adult population:

- Current drinkers - 44%,
- Former drinkers - 22%,
- Lifetime abstainers - 34%,
- Abuse and dependency in the past year - 7.5 - 9.5%, and
- Lifetime prevalence of alcoholism - 13.5 - 23.5% (note that this figure differs from the 29% statistic provided by the National Institutes of Health).

Alcoholism is more than twice as prevalent in men as it is in women, but women certainly aren't immune. The typical age of onset of problem drinking in females occurs later than in males. However, progression is more rapid, and females usually enter treatment earlier than males. Women are more likely to combine alcohol with addictive prescription drugs than are males. Women living with substance-using men are at especially high risk for this. Alcohol problems are less likely to be recognized in women, and women are less likely to get treatment.

Women don't metabolize alcohol as efficiently as men; they tend to become intoxicated faster and take longer to sober up. This gender difference is due to variations in the amount and activity of *alcohol dehydrogenase (ADH)*, the enzyme responsible for metabolizing alcohol. Males have highly active forms of ADH in their stomach as well as their liver. The presence of ADH in the stomach of males can reduce the absorption of alcohol by 30%. By contrast, females have almost no ADH in their stomach and they therefore absorb more alcohol into their bloodstream. Additionally, the ADH in the liver of females is much less active than the ADH in the male liver. These gender differences contribute to the increased blood alcohol concentrations for females compared to males – pound for pound – if they both consume the same amount of alcohol.

Minimum legal drinking ages around the world vary quite a bit. Most such laws apply only to drinking alcoholic beverages in public locations. The only country with a minimum legal age for consuming alcohol at home is the United Kingdom, which prohibits drinking below the age of six. In the U.S., some states allow underage drinking if a family member consents and/or is present. In some states those under 21 may drink in any private location. A majority of states permit under-21 drinking; 30 states allow parents to provide their children with alcohol in their own home. In the remaining 20, parents are barred from providing their children with alcohol until the child's 21st birthday. Many of the states in the U.S. that have chosen to prohibit alcohol consumption by those under age 21 have a variety of exceptions.

The average minimum legal drinking age around the world is 15.9. The majority of countries have a drinking age of 18. In fifty countries the minimum age is lower than 18, in 12 countries it's higher than 18, and 19 countries have no age restrictions for drinking. The enforcement of minimum legal drinking ages also varies widely between countries and often within countries. In many nations the law isn't generally enforced unless alcohol is abused. In some European countries McDonald's serves alcohol. Beer is available in vending machines and by street vendors in Japan.

Many high school cafeterias in Europe serve alcohol to students. Internationally, the average age at which drinking alcohol first occurs is 12 years. According to WHO, about 80% of young people worldwide begin drinking alcohol regularly at age 15 or younger.

Alcohol is the most commonly used drug by children and adolescents in the United States. Trauma is the leading cause of death in children, and alcohol use is linked to a 300-700% increased risk of trauma. Alcohol use is also strongly linked to other risk-taking behaviors that can lead to trauma, assault, other drug use, and teenage pregnancy. About 40% of the 10,000 annual non-automotive child deaths (usually drownings and falls) are associated with alcohol.

More than three quarters of all foster children in the United States are children of alcohol- or drug-dependent parents. From 60-70% of reported domestic violence incidents involve alcohol. Half of all violent crime is alcohol- or drug-related. Children of parents with alcoholism have a 2-fold to 4-fold increased risk of alcoholism. Whether reared by biological or adoptive parents, sons of males with alcohol problems are 4 times more likely to have problems with alcohol than are sons of persons who are not problem drinkers. Data from adoption studies on daughters of persons with alcohol problems are less clear. Daughters might be at increased risk if the biological mother has alcoholism.

Young children often present to the ER after drinking discarded alcoholic beverages left within their reach during and after parties or after ingesting a fluid that contains alcohol (cough syrup, gripe water, etc.). This occurs most often when they drink a liquid not meant for consumption, such as perfume or cleaning agents. Frequently, other chemicals in the ingested substance are more toxic than the alcohol.

Compare the alcohol concentrations in these common household substances to that of alcoholic beverages:

- Liquid cold remedies, 2-25%,
- Mouthwashes, 7-27%,
- Rubbing alcohol, 70% (contains isopropanol),
- Aftershave lotions, 15-80%,
- Perfumes and colognes, 25-95%, and
- Alcohol concentrations in some common alcoholic beverages are:
    - Whiskey, 40-60%,
    - Liqueurs, 22-50%,
    - Wine, 8-16%, and
    - Beer, 3-7%.

Infants and toddlers react differently to alcohol than do adolescents and adults. Alcohol ingestion - even very small amounts - can lead to marked hypoglycemia (dangerously low blood sugar) in infants and young children. Alcohol can also lead to respiratory depression and hypoxia (dangerously low oxygen levels) in the very young, much like opioids do in older people. Alcohol's sedating effect can make it look like the child is simply tired or asleep, and it may not be evident when they go into a coma from low blood sugar and low oxygen. If this happens the child will likely never wake up again unless given emergency medical attention.

In children, the classic triad of signs of alcohol ingestion is: 1) coma, 2) hypoglycemia, and 3) hypothermia (very low body temperature). They may have seizures from the low blood sugar, which is different from the alcohol withdrawal seizures seen in adults.

In the 2011 U.S. Youth Risk Behavior Survey, 21% of high school students admitted to drinking alcohol before age 13. The survey also found that 71% drank alcohol and 39% had at least one drink in the 30 days prior to the survey. Even more alarmingly, 24% rode in a vehicle with a driver who was drinking alcohol and 8% drove a vehicle themselves after drinking alcohol.

With regard to pregnancy, fetal alcohol syndrome (FAS) is the leading cause of mental deficiencies in the U.S. (1 in 1000 births). Even small amounts of alcohol consumption may be risky in pregnancy. One study demonstrated that children whose mothers consumed even small amounts of alcohol in pregnancy had more behavioral problems. Another study showed that moderate alcohol consumption while pregnant resulted in a higher incidence of problem drinking in the child by age 21 years, even after controlling for family history and other factors. All women who are pregnant or planning to become pregnant should avoid alcohol.

Alcohol has a long history in human society. Before the advent of water treatment centers and other public health measures, people in many areas drank alcoholic beverages – usually beer or wine – because it was the only way to safely drink the water. Alcohol is highly toxic to microbes, so the alcohol content made the water safer to drink. We know from jugs that have been excavated that people were making alcoholic beverages in the Stone Age, about 10,000 years ago. The ancient Egyptians were particularly heavy drinkers of beer, and they used the phrase *bread and beer* as a common greeting, like saying *hi*. Indeed, the oldest known recipe to be excavated is for beer.

Although mostly forgotten today, the "chemists' war of Prohibition" remains one of the strangest and most deadly decisions in American law-enforcement history. As one of its most outspoken opponents, Charles Norris, the chief medical examiner of New York City during the 1920s, liked to say, it was: *our national experiment in extermination*. Although I don't want to veer too far off-topic, I like to tell this story because although it's weird and shocking, I can't help but to draw parallels between the "chemists' war" and the war on drug possession.

During the U.S. prohibition era (1920-1933), rigorous enforcement had managed to slow the illegal flow of alcohol from abroad. Crime syndicates responded by stealing massive quantities of industrial alcohol – used in paints and solvents, fuels, and medical supplies – and redistilling it to make it drinkable. Well, sort of drinkable. The U.S. Treasury Department, charged with overseeing alcohol prohibition enforcement, estimated that by the mid-1920s, some 60 million gallons of industrial alcohol were stolen annually to supply the country's desperate drinkers.

In response, in 1926 President Calvin Coolidge's government decided to turn to chemistry as an enforcement tool. Toxic chemicals were added to industrial alcohol, knowing full well that much of it would end up being consumed by people. The new chemicals included some notable poisons—kerosene and brucine (closely related to strychnine), gasoline, benzene, cadmium, iodine, zinc, mercury salts, nicotine, ether, formaldehyde, chloroform, camphor, carbolic acid, quinine, and acetone. The Treasury Department also added the highly toxic methyl alcohol ("wood alcohol," which causes permanent blindness, and death) – up to 10 percent of the total product. It was the methyl alcohol that proved most deadly.

In 1926, in New York City, 1,200 people were sickened by purposely poisoned alcohol; 400 died. The following year, the deaths climbed to 700. These numbers were repeated in cities around the country.

One would hope that the U.S. government would have outgrown such a mentality after the 1920's. However, the U.S. government made a controversial decision in the 1970s to spray Mexican marijuana fields with paraquat, an herbicide. Its use was primarily intended to destroy crops, but government officials also insisted that awareness of the toxin in the dope would deter marijuana smokers. They echoed the same official position as that of the 1920s – if some citizens ended up poisoned, well, they'd brought it upon themselves.

*

Even though many people view alcohol as a relatively safe substance because it's so widely available, it's actually one of the most dangerous drugs to withdraw from after chronic use. Because of this, people who've been using alcohol heavily or repeatedly should consider discussing the issue with their doctor before stopping their alcohol use (medications can be prescribed to reduce the risk of the most serious withdrawal effects), or should consider attending a seven-day detoxification facility. Certainly, people should not withdraw from alcohol at home alone where no help is available if they get into trouble.

Habitual use can result in specific withdrawal symptoms when individuals stop or reduce their alcohol intake. These withdrawal symptoms are collectively known as *alcohol withdrawal syndrome (AWS)*. Generally, the severity of AWS symptoms depends on how much and for how long a particular individual has been drinking, but other factors come into play (such as general health, genetics, gender, and age). Withdrawal symptoms usually appear about six hours after the last drink, although with chronic drinkers the symptoms can appear much sooner. Symptoms usually peak between 24 and 72 hours after they start, and improve by seven days, although they can last weeks in some people. Alcohol withdrawal syndrome includes five specific withdrawal disorders:

- Simple withdrawal (i.e. a "hangover"),
- Alcohol withdrawal seizures,
- Delirium Tremens ("the DTs"),
- Alcoholic hallucinosis, and
- Post-acute withdrawal syndrome (PAWS)

People can experience some or all of these types of withdrawal after reducing or stopping their alcohol intake, even after a single episode of binge-drinking.

Withdrawal from alcohol use – even following one binge – typically results in a "hangover." Most people are familiar with the sickness that follows a night of drinking: nausea and vomiting, tremors (shaking), heavy sweating (diaphoresis), anxiety, a general unwell feeling (malaise), depressed mood, muscle spasms, and headache.

Alcohol withdrawal seizures occur in just over 5% of frequent drinkers when they withdrawal from alcohol. The risk of seizures arises by about 24-48 hours after the last drink, although they can appear within two hours in heavy drinkers. More than 90% of seizures occur within the first 48 hours after the last drink, but about 3% of seizures occur late: up to three weeks after the last drink. The risk of seizures is especially high in individuals who've previously undergone multiple withdrawals from alcohol, an effect known as *kindling*.

Alcohol withdrawal seizures can be fatal, and are always a medical emergency. They occur due to the hyper-excitability of the brain following withdrawal from the brain-slowing alcohol. These seizures are scary to witness, especially when they happen to a loved one. They usually consist of *generalized tonic-clonic (GTC)* seizures, the ones you may know of as "grand mal" seizures. The person loses consciousness and falls to the floor. Their body stiffens with the legs extended and the arms fully bent at the elbows so that the fists are on the chest. There may be grunting, drooling, and frothing at the mouth. This lasts about a minute and then the person starts shaking rapidly, which lasts a few minutes. After the seizure the person may be difficult to rouse, and remain in a deep sleep for hours. An alcohol withdrawal seizure is always a medical emergency and a 911 call should be made for immediate medical help.

Delirium tremens ("the DTs") is the most severe form of alcohol withdrawal, and is fatal in about 5-25% of cases. It occurs in 5-20% of chronic drinkers when they withdraw, and about one third of individuals who experience seizures will also get the DTs. Factors that increase the risk of experiencing DTs include older age, poor overall health, previous history of withdrawal seizures and/or DTs, and poor liver function.

In most cases, by 48 hours withdrawal symptoms begin to improve, and individuals start feeling better daily. However, sometimes the withdrawal will continue to increase in severity and progress to the DTs. The DTs are characterized by hallucinations that are indistinguishable from reality, severe confusion, anxiety, seizures, severe shaking, high blood pressure, diaphoresis (drenching sweats), rapid heart rate, and fever. Individuals with DTs are a sorry sight. They're drenched in sweat, disheveled, usually unaware of who or where they are, terrified by hallucinations, shaking badly, and may fall to the ground and have a seizure. As with seizures, the DTs are a medical emergency, and a 911 call should be made for immediate medical assistance.

Alcoholic hallucinosis is the withdrawal condition where the individual has hallucinations, but they're different from the hallucinations that occur with the DTs. These involve visual and auditory hallucinations (seeing or hearing things that aren't there), and tactile hallucinations (i.e. feeling things, such as bugs crawling on the skin). Unlike the hallucinations that occur with the DTs, people who experience alcoholic hallucinosis realize that the hallucinations aren't real. Nevertheless, they're a frightening experience. If alcoholic hallucinosis occurs, it usually begins 12-24 hours after the last drink, and lasts about 48 hours once the hallucinations begin.

Post-acute withdrawal syndrome (PAWS) – sometimes referred to as protracted withdrawal syndrome – develops in some people after they've passed through acute withdrawal, and may last for a year or more. Basically, PAWS is simply acute withdrawal symptoms that don't go away after the usual amount of time in abstinence, especially: anxiety, sleep disturbances, low energy, fatigue, depressed mood, apathy, elevated blood pressure, elevated body temperature, and rapid heart rate.

*

In the Western world about 15% (this figure varies between countries) of people who drink become alcoholics at some point in their lifetime. About half of people with alcoholism will develop significant withdrawal symptoms upon reducing their use, with four percent developing severe symptoms. People who've had repeated bouts of heavy alcohol use followed by withdrawal (the so-called "chronic relapsers") are at particularly high risk for severe AWS, including the DTs and seizures.

The medical management of alcohol withdrawal includes measures to make the individuals more comfortable, and to prevent serious complications. This includes:

- Supportive care – severe dehydration is often present in alcoholics who come to a detox center or the hospital, and they may require fluid resuscitation (giving fluids by intravenous infusion). As well, other complications of chronic alcohol intake may require management, such as: rapid heart rate (tachycardia), high blood pressure (hypertension), low blood sodium (hyponatremia), low blood potassium (hypokalemia), and low blood sugar (hypoglycemia). Other potential complications can be identified and addressed, such as malnutrition, inflammation of the pancreas (pancreatitis), etc.,

- Seizure prevention – a type of sedative medication known as a "benzodiazepine" (such as diazepam or chlordiazepoxide) is given to prevent seizures, usually for the first five days. Besides helping to prevent seizures, these medications also help calm the anxiety that accompanies alcohol withdrawal,
- Magnesium – chronic alcohol use is often associated with significant malnutrition. In cases of severe malnutrition, low magnesium levels in the blood (hypomagnesemia) may be present, and may precipitate serious complications, such as potentially fatal irregularities of the heartbeat,
- Insomnia – this is a common symptom of alcohol withdrawal, and may last for weeks. Insomnia is a risk factor for relapse, so it should be addressed. However, many traditional sleep aids (including benzodiazepines) are ineffective due to cross-tolerance with alcohol. Magnesium and the medication trazodone usually work well. Trazodone is not cross-tolerant with alcohol and has low abuse potential, and
- Thiamine – also known as vitamin B1, thiamine is administered to prevent or treat "wet brain" (which we'll discuss shortly).

At some point in early recovery a complete physical exam and lab tests and imaging should be done to assess overall health and to identify any health issues that may have arisen from chronic alcohol use. Liver health, in particular, should be checked. Other substance use and co-existing mental health issues should be screened for as well.

*

There's a long-term complication that can develop after chronic alcohol use, known as "wet brain" (properly referred to as *Wernicke-Korsakoff syndrome (WKS)*). Wernicke-Korsakoff syndrome is actually a combination of two separate conditions, *Wernicke's encephalopathy* (an encephalopathy is a condition that affects how the brain works, causing an altered mental state) and *Korsakoff psychosis* (psychosis is a loss of touch with reality, and may include delusions, paranoia, hallucinations, and strange behaviors). It's possible for chronic alcoholic users to develop either condition separately, but they share a common cause and therefore usually end up occurring together. Wet brain is almost exclusively seen in alcoholics, but isn't directly caused by alcohol. It's actually a disease of malnutrition, specifically a severe deficiency of vitamin B1 – thiamine – which often occurs in the "advanced" alcoholic. Remember a few paragraphs ago, when I mentioned that when people detoxify from alcohol they're given thiamine shots for three days? That's done to prevent or arrest wet brain.

As alcoholics become more and more destitute, the bits of money that do come along end up going into alcohol instead of food. The inflamed stomach, liver, and pancreas – and the associated vomiting – result in poor absorption of any food that they do manage to obtain. Thiamine is a vitamin, which means that our body can't produce it, so it must come from food. So, the body's supply of thiamine runs out. Lack of thiamine interferes with the delivery of proper nutrition of the brain. The brain is a hungry organ: it uses up to 60% of our body's total energy (when we're at rest) and when it's not properly fed it'll start to digest itself. This is exactly what happens; the brain progressively withers, resulting in WKS.

Usually the symptoms of Wernicke's appear first. These are typically from three main categories: 1) changes in mental state (confusion, lack of interest in anything, inability to concentrate, and lack of awareness of their immediate situation), 2) visual changes (rapid eye movements, partial paralysis of eye movements, reduced vision), and 3) unsteadiness standing and walking. Left untreated, Wernicke's leads to coma or death. These symptoms come on suddenly, usually starting with the individual appearing confused. This can be hard to diagnose in a person who's habitually intoxicated, because they tend to be alone by this point in their drinking career, and their confusion is easily confused with drunkenness. Unlike drunken confusion this confusion is constant, even when the individual isn't intoxicated.

Later the ominous symptoms of Korsakoff psychosis appear. As mentioned earlier, psychosis is a loss of touch with reality, so the symptoms of Korsakoff psychosis are: hallucinations, memory loss, confabulation (making up stories to compensate for the memory loss), inability to form new memories, and nonsensical speech.

You may have seen someone with WKS. These unfortunates are usually dismissed as "crazy drunks." They're usually badly disheveled and unkempt, bottomed-out drunks by this point. They appear thin and poorly nourished. Their eyes vibrate and often don't line up properly. They appear to be in another world, and it's difficult to get and hold their attention, although they will follow simple commands. They talk to themselves, often repeating the same random phrase. They stagger when walking and fall easily. They're the extreme endorsement of the saying that no one ever drank themself smart, successful, or happy.

The onset of Wernicke's encephalopathy is a medical emergency. If treated promptly, it may be possible to prevent the development of Korsakoff psychosis and therefore prevent it from developing into full-blown WKS. At the very least treatment can reduce its severity. Treatment can also reduce the progression of the damage if there's already WKS, but will not completely reverse existing deficits. For such a devastating and deadly disease, treatment is cheap and easy: thiamine given intravenously once a day for three days. That's why it's so sad to see cases go untreated.

Treatment is not guaranteed to be effective and WKS will continue to be present, at least partially, in 80% of individuals. However, it's also important to continue supplementing with thiamine until a normal diet is in place, but many of these unfortunate people end up back out on the street picking up where they left off. What about those with WKS who do manage to find sobriety? It depends on how soon in the process the drinking is stopped and the thiamine deficiency is treated. Most of those who do find their way into recovery will be able to regain much of the functioning that was lost to WKS. Some will suffer lingering effects, but are usually able to adapt and find a better life away from alcohol. The amnesia from Korsakoff psychosis seems particularly permanent, and 80% of these people will always have problems with forming new memories. No matter what, finding sobriety is by far the best thing for them.

Sadly, only about 20% of cases of WKS are identified before death, so no treatment is provided. This is because most people who develop WKS are chronic daily drunks, so their symptoms are just assumed to be from being drunk. As well, many of them are long estranged from their family and friends, even homeless, so there may not be anyone around who cares enough to notice. Their disheveled appearance and strange, psychotic behavior – such as staggering around repeating weird statements – scares people and they tend to be avoided and shunned. This failure in diagnosis of WKS and thus treatment of the disease leads to death in 20% of cases, while 75% are left with permanent brain damage. About 25% require long-term institutionalization in order to receive effective care, but many never get this care. Instead, their behavior and socially unacceptable demeanor lands them in jail and the local Emergency Room, but their fate is usually the street.

Opioids

Opioids are a class of drugs found naturally in or derived from the opium poppy plant. They're commonly prescribed medications; the most frequently prescribed medications in America. Opioids are used primarily for pain management, although they have a few other medical uses. Not all opioids are used medically; for example, heroin has no medical uses whatsoever in most countries.

Unfortunately, opioids have gained much notoriety and fame over the past two decades, as the death rate from opioid addiction and overdose has reached horrifying levels. So much so that in 2017 the U.S. Department of Health and Human Services declared the opioid addiction crisis a public emergency in America.

You may have heard the words "opiate" and "opioid" used to describe these addictive drugs, and the two terms are often incorrectly used interchangeably. "Opiate" refers to naturally occurring compounds that are harvested directly from the opium poppy (of which there are four), and "opioid" refers to all drugs that act on opioid receptors in the brain, which includes opiates (such as morphine, and codeine), semi-synthetic derivatives of opiates (e.g. heroin, and oxycodone), and fully synthetic opioids (e.g. fentanyl, and methadone). If in doubt, the term "opioid" is the one you should use; it applies to all these drugs.

Another term you may have heard in use is "narcotic." Although this term is often applied to any addictive drug, it's really only properly used when referring to opioid drugs.

Opioids/narcotics present a real "catch-22" situation to society, and particularly to the medical professionals who prescribe them. Opioids have useful medical benefits, but the cost of their use includes a significant risk of addiction. Medical professionals, lawmakers, and society are struggling to find a balance between the important medical uses for opioid narcotics and their terrible potential for harm.

The medical uses for opioids include:

- Pain management,
- Anesthesia,
- Sedation,
- An anti-diarrheal,
- Cough suppression (i.e. antitussives),
- Treating heart attacks (by lowering blood pressure and relieving stress on the heart),
- Reducing respiratory distress in people who're dying, and
- Treatment of withdrawal symptoms in people in recovery from opioid addiction.

Opioids are abused for their euphoric and sedating effects.

As we discussed in chapter 1, opioids are very widely prescribed – and abused. The CDC gives us the following statistics for the U.S. for the year 2017:

- 58.7 opioid prescriptions were issued per 100 persons (down from 81.3 per 100 persons in 2012),
- In 16% of counties enough opioid prescriptions were issued for every man, woman and child to have one,
- Two out of three drug overdose deaths involved an opioid,
- 36% of opioid overdose deaths involved opioids that were obtained by prescription, and
- More than 130 Americans died every day from drug overdose, 46 of which were from prescription narcotics.

The most widely prescribed opioid in the U.S. is hydrocodone. In 2010, the worldwide production of hydrocodone was 36.3 tons, and Americans consumed 99.7% of the world's hydrocodone. The second most prevalent opioid in the U.S. is oxycodone, followed by prescription fentanyl.

*

As we discussed in chapter 1, prescription opioids are a major pathway to addiction, and "harder" drug use. And dealing in prescription opioids is a big business. Data from the 2018 NSDUH show that street drug dealers admitted that prescription opioids are a major part of their business. More than half of them reported that they obtain their opioid supply from clinics with lax prescribing habits and by "doctor-shopping" at an average of 4-5 different clinics per month. Just under half of the dealers reported that they obtain their supply by purchasing opioids from people in their community who've been prescribed opioids.

We discussed in chapter 1 how people subtly transition from proper use of prescription opioids to misuse, and then to addiction. As this occurs, tolerance develops, so that the addicted individual needs increasingly larger amounts of the drug. Typically, their prescription begins running out early, and they request early refills and dose increases from their doctor, or they begin seeing multiple doctors to request more prescriptions ("doctor-shopping").

Often the prescribers will stop writing scrips for opioids when they become suspicious because of continuing use, or requests for early refills, or self-administered dose increases; prescribers refer to this as "drug-seeking" behavior. If they find out that their patient is doctor-shopping they almost invariably cut off prescriptions (many countries have safeguards against doctor-shopping, such as the Prescription Drug Monitoring Programs (PDMPs) in the U.S.). At this point, people will often begin buying their opioids on the street, and many will transition to the cheaper and easier to obtain heroin. This is when the opioid use really begins to escalate and the risk of overdose skyrockets. Many "pharmaceutical opioids" that are sold on the street are actually fake; they're homemade pills containing a super-potent opioid (such as fentanyl or carfentanil). Most of the illicit heroin supply is likewise badly tainted.

So, if doctors are one of main the culprits in putting so many opioids on the street, why do they do it? Is it because they don't care? Are they on the pharmaceutical industry's payroll? Why do they keep prescribing so many opioids in the midst of the opioid addiction crisis? Why are these harmful drugs even available by prescription?

Well, I don't want to paint every prescriber with the same brush, but in general there are a few reasons that answer these questions. First of all, many prescribers come from relatively sheltered backgrounds where they haven't been exposed to many people in active addiction, and may be somewhat naïve when a patient is beseeching them for drugs. As well, even today medical education about addiction is woefully inadequate. By the time you finish reading this book you will definitely have a much better knowledge and understanding about addiction than the vast majority of doctors currently in practice. As well, doctors really want to help people, and when their patient is in pain – the very worst symptom that anyone can have – they especially want to help.

When someone comes to a doctor with a painful condition that would substantiate an opioid prescription, it puts the doc in an awkward position. Maybe the person is faking and has no pain – there's no test to prove or disprove pain. Many (but not all) painful conditions can be verified through some kind of test, but the amount of pain cannot be. So, often the prescriber is faced with a decision to make with little or no objective evidence to back up the patient's stated symptoms. My policy as a prescriber was that I gave people a reasonable benefit of the doubt until they gave me reason not to. Statistically, I know that I gave people a prescription that did nothing more than feed their addiction, but I didn't want people who really needed pain meds to suffer by cutting off all prescribing for everyone.

Even in legitimate cases of significant pain requiring opioid pain medications, the doctor knows there's a good chance the patient will become addicted or dependent. But there's no way to know who or when. But, should the doctor just leave them to suffer in pain, just in case they might become addicted? When does the stay-at-home mom with a kidney stone cross the line from using a prescribed opioid for pain relief to using it for its euphoric effect? And how can the doctor know when that is? Perhaps the woman with the kidney stone will enjoy the euphoric effects of the drug but only take it as prescribed and never touch it again after the pain is gone. Or perhaps not. There's no way to know. Most doctors would prefer to never prescribe opioids again, but the fact is that pain is the most common reason that people seek healthcare (according to the Pain and Emergency Medicine Initiative (PEMI) study, 78% of ER visits are for a pain complaint), and doctors have an ethical obligation to alleviate suffering.

Prescribers' caution and reluctance to prescribe opioids to prevent being part of the addiction problem has proven to be a double-edged sword. The CDC has expressed concern that prescribers are now under-prescribing badly needed opioids to people with significant pain, or are abruptly cutting off people's prescriptions or dismissing them from their practice because of opioid use. This problem of people with a real need for pain relief being unable to get the help they need is referred to as "the other opioid crisis." The World Health Organization's (WHO) Access to Controlled Medications Programme has estimated that over 80% of people in the world who suffer from moderate to severe pain are inadequately treated even though medical science has the ability to treat their pain. The top two reasons identified for this problem are regulations that prevent prescribers from properly treating significant pain, and inadequate knowledge and negative attitude among prescribers.

When people with legitimate pain are unable to get the help they need from the medical system, some end up buying pain medications on the street, and eventually switching to heroin, again due to cost and availability.

One false belief is that doctors somehow profit from prescribing opioids, which is mostly false. In most Western countries, it's illegal for doctors to directly profit from their prescribing choices. Pharmaceutical companies used to give gifts to doctors as indirect rewards for prescribing, but regulations have long been in place to curb these efforts. However, two situations exist whereby prescribers can directly profit from opioids. One is when they sell prescriptions for opioids, which is illegal, and the other is when they operate a "pill-mill," where they crank out prescriptions for anything, no questions asked. When they do so, they're able to see so many people in a day that they make a fortune in billing. Fortunately, most countries put a great deal of effort into identifying and shutting down such prescribers.

So, you can see that there's no easy solution to the prescription opioid problem. The pharmaceutical industry is constantly making efforts to produce opioid formulations that are "abuse-resistant," but people find ways around these measures very quickly once they come to market. Besides, these "abuse-resistant" formulations are very expensive, and many individuals are unable to afford them, so they're prescribed regular opioids instead.

*

One of the most serious problems with opioid drugs is that it's *very* easy to overdose on them, and overdoses are often fatal. The problem lies in the fact that opioids suppress the brain's natural drive to breath. The brain is very sensitive to low oxygen and high carbon dioxide levels in the blood, and when it detects these situations the brain makes us breath deeper and faster. That's why we huff and puff when we exercise and our oxygen levels drop because of increased oxygen use. Opioids suppress the brain's response to inadequate oxygen intake. Opioids taken in dangerous doses put people to sleep, make the brain "forget" to keep breathing, and relax the breathing muscles. The result is that when people consume too much opioid (i.e. overdose), they fall asleep and stop breathing. If they're not rescued within seconds to minutes they suffer brain damage, coma, and then death.

The dose of opioid required to overdose can be perilously lowered if the individual also takes a "CNS depressant" drug (see the next section) together with the opioid, particularly a benzodiazepine sedative. Unfortunately, many medical professionals prescribe opioids and benzodiazepines together, which puts people at significantly higher risk for overdose. In fact, one study found that nearly 60% of people who were prescribed opioids were also concurrently prescribed medications that increase their risk of overdose. The same effect can occur when alcohol, muscle relaxants, or other sedatives are combined with opioids.

One situation where overdose commonly occurs is when people in recovery from opioid addiction relapse. If they've been in recovery for a while, they will have lost their tolerance to opioids, so their body is no longer used to the drug. However, relapsing addicts commonly resume their drug use at the same doses that they were using when they were in active addiction with high tolerance. The result can be overdose early in relapse, often right at the very beginning of the resumption of opioid use.

Another common overdose situation is when people inadvertently use ultra high-potency synthetic opioids, such as fentanyl or carfentanil. These are produced illicitly and come in a powder. They're so potent that even a few grains can be the difference between life and death. According to the CDC, these synthetic opioids are involved in 67% of opioid deaths in the U.S. Ultra high-potency opioids are cheaper and easier to import than are other drugs, so dealers commonly use them to make fake drugs. I've heard a number of dealers say that they put a pinch of these drugs into the heroin or fake pills that they make, with no measuring or weighing; they "eye-ball it." Often the drugs for sale on the street are made up entirely of ultra-high opioids, with not even a little of the real drug in them. I've interviewed a number of individuals in the hospital following a heroin overdose where their lab tests showed that they didn't have even a trace of heroin in their system; it was all fentanyl. They thought they were purchasing heroin, but it was "fake" heroin – fentanyl added to cutting agents to make it look like heroin. Imagine their surprise. I've been told by many heroin addicts that with each bag (dose) of heroin that they buy, they don't know if they'll survive because they have no way of knowing what exactly is in it, and how much. Each time they put the needle in their arm they don't know if they'll wake up again. Scary.

*

Withdrawal from opioids is notoriously difficult, and fear of withdrawal is a significant barrier to stopping their drug use for opioid addicts. In fact, as tolerance to opioids develops and individuals no longer feel much of a "high" from them, avoiding withdrawal becomes the main motivation to continue the substance use.

Although withdrawal from opioids is much feared and a major driver of continued opioid use, opioid withdrawal and detoxification – unlike withdrawal from alcohol – is seldom dangerous. Deaths from opioid withdrawal have been reported, but they're mostly in people who developed diarrhea and vomiting that was so severe that they dehydrated, and they were alone (usually in a jail cell) with no medical help available.

Typical symptoms of opioid withdrawal include:

- Watery eyes and runny nose,
- Intense sweating ("diaphoresis"),
- "Goose flesh" skin bumps,
- Nausea and vomiting,
- Diarrhea,
- Loss of appetite,
- Dilation of the pupils and sensitivity to light (photophobia),
- Muscle tightness, cramps, and overactive reflexes,
- Fever, chills, hot and cold spells,

- Rapid heart rate, heart palpitations, rapid breathing,
- High blood pressure,
- Yawning,
- Fatigue and lethargy,
- Anxiety,
- Depressed mood,
- Intense drug cravings, and
- Insomnia.

These withdrawal symptoms usually last four to ten days. The exact duration depends on the specific opioids being used (i.e. the half-life of the opioid), the duration and amount of substance use, and individual physical characteristics, such as age, gender, overall health, and so on. Afterwards, there may be protracted withdrawal symptoms that may last for months. These are mostly psychological symptoms and may include:

- Inability to experience pleasure (*anhedonia*),
- The "pink cloud effect" (excessively happy feelings, often resulting in ignoring the reality of life),
- Addiction-related negative feelings: guilt, remorse, anger, self-loathing, low self-esteem,
- Emotional blunting,
- Fatigue,
- Depression, anxiety,
- Difficulty concentrating,
- Irritability,
- Cravings and invasive thoughts about drug use, and
- Relapse dreams.

These protracted psychological symptoms are a potent cause of relapse, and are therefore a major focus of addiction treatment programs. We'll be discussing these symptoms in more detail in upcoming chapters.

As with other addictive substances, withdrawal from opioids can be made much easier and safer when people attend a detox facility for medically assisted detoxification. This includes using medications to reduce withdrawal symptoms, such as anti-diarrheals, and sedatives. Unlike with other addictive substances, opioid detoxification includes the option of "opioid replacement therapy" to alleviate or completely avoid withdrawal. Withdrawal, detoxification, and opioid replacement therapy will be discussed in more detail in chapter 11.

Opioid withdrawal can occur in individuals who're taking prescribed opioids for proper medical reasons, if they're not properly tapered off the medications at the end of their prescription. There are cases where individuals ended up buying opioids on the street because their prescriber did not properly taper them off their prescription opioid, as not all prescribers are skilled in the use of these medications. As such, a plan for properly discontinuing opioid medications should be included in the treatment plan whenever these potentially dangerous medications are prescribed.

Central Nervous System (CNS) Depressants

The central nervous system (CNS) consists of the brain (and spinal cord), so CNS depressants are drugs that slow brain activity. Because they slow brain activity, they're used medically to treat conditions where the brain is overactive (such as anxiety, seizures, acute stress reactions ("mental breakdowns"), and insomnia), and they're also used as part of an anesthetic cocktail to put people to sleep during surgeries, or to sedate them during other medical procedures. As well, the CNS depressant butalbital is used in combination with other medications to treat certain types of headaches and CNS pain.

CNS depressants include three basic types of drugs:

- Barbiturates (e.g. pentobarbital, and phenobarbital),
- Benzodiazepines (BZDs) (e.g. lorazepam, and diazepam), and
- Non-benzodiazepine sedative-hypnotics (sleep aids such as zopiclone, and zolpidem).

As well, many other types of drugs have CNS depressant effects, such as alcohol, muscle relaxants, and opioids. Basically, virtually any class of drug associated with addiction – with the exception of stimulants (we'll talk about those in the next section) – has a CNS depressant effect.

When more than one CNS depressant are used together, their effects are additive, increasing the risk of overdose. Overdose on CNS depressants results in sluggish thinking, speech, and movements, drowsiness, shallow and inadequate breathing, and – in severe cases – coma, brain damage, and death.

The addiction potential of CNS depressants lies in their calming and sedating effect, making individuals feel detached from the world. This effect may be attractive to individuals who're having difficulty coping with stress, or who seek to relieve mental health symptoms, particularly anxiety. Tolerance and dependence develop quickly with these drugs, often leading to rapidly escalating use. The CNS depressants are also often used by individuals to calm themselves when they're "coming down" from a "high" on stimulants.

As you may expect, symptoms of withdrawal from CNS depressants result from the rebound hyperactivity of the brain when the depressants wear off. The overactive brain then causes symptoms such as:

- Seizures,
- Shaking (tremors),

- Hallucinations,
- Agitation,
- Anxiety,
- Insomnia,
- Severe cravings,
- Muscle tightness and overactive reflexes, and
- Rapid heart rate, high blood pressure, and high body temperature.

People who were regularly using CNS depressants – especially if they were mixing them or taking high doses – and suddenly stop taking them may experience severe withdrawal symptoms, which may be life-threatening. Medical supervision of withdrawal in those situations is strongly advised.

Stimulants

Stimulants, which include cocaine and the amphetamines, have a somewhat different profile than most other addictive substances in that they are not CNS depressants, but CNS stimulants.

Stimulants – sometimes referred to as "uppers" – have a checkered past. They were used soon after their development by many countries' militaries in World War 2 as performance enhancers to help their soldiers remain awake and alert for prolonged periods, and were especially popular with fighter pilots. After the war they were marketed extensively as an antidote for depression. However, it soon became obvious that there were some serious addiction problems arising from their widespread casual use, so their medical use declined.

Many stimulants remain in common use today and are available without a prescription, such as caffeine, nicotine, pseudoephedrine (used as a nasal decongestant), and phenylpropanolamine (a cold medicine).

Although stimulants are a widely used street drug, several synthetic amphetamine stimulants are used for a few medical indications such as attention deficit disorder (ADD), weight loss, and narcolepsy. For example, the stimulant methylphenidate is commonly used to treat ADD in children, and sometimes in adults.

Methylphenidate was first synthesized in the lab in 1944 by a chemist who developed the drug to treat his wife's low blood pressure. Her name was Rita, so he called the drug "Ritalin." The drug was used for a variety of purposes, and today it's commonly used to treat ADD. Besides Ritalin, methylphenidate is available in a number of pharmaceutical short- and long-acting preparations. As a stimulant, it has a high abuse potential, and is commonly sold on the street as a "recreational" drug.

Dextroamphetamine is another stimulant that's available by prescription, and is similarly use in short- and long-acting formulations to treat ADD, and narcolepsy. Even cocaine is used medically, although not for its stimulant properties. It's used in topical anesthetics for eyes; and ears, nose, and throat (ENT) specialists will sometimes use it to stop nosebleeds.

Misuse and diversion of prescription stimulants to the street is a serious concern.

*

Although stimulants are "uppers" and some people see them as a way to accomplish more in a day, the illicit stimulants that are in use by addicts are especially nasty and life-consuming.

Powder cocaine, for example, stands out from other addictive drugs due its monetary cost. Robin Williams once said: *cocaine is God's way of saying that you're making too much money.* I've met a number of people with powder cocaine addiction who spend over $1,000 a day on their drug – if they have it. Many wealthy people have been left penniless by cocaine addiction. The two other major illicit stimulants that are in widespread use – crystal methamphetamine and "bath salts" – are cheaper, but they're especially pernicious to the physical health, and horribly devastating to the mind.

The "high" from stimulants is different from other addictive substances, mainly because they're a CNS stimulant rather than a CNS depressant. People who take stimulants still get the euphoria, but they also get stimulation effects, such as:

- Increased energy, reduced fatigue,
- Increased sexual drive (libido),
- Increased self-confidence,
- A feeling of well-being,
- Reduced appetite, and
- Hyper-alertness.

Stimulants are associated with a number of dangerous adverse effects. These are related to over-stimulation of the mind, as well as the body. They super-charge the *autonomic nervous system*, which is that part of our nervous system that gets us charged up in situations where "fight or flight" is necessary, such as situations of danger or conflict. In other words, they not only stimulate the brain, but much of the rest of the body as well. The most commonly seen adverse effects of stimulants include:

- Insomnia,
- Irritability,
- Jitteriness (*psychomotor agitation*),
- Anxiety,
- Behavioral consequences due to impulsivity, confusion, and grandiosity,

- Tight muscles and overactive reflexes (*hyper-reflexia*), high body temperatures (*hyperpyrexia*), rapid heart rate (*tachycardia*), high blood pressure (*hypertension*), and rapid shallow breathing (*tachypnea*) due to over-stimulation of organs (*adrenergic hyper-stimulation*),
- Convulsions and seizures,
- Psychosis – paranoia, delusions, flashbacks, and hallucinations (psychosis may persist for years into abstinence following amphetamine use),
- Stroke by bleeding into the brain, or from a cut off blood supply due to narrowed arteries and/or blood clot formation (*cerebral hemorrhage*, or *infarct*),
- Heart attack or abnormal heart rhythm (*cardiac ischemia*, or *arrhythmias*),
- Arrested breathing (respiratory failure),
- Serious muscle injury that may be life-threatening (*rhabdomyolysis*), and
- "Tweaking" – picking at the skin due to tactile hallucinations (*formication*).

Stimulant addiction often takes on a unique pattern of use that differs from other drugs. In some stimulant users, their use occurs in cycles of binging followed by abstinence. During binges, individuals take the drug repeatedly to try to maintain their "high." Binges usually last twelve hours or more with cocaine, but can last days with methamphetamine. Most of the binge-users that I've spoken with told me that their binges usually ended when they ran out of money, when their body was crashing from utter exhaustion or – more commonly – a combination of both factors. After the binge, the individuals' bodies are so exhausted that they "crash," and this crash begins the abstinent part of the cycle. The crash is very uncomfortable and produces symptoms that may last weeks. As you might expect, the crash symptoms are the opposite of the high produced by the stimulants, and typically include:

- Persistent extreme sleepiness (*hypersomnolence*),
- Depressed mood,
- Inability to feel pleasure (*anhedonia*),
- Lethargy, low energy, lack of motivation, and
- Powerful drug cravings.

People who're "crashing" from stimulant use often use other drugs – specifically CNS depressants – to sedate themselves while they crash. Most commonly, they use alcohol, benzodiazepines, or both. There are currently no specific approved medications for treating stimulant addiction or withdrawal.

Medical treatment is supportive (giving fluids, treating side effects of the drug, and sedation).

Not everyone who uses stimulants binges. Most of the stimulant addicts that I've spoken with use their drug every day if they can. For example, I spoke with one young man who told me that he got up every morning for work and smoked crystal meth before leaving for his very dangerous job as a roofer. He said that the entire roofing crew that he worked with did the same; it was how they "got through their days."

Overdose from stimulants is a frequent occurrence. According to the CDC, in 2019 12.7% of drug overdose deaths in the U.S. occurred from stimulant use alone, and 32.6% of overdose deaths involved a mixture of stimulants and opioids. Many more overdoses occur that are non-fatal, but the numbers are impossible to gather because many addicts will not seek medical care for stimulant overdose due to fear of arrest. The symptoms of stimulant overdose include those of physical and psychological distress:

- Psychological distress – psychosis (paranoia and hallucinations), confusion, anxiety, panic, extreme agitation, and
- Physical distress – chest pain, stroke (sudden onset of numbness, weakness, or reduced level of consciousness), shortness of breath, overheating, shaking, seizure, paralysis, vomiting, and death.

Overdose causes only about a third of the deaths associated with stimulant use. The vast majority of stimulant-related deaths are caused by homicide, suicide, and motor vehicle collisions and other accidents as a result of the drug's mind-altering properties. These are dangerous drugs.

Let's now look at the three main stimulants that are involved in the addiction epidemic: cocaine, crystal methamphetamine, and bath salts. We'll also take a look at the stimulant MDMS ("ecstasy") because of its popularity among adolescents.

*

Cocaine is a naturally occurring compound that's extracted from the leaves of the coca plant, which is native to South America. It's the most powerful central nervous system stimulant found in nature. Three countries: Colombia, Peru, and Bolivia account for all the coca production in the world.

There's no doubt that cocaine is everywhere. After marijuana, cocaine is the second most used illicit drug in the United States, and the second most trafficked drug in the world. According to one study, trace amounts of cocaine can be found on four out of every five dollar bills in circulation in the U.S. More than 400,000 babies are born addicted to cocaine each year in the U.S.

As a street drug, cocaine looks like a fine, white powder with tiny sparkly crystals. The powder is water-soluble, so it can be snorted, or dissolved and injected intravenously. The powder form is not smoked because high temperatures destroy its psychoactive ingredients. Base cocaine (i.e. crack), on the contrary, can be vaporized and inhaled. Dealers often combine cocaine with heroin to produce an injectable combination drug known as "speedball."

Crack is considered to be the most addictive form of cocaine. All the cocaine coming into the United States arrives as powder cocaine and some is modified and made into crack once in the country. It's processed to make a rock crystal (also called "freebase cocaine"), and the crystal is heated to produce vapors that are inhaled into the lungs. The name "crack" refers to the crackling sound of the rock as it's heated.

The slowest onset of cocaine's effects occurs when it's snorted, and this can take up to 20 minutes. The effects last up to 60 minutes. When injected, cocaine reaches the brain within one minute and the effects last for up to 30 minutes. Crack cocaine (i.e. smoked cocaine) takes about 20 seconds to reach the brain, and its effects last for a few minutes to half an hour.

Many people who use cocaine also drink alcohol at the same time, which is particularly risky and can lead to overdose. Others mix cocaine with heroin, another dangerous – and deadly – combination. Ingesting cocaine and alcohol together causes more deaths than any other drug combination. The effects of cocaine and alcohol combined cause the liver to produce a substance known as cocaethylene. Cocaethylene enables users to consume more alcohol than usual when ingesting cocaine at the same time. This increases a person's tolerance to alcohol, leading to highly toxic levels in the blood. Over time, cocaethylene accumulates inside the liver, causing long-term heart problems and increased risk of overdose with each successive use.

In interviews with people in various stages of addiction or recovery, I've heard a number of individuals say that they began using cocaine to counter the CNS depressant effects of alcohol. They found that when they used alcohol first thing in the morning (an "eye opener," a common practice among alcoholics) they would crash and feel like passing out by lunchtime. Therefore, they would use cocaine with their morning alcohol to counter the sedating and depressant effects of alcohol. Conversely, a lot of cocaine users report using alcohol to slow down at the end of a cocaine binge.

As well, there's a rapidly rising threat of cocaine overdose as dealers add ultra-potent opioids to cocaine. One former dealer told me that he would make fake cocaine by adding fentanyl to a cutting powder that resembled cocaine, and then add some numbing agent (such as lidocaine) to the mixture, so that users would get the same numbing sensation when they snorted the powder as they get from real cocaine. As such, he was able to sell cheaply made fake cocaine as the real thing and turn a huge profit. The risk of unintentional overdose in that situation is very high, because if cocaine users are not also regular users of opioids (which they often aren't) they'll have little or no tolerance to the fentanyl and will overdose at very low doses. Because Naloxone (the drug used to rescue opioid overdose victims) doesn't work for cocaine, many cocaine users are not familiar with the life-saving drug, nor do they have access to it, because they're not even aware they're using fentanyl.

Another way in which dealers try to increase their profits is by tainting cocaine with impurities as a way of increasing its volume – a practice known as "cutting." Apparently, everybody in the illicit supply chain who touches the real cocaine "cuts" it before in turn selling it, so they can increase their profits at the expense of their customers. By the time it reaches the users, there may not be very much real cocaine left in what they're purchasing. Unfortunately, most of the substances used to dilute cocaine are themselves very toxic when snorted, injected, or smoked. These are known to include: cornstarch, talcum powder, laundry detergent, boric acid, laxatives, and flour.

Yet another way of ripping off their customers to maximize profits is by selling other, cheaper stimulants as cocaine. This is usually done with the very cheap (and dangerous) "bath salts" stimulants, which we'll discuss shortly.

Cocaine use can cause some serious health problems, besides the usual problems caused by addiction. Cocaine has been described as the "perfect heart attack drug" because it increases blood pressure, constricts arteries, and thickens heart muscle walls. These abnormalities persist long after the intoxication effects of cocaine have worn off, even in occasional users. Some of the most frequent and severe health consequences leading to cocaine overdose involve the heart and blood vessels (including irregular heart rhythm and heart attacks), and the brain (including seizures and strokes). During my time as an ER doctor I treated a number of young people for heart attack and stroke from cocaine use.

Cocaine causes significant tooth decay because it dehydrates the mouth and causes bruxism – involuntary teeth grinding. Other long-term effects of cocaine use include being malnourished (because cocaine decreases appetite and burns Calories), and movement disorders, including Parkinson's disease, which may occur after many years of use. In addition, people report irritability and restlessness resulting from cocaine use, and some also experience paranoia, in which they lose touch with reality and have frightening auditory hallucinations – hearing noises and voices that aren't real. Chronic cocaine snorting can destroy the nasal septum – the cartilage separating the nostrils inside the nose. I've seen photos of individuals whose nose was completely eroded away from cocaine use.

*

Synthetic methamphetamine ("crystal meth") is a potent stimulant that has no medical uses. It may be smoked in a glass pipe, snorted, injected, swallowed, or inserted into the rectum. It's colorless (sometimes with a blue hue), opaque, and odorless. It comes in fragments of various sizes that look like crystals. Due to its appearance, it's sometimes called "ice," "blue-ice," "glass," or simply "meth."

Smoking or injecting methamphetamine causes an immediate, intense "rush" that lasts anywhere from a few minutes to up to half an hour. Snorting does not produce the intense rush but rather a euphoric high within 3-5 minutes of ingestion. The oral effects can be felt within 20 minutes. Following the initial "rush," there's a sense of energy, hyperactivity, and alertness that lasts for 6-24 hours, depending on how it was ingested. This part of the high is sometimes referred to by users as "the shoulder." This is a much longer duration than the high associated with cocaine.

Because the "high" from meth starts and fades quickly, users most often end up taking repeated doses in a "binge and crash" pattern. Many users end up in a form of binging known as a "run," giving up food and sleep while continuing to take the drug every few hours for up to several days. Unlike cocaine – which is rapidly metabolized and removed from the body – meth remains in the body much longer (by comparison one-half of cocaine is removed from the body after one hour, versus twelve hours for meth). Users try to maintain the high by taking more of the drug before the first dose wears off. Some users binge until they finally run out of money and the drug, they "tweak," and/or they crash.

During a run (i.e. a binge) the repeated use of meth results in the user experiencing less and less of a high each time, until it gets to the point where little or no rush is felt. At the end of a run, when the high is no longer achievable, users describe the experience as "tweaking." They feel horribly unwell, down and depressed, and they crave the high. They're utterly exhausted. Their mind begins to play tricks on them: they become psychotic, completely out of touch with the world around them. They experience tactile hallucinations – feeling like they have bugs crawling under their skin – and begin to scratch and pick at their skin. They have vivid visual and auditory hallucinations that they believe are real, and become terribly paranoid. They become defensive, aggressive, hostile, and even violent. They're dangerous to themselves and others, and may self-mutilate or confront and assault total strangers. I've seen meth addicts tweaking in public, and it isn't pretty. They'll wander aimlessly around a public place yelling and screaming at their hallucinations and making violent gestures. They scare people, and rightfully so; they can be dangerous.

The "crash" occurs when the body shuts down, and the user becomes lifeless for one to three days. This is followed by the meth "hangover," where the utterly exhausted meth user is physically and mentally spent. Withdrawal begins gradually – often as much as thirty days or more after the binge. Withdrawal from meth is painful, and typically lasts much longer than that experienced by cocaine users. Withdrawal usually lasts three to four weeks, with the first week being the "crash." The prolonged withdrawal is one of the reasons that meth is such a difficult drug to break away from, and why it has such a high relapse rate. Typical withdrawal symptoms include:

- Severe overall feeling of being physically sick,

- Agitation and anxiety,
- Drug craving,
- Profound depression,
- Fatigue and insomnia,
- Psychosis,
- Emotional turmoil,
- Lack of motivation, and
- Vivid or lucid dreams.

Crystal meth is highly addictive, and is a serious problem in many places around the world. One of the problems with the drug is that – unlike cocaine – it's cheap to buy. A hit can usually be purchased for around $10; about what a high-school kid has for lunch-money. Unlike cocaine – which must be imported from South America – meth can be made locally with commonly available ingredients, although government controls are making these ingredients more difficult to obtain.

Most of the meth found in the United States is made in clandestine "super-labs" in the U.S. or, more often, in Mexico. However, huge amounts of domestic meth are produced in "Mom-and-Pop" cook labs in home kitchens, workshops, recreational vehicles [like "Eisenberg" from *Breaking Bad*], and rural cabins.

Some of the ingredients needed to cook meth are found in over-the-counter products, such as pseudoephedrine, a common ingredient in cold medicines. To curb production, the law requires pharmacies and other retail stores to keep a purchase record of products containing pseudoephedrine. A person may only buy a limited amount of those products in a single day. Other key chemicals needed for its production are similarly controlled (by the Combat Methamphetamine Epidemic Act of 2005). However, labs in the U.S. have skirted these regulations by obtaining methamphetamine (mostly from Mexico) smuggled into the U.S., and the small labs in the U.S. convert it to crystal meth.

Illicitly manufactured methamphetamine may include drain cleaner, antifreeze, lantern fuel, battery acid, anhydrous ammonia (fertilizer), hydrochloric acid, acetone, red phosphorus (from matches or road flares), and lye; not your basic list of healthy natural ingredients. As well, meth is often tainted with other illicit drugs – especially fentanyl.

Increasingly, dealers are pressing meth into pill form and selling it as ecstasy, so as to rip off their customers and introduce unsuspecting new people to meth addiction.

*

During World War II, methamphetamine was sold in tablet form under the brand name Pervitin by a German pharmaceutical company. It was used extensively by all branches of the German armed forces of the Third Reich for its performance-enhancing stimulant effects and to induce extended wakefulness. However, its side effects were so serious that the military cut back its usage in 1940. Some soldiers turned very violent, committing war crimes or attacking their own officers. Historian Lukasz Kamienski says: *a soldier going to battle on Pervitin usually found himself unable to perform effectively for the next day or two. Suffering from a drug hangover and looking more like a zombie than a great warrior, he had to recover from the side effects.*

In the 1950s methamphetamine came into use as a legal pharmaceutical (marketed under the brand name Obetrol) for treating obesity. Unsurprisingly, Obetrol became a popular diet pill in America in the 1950s and 1960s, as many people became addicted to its stimulant effects. Eventually, as the addictive and other detrimental properties of the drug became known, governments began to strictly regulate the production and distribution of methamphetamine. Currently, methamphetamine is sold under the trade name Desoxyn in the U.S., as a last-resort way to treat ADHD. Note that Desoxyn is prescribed in doses far lower than the amount used by typical meth addicts.

In low doses, methamphetamine can elevate mood, and increase alertness, concentration, and energy in fatigued individuals, reduce appetite, and promote weight loss. It brings on increased activity and talkativeness, decreased appetite, and a sense of well-being or euphoria. It removes tiredness and brings a feeling of power and self-control. Sounds great... but the price is high.

Few people are able to use meth "responsibly." Meth is highly addictive, and tolerance develops especially rapidly with it. Meth is known to possess a high addiction liability (i.e., a high likelihood of compulsive drug use) and high dependence liability (i.e. a high likelihood that withdrawal symptoms will occur when use ceases).

*

Meth is one of the nastiest drugs in circulation. Users typically lose a lot of body weight because during binges (runs) they neglect eating, and they're hyperactive and not sleeping for days on end, burning lots of Calories (remember, in the mid-Twentieth century meth was used as a weight-loss drug). Even between binges they sleep a lot and neglect self-care, and have probably used all their money to buy drugs. They end up looking malnourished and gaunt. The skin picking and scratching that occurs during tweaking results in numerous open, raw sores around the body, and especially on the face. As well, the dry mouth and teeth grinding that are side effects of the drug – as well as neglected self-care – result in serious deterioration of the dentition, so that they have missing, broken, and rotten teeth. This is so common in meth users that it's referred to as "meth mouth." The Internet is full of before-and-after photos of meth users, and it's worth doing a Google search to see the shocking changes that occur in a short period of time with meth use.

In addition to their physical appearance, meth users are often affected by serious psychological and behavioral problems, even when they're not actively using. Exposure to stress when they're in recovery may re-activate psychosis. They often develop psychosis that may persist months or years after their last use. Meth users also commonly suffer from irritability, sleep disturbances, anxiety, confusion, and violent behavior, even when they're not using. The end result is that meth users end up looking and acting as horribly as they feel.

Fortunately, many – but not all – of the brain changes and damage that occur from meth use are reversible when these individuals are in recovery and abstinent from substance use. Much of the damage becomes reversed in the first two years in recovery. I know a lot of former meth users who're in stable long-term recovery and now lead normal, happy, and productive lives.

*

"Bath salts" is the innocuous-sounding commonly used term for a truly scary type of stimulant drug. "Bath salts" refers to synthetic *cathinones*, human-made drugs chemically related to a stimulant found in the Khat plant. Khat is a shrub grown in East Africa and southern Arabia, where people chew its leaves for the mild stimulant effects. Synthetic variants of cathinone can be much stronger than the natural product found in Khat.

Despite their street name, "bath salts" should not be confused with actual bath salts such as Epsom salts, the stuff we use in the tub. Those have no mind-altering properties, although they're pretty nice for calming the mind in a hot bath. The street name came about because synthetic cathinones were originally sold disguised as true bath salts, and they do resemble real bath salts as well.

Synthetic cathinones are marketed as cheap substitutes for other stimulants, or are passed off as fake cocaine or crystal meth by dealers to rip off their customers. Synthetic cathinones are included in a group of drugs that public health officials refer to as "new psychoactive substances" (NPS). The NPS are unregulated addictive substances that have become newly available on the market and are intended to copy the effects of illegal drugs. Some of these substances may have been around before but have re-entered the market in altered chemical forms or due to renewed popularity. They're ahead of the law, in that they're as yet unregulated and therefore exist in a legal grey area that allows them to be easily obtained.

Bath salts are thought to be mostly made in China, in tablet or powder form. These substances are often sold over the Internet, as well as in convenience and tobacco stores, gas stations, head shops, truck stops, pawn shops, tattoo parlors, and on the street. The drug's packaging often states "not for human consumption" in an attempt to circumvent drug laws. The legal system is slowly catching up with these dangerous chemicals and their distribution. Meanwhile, they're often easier for young people to obtain than are cigarettes and alcohol.

Bath salts comprise a number of chemically similar recreational "designer" drugs. Bath salts contain some form of a synthetic cathinone, typically MDPV (methylenedioxypyrovalerone), methylone, or mephedrone. Sometimes also seen are pyrovalerone or pipradrol. However, the chemical composition varies widely due to amateurish production and cutting with various impurities. In Europe the main synthetic cathinone is mephedrone, whereas in the U.S. MDPV is more common. They're all synthetic stimulants with different chemical structures but similar effects on the user.

Bath salts are sometimes referred to on the street as "zombie" or "cannibal" because it has been reported that a person who engaged in murder and cannibalism may have been intoxicated on the substance. Some of the other street names include Plant Food, Red Dove, Blue Silk, Energy 1, Vanilla Sky, Purple Wave, Ivory Wave, Bliss, White Lightning, White Dove, Super Coke, Tranquility, Zoom, and Magic. Mephedrone also has street names like meow, drone, and meph. One bath salt, referred to as "Cosmic Blast" or "synthetic cocaine," contains MDPV and Naphyrone, another synthetic cathinone.

A majority of U.S. states have made a number of the active ingredients in bath salts illegal at the state level, and the U.S. federal government has made MDPV illegal due to the drug's tendency to cause psychosis and violence in users. The Drug Enforcement Agency (DEA) now lists a number of the active ingredients found in bath salts as schedule I drugs, meaning they're illegal because they have a high potential for addiction, no accepted medical use, and no accepted safe use.

In July 2012, U.S. federal drug policy was amended to ban bath salts. The drug policy of Canada since the fall of 2012 categorizes MDPV as a schedule I controlled substance, placing it in the same category as heroin and MDMA. Mephedrone and methylone are already illegal in Canada and most of the US. In the United Kingdom, all synthetic cathinones were made illegal in April 2010.

Bath salts intoxication is characterized by:

- Feeling euphoric ("high"),
- Sexual hyper-stimulation,
- Thinking one is more focused, and
- High energy levels for 2-4 hours after taking the drug.

Those symptoms tend to be followed by a withdrawal characterized by depressed mood, anxiety, shaking, and psychosis (particularly paranoia) for several hours or days thereafter.

Aggressive behavior, wildly unpredictable acts of violence, self-mutilation, and suicide are commonly seen with bath salts use. Often this is brought on by psychosis. The risk of psychosis is highest when the user is sleep deprived, using high doses, or using frequently. The psychosis and agitation can outlast the high, lasting for days.

An example of the psychosis associated with bath salts happened to a man who barricaded himself in his attic with a rifle wanting to kill monsters before the monsters killed him. Another bath salts user tried to remove her own liver with a mechanical pencil. A lot of people who've used bath salts say that they didn't enjoy the high due to the frightening paranoia. Even though the psychosis may make bath salts "trips" miserable, people report that the cravings for repeated use are intense and drive further bath salts use. Overdose on bath salts is common, often brought on by brain damage from very high body temperature (hyperthermia).

*

Ecstasy – properly known as MDMA (3,4-methylenedioxy methamphetamine) – is a stimulant that also has the properties of a hallucinogen. It's used as a "party drug" by young people due to its stimulant properties and lowered inhibition. Commonly referred to as Molly (short for "molecular"), this drug is taken orally as a pill or in liquid form, or snorted in its crystalline powder form, which is usually sold in capsules. In many cases, individuals who think they're buying MDMA are actually buying the much cheaper and more dangerous bath salts, as their dealers rip them off to increase profits. MDMA is frequently mixed with alcohol or marijuana at parties. Much of the ecstasy that has been seized and tested by authorities in the U.S. contained cocaine, ketamine, cough medicine, and/or bath salts instead of or in addition to MDMA.

People use ecstasy as a "party drug" because its stimulant properties give them stamina for partying all night, although they usually have to take another dose after the drug wears off after 3-6 hours. The drug gives them energy, euphoria, and makes them hyper-sexual and disinhibited. It also causes excessive sweating, muscle cramping and teeth clenching, blurred vision, and nausea.

After using ecstasy, individuals often feel unwell – hung over – for up to a week. The withdrawal effects may include:

- Irritability and aggressiveness,
- Depressed mood,
- Anxiety,
- Impulsiveness,
- Reduced appetite,
- Memory and attention deficits,
- Loss of sexual interest, and
- Sleep disturbances.

Ecstasy appears to have much less addiction potential than do cocaine or meth. Many individuals who use the drug only use it at specific times, such as at all-night rave parties, and don't use it in between. One of the reasons that dealers put other drugs into ecstasy is to increase its addiction potential so as to get themselves repeat customers.

I've had some horrible clinical experiences with ecstasy in my time as a doctor. On nights that I was working in the ER, if there was an all-night rave party going on somewhere in the area we would get a constant stream of ambulances bringing in partygoers who had collapsed from using ecstasy. There were many cases where the paramedics thought the patients were dead because they had no discernable vital signs, but we were able to resuscitate them in the ER. The problem was that we had no idea exactly which drugs these people were actually taking, because ecstasy is notoriously tainted with impurities, many of which we have no tests for in the medical lab. As well, I've seen cases where young people became schizophrenic (schizophrenia is a permanent psychotic disorder) after ecstasy use. In some cases the individuals involved were adamant that they had only tried ecstasy once. I don't know if the drug simply unmasked a predisposition for schizophrenia, or if it outright caused it. Either way, I have seen young lives derailed and ruined by the effects of the drug.

Hallucinogens

Hallucinogens are drugs that cause distortions in perception, including (but not limited to) hallucinations. Hallucinogen drugs are classed into two categories:

1) **Classic hallucinogens** – these produce distortions in perception and disturbances in emotion, memory, and judgment. Classic hallucinogen drugs include, for example, LSD, and psilocybin (the active drug in magic mushrooms), and
2) **Dissociative drugs** – these produce a feeling of being detached from oneself. Dissociative drugs include ketamine, PCP, and dextromethorphan (that's right, the over-the-counter cough medicine).

A "high" from a hallucinogen drug is often referred to as a "trip." Hallucinogens produce a variety of effects, including:

- Hallucinations, which can be auditory (hearing things that aren't really there), visual (seeing things that aren't really there), or sensory (such as tasting or smelling things, feeling things touching or crawling on the skin, or feeling the internal organs moving around),
- Mixed senses, such as "seeing" sounds, or "feeling" colors,
- Intensified sensory experiences,

- Altered perception of time: feeling like time is moving super-slowly,
- Increased energy,
- Rapid heart rate, high blood pressure, high body temperature, rapid breathing,
- Dizziness, and
- Nausea, and vomiting.

As well, hallucinogens are notorious for causing symptoms long after the last drug use, especially psychotic episodes ("flashbacks"), and breathing and heart irregularities.

Generally, people's motivation for using hallucinogens differs somewhat from other drugs. Hallucinogens have been used for millennia to bring about "visions" and religious experiences. Even today, some people believe that hallucinogens help them to achieve "enlightenment" or deeper levels of thinking. However, just like with other addictive drugs, some individuals use hallucinogens because they enjoy the "trip," or to dissociate themselves from reality as a way to escape from stress or mental illness symptoms.

Are hallucinogens addictive? Yes and no. They all produce tolerance, which is a characteristic of addiction, but not all of them seem to produce the obsessive repeated drug use that characterizes addiction. For example, LSD is not considered to be particularly addictive, but PCP is highly addictive. The difference is that PCP produces a withdrawal that includes intense cravings.

Cannabis

Cannabis – marijuana – comes from the dried parts of the *Cannabis sativa* or *Cannabis indica* plants. These plants produce over 100 unique compounds known as "cannabinoids." The vast majority of these cannabinoid compounds have not been investigated, so we know little about them, but some are believed to have medicinal properties. The two cannabinoids of greatest interest are THC (tetrahydrocannabinol), and CBD (cannabidiol). These two compounds have been at least partly investigated, although there remains much we don't know about them.

Based on our current knowledge of cannabinoids, almost all the medicinal properties that may come from cannabis are due to CBD; the THC component of marijuana doesn't appear to have many medicinal properties (THC is used as a second-line treatment for nausea in some patients). THC is the cannabinoid that makes people high and is the main cause of the adverse effects of cannabis. Another crucial difference between the CBD and THC is that THC is psychoactive and addictive, while CBD is non-psychoactive and non-addictive. Anyone who wishes to explore the medicinal effects of cannabis should consider CBD-only preparations (with less than 0.3% THC), which are widely available. The CBD-only preparations have all the medicinal benefits without the side effects and mind-altering addictive potential of THC.

The typical "high" that people experience from THC depends on the individual and the particular strain of cannabis plant, but the high usually involves feeling relaxed, dream-like, and being disconnected from the world. There may be euphoria, and a feeling of heightened sensory perception.

An increasingly common practice involves making THC-rich extracts from the cannabis plant; a process known as "dabbing." Dabbing has resulted in a spike in cannabis overdoses and hospitalizations. As well, the preparation of these potent THC extracts is dangerous in itself. The process requires the use of butane – which is volatile and highly flammable – and a number of fires, explosions, and burns have resulted from attempts at dabbing.

There's a common belief that cannabis is a "soft drug" and not addictive. However, data from large U.S. surveys show that nearly a third of cannabis users are addicted to the drug. As well, contrary to popular belief, cannabis is very much a "gateway drug" that leads to the use of harder drugs. Overwhelming research data have shown that cannabis creates the physical and psychological brain changes (that we'll discuss in upcoming chapters) that predispose to other substance use and addiction. Indeed, a large U.S. national survey showed that 44.7% of chronic cannabis users go on to use other illicit drugs.

My experience as a doctor has been that the majority of the people who seek help for cannabis addiction are young – in their teens or twenties. Typically, they need to smoke up in order to get out of bed in the morning, and continue to smoke to get through the day, and they are often deeply in debt or in financial trouble because of the expense of their "weed."

One of the sad ironies about cannabis use is that many individuals who use it regularly began using the drug in order to "self-medicate" mental illness symptoms. The irony is that although the calming and detached feeling they get from the cannabis high may provide some relief for a while, cannabis can itself trigger mental illness, particularly psychosis. Cannabis use is known to cause acute psychosis, and can precipitate chronic psychiatric illness, including schizophrenia.

It's especially distressing to see young people using cannabis, because of the drug's adverse effects on the developing mind. The brain doesn't fully mature until around age 25, and the immature mind is exquisitely sensitive to the physical changes that bring about addiction when exposed to psychoactive substances. To be sure, the same brain effects may happen even after brain development is complete, but the young mind is especially sensitive. Research has identified a number of adverse outcomes of cannabis use, including:

- Poor educational outcome, increased likelihood of dropping out of school,
- Permanent impairment of cognitive functions (thinking, planning, decision-making, etc.),
- Reduced IQ,

- Reduced achievement in life,
- Reduced life satisfaction,
- Addiction,
- Impaired brain development, and
- Chronic bronchitis symptoms, such as cough, reduced lung capacity, and shortness of breath.

Cannabis withdrawal symptoms are usually relatively mild, but may include:

- Irritability,
- Anxiety,
- Insomnia,
- Reduced appetite, and
- Cravings.

No medications are currently approved to treat marijuana addiction.

Inhalants

Inhalants are volatile substances that have a psychoactive effect when inhaled. These include:

- Aerosols – sprays that contain propellants, such as spray paint, hair spray, deodorant, and spray cooking oils,
- Volatile solvents – such as gasoline, paint thinners, liquid paper, felt-tipped markers, and glues,
- Gases – such as butane lighters, propane tanks, medical anesthetics (nitrous oxide, chloroform, and ether), and refrigerants, and
- Nitrites – such as amyl nitrite and butyl nitrite. These are known as "poppers" on the street. They're used to facilitate anal sex, because they relax sphincter muscles and increase blood flow to the penis. They also provide a brief high. Most of the poppers found on the street in Western countries have been made in illegal labs.

Although inhalants do not receive much attention in the newspapers, national surveys have found that 21.7 million Americans have used inhalants at least once in their life, and by eighth grade 13.1% of children have used them.

Withdrawal from inhalant use may cause mood swings, insomnia, irritability, and insomnia. There are no medications approved for treating inhalant addiction.

Polysubstance Use

"Polysubstance use" refers to using more than one class of addictive substance, although not necessarily at the same time. While most people in active addiction prefer a specific drug or class of drugs (often referred to as their "drug of choice"), the majority are polysubstance users. Use of one substance (even nicotine) greatly increases one's likelihood of using other addictive substances.

The use of more than one substance in the same person magnifies the risks of adverse events – especially overdose. Polysubstance use complicates addiction treatment, including withdrawal and detox, and increases the risk of subsequent relapse.

Overall, people who're addicted to one substance report using an average of 3.5 different substances. A recent large U.S. public health study found that more than 90% of people who're addicted to opioids are polysubstance users at the time they enter treatment.

There are several main reasons for polysubstance use:

- Balancing effect – the classic example is individuals who combine "uppers" (i.e. stimulants, such as cocaine or meth) with "downers" (i.e. CNS depressants, such as sedatives or alcohol) in order to balance the effects and function properly,
- Substitution – when the "drug of choice" isn't available or the user doesn't have enough money to buy it, a cheaper and more easily obtained substitute may be sought. Substitution likely has a lot to do with the huge increase in crystal meth use in recent years, as meth is cheaper and more easily obtained compared to other drugs,
- Chasing the high – as people progress in their addiction, they get less and less of a high as tolerance develops. They may try using more of the drug, but soon they feel little or no high. Adding another drug to the mix is a common approach to chasing the high,
- Dealing withdrawal symptoms – people often use other drugs to help reduce their withdrawal symptoms. Benzodiazepines are frequently used for this purpose,
- Social influence – people who use substances tend to congregate, and provide each other access and advice on substance use. Many are thus exposed to different substances and opportunities to use them, and
- Brain changes – once addicted, people lose the ability to properly reason and make decisions, and they're psychologically adjusted to seeing themselves as substance users. As such, adding another substance to the mix isn't a great leap.

The take-home message here is that polysubstance use is the norm rather than the exception, and it greatly complicates treatment and recovery from addiction. As such, it's a significant factor in diagnosing and treating addiction, and it should be carefully identified early in the treatment of addiction.

4

The Core Symptoms and Behaviors of Addiction

An alcoholic is someone who can violate his standards faster than he can lower them.

– Robin Williams

Secretive substance use, covered by lies and excuses; selfish behavior, dropped obligations and responsibilities, failed promises and resolutions, alienation of family and friends, inability to initiate action – are all typical behaviors of addiction. The erosion of life and character brought on by addiction leads to a progressively worsening negative mindset characterized by guilt, shame, and self-loathing. Despite the hard, arrogant, know-it-all exterior, addicts are hurting inside, and don't like who they've become.

When someone becomes increasingly drawn into addiction, they develop a set of behaviors that may make them seem like a totally different person. When we watch a loved one go through this transformation, it's dreadfully distressing. A once caring and loving individual now seems distant, selfish, uncaring, and hurtful. To make matters worse, they're totally defensive and unapproachable. You can't talk to them anymore without it turning into a fight.

It may seem impossible to understand how someone you love can undergo such a drastic transformation for the worst. But you're not alone; people who go through addiction don't understand the transformation either. In fact, they're tremendously burdened by guilt, remorse, regret, and even self-loathing because of their behaviors, declining relationships, and shirked responsibilities. They don't like what they've become any more than you do. Indeed, trying to cope with these negative feelings are a major driver of their continuing substance use.

When I went through addiction, I had been practicing as a doctor and psychotherapist for a number of years, so I thought I had the human body and mind pretty much figured out. However, I couldn't understand my own behaviors, especially the terrible things that I would do and say. I couldn't understand why I kept self-destructing. I was just watching it happen to me without being able to do anything about it. My mother used to say: *you're so miserable and sick, and you're ruining your life... why don't you just stop?* But you know what? I couldn't answer that question. I, too, wondered: *why can't I just stop???*

People in active addiction get dismally down on themselves because of their behaviors. Each of them sees their unlovely actions – where they put obtaining and using their substance ahead of all other priorities, no matter how dearly those priorities were previously held – as being evidence that they're a bad person. They're hurting inside and they know they're hurting everyone around them. Yet they respond with anger and become defensive the moment anybody tries to help them. It just doesn't make sense. All human beings have a need to feel good about themselves, and people in active addiction don't feel good about themselves at all. They get so down on themselves that they need their substance use to numb the terrible feelings. However, there's one thing that most of them – and maybe their loved ones – may not realize: all those behaviors – as ugly as they are – are simply the typical symptoms of addiction.

One of the benefits of the disease model of addiction is that it helps people in active addiction and their loved ones to remember that the ugly behaviors of addiction don't mean that addicts are bad people, it means that they're people who're displaying the typical symptoms of a brain disease. They're people who're unwell and need to get healthy, not bad people who need to become good. In other words, the disease model of addiction helps us to separate the sickness from the person. As a doctor, when I have a person in my office who's schizophrenic and acutely unstable, and that person is causing disruption and chaos, I always remember that I'm dealing with a person who has a disease that needs treatment, not a person who's a jerk. The same applies to the awful behaviors that we see from addicts. But remember: addiction doesn't *excuse* the behavior, but it *puts it in context*. Just because they have a sickness doesn't mean they're off the hook for their actions.

Personally, I felt immense relief when I realized that I was the same as the millions of people who came before me and went through addiction, and that treating addiction meant that the same old good person could emerge once again. This realization helps addicts to see themselves as worthy of recovery, and provides powerful motivation for beating their addiction. However, even though we try to separate the sickness from the person, their addiction doesn't excuse addicts' horrible antics, and we must hold them responsible when the time is right – for their sake and for ours. In fact, part of the addiction treatment and recovery process requires that addicts take ownership and responsibility for their past actions, and that they make meaningful amends to those they've harmed. It's how they heal, and it's how they help those they've harmed to heal. The overall lesson: people in addiction are sick people who need to get well, not bad people who need to become good. That may be difficult to remember when they're pulling your strings and pushing your buttons, but it's true.

As your addict loved one slowly changes for the worst, you may feel you've lost the person you once knew and loved. But take heart: once people have participated in a treatment program that addresses the causes and effects of addiction and are in successful recovery an entirely different person emerges: usually the same likeable and loving individual you once knew. In fact, many are more functional and resilient than they were before their addiction, because issues that had long bothered or affected them have been identified and addressed. As part of their relapse prevention therapy they would have learned how to handle life in a much healthier way, and to interact with others in a more convivial way. You may find your loved one in recovery to be more likeable than they were even before the addiction.

In this chapter we'll review the cluster of symptoms that form the core symptoms and behaviors of addiction. While not everybody will display the exact same symptoms in the exact same way, the symptoms and behaviors of addiction are remarkably uniform in different people. I've always been amazed how different people of different age groups, who come from different cultures and countries and speak different languages display remarkably similar symptomatology when they're in active addiction. See if any of these symptoms remind you of the behaviors you've observed in your loved one, and always try to remember that these symptoms are a reflection of how addictive substances affect the brain, not a reflection of who addicts are as people.

*

A good place to start when looking at the symptoms of addiction is by reviewing the medical definition of addiction – or, as the medical books call it, a *substance use disorder*, or SUD. Medical professionals all over the world rely on a standardized manual for diagnosing mental health disorders, a huge (and very boring) tome that's known as the *Diagnostic and Statistical Manual of Mental Disorders, 5th edition*, or "DSM 5" for short. Since addiction is classified as a mental health disorder, its definition is included in the DSM 5. Personally, I view addiction as a neurological disorder – a disease of the brain – but given the blurring of boundaries between the brain and mind, classifying it as a psychiatric disorder – a disease of the mind – isn't such a stretch.

The DSM 5 criteria for an SUD require the presence of two or more of the following symptoms within a 12-month period:

- Hazardous substance use (participating in risky behaviors while under the influence of psychoactive substances, such as driving while impaired, sharing needles, or engaging in unsafe sex),
- Continued substance use despite obvious social or interpersonal problems arising from the substance use,
- Neglect of major roles or giving up important or cherished activities due to substance use,
- Problems with family, relationships, job, school, or the law due to substance use,
- Withdrawal symptoms when use is reduced or stopped,
- Tolerance develops, so that higher and higher doses are required to achieve the same effect,
- Using larger amounts of substances and/or for longer than intended,
- Repeated failed attempts to control or stop the substance use despite an earnest desire to do so,
- Spending an inordinate amount of time obtaining, using, or recovering from substance use,
- Continued use despite physical and/or psychological problems that arise due to substance use, and
- Cravings, and obsessive, invasive, or perseverative thoughts about substance use.

The severity of the SUD is rated by the number of criteria that are present out of the 11 on the list: 2-3 = mild, 4-5 = moderate, 6 or more = severe. Most of the addicts that I meet in my research check all those boxes, just as I would've while I was in active addiction. These criteria are for diagnostic purposes, and fall far short of providing an adequate description of the symptomatology of addiction.

The DSM 5 diagnostic criteria for an SUD provide a good generalized characterization of addiction, but they don't provide a picture of the daily life, mindset, and social interactions of people in active addiction; the kinds of things that we observe when someone we care about is living addiction before our eyes. As such, in this chapter we'll review the typical symptoms that take over people's life when they're in active addiction. Then, in the following two chapters we'll discuss exactly what addictive substances do to the brain and mind and how these effects bring about these symptoms. This not only helps us to recognize addiction in someone who's trying to hide their problem from us, but it also helps us to understand and predict their behavior, and it forms the basis for helping them beat addiction and heal.

One of the main themes of this book is that the thought processes and behaviors – the symptoms – of addiction are driven by the physical effects of addictive substances on the brain, not by individuals' lack of intellect, morals, character, or willpower. It's easy to be judgmental of individuals who're wrapped up in obsessive substance use and behaving like complete louts. After all, they display some really dastardly behaviors and say some really ugly things and do some really stupid stuff. And they hurt others with no apparent remorse. However, we must remember that our overall goal is to help our loved one beat addiction and heal, so that we can get back the fully functional and healthy individual we once knew. To this end, it's important that we do our best to maintain our compassion, patience, and love by doing our best to separate the person from the disease and its symptoms. That's not easy to do sometimes, but when we understand the symptoms and why they occur, peering through the ugly exterior to see the hurting person underneath makes much more sense. This knowledge also forms a foundation for helping move our loved one toward a readiness to accept help, and for supporting them in recovery. When we understand them, it's much easier to break down the walls and form a productive bond with them.

*

Addiction – like any other disease or illness – tends to follow a distinctive pattern of onset and progression. Medical people refer to this as a disease's *natural history*, meaning that it's how a disease will play out if some kind of preventive intervention or treatment isn't initiated. In Chapter 1, we laid out the reasons that people begin repeatedly using psychoactive substances, initiating the addiction process. You may recall, for example, that some people begin using addictive substances through a prescription for a legitimate medical reason, some start their use as a way to "self-medicate" mental health symptoms, some just plain enjoy the high, and so on. However, regardless of the reason for the initial substance use, the progression to addiction typically follows the same four stages:

1) **Experimental use** – this is sometimes referred to as "recreational" use. In this early stage of addiction, individuals begin using the substance (or substances) for the euphoric or sedating effects. They begin using the substance outside of "casual" social use (for example, drinking alcohol while alone for the high, rather than drinking in social settings), or – for prescribed drugs – taking the drug for the high in addition to or instead of its intended use. During the experimental use phase, people also begin taking the substance at higher doses or more often, in order to attain the desired effect,

2) **Regular use** – in this stage, individuals begin relying on the drug's effects to cope with getting through their days, so the substance use

becomes regular, with increasing frequency. They begin using the substance to "fix" negative feelings or stress, or because they feel they can perform better with the substance. Tolerance and cravings develop as the body becomes accustomed to regular exposure. In this stage of addiction, individuals may become erratic in their day-to-day responsibilities and activities, such as declining attendance and performance at school, work, or home. They often begin to socially isolate. Individuals start becoming preoccupied about their substance throughout the day, and worries about not having enough of the drug may become a major distraction for them. They expend considerable thought into how they will obtain enough of their substance, as they develop fears and anxiety about having to face their days without it,

3) **Problem or risky use** – at this point, individuals begin prioritizing obtaining and using their substance over just about anything else, including their own safety. They lose motivation for school, work, relationships, and normal activities, especially if those activities interfere with substance use. Obvious behavior and attitude changes occur, and loved ones notice that the individual has become secretive and socially isolated. Difficulty in obtaining enough substance causes desperation, and individuals may resort to risky, illegal, or dangerous measures in order to ensure their supply of drug. For example, people in this stage of addiction may begin trying to manipulate healthcare providers for prescriptions, dealing drugs, obtaining drugs on the street, resorting to drugs that are cheaper and easier to obtain (such as heroin or meth), and crime. Usually individuals have developed serious financial problems by this stage, and they may begin diverting their rent or grocery money into purchasing their substance. Family members may be constantly bombarded with requests for money, always with the excuse that the money is needed for basic necessities, such as rent or groceries. Family members may begin noticing that their loved one has become manipulative, and

4) **Full-out addiction** – by this time, the individual's life becomes focused on their substance use. They feel that they cannot face life without drugs or alcohol. Tolerance makes their substance use less and less enjoyable, and substance use becomes about avoiding withdrawal and escaping from life rather than enjoying a high. Physical and mental deterioration, and significant losses occur. Important aspects of life structure are lost, such as job, marriage, relationships with children and family, savings and significant possessions, and so on. Multiple desperate attempts to stop or control substance use fail. Depressed mood and suicidal thoughts or actions often develop. Serious behavioral problems arise, and interactions with the family may be turbulent and even violent. Desperation to

obtain money to buy drugs may result in desperate measures, such as prostitution and felony crime. The addict may disappear for days or weeks on end without contacting their family.

*

In this section, we'll go through the core behavioral symptoms that are typical of active addiction.

Tolerance and withdrawal. Tolerance and withdrawal are important symptoms of addiction because they're one of the major drivers of continued and escalating substance use. They're also a major barrier to recovery, and play a key role in drug overdoses.

Tolerance is the diminished intoxication effect felt from a substance with repeated use. Tolerance also results in the body becoming able to tolerate higher doses of the drug without overdosing. If someone who's never taken an opioid before were to take the same dose as an opioid addict it would likely kill them.

Tolerance occurs as the body adapts to repeated exposure to the drug. The more tolerance develops, the more individuals will increase their dosages as they "chase the high." Conversely, the more they increase the dosage the more tolerance they develop. Thus, a vicious cycle of mounting tolerance and increasing doses occurs, until individuals are using tremendously high doses with little effect. For many types of drugs, the users reach a point where they feel little or no "high," and their continued drug use becomes about avoiding withdrawal because the drug use itself is no longer enjoyable. They describe that as the point where their substance use was no longer "fun," and the point at which they needed their substance to feel "normal."

Because of tolerance people often end up using doses that would be lethal to anyone who was not used to them. Tolerance is part of the reason that there's such a high incidence of overdose in relapse situations, especially with opioids. When people are abstinent from substance use their tolerance begins to lower as their body re-adjusts to the new normal. Many people who relapse go back very quickly to the same high doses of the drug that they had been using during their active addiction, but since their tolerance has lowered while they were in recovery, the high doses are now lethal for them, and overdose occurs.

Withdrawal is a cluster of uncomfortable symptoms that occur after the drug effects wear off and the drug is cleared from the body. Like tolerance, withdrawal occurs as a result of the brain's desperate effort to adjust to the repeated exposure to the psychoactive substances. The brain adjusts itself so that it's used to having the drug, then when the drug is decreased or stopped the brain reacts negatively.

Generally, the higher the tolerance an individual has, the more pronounced the withdrawal symptoms. Avoiding withdrawal is a major driver of addiction, and often becomes the main motivator for continued substance use in the later stages of addiction. Each drug has its own withdrawal symptoms, which were discussed in chapter 3. People in active addiction usually have an intense fear of withdrawal, and this fear is a powerful barrier to recovery. Many won't even try to stop their drug use out of fear of withdrawal. Fortunately, there are drug and alcohol detoxification facilities that are there to help people get through their withdrawal safely and comfortably. Once people are "over the hump" of withdrawal, they can focus on their recovery.

Motivation. Motivation is the main driver of behavior in humans. Most of the things we do are determined by our motivations. This may be simple behaviors, such as brushing our teeth because we're motivated to be healthy and have a nice smile, or much more complex behaviors, such as doing a college degree because we're motivated to have a better job. As such just about everything we do is goal-directed behavior, intended in some way to bring us closer to a certain goal. Goal-directed behavior is crucial to our ability to survive and thrive, because the goals that motivate us are directed toward our needs, wants, and overall betterment.

Our brain has a reward system that's responsible for motivation. This will be discussed in more detail in chapter 5, but our brain's reward system gives us a little shot of feel-good chemicals when we achieve a goal. These "reward neurotransmitters" give us a bit of a high for accomplishing something, and seeking this natural high is largely what motivates us. For example, when we're hungry, and we find food and eat, we feel pleasure because our brain's reward system is activated in response to this goal-directed behavior. That reward is important for our survival, because it motivates us to seek out food when we're hungry and our body needs fuel.

Unfortunately, addictive substances have a potent effect on the brain's natural reward system, inducing it to release feel-good chemicals in amounts that are far, far greater than normal. That's why people feel so good – euphoric – when they're high on alcohol or drugs. This skyrocketed reward level leads to a motivation for further substance use that overpowers all other natural motivations, including very basic needs such as food or shelter. The motivation to obtain and use drugs becomes so powerful that everything else becomes a distraction, even things that were previously very important to the individual.

Many of our motivations are not only based on reward, but also based on avoiding punishment. For example, when we're hungry, our motivation for seeking food isn't only to attain the reward of a delicious meal, but also to avoid the painful feeling of a hungry belly. Because withdrawal from drugs and alcohol is so agonizing, avoiding withdrawal is another reason that people in addiction are motivated to continue using their substances.

As substance use becomes the dominant motivation in life, all other normal human motivations and goal-directed behaviors fall away. Even the most basic of all human motivations – such as food and shelter – become compromised. The reason that most people who remain in addiction become homeless at some point – if they continue with their substance use long enough – is because they devote all their resources to substance use. Even their rent and grocery money is diverted to buy their drug. I see this in my work with homeless addicts; they receive their government welfare checks at the beginning of the month, and they disappear for a few days on a substance-fueled binge. When the money's all gone – usually after 3-5 days – they don't have a cent left for food, lodging, clothing, or anything. They spend the rest of the month penniless. When the check arrives the next month, they do exactly the same thing, and once again end up penniless.

As these fundamental motivation shifts occur, suddenly things that used to be important simply don't matter anymore. Even things that were *very* important cease to matter. I've seen many mothers who once put their children before anything else in the world suddenly stop properly caring for them. Job, education, children and family, friendships and relationships, investments, home, all cease to matter and become neglected. Nothing else matters unless it helps in some way to obtain the drug. Life comes to be about obtaining and using the substance, and that's it. This is distressing to watch in a loved one, because they seem cold, uncaring, and detached from life; it's deeply hurtful.

As motivation shifts from normal life activities to substance use, some of the classic symptoms of addiction begin to appear:

- Continued substance use even though it's obviously causing problems at home, work, school, with relationships, with finances, and even legal problems,
- Neglect of basic self-care and appearance,
- Irrational decision-making,
- Shirking responsibilities and neglecting normal activities, including activities that were previously enjoyable or important for the individual,
- Sudden change in friends, leisure activities, and hangouts,
- Unexplained financial problems, constantly asking for money, borrowing or even stealing money from family and friends, and
- Making excuses for unmet responsibilities and shortcomings, and the excuses become increasingly frequent and difficult to believe.

Part of the crucial process in helping a loved one to escape addiction and return to good health and function involves diverting their motivation away from substance use and back to the things that matter in life, such as children, family, career, health, and so on. Family members can play a huge role in helping to bring about this important shift in motivation and making it stick. We'll discuss how you can be a positive part of this process in upcoming chapters.

Deception. Even the most honest of individuals become masters of deception when they're in active addiction. They'll lie to cover up their drinking or using, then they'll lie to cover up those lies. They'll lie to cover up the things they do while intoxicated, to cover for their absences from work or other responsibilities, and for what happened to their money. They'll also lie by putting on an outward appearance that all is well when things are definitely not well. It can be frustrating to be constantly lied to by a loved one who's obviously using or drinking, but it really helps to try to remember that these people aren't liars; rather, the deceit and lies are simply typical symptoms of addiction.

People in active addiction even lie to themselves about the reality of their life and how bad things have gotten; in other words, they engage in serious denial. They usually even become defensive or hostile when confronted about their substance use. This is a real problem, because the very first requirement for dealing with a problem is acknowledging that there is a problem. Why bother worrying about trying to fix a problem if there is no problem, *right?*

The deception that's associated with addiction is driven primarily by fear: fear of being exposed as addicts, fear of getting in trouble at work or at home if their problem is discovered, fear of losing access to their substance if they're exposed, fear of arrest. As well, many people are embarrassed and ashamed by their substance use and related behaviors, and try to hide these behaviors. As we'll discuss in chapter 6, there are other fundamental psychological reasons for addicts' denial, and addressing these reasons is a necessary part of helping an addict become ready to accept help.

The deception that's typical of active addiction often creates considerable friction between addicts and their loved ones. I've seen time and again situations where choleric conflict between addicts and their loved ones over the lies and deceit is a daily occurrence. The family member is concerned, frustrated, and angered by the lies and deceit, especially when the contradictions between the truth and the lies are obvious, and confronts the addict about the lies. The result of these confrontations is seldom productive; nothing gets fixed, and nothing changes because of it. Rather, it just further worsens the wedge between the addict and the loved ones, and it drives the addict further underground into secrecy and isolation. It's frustrating for all involved. Even simple discussions turn into arguments, and arguments turn angry and explosive; ultimatums are issued, feelings are hurt, horrible things are said, and nothing whatsoever is accomplished from it. Perhaps one of the most difficult aspects of learning to help a loved one in addiction is learning to handle the lies and deceit in a way that's more productive, and leads toward the end goal: a healthy loved one in recovery.

The first thing to realize when learning to handle the lies is to recognize that exposing lies and deceit from a loved in addiction can be a hollow victory, and that the greater good is often served by a less confrontational and emotional reaction. Repeatedly proving to the addict that you know what's going on is non-productive and only serves to increase conflict and anger. Showing the addict that you've discovered another stash of drugs or alcohol, or a pipe, or needles, or empty bottles, or whatever, serves only two purposes: 1) to prove what you both already know – that your loved one has a problem, and 2) to start another horrible fight. I suggest only confronting the addict with evidence of their deceit when it'll serve a specific purpose, such as:

- Guiding (not forcing) the individual to admit that there is a problem. This doesn't have to be coupled with a call for a commitment to getting help. One step at a time. Getting the problem out in the open and breaking down the lies, deceit, and denial is a great step forward. Leave it at that for the time being,
- Cutting off enabling. Families are often drawn into being enablers of substance use by the manipulative addict. An addict knows that family members care and would do anything to help, so they make emotional appeals for money lest they be evicted, or grocery money lest they go without food. However, one should never give an addict money. Never. It will always go to drugs or alcohol. Always. Confronting an addict with evidence of abuse of your charity is a good way to stop any enabling behaviors that you've been manipulated into, and
- To establish or enforce rules. If you decide that you want to limit the addict's access to amenities, people, or even to evict them from your home, the correct time to do so is when it's coupled with evidence of their rule-breaking. It's the perfect time to set boundaries, make rules, or enforce actions in response to established rules that have been broken.

When you confront an addict with evidence of lies and deceit, be sure to do so with a purpose in mind, and in an unemotional and matter-of-fact way. Achieve your purpose, and be sure not to be drawn into an emotional exchange, because addicts can become polemical when confronted. That's especially the case if they believe they're losing a source of money for obtaining their substance. Just get across the point that you do not accept the denial and state your purpose, and then walk away.

I advise people to always make two points when confronting a loved one with evidence of lies or deceit, because these are helpful in moving addicts toward readiness to accept help. They are:

1) That you understand that lies, deceit, and denial are typical symptoms of addiction, and that you do not see the individual as a liar or a bad person, and
2) That addiction is 100% beatable by every individual, no matter how bad off they think they are, and that you have information about how

your loved one can do that when they're ready for help. And then leave it at that. That little piece of information sticks in the minds of addicts every time they drink or use, and provides a seed by which they begin to accept that there is a viable way out, and that they need only to reach out when they're ready.

You should be the one to end the conversation, or the addict will almost certainly drag it out into an argument. They believe that if they argue and push hard enough they'll get their money, or whatever it is they're looking for. You're not there to argue. You're there to demonstrate that you're aware of the lie or deceit, to express an understanding that the lie is part of the addict's struggle, to state and achieve your aim (establish a rule, help the individual overcome denial, etc.), and to express that there is effective help available when the individual is ready to accept it. Anything more is non-productive. End the conversation as soon as you've accomplished these aims.

When I suggest that you should confront the addict about lies or deceit in a non-judgmental way, you may wonder how that can be done. After all, lying and deceiving are wrongdoings, so how can we be non-judgmental? Well, the addict knows very well that these are wrongdoings, and addicts carry considerable guilt, remorse, and self-loathing over such behaviors. Coping with these negative feelings is a big part of why they continue with their substance use. If you turn the discussion into a lecture about how obvious or bad the behaviors are, you compound that guilt, and enlarge an already significant barrier to recovery. They know that what they're doing is wrong and hurtful to others, they don't need to be lectured on it. They're unlikely to come to you for help if they think doing so will just result in more lectures and admonishments. Rather, make sure that they understand that you know that their behaviors are part of the disease of addiction, and not something that defines who they are. We need them to know that there's still a good person inside that can be salvaged when they get help.

As we'll discuss in upcoming chapters, stopping the tendency to lie and deceive is a necessary part of maintaining sobriety in recovery. Lying and concealing are addiction behaviors, not behaviors that are consistent with healing and living sober. Secrets are what keep addicts sick. Honesty is hugely therapeutic, and individuals in recovery widely express relief at unburdening themselves of old secrets that weighed on their shoulders for years.

When people in recovery begin keeping secrets and hiding things, they may be beginning the downward process of relapse. Family members can play an important role in relapse prevention by reminding their loved ones in recovery of this fact, and by challenging them on apparent untruths. It's healthy, and it's an important way that you can help your loved one stay strong in recovery. We'll talk much more about how to confront and talk and connect with an addict – one who's in active addiction as well as one who's in recovery – in chapter 8.

Denial, self-deception. Denial that their substance use is a problem is a common symptom among addicts. We'll see in the next two chapters that there are reasons for self-deception and denial that are largely outside of the conscious control of people whose brain is repeatedly exposed to addictive substances.

A number of mental illnesses are characterized by what physicians refer to as *lack of insight* (also known by the horrible term *anosognosia*), where the affected individuals are unable to perceive their illness and symptoms. Schizophrenia and bipolar disorder are classic examples of mental health disorders characterized by lack of insight, but addiction, too, is characterized by considerable "anosognosia."

All addictive substances affect the part of the brain that's responsible for *interoception* (our ability to sense what's going on inside our body), and self-awareness. This results in an impaired ability to sense or detect signals that something may be wrong, and addicts therefore have a faulty self-image. Addictive substances also affect the part of the brain that processes information in general, resulting in poor information analysis, judgment, and decision-making. The end result is a defective ability to fully understand what's going on with oneself. These impairments occur not only while the individual is intoxicated, but also in between bouts of substance use, creating an impaired ability to fully understand one's situation; i.e. a lack of insight.

Besides this very physical cause of impaired insight, denial in addiction also occurs for psychological reasons; most notably due to *cognitive dissonance*. We'll discuss this important psychological concept further in chapter 6 because it's central to the addicted mind, but in the meantime I'll tell you that cognitive dissonance is the bad feelings that we have when our actions aren't in keeping with how we believe a good person should act. Normally, this bad feeling makes us adjust our behavior so that it's more aligned with our beliefs and standards about how we should act. However, in addiction that would mean stopping the substance use, and for people in active addiction that's not within their power. So, they carry around a lot of guilt and shame about their actions, and their mind tries to reduce these bad feelings by rationalizing and minimizing their offending behaviors. They try to – in their own mind – justify their substance use (*you'd use too if you had my life*), blame others for their predicament, or downplay how bad their problem is. They're trying to fool themselves so that they don't feel so bad.

This combination of impaired brain function and cognitive dissonance is the perfect recipe for some hard-core denial and attempts at deception of the self and others. Addicts do this largely unconsciously – without being fully aware of it – but they also make conscious efforts at deception. The conscious efforts result from a desire to protect the continued substance use by avoiding detection and censure. They're afraid that if others find out about the true extent of their problem they'll intervene and interfere with the substance use.

Some of the symptoms of addiction result from these efforts at denial and self-deception, such as:

- Making excuses to use drugs or alcohol,
- Making empty promises to stop or control the substance use,
- Secretive or suspicious behavior,
- Appearing fearful, anxious, and even paranoid,
- Lying,
- Sudden changes in friends, leisure activities, and hangouts (a preference for people and places where they don't have to hide their substance use), and
- Defensive, hostile, and even aggressive reactions when confronted about substance use.

One odd manifestation of denial that's commonly seen among addicts is the so-called "geographical cure." This interesting phenomenon is where an addict will decide that moving to another town, state, or even country is the answer to their problem. They seem to believe that all their problems stem from the people and places in their life, so they move away to start fresh and wipe away all their problems in a different place. Naturally, geographical cures never work, no matter where they go to start over. The place isn't the problem.

Even when people in addiction come to accept that they have a problem, the denial usually switches to that of denial of a need for help. The addicted mind is characterized by a persistent belief that one can control or stop the substance use on one's own, despite repeated failures to do so in the past. It's uncanny to watch someone in this stage of denial because it's so illogical. The thing is that they really believe it. Addicts will make repeated promises that *this* time they're done with the substance use and are stopping for good... and they mean it in all earnestness. They may make it a few days, even a few weeks in some circumstances, but when they try to stop their substance use on their own and in their own way they almost inevitably fail. Then, not long after, they're once again convinced they can stop on their own and the cycle repeats itself. When I hear addicts insisting they can stop on their own and in their own way, I always say: *Oh, yeah? How's that worked out for you so far?*

Denial is a major barrier to recovery, because it's impossible to deal with a problem that one doesn't believe exists or won't admit to. Too, why would anyone commit to a treatment program if they don't believe they need it? People really must be past the denial stage before they're ready to commit to treatment and recovery. That means that they must have fully accepted that they have a serious problem, and that they can't stop the substance use on their own, doing it their own way. This is the critical mindset that addicts must achieve before they're ready to accept help, and we'll be talking about how you can help your loved one get to that mindset.

We'll talk about this in more detail in chapter 9, but family members can help loved ones work their way toward acceptance of their problem and of their need for help by demonstrating an understanding of addiction, and by being firm in reminding the addict of the facts. It's important to pick your moments and to not cross the line into "nagging," lest you become shut out. A good time to bring up the discussion is when your loved one tells you that they're done with the substance use and intend to quit. That's the perfect time to point out that this has never worked in the past and never will unless the proper help is in place. And then leave it at that. Make it understood that you've done some learning about addiction and that you wish to listen to the addict to learn more and to understand their struggles, and that the proper help is available when the addict is ready. If you come across as understanding and non-judgmental, the addict is far more likely to come to you than if you come across as nagging and punitive. By the end of this book, you'll be an expert in how to interact with an addict at any stage of addiction or recovery.

Need for control. People in active addiction have an obsessive need for control, which is ironic given that their lives are totally out of control. However, their need for control centers on their need to keep open a pathway to obtaining and using their substance. Addicts will go to great lengths to ensure that they have the freedom of movement to get away to do what they need to do to obtain and use their substance.

This need for control is a significant barrier to recovery, because the need for control prevents them from fully committing themselves to recovery. Addiction is a serious disease and it requires a serious commitment and determination to beat. Addicts who aren't yet mentally ready to surrender this need for control will lack the necessary commitment. They'll hold back so that they can access their substance "just in case:" just in case recovery is too hard, or just in case they're having a really bad day and need to drink or use.

Until they're willing to let go of this need for control – even when they've acknowledged that they have a problem and conceded that they need help – they'll pick and choose what help they accept, so that they have one foot in the recovery program and one foot out, and they can bail anytime they need to. This less than 100% commitment just won't work; beating addiction requires an "all-in" commitment. If addicts leave the mental doorway that leads back to substance use open even a crack, they *will* go through it at some point. They need to shut that door in their mind. A half-in commitment or picking and choosing bits of help here and there virtually never produces success.

The Twelve Step program has a saying that people must "reach their bottom" before they can beat addiction. What they mean is that people must get to a point where they are *so* fed up with addiction and *so* desperate for recovery that they're ready to do *anything* – whatever it takes – in order free themselves from addiction. It's only at that point that addicts are ready to let go of that need for control – that need to keep the pathway back to their substance use open "just in case" – and to fully commit to a recovery program. Only then are they in the correct frame of mind to succeed in long-term recovery.

So, when do people in active addiction "reach their bottom?" Well, every person is different. Many reach their bottom and commit to recovery before they've lost too much, while their family, job, finances, and health are still intact. Others have lost everything and are living under a bridge before they reach their bottom. Sadly, many reach their grave before they reach their bottom. Reaching their bottom doesn't depend on how much an individual has lost, or how much they drink or use; rather, it's about when they reach the frame of mind that they're thoroughly done with substance use and ready to relinquish their need for control.

Helping a loved one to "reach their bottom" before too much is lost is a major accomplishment, because it brings the individual to the point where recovery is finally possible. In chapter 9 we'll focus on how to accomplish that goal.

Selfishness. The selfishness of people in active addiction is one of the most hurtful symptoms to loved ones. The drive to obtain and use their substances is so strong that it overtakes all other motivations, no matter how important or cherished those motivations once were. Thus, they'll sacrifice obligations and responsibilities to their children and family, workplace, and virtually any other person or thing in order to partake in their chemical misadventures. I've seen individuals in active addiction go to extraordinary and shocking depths of selfishness, including unspeakable acts affecting their own children. However, there's one particular example that I like to use to illustrate the selfishness of the addicted mind:

> Recently, in my community, a couple of guys stole a large delivery truck, and then – in the dark of night – drove it to a little "mom and pop" convenience store and proceeded to use the truck to smash through the exterior wall of the store. Once inside, the hoodlums tied a rope to the ATM machine and pulled it out with the truck. Then, they loaded the ATM into the truck and made off with it into the night. A few miles away they transferred the ATM to their own vehicle, set fire to the stolen delivery truck, and drove off with their loot. All the while, the terrorized family who operate the convenience store were cowering in their apartment above the store, without a clue about what was going on beneath them.
> It didn't take long for the police to find the two hapless criminals. They had managed to get about $2,000 in their little enterprise that night, and the money was all gone within two days. It turned out that they were cocaine addicts who were so desperate for money to get their drug that they resorted to this insane venture. The price-tag to

others for their little escapade was in the hundreds of thousands: they caused $150,000 of damage to the convenience store, the delivery truck they stole and burned was worth over $100,000, and they put the convenience store – one family's sole source of income – out of business for weeks while repairs were done. I'm sure the store owners and their children were deeply traumatized by the experience as well. These two guys caused all that damage and mayhem to other people's lives to get $2,000 for themselves, and then it was gone up their noses in a couple of days. The level of selfishness involved is incomprehensible, but it's not uncommon to see such depths of selfishness from people in active addiction. Woe to anyone or anything that stands between the addict and their drug.

By all accounts, the two men involved were – prior to their addiction – ordinary, productive, and nice people. One even had a wife and kids. I've never met them, but it sounds like they were ordinary guys who were driven to extraordinary acts of selfishness by their addiction.

Irrelevance of willpower. By the time addicts finally become willing to seek and accept help, they've likely tried multiple times and many ways to stop their substance use on their own, in their own way. Addicts strangely place great faith in their willpower, as they seem unable to accept that they just can't stop on their own. So, they keep trying.

Most people can cut back or stop their use of alcohol or drugs once they realize that it's becoming a problem. The human mind is capable of great feats of the will, and even the draw of drugs or alcohol can be beat. However, for those who've crossed the line into addiction, strong-arming their drive to drink or use with willpower doesn't work. No matter how much willpower they may have, how disciplined they are, how hard-working they can be, and how intelligent they are, once they've crossed the line into addiction they aren't able to think or will themselves out of it. If they did have the ability to stop or control their substance use on their own, they would've done so long ago, when their life began falling apart and they became miserable. They need help.

"Willpower" is the term we use to describe our ability to control our actions and restrain ourselves in the face of urges or impulses; in other words, willpower is our ability to exert self-control. The brain has specific networks that provide us with the ability to apply self-control in the face of temptation; these are known as *inhibition circuits*, and these brain networks are the basis of our willpower. Unfortunately, these circuits are contained in precisely the part of the brain that addictive substances directly interfere with. Under normal circumstances, our brain's natural decision-making mechanisms weigh out the consequences of our actions and can over-ride the desire for immediate gratification in favor of future rewards. Sadly, these reflective processes are significantly disrupted by the effects of repeated exposure to addictive substances; immediate gratification overrides any consideration for future rewards and consequences.

Not only do addictive substances disrupt the brain's mechanisms for inhibiting unwise or harmful behaviors, but they also interfere with the brain circuits that enable people to learn from experience and to change behaviors based on probability of error. In other words, addicts cannot even learn from their mistakes.

Even when people in addiction try their very best to apply their willpower to their substance use, their willpower burns out. This is because of the nature of how willpower works in the human brain. Willpower is not available to us in infinite quantities; rather, it's a limited resource that becomes depleted. When people face compulsive urges to drink or use, resisting the urge diminishes their strength for resisting the next temptation. This is why some people find that they're able to withstand the temptation to use drink or use in the early stages of their addiction, but soon find that they can no longer prevail when they try to apply their willpower.

Even in recovery, success doesn't come from developing the ability to use willpower to overcome addiction. Willpower is an internal process, where people keep the problem within themselves, thereby relying on a person who's mentally and physically sick and unreliable – themself. Trying to rely on willpower prevents individuals who need help from letting other people in. Studies have shown that even among people who are high in willpower, willpower has no effect on success in beating addiction. This is likely because people who've had success in the past accomplishing goals by applying willpower may place too much belief in their own ability to stop their substance use, which can significantly delay their readiness to accept outside help.

Even when in recovery, people can err in their belief that they can try using drugs or alcohol again, and this time control it and not let it get out of hand. Experience and significant research data have shown that this almost never works. As such, a forlorn belief in one's ability to exert willpower over substance use after a period of abstinence is a common cause of relapse. Indeed, studies have shown that trying to rely on willpower to prevent relapse not only doesn't work, but is probably actually harmful. In fact, addiction counselors in treatment programs don't waste any time trying to teach their patients how to increase their willpower.

So, it can be said that people who're in active addiction and those who're in recovery need to accept one truth before they can succeed in recovery: *they cannot now, and never will be able to control their substance use through willpower*. This is even true of people who've been in recovery for decades. In my clinical work I've met many, many individuals with significant abstinent recovery time who talked themselves into relapse by allowing themselves to believe that enough time had lapsed so that they could drink or use and keep a lid on it. Famous last words. I will say this, though: there is a way that willpower can be used to great success in recovery from addiction, and that's through applying willpower to continue doing recovery activities every day, on an ongoing basis. Using willpower to go to a recovery group meeting rather than staying home and watching TV, or using willpower to do 20 minutes of recovery reading every day, and so on, is an effective way to use willpower to recover from addiction. However, using willpower to try drinking or using again in a controlled way is not going to work.

So, knowing what you now know about willpower and addiction, I suggest an important lesson is that, when dealing with a loved one in active addiction, you should never use the admonishment: *why don't you just stop???* The proper response to that question is this: *because substance use has disabled the part of their brain that controls willpower.* Asking an addict this question only serves to demonstrate to the addict that you don't understand the nature of addiction and what the addict is going through, and worsens the gulf between you and your loved one. An addict will never come to someone for help or advice or even just to talk if they think that person doesn't understand or can't understand their struggles.

The other lesson here is that when your loved one is in active addiction and keeps promising: **this** *time I'm done with drinking/using,* **this** *time I'm going to stop!* you should gently remind them that you have information that willpower is of no use in addiction, and that if they had the ability to stop or control the substance use, they would've done so long ago. The suggestion should then be made that if they really want to stop they need to accept help. And then leave it at that and walk away; don't allow the addict to turn it into a debate or draw you into an argument. As well, when your loved one is in recovery and begins talking about trying drinking or using again – because *this* time they'll be able to handle it – you should remind your loved one that you have information that this idea amounts to pure folly. Better that they use their willpower to pick up on their recovery activities so that they stop thinking such nonsense.

Living in the here and now. One of the odd symptoms of addiction is related to the breakdown of willpower: the addict's apparent complete lack of concern for consequences. The here and now is all that matters, especially as it pertains to substance use. A typical example is how addicts will spend their rent money on drugs or alcohol, satisfying their immediate desires at the expense of later problems.

One of the reasons that humankind has thrived as a species is because of our capacity to engage in goal-directed behaviors, undertaking complex behaviors and being willing to make sacrifices now in order to achieve greater goals in the future. Willpower is about determination to put off gratification and to suffer difficulties now in favor of future benefits. However, addiction is defined by continued substance use now regardless of obvious negative consequences in the future. The addict's focus is completely on the here and now: instant gratification and escape from reality. Again, this is related to the toxic effects of psychoactive substances on the part of the brain that allows us to exercise judgment, make decisions based on our goals and needs, and plan out goal-directed behaviors. We'll discuss these brain changes in more detail in the next chapter.

Manipulation. The drive to drink or use is so overwhelming that people in active addiction will resort to virtually any measures to obtain their substance. This is one of the saddest symptoms of addiction, because people can be driven to extremes of behavior that they ordinarily wouldn't even think about. Although extremes of behavior usually appear later in the addiction process, when the substance use is expansive and resources are depleted, manipulative behaviors usually appear early on.

Sadly, addicts begin to take on the characteristics of narcissistic and antisocial personality disorders, where they view people solely in terms of their usefulness for obtaining money for drugs. When family and friends recognize this mindset in their addicted loved one – that the addict sees them as more of a puppet than a person – they can feel deeply hurt. However, once again it's helpful to remember that it's nothing personal – it's just a typical symptom brought on by the toxic effects of substance use on the addicted brain.

The classical manipulation among addicts is centered on their efforts to obtain money for their substance use. There's usually a progression in terms of financing their substance use that parallels the progression of their addiction. Initially, addicts use their own financial resources. When those dry up – which is often precipitated by losing their job and/or by estrangement from their spouse – they'll borrow money from family and friends. When that source, too, dries up, they may resort to manipulating and even stealing from family and friends.

Manipulation to obtain money is usually based on tugging on your heartstrings. They'll spin sob-stories where they'll be evicted from their apartment, or go without groceries, or have their power shut off, or they need money to get their terrible toothache looked after, and so on, unless their loved one gives or lends them some money. They'll tell you their rent money was stolen from their car. They'll tell you their kids need groceries. The money, however, will go where the rest of their money went: toward obtaining their substance. If you give an addict money under any pretenses, it *will* be used to purchase drugs or alcohol. No matter how sad the story they paint, and how much they promise otherwise, the money *will* go to their dealer or the liquor store.

I frequently see around town people I know from my work at the local detox center, out panhandling for money. They're usually holding signs saying that they lost their job and their children are starving, but I know that that they're using the money they're given to buy drugs or alcohol. I know this because they've told me so when I interviewed them at the detox center. One individual I know has Wernicke-Korsakoff syndrome (remember "wet brain" from chapter 3?) from chronic alcohol use, so he looks horrible. He's emaciated and obviously in poor health. Frankly, he looks like he's been dragged behind a car. He sits outside one of the local grocery stores panhandling for change, holding a sign requesting change for food. As soon as he gets enough money he runs into the store and buys a bottle of mouthwash, sits out back while he drinks it, and then resumes his panhandling "for food." He takes advantage of his sickly appearance and people's goodwill to fuel his alcohol addiction.

When you're dealing with a manipulative addict, it's very easy to cross the line from helping your loved one to becoming an enabler for the substance use. Enabling is a form of accommodation that makes it easier for an addict to obtain drugs, and protects the addict from fully experiencing the consequences of their substance use. Many family members and friends of addicts don't even realize it when they're being manipulated into being an enabler, or they try to walk the fine line between helping the addict and enabling the addict, but fail. When you try to play that game, the addict will win every time. Stopping the enabling requires some tough love, some well-informed skepticism, and unyielding resolve. It requires well-defined and well-enforced boundaries. By the time you finish this book you'll be thoroughly familiar with how to help without enabling, and how to shut down the manipulation.

I suggest never giving an addict money; you can safely assume it will be diverted to substance use. Even in recovery, suddenly receiving money is a common trigger for relapse. There are many ways to help an addict financially without giving them money. For example, if you wish to help your loved one avoid eviction, I suggest giving the rent money directly to the landlord with instructions not to refund the money to your loved one under any circumstances. By telling the landlord that you will now be paying the rent, and that the landlord should contact you directly with any rent concerns or trouble with the tenant, you cut the addict out of the loop and close the purse strings to the addict. We'll talk much more about these sorts of things in later sections of this book.

Labile moods and emotions. Moods and emotions in people in active addiction are often unstable, easily aroused, and subject to rapid changes. Most people who've lived with or spent time around someone in active addiction are probably very familiar with this symptom of addiction.

Our moods and emotions are controlled by specific brain areas that rely on certain chemicals (*neurotransmitters*) to transmit emotional responses to the parts of the brain that control behavior. Addictive substances cause abnormally large spikes followed by profound drops in these neurotransmitters, causing moods and emotions to fluctuate wildly as individuals cycle between acute intoxication, withdrawal, and the after-effects between periods of intoxication. Because these emotion circuits are closely tied in with the brain's behavioral circuits, these wildly fluctuating moods and emotions are expressed in behavior. Anger may be expressed by more than just facial expressions and harsh words – there may be aggressive or violent behavior as well.

As well, the parts of the brain that are responsible for our emotions are closely tied into our motivational circuits. As we've previously discussed, substance use becomes the dominant motivation for addicts, taking precedence over all else. Anything that threatens an addict's access to substance use – such as cutting off money or confiscating their stash – will likely result in a mercurial emotional reaction, accompanied by emotionally-driven behavior. This is partly why addicts who're subjected to one of those ambush-style "interventions" like you see on TV and dragged off to rehab against their will go kicking and screaming. It makes for great television, but not for great recovery.

The labile moods and emotions may also be tied to underlying mental health problems. More than half of people who develop addiction also have a co-occurring mental health disorder. Many mental health disorders also cause mood and emotional fluctuations, and this can have an additive effect when combined with substance use. People who were previously stable and in remission from a mental health disorder due to medications or other treatments often find their symptoms becoming active again, as addictive substances negate the stabilizing effects of the medications and treatments used for mental health disorders. Because of this, the medications may cease working properly, and symptoms may re-emerge.

With or without an underlying mental health disorder, the neurotransmitter instabilities caused by addictive substance use commonly result in observable symptoms related to mood and emotion, including:

- Sudden mood swings, rapidly going from very sad to happy, or vice-versa,
- Angry or violent emotional outbursts, particularly if access to substance use is threatened,
- Dramatic expressions of various emotions (happiness, fear, sadness, disgust, anger, surprise),
- Irritability,
- Psychosis (loss of touch with reality, paranoia, auditory or visual hallucinations),
- Depressed mood, and
- Anxiety, panic.

Social isolation. Social isolation is often one of the first observable symptoms that tips us off that there's something not quite right with a family member. Typically, addicts begin avoiding the family, staying in their room, taking meals on their own, wearing headphones and avoiding conversation, and acting annoyed when anyone "gets in their space." They may begin hanging around with a whole new set of friends who're unknown to the family.

Social isolation initially occurs because people in active addiction don't want their substance use and related behaviors to be discovered. As such, social isolation is part of their secretive behavior. However, once their problem has been discovered, they socially isolate to avoid the "nagging" from family and friends about their substance use, dropped responsibilities, and errant behaviors.

There's a distinct psychological compulsion that underpins social isolation. We previously discussed cognitive dissonance, where individuals feel bad about themselves because their behavior doesn't align with how they think a good person should behave. Being exposed to people who're living normal, functional lives without substance use forces on the addict an *upward social comparison*, which highlights the addict's errant behavior. Addicts therefore prefer the company of others who're also using substances, because avoiding upward social comparison is psychologically soothing for them. Nothing reduces guilt and cognitive dissonance like *downward social comparison.*

Regardless of how any individual's substance use began, at some point it becomes a dysfunctional coping mechanism. Like substance use, social isolation is a form of escape/avoidance coping, running away and hiding from the unkind world and all its pressures and stresses. As such, substance use and social isolation tend to occur together as part of an escape/avoidance way of dealing with life.

Social isolation can be further deepened by social rejection. Addiction is a socially unacceptable behavior with significant stigma attached to it. As well, the appearance and behavior of people in active addiction often leads to significant social rejection. Behavior while intoxicated, an unkempt appearance, and anti-social behaviors (such as theft, etc.) tend to deepen the social rejection experienced by people in active addiction, including from their own family. By the time addiction has progressed to the point where social rejection occurs, social isolation is usually profound, with addicts living in their own world, detached from others and reality.

One of the necessary aspects of addiction treatment and relapse prevention is to connect recovering addicts with other people, especially other people in recovery. Overcoming their tendency to socially isolate in the face of problems and stressors helps keep them engaged in life rather than reverting back to their escape/avoidance mindset. When an addict in recovery begins socially isolating again, it may be an early red flag that a relapse is in the making.

Criminal behaviors. The drive to obtain and use substances is so overwhelming that people who ordinarily would never even consider engaging in criminal activity may resort to criminal acts to fund their substance use. Addiction is a costly enterprise, and people usually burn through their financial resources quickly as their substance use progresses. This may be compounded by loss of job and income, and estrangement from family, and it may occur especially quickly if they're using expensive substances (an addict can easily burn through upwards of $1,000 of powder cocaine a day, for example).

Addictive substances impair the brain's capacity for judgment and inhibition, which may further contribute to a propensity for criminal activity. The kinds of criminal activity that I commonly see among people in active addiction are theft, robbery, break and enters (B&Es; i.e. burglary), drug trafficking, and prostitution.

We've already discussed the typical progression of money-seeking behaviors once addicts' own financial resources run out; it begins with borrowing from family and friends until the lenders figure out what the money is being used for and cut them off. When family cuts off the money, addicts may begin to steal from family and friends. When that's no longer possible, desperation to obtain that next drug or drink may drive them to acts of crime.

I've met a lot of addicts who've been involved in serious crime, including individuals who started from very high places; addiction has the power to humble even extraordinary people. Fortunately, not everyone in active addiction ends up becoming reliant on criminal behavior. However, substance use frequently leads to other kinds of trouble: arguments, fights, school or work problems, legal troubles, and impaired driving charges are common consequences of addiction.

Intoxication and "hangovers." In chapter 3 we discussed the intoxication and withdrawal ("hangover") effects of the various classes of addictive substances. Addicts will go to great lengths to conceal the symptoms of intoxication and withdrawal from family and friends, but the symptoms are difficult to hide. Seeing the symptoms of intoxication and withdrawal may be your first indication that your loved one is involved in substance use, and seeing these symptoms repeatedly may be your first indication that a real problem exists. At first these may be shrugged off as simply "recreational" drug or alcohol use, but serious concerns may arise as they become more frequent and severe.

Although each type of substance has its own characteristic effects and after-effects, in general intoxication and withdrawal symptoms may include:

- Confusion,
- Change in demeanor or personality,
- Euphoria,
- Slurred speech,
- Poor coordination,
- Hyperactivity,
- Sedation, dozing off during the day or while sitting or driving,
- Shaking,
- Nausea and vomiting,

- Bloodshot eyes,
- Unusual smells on the breath, clothes, or body, or in the living space (such as a teenager's bedroom),
- Changes in habits, appetite, sleep patterns,
- Depressed mood, anxiety, psychosis, and
- Seizures.

People who're involved in repeated substance use often try to explain off their withdrawal symptoms to concerned family members as simply "feeling ill," or "being sick." However, as absenteeism begins to mount at school or work, and the "sickness" becomes a regular occurrence, concerns arise, and family members realize that something's wrong. They're usually correct; remember: addicts are secretive and they will lie to conceal their substance use and to cover up the consequences of their substance use. Addicts will deny their family's suspicions, but my experience has been that families are almost always right when they suspect something is wrong.

Self-pity, blamefulness. We'll discuss what goes on in the addicted mind in chapter 6, but in the meantime suffice it to say that addiction is characterized by what I refer to as a "negative psychology." This is a state of mind that's dominated by pessimism, low self-esteem, a negative self-image, a focus on problems, and an overall negative outlook on the self, other people, and the world. Addicts usually progress to a state of mind known as *learned helplessness* – where they feel that no matter what they do, they won't be able to solve their problems – and they develop an *external locus of control* – where they believe that their fate is controlled by other people and things that are beyond their control. They view the world as an unkind, hostile place, and they feel that they're a victim of other people and the world and even God. Like any "victim," they're angry and resentful. Their problems feel overwhelming and beyond their ability to solve, and they try to find solace in blaming others and feeling sorry for themselves.

The self-pity and blamefulness that tends to predominate the addicted mind can make addicts difficult to be around. As you can imagine, anyone who feels like a helpless victim is angry, and family members usually bear the brunt of this anger. Addicts blame everybody and everything except themselves for their situation. I refer to their attitude as the "addict's blamethrower." Even when loved ones try to help the addict, they're met with hostility. It makes addicts seem unapproachable.

Rumination. Although it's not officially classified as such, addiction is very much an obsessive-compulsive disorder. The addicted mind is taken over by persistent, invasive thoughts about substance use (these dominant thoughts are known as *obsessions*) and overwhelming anxiety that can only be satisfied by fulfilling the object of the obsessions – obtaining and using substances (these must-do behaviors are known as *compulsions*).

The addicted mind – clouded by pessimism, negativity, and fear – also tends to become obsessive about problems. Addicts ruminate, obsessing about past events and what the future may hold, running through them in their mind over and over again, blowing them out of proportion. They focus on past negative events and perceived failings and beat themselves up over them. They project their problems into the future and engage in neurotic rumination about future events that likely will never occur.

These ruminations about the future create significant fears that have an operatic self-destructive effect on the mind, swirling around and provoking pessimism, dread, and anxiety. This neurotic fear is a cornerstone of the extreme negative psychology of addiction. These ruminations are uncomfortable, and even painful. They're negative, problem-focused, and self-berating. Ruminations are a powerful driver of substance use as individuals seek to escape them by numbing their mind and distracting themselves with substance use. Many addicts see substance use as their only escape from ruminative thoughts. Addressing rumination is a major focus of addiction treatment.

Risky behavior. The human brain has a defense mechanism against behaviors that may lead us to harm. Our executive brain functions allow us to think, recognize risks, anticipate outcomes of our actions, and use judgment to decide if a particular action is likely to cause us harm. Therefore, we reject actions that may cause us peril, even if that harm may occur much later on. However, as we discussed in the previous chapter, the toxic effects of addictive substances impair the brain's executive functions, so that this normal defense mechanism against foolhardy, dangerous, or outright stupid actions isn't working very well. This occurs even when the addict isn't acutely intoxicated, so that addicts are likely to engage in unwise and dangerous behaviors even when sober. So, it's hardly surprising that engaging in risky behaviors that they would otherwise avoid is a characteristic symptom of addiction.

Many of the risky behaviors don't result in any harm because the addicts get lucky. It's a safe bet that every addict drives while impaired – probably multiple times – and they may get lucky and not get into an accident and not kill anyone. However, many risky behaviors are repeated multiple times, increasing the risk of serious long-term harm. For example, substance use is associated with increased risk of infections – including Hepatitis B and C, endocarditis (heart infection), and HIV. This isn't just among those who share needles; substance use has been associated with risky sexual behaviors, including unprotected sex with strangers. As well, substance use – even in non-addicts – mixed with driving puts the driver, passengers, pedestrians, and other drivers at risk for serious injury and death. After alcohol, marijuana is the leading cause of impaired driving, as marijuana use is known to cause lane weaving, poor reaction time, and lack of attention to the road.

Early in my medical career I worked on a trauma team in the ER of a large hospital, and the majority of the serious injuries that we treated involved substance use of some kind. Even intoxicated people who were not necessarily addicts were engaging in risky behaviors that led to falls, injuries from fights, motor vehicle accidents, and so on. Substance use in general leads to risky behaviors. Even non-addicts, who haven't had the brain changes that cause addiction, will succumb to the disinhibiting effects of drugs and alcohol while intoxicated and do stupid things, and they'll do those things with impaired coordination.

Substance use has also been associated with a higher risk of tobacco use, which carries significant health risks. Of course, addicts – who cannot control their substance use – commonly continue their drinking and/or drugging while pregnant, putting the fetus at considerable risk for health problems in the neonatal period and for life. When I was an intern I worked in a neonatal ICU in a pediatric hospital for a few months, and the vast majority of our tiny, innocent patients were there because they were born addicted to heroin, cocaine, or other drugs, and/or had significant birth defects from exposure to drugs or alcohol during the pregnancy.

Adolescents appear to be especially likely to engage in risky behavior with substance use. This is likely because even without drugs or alcohol involved, adolescents are more likely than other age groups to engage in risky behaviors.

Of course, illicit drug use is in itself risky, given that there's no way to know exactly what's in the stuff the dealers are selling. Most overdoses are accidental, usually from dangerous cutting agents and ultra-potent additives. I've been told by many addicts that every time they use, they have no idea if they'll survive or not. Many don't.

Fear. You may have noticed that the word "fear" has popped up quite a few times during our discussion. That's because the addicted mind is ridden with fear. Don't let the addict's arrogant, know-it-all demeanor fool you; despite their outward façade, they're full of fear on the inside.

The profound negative psychology of the addicted mind generates a pessimistic view of life, the world, and the self. Addicts tend to see the worst in everything, and project the outcome of their stressors into worst-case scenarios, creating significant fear and anxiety. Of course, these fears are magnified by rumination.

Much of this negativity and fear comes from the fact that their life is crashing down around them, making them naturally pessimistic. However, alcohol and drugs also have a biochemical effect on the brain – activating alarm circuits – that produces anxiety even when all is well. As one addict puts it: *we're not always sure what we're afraid of; sometimes it is just a vague, generalized, nameless fear* (*Living Sober,* p. 38).

Fear is a significant barrier to recovery, so we'll be discussing it more in the chapters to come, as well as how you can play a huge role in breaking down these fear-filled barriers to recovery.

*

As with any disease, the symptoms of addiction can all be explained by the effects of the disease on the body. Addiction is mostly a disease of the brain and mind, so naturally most of the symptoms involve dysfunctional thought processes and behaviors. Many of these symptoms make addicts unlikeable (to say the least), but it's important to remember that these symptoms are reversible with proper treatment and care. The disease model of addiction gives us a basis for separating the person from the disease and its symptoms so that we remember that underneath all the ugly words and acts there's a hurting person who needs help.

It's helpful for addicts and their loved ones to understand the link between the toxic effects of psychoactive substances on the brain the symptoms so that they can understand that the person they once knew and loved is still there underneath the horrible veneer. This helps reduce stigma, and helps people in addiction and their families take hope in the fact that addiction is a treatable disease and that people can expect a full return to better health and function with the appropriate help, support, and effort.

To that end, in the next two chapters we delve into what happens to the brain and mind from repeated exposure to substances of addiction.

5

The Addicted Brain

She put that bottle to her head and pulled the trigger.

– *Whiskey Lullaby* (Brad Paisley and Alison Krauss)

Addiction is primarily a disease of the brain. Thanks to significant innovations in our ability to study the brain, our understanding of the effects of addictive substances on the brain has advanced considerably over the past two decades. Our newfound understanding of how addiction transforms the structure and function of the brain has vastly increased our understanding of the symptomatology of addiction, and provides great insight into how we can treat this horrible disease.

The brain changes seen in addiction are responsible for and correlate with most of the behavioral symptoms that we discussed in the previous chapter. The rest of the symptoms result from the psychological effects of substance use; in other words from the addicted mind. We'll discuss the effects of addiction on the mind (as well as what, exactly, the difference is between the brain and the mind) in the next chapter.

Addiction exists simply because addictive substances have a remarkable ability to activate and adulterate key brain structures in a way that propagates substance use and promotes relapse in recovery. Addiction results primarily from the effects of psychoactive substances on two important brain systems:

1) **The executive control system** – this is the part of the brain that allows us to engage in higher level thinking, such as reasoning, planning, and decision-making. It protects us from harm by giving us judgment and self-control, and helps us to achieve our short- and long-term goals by coordinating our behaviors so that they are goal-directed. The executive control system is the part of the brain that decides what we do, how we do it, and when; therefore, it may be thought of as the "CEO of the brain," and
2) **The learning system** – this is the system that enables us to adapt to our environment and meet our goals by learning new information and behaviors. This important brain system also helps us to learn from our mistakes and our successes, so that our future actions are improved by lessons learned from our past actions. Much of the learning that occurs in our brain involves a reward system that releases feel-good chemicals into the brain that give us a bit of a "high" when we accomplish something good. We learn to repeat behaviors that earn us a reward, and we avoid behaviors that don't result in a reward. As such, much of our learning is reward-based (reward-based learning is known as *conditioning*). The learning system is also involved in memory and motivation.

Once the brain has undergone the physical changes that create addiction, the effects of addictive substances on the brain occur independent of intoxication, so that they disrupt behavior even when the individual is sober. Unfortunately, many of the changes to the brain in addiction are long-lasting and time-stable. This means that although people in recovery can return to normal function and behavior, the addicted brain can be re-activated by re-exposure to addictive substances years – even decades – after the last drink or drug. When an addict is in recovery, even a single exposure to drugs or alcohol can re-activate these enduring brain changes, resulting in a rapid resumption of the same behaviors and dysfunction that occurred in the original bout with addiction. In my work with addicts I've seen innumerable cases of people with many years of sobriety relapsing right back to where they were with even one drink or drug. This is why relapse prevention is such a critical part of addiction treatment and recovery.

*

The human brain is a fascinating contraption. It has justifiably been described as the most complex object in the universe. It's a collection of 86 billion nerve cells – known as *neurons* – that work together in ways that we're only beginning to understand. This most formidable of machines – capable of the most wondrous of achievements – can be manipulated by addictive substances into shattering lives, and the mind becomes powerless to do anything about it. In his New York Times column Harold M. Schmeck Jr. aptly observed: *the ultimate goal is to understand the human brain – that incredible three-pound package of tissue that can imagine the farthest reaches of the universe and the ultimate core of the atom but cannot fathom its own functioning.*

The brain is not a homogenous organ, but operates on a modular basis. It consists of a number of separate structures that all have different functions. These different structures are all semi-autonomous, but they interact together in different combinations, depending on the task on hand. In order to accomplish coordination between the various structures of the brain, there are wondrously complex and intricate interconnections between the various parts.

The human brain weighs 3.3 lbs. (half of what our skin weighs), making up about 2% of our body weight. It contains 86 billion neurons – the gray matter – and billions of nerve fibers – the white matter. Each of the 86 billion neurons has up to 10,000 connections to other neurons. A piece of brain the size of a grain of sand contains 100,000 neurons and 1 billion interconnections. Despite the trillions of inter-connections that crisscross and run in all directions, the brain's functions are harmonious and sophisticated beyond measure; its abilities are boundlessly greater than the sum of its parts. The entire body is there to support the brain, and it alone is responsible for all humankind's actions and interactions, society, history, and accomplishments.

Even though the brain makes up only 2% of our body-weight it uses up to 60% of our total energy and oxygen intake. It's composed of 73% water, yet it takes only 2% dehydration to disable its function. The brain is the fattiest organ in the body, being 60% fat. A quarter of all the cholesterol in our body is contained in the brain, which needs it: without enough cholesterol, brain cells die.

The brain works by transmitting information between neurons, which is why there are so many inter-connections. None of the brain cells actually touch. There's a tiny, microscopic gap between them, and the brain cells communicate by releasing various chemicals across the gap to transmit messages between them. These message chemicals are known as *neurotransmitters*. Each of the many different neurotransmitters means different things to different brain cells at different times and in different amounts. The sending brain cell produces and releases the neurotransmitter, and the receiving cell picks up these signals on receptors, which recognize the signal and understand the message. The receiving neuron then passes the signal along to the next neuron in the pathway. Thus, the message is passed along the sequence of neurons that form the pathway.

There are many different neurotransmitters, and they all have various functions. Of course, if the neurotransmitters become disrupted for any reason the messages will get mixed up and it'll affect brain function and lead to many different problems and disorders. These include Alzheimer's disease, Parkinson's disease, depression, schizophrenia, and so on. Addiction is also included on the list. Alzheimer's disease causes specific neurotransmitter disruptions that cause the specific symptoms of Alzheimer's disease. The same is true for Parkinson's disease, and depression. Likewise, addiction causes specific neurotransmitter disruptions that cause the specific symptoms of addiction. Besides using neurotransmitters, neurons can also pass messages along by direct electrical impulses, and these, too, are affected in addiction. However, the main problem in the addicted brain lies in the disordered neurotransmitters.

Although they all have different ways of disrupting neurotransmitters, the neurotransmitter dopamine is the common end-point for all drugs of addiction, as well as for addictive behaviors (such as gambling, compulsive shopping, and so on). Dopamine has been implicated in addictive behavior in both animal and human studies, so we're sure it's the culprit. It's responsible for the feel-good euphoria that's brought on by these drugs, which provides positive reinforcement for continued drug use. Conversely, removal of the drug causes reduced production and release of dopamine in the brain, which causes the opposite of a high: a depressed mood and low energy, which makes the individual seek the drug to stop the negative feelings. Thus, there is positive and negative reinforcement involved in drug-seeking behavior. This reinforcement, positive and negative, is a form of learning known as *conditioning*.

In normal life, rewards usually come only with time and effort. Substance use gives the brain a much bigger and faster burst of reward without all the work involved, providing a shortcut, flooding the brain with dopamine and other feel-good neurotransmitters.

The brain is not naturally exposed to these huge substance-induced bursts of dopamine, so it compensates by trying to reduce dopamine levels, trying to get things back to normal, a process known as *homeostasis*. The brain reduces the number of receptors that are stimulated by dopamine release, and we become sensitized to dopamine, so that the good feelings from its release are reduced. Then the brain starts to "down-regulate" the production of dopamine in order to further compensate for the repeatedly high levels produced by the addictive substances. As a result, people who repeatedly use substances need more and more of the drug to get the same effect. This is what's known as *tolerance*.

This lowered dopamine production that occurs as the brain compensates in response to addictive substances results in lower-than-normal levels of dopamine when the substance isn't present. Therefore, when addicts are not "high" or "drunk," their baseline dopamine levels are now way below normal levels, and they feel depressed, lifeless, lacking energy, and unable to feel pleasure. They're now the opposite of rewarded. They no longer feel any reward for anything at all, including such normally rewarding things such as eating, accomplishing tasks, or finding a fulfilling relationship. They need their drug just to feel normal, let alone "high." Trying to overcome this depressed feeling is a major driver of continued substance use even when tolerance has rendered it no longer fun.

This is how substances of addiction insert themselves into the brain's communication system – the neurotransmitters – and interfere with the way neurons normally communicate. Anything that we put in our body that messes with our neurotransmitters is referred to as being *psychoactive*. All substances of addiction are psychoactive, including anabolic steroids. Some drugs, such as marijuana and heroin, have a chemical structure that mimics that of a natural neurotransmitter, especially dopamine. This "fools" receptors and allows the drugs to activate the feel-good reward system directly. Although these drugs mimic the brain's own chemicals, they don't activate neurons in the same way that natural neurotransmitters do, and they lead to abnormal messages being transmitted through the neural network. Other drugs, such as stimulants, cause neurons to produce and release abnormally large amounts of natural neurotransmitters or prevent their normal break-down. This disruption produces a greatly amplified message, ultimately disrupting communication channels and producing symptoms consistent with these high levels of neurotransmitters. While this results in an extremely high feel-good state, it also significantly disrupts normal brain functions.

Although we've so far mostly limited our discussion to the neurotransmitter dopamine – because that's the one that's most relevant to addiction – addictive substances also affect myriad other neurotransmitters, most of which are involved in crucial brain functions. Critically, the neurotransmitters that cause depression, anxiety, psychosis, and other mental health problems (such as the neurotransmitters serotonin, norepinephrine, and GABA, for example) are also affected, which explains why there's so much overlap between mental health issues and addiction.

In addition to its role in the reward system, the neurotransmitter dopamine is also involved in a number of other brain processes, including those that regulate movement, emotion, motivation, and, oddly enough, screening our thoughts. Because of this, imbalances in dopamine, such as the highs and lows brought on by addictive substances, can have other serious consequences. High levels of dopamine cause the symptom of psychosis, which is defined as a loss of touch with reality. The high levels of dopamine interfere with our brain's system for screening out nonsensical subconscious thoughts before they're allowed through to our consciousness, so thoughts that would normally be rejected as unreal are allowed through. The result is psychosis. Symptoms of psychosis include hearing or seeing things that aren't there (auditory and visual hallucinations), receiving weird but compelling instructions, paranoia, ideas of reference (believing that people on TV and the radio are talking about us), catatonia (holding absolutely still in statue-like poses for prolonged periods of time), and general weird behavior. Some addictive substances are especially tied into psychosis, particularly marijuana, MDMA, and methamphetamine. Unfortunately, violent behavior is common during psychosis, especially if there's paranoia. Some drugs are known to cause permanent psychosis, which is known as schizophrenia.

There are other effects from the extreme highs and lows of dopamine that come with psychoactive substance use. For example, low levels of dopamine is the cause of Parkinson's Disease, so the lower than normal levels of dopamine that occur when withdrawing from substance use cause shaking and unsteadiness. As well, dopamine is involved in regulating emotions, so the ups and downs of dopamine have much to do with the sudden alterations and extremes of emotions that we see in addicts as they cycle through their substance use and withdrawal.

Now, let's take a closer look at the first of the two brain systems that are affected by substance use: the executive control system, the "CEO of the brain."

*

The executive control system is that part of our brain that gives us the ability to think, and to control and regulate our behaviors. It's responsible for giving us the ability to reason, plan, self-monitor, self-control, organize, and adapt (these are referred to as our *cognitive* functions). Importantly, it's also involved in inhibition, so that we don't get derailed from our longer-term goals by choosing immediate gratification when it'll interfere with our goals. The executive control system is seated in the *pre-frontal cortex* (PFC) of the brain. The PFC is the forward-most part of the brain – sitting in the front part of the frontal lobe – located directly behind the eyes and forehead.

It's unfortunate that addictive substances disrupt the PFC, because it's a very important part of the brain. The PFC is heavily involved in personality expression, control of social interactions, and our ability to think, make decisions, and to plan out our actions. It's the part of the brain that allows us to compare conflicting ideas and choose the best option, determine the future consequences of our decisions, set goals and work toward achieving them, and interpret our interactions with other people. Disruption of circuits in the PFC from the toxic effects of addictive substances results in profoundly disrupted overall ability to function. This is why addicts are virtually incapable of goal-directed behavior (for any goal other than substance use), judgment, self-control, flexibility, inhibition, and sound decision-making. It's not hard to see why disruption of this critical part of the brain would result in someone suddenly seeming to have a different personality, choosing immediate gratification despite the consequences, and being overall prone to making stupid decisions.

The association between substance use and significant perturbation in the PFC has been solidly established by extensive research. Indeed, the symptoms of addiction resemble very closely the symptoms of "dysexecutive syndrome," which occurs in people who have a stroke or other brain injury to the PFC.

The symptoms dysexecutive syndrome are virtually the same as many of the symptoms of addiction:

- Impulsivity,
- Euphoria,
- Impaired inhibition,
- Untruthfulness, confabulation,
- Poor ability to plan,
- Difficulty with time and sequencing,
- Lack of insight into one's own dysfunctional behaviors,
- Aggression,
- Restlessness,
- Apathy and lack of drive,
- Perseveration (obsessive or repeated thoughts or actions),
- Knowing-doing dissociation (i.e. undertaking unwise actions despite knowing better),
- Distractibility, poor concentration,
- Poor decision-making,
- Lack of social awareness, and
- Lack of concern for social rules.

Sounds a lot like the behaviors we see in addicts, right? Some of the PFC's functions are also disrupted in some mental health disorders, which provides a further explanation for the overlap in symptoms between addiction and other mental health disorders.

*

The other major brain system that's disrupted by addictive substances – the learning system – uses motivation and reward to direct our attention toward things that matter and that will help us to achieve our goals. The learning system motivates us to perform activities that help us survive and improve our situation in the world, and it provides us with a mechanism for remembering the things that help us to function better and avoid calamity.

We're able to interact with the world around us because of the connections that we form between neurons in our brain. These brain cell connections allow us to learn, store memories, remember things, interpret what we see and hear, communicate, plan, make decisions, engage in thought processes, interact with other people, and so on. We discussed earlier how each brain cell has up to 10,000 connections to other brain cells. When brain cells connect in a series, we call that series of connections a *pathway*. When the series of brain cells (neurons) in a pathway send a signal along that pathway, we say that the pathway *fires*. When we learn something new, new neuron connections forming a pathway are laid down, and these pathways become part of our memory. When we access that memory, the series of neurons that form that pathway fire, and we recall the memory.

The most important thing about our learning system is that it's adaptive. It helps us to learn from experience and adjust our behaviors so that we can adapt and become better at achieving our goals as our situation changes. Unfortunately, addiction corrupts these otherwise highly beneficial learning processes in order to direct behavior exclusively toward a single goal – obtaining and consuming addictive substances, at the cost of all other goals and motivations. Addiction's effects on the learning system is one of the great paradoxes of addiction: it takes the brain's learning system – which is designed to be adaptive to help us to improve our ability to survive and thrive – and usurps it so that it becomes maladaptive and causes addicts to adopt behaviors that lead to self-destruction and death. As such, addiction turns one of the most biologically useful neural processes into a dysfunctional and harmful trap. Let's have a look at how the brain learns, and how addiction takes over this process.

Learning is driven by motivation. There must be an attractive goal to motivate the mind to learn to behave in a way to attain that goal. When there's a barrier to attaining that goal, the mind is motivated to learn to behave in a way that overcomes that barrier. When we achieve something that helps us survive – such as finding food when we're hungry – or that improves our situation in the world – such as getting a job promotion – our brain rewards us by releasing feel-good neurotransmitters (including dopamine) that provide us with a small "high" as a reward for our good behavior. This little "high" provides us with motivation to do things that'll get us another reward. That's how our mind teaches us to repeat good behaviors – such as getting food every time we're hungry – or to work toward long-term goals – such as getting a promotion at work. Our executive brain functions allow us to use judgment and self-control so that we can put off immediate gratification (such as goofing off at work) in order to achieve a bigger gratification later on (such as a job promotion).

Our brain's reward system is the main motivator for learning: people are motivated to learn behaviors that lead to a reward. This is known as *positive reinforcement*, because we get a positive reward for doing something good. Conversely, we also learn by *negative reinforcement*, which means that we learn how to avoid punishments. For example, if we touch a hot stove we get a painful burn (a negative reinforcement), so we learn to avoid touching hot stoves. In order to illustrate, let's look at some basic learning: food acquisition.

We need food to survive. So, in order to make sure that we learn to give our body food, our brain gives us a nice shot of our feel-good reward chemicals when we eat when we need to. That's why we feel pleasure when we have a good meal when we're hungry. Because of the reward, we learn to seek out food when we're hungry. Conversely, if we don't seek out food we get hunger pains and feel weak and unwell – a punishment. So, we learn to obtain food when we're hungry because it helps us to feel pleasure (positive reinforcement), and to avoiding the punishment of hunger pangs (negative reinforcement).

The link between addiction and learning lies in the fact that addictive drugs stimulate our brain's reward system to release feel-good chemicals at levels that are far higher than natural. Rather than the small high that people get from feel-good rewards when they accomplish something good, addictive drugs provide a huge burst of feel-good neurotransmitters that creates a huge high, known as *euphoria*. Because the reward from addictive substance use is so high, obtaining and consuming addictive substances becomes the dominant motivation in vulnerable individuals. Their substance use is driven by positive reinforcement. This is why addicts will sacrifice all other motivations – including such things as eating, sleeping, and accomplishing goals – in order to pursue their substance use; the reward is much bigger.

Conversely, once substance use becomes regular, very uncomfortable withdrawal symptoms occur – a punishment – after the drug wears off, so people are motivated to seek out the drug to avoid punishment. In other words, negative reinforcement also plays a role in propagating substance use. In early addiction, motivation is driven by reward because the high from substance use is still huge and there's very little withdrawal, but as addiction progresses the euphoric "high" becomes diminished while withdrawal symptoms become more pronounced. As such, later in addiction motivation is primarily driven by avoiding punishment (negative reinforcement) rather than obtaining a reward (positive reinforcement). The normal thought processes, logic, needs, motivations, and desires of the brain become derailed. The brain's learning system is focused on one single goal: obtaining and using substances – the brain is now addicted.

Of course, most people who use alcohol and drugs become high and have the same rush of feel-good neurotransmitters, but they don't become addicted. *Why is that?* Well, as we discussed in chapter 1, addiction occurs in people who're vulnerable to the brain changes, and vulnerable to seeking repeated highs. I'm a good example of this. I was able to go through my whole life able to drink alcohol, and I even tried drugs, without developing addiction. I drank or used drugs and felt high, but I was able to shake it off and get on with life the next day. I wouldn't use alcohol or drugs for months at a time, and I wouldn't even think about it. I wasn't addicted. However, when my life stressors became overwhelming for me and I developed symptoms of depression, the high of alcohol and drugs became an escape from my stress and a relief from the pain of depression, and that made me use alcohol and drugs repeatedly. With repeated exposure – it became daily – my brain underwent the changes of addiction. Now I was addicted. As we discussed in chapter 1, people can be vulnerable to addiction because of their genetics and because of their life situation and ability to cope. I had a genetic vulnerability – my father was an alcoholic – and my life situation and inability to cope became overwhelming, creating the perfect storm for addiction.

The powerful motivation provided by addictive substances results in the complete usurpation of people's normal needs, goals, and motivations. As addiction progresses, individuals progressively sacrifice previously held motivations as their focus becomes increasingly narrowed on obtaining and using substances. That's why even the threat of loss of employment, savings, family, home, and friends doesn't stop the substance use. It's why addicts will use their rent and grocery money to obtain their substance. It's why they'll even forsake the care of their children, even if they were previously dedicated, caring parents. This is why cajoling addicts with threats will not make them stop their substance use or commit to treatment.

The type of learning we've been discussing so far is known as *operant conditioning*. This is the psychological term for learning by responding to positive and negative reinforcements. There's another type of learning that's important to addiction, known as *classical conditioning*. Let's take a look at that now.

*

You may remember the story of Pavlov's dogs from high school biology or psychology. Ivan Pavlov was a Russian psychologist who demonstrated what we now refer to as *associative learning*, where our brain is geared to learn to relate things in our environment that lead to rewarding goals. Pavlov was able to demonstrate that when he rang a bell immediately before feeding his dogs, his dogs would eventually begin salivating as soon as they heard the bell, even though they hadn't yet been given the food. This is because – after only a few times hearing the bell while they were being fed – the dogs learned to associate the sound of the bell (the cue) with being fed (the reward). We now refer to this kind of learning – where we associate cues with a reward – as *classical conditioning*. This kind of learning plays a huge role in addiction and relapse.

As addiction develops and people become increasingly motivated to obtain their substance-based "reward," they devote increasingly more of their attentional resources to their substance. This also means that anything associated with their substance gets their attention, and they begin to learn the associations between these cues and the substance-related reward. As such, they begin to associate certain people, places, and things with their substance use, just like Pavlov's dogs associated the sound of the bell with the reward of being fed.

As addiction develops people begin using their substances more and more frequently, and it often becomes a daily occurrence. As the substance use continues, over the weeks, months, and even years, these associated learned cues become deeply embedded in the brain's memories. Not only does the high frequency of the substance and cue pairings cause the learned associations to become deeply embedded, but the very high levels of reward and emotion associated with the substance use also further cement the learned cues. As people in addiction learn cues that become associated with their substance use, these cues in turn trigger drug cravings and extraordinary efforts to satisfy the cravings. In other words, these cues become triggers for them to crave and seek substance use. For example, an alcoholic may learn to associate the street that her favorite bar is on with drinking, so every time she sees the street it initiates cravings for alcohol use. Similarly, a drug addict may associate the area where his dealer operated with substance use, and may experience powerful cravings whenever he passes near that location.

One of the unfortunate consequences of addiction learning is that these substance-related cues become permanent memories, embedded in the subconscious mind. This is why even decades into recovery people can be triggered into relapse by exposure to substance-related cues, especially if they're vulnerable at the time (such as if they're under a great deal of stress, or experiencing mental health symptoms).

The development of brain pathways that establish cues and triggers is just one example of the addiction-related learning that occurs with repeated substance use. Many other pathways that are responsible for obsessive and uncontrollable substance use also develop. These learned pathways are primarily involved in creating automatic behaviors, where addicts react in specific ways to stimuli (such as exposure to cues, or to interactions with other people) without even thinking first. In other words, addiction becomes automatic. This is one of the reasons that addiction is difficult to break. Over-riding these automatic behaviors and re-asserting thinking control over behavior is one of the main focuses of addiction treatment. This is only possible when the addicts are substance-free, so that their brain's "CEO" (executive control system) can begin functioning properly again.

*

Another way that the brain learns new behaviors bears mentioning here, because it plays a role in the development of addiction, and it can be turned around and used to have a powerful effect on recovery and relapse prevention. *Social learning* involves learning new attitudes and behaviors by observing and emulating how other people behave. This process is an integral part of how we grow and learn, especially in childhood and adolescence. Children and adolescents notice, register, and model the behavior of important others as they learn to survive and thrive in a complex world. As such, our brain is geared to notice what other people are doing and to take on their behaviors for ourselves.

Social learning is especially potent among adolescents, who're intensely driven to fit in and be accepted by the crowd. As such, if there's a group of people who an adolescent admires or wishes to fit in with, the adolescent will be driven to adopt their attitudes and behaviors in order to be accepted into the group. If that group is involved in substance use, then the substance use is likely to be adopted as well.

Social learning can be especially intense among people in addiction. As they become alienated from their "nagging" family and friends and increasingly rejected and marginalized by society, addicts crave acceptance with some group of people – any group. Of course, the group most likely to accept them for who they are is other addicts. Being around other people who're engaging in the same behaviors helps addicts feel better about themselves, because it reduces cognitive dissonance. After all, when you're doing something "bad," it can't be all *that* bad if everyone else is doing it too, right?

Unfortunately, social learning tends to escalate substance use, and it's also a common pathway to trying new drugs, when friends within the group expose each other to new drugs and ways of doing drugs. Social pressure from the group is a powerful deterrent to recovery, due to a phenomenon that I refer to as the "misery loves company effect." Addicts don't like it when their friends get sober and healthy, because it highlights their own continuing substance use and magnifies their cognitive dissonance. They'll try very hard to talk their friend out of recovery and do their very best to get them to relapse. I see this happening all the time in my work with people in early recovery. Misery loves company, and the selfish addict mind can't stand seeing someone else escaping the misery of addiction. It's one of the reasons that addicts in recovery need to stop associating with their old substance-using friends.

Social learning forms a fundamental part of virtually all credible addiction treatment and relapse prevention programs. The application of social learning to recovery includes:

- Ceasing contact with the people and places that previously served as models, triggers, and peer-driven influences for substance use,
- Developing a new network of friends and family who support recovery,
- Inclusion in a recovery support group, during treatment and after, that involves immersion in a culture of recovery, where recovery-based attitudes, behaviors, and values are modeled and rewarded,
- The use of vicarious experiences for providing modeling and motivation for recovery, to increase self-efficacy beliefs (we'll discuss this in the next chapter), and to show the way to recovery,
- Establishing and using a supportive network for a healthy approach to dealing with stress and adversity, and
- Learning skills and the self-confidence to respond appropriately to negative peer pressure.

Social learning plays a significant role in the development and propagation of addiction, and it must be leveraged to play a significant role in recovery.

Those are the three important ways in which the brain's learning systems are adulterated in the process of developing addiction – operant conditioning (seeking rewards and avoiding punishments), classical conditioning (making associations between substance use and cues), and social learning. Of course, the obvious question is: *if addiction is a learned behavior, can it be unlearned?* We'll answer that question in chapter 11, and lay out how you can be a vital part of the process of "unlearning" addiction.

*

You may have heard the term *neuroplasticity*, as it's one of those medical terms that gets bandied about in the popular media. All it refers to is the brain's ability to adapt, to change according to our needs. The term "plasticity" in general refers to the ability of our body tissues to adapt to our needs. For example, muscles have plasticity: if we lay around and don't use them they shrink and lose tone. They become weak and diminished. After all, our body sees no point in maintaining big muscles if we never use them. However, if we exercise and stay active, our muscles respond by growing in size and strength to meet our needs. Likewise, laying around and watching TV requires little brain effort, so our brain will respond accordingly. However, if we use our brain and challenge it, it will grow in capacity and ability. It really does work like that. This is neuroplasticity – brain plasticity.

The brain is one of the most "plastic" organs in the body; it's built to adapt. The brain is geared to re-wire itself, and modify or form new connections so that we can learn and adapt rapidly. We can see examples of neuroplasticity all through life: every time we learn something new, our brain has changed so that we can learn the new information or skill to help us function more effectively. As we develop from infancy to adulthood our brain learns how to control our muscles, communicate in the language of those around us, and to behave appropriately in society. Without neuroplasticity, none of this would happen and we'd go through life as infants.

Neuroplasticity is both friend and foe when it comes to addiction. As we just discussed, addiction is a learned behavior, where the brain forms new associations, learns to perform new behaviors, and adapts to optimize the addict's ability to obtain and use drugs or alcohol. As such, addictive substances use neuroplasticity to entrap the brain into addiction. However, neuroplasticity can also be used to overcome addiction and prevent relapse, and all credible addiction treatment programs leverage neuroplasticity to great effect.

The neuroplastic changes that occur in response to repeated exposure to addictive substances in vulnerable individuals – i.e. those who develop addiction – are deeply embedded in the fabric of the brain. In fact, these changes occur in how the brain cells are connected, and how the brain cells communicate with each other to pass on information. As well, changes occur right down to the molecular structure and function of brain cells, including changes in the brain cells' DNA.

The alterations to DNA caused by exposure to addictive substances are known as *epigenetic* changes. That means that the DNA itself is not changed, but previously inactive genes are activated. Activation of these otherwise dormant genes changes how the brain reacts when exposed to addictive substances. While there is no single "addiction gene," many genes that promote addiction have been identified, and there may be hundreds of them. The more of these genes that a particular individual possesses, the more likely that individual is to develop addiction when exposed to addictive substances. Most of the genes involved in making someone prone to addiction are genes that act on the brain. Many "addiction genes" lie dormant, but repeated exposure to drug or drink will activate them, thereby promoting the development of addiction.

Brain cells – neurons – are changed in a fundamental way as the brain changes from the normal to the addicted state. These changes alter how the individual responds to exposure to addictive substances or behaves in response to substance-related cues. The changes are usually permanent, so that once addiction occurs the brain is highly likely to revert to the same way of responding to addictive substances and related cues for the rest of the individual's life, even after years of recovery.

We're not exactly sure how addictive substances manage to take control of our brain and alter it in such fundamental ways. However, it appears to have to do with the ability of these toxic substances to trigger the brain's immune system (the *neuroimmune system*). Neuroimmune activation can have a significant impact on brain function, and has been found to play a role in a number of neurodegenerative diseases, psychiatric disorders, as well as addiction. Repeated exposure to drugs of addiction creates a low-grade brain inflammation. The inflammation irritates the brain cells, making them vulnerable to the neuroplastic changes that we see in addiction. The resulting alterations enhance the rewarding effects of addictive substances, increase craving, magnify withdrawal symptoms, and promote the development of substance dependence. Although the exact mechanism of how this happens is not yet understood, these substance-induced neuroimmune effects have been clearly implicated in the development and propagation of addiction.

The neuroplastic changes that occur in addiction are in the very fabric of the brain tissue, right down to the molecular level inside the brain cells. They include changes to how each brain cell responds to addictive substances (through alterations in *intracellular signaling*), how DNA is expressed (*epigenetic* changes), how DNA is used (*DNA transcription*), how neurons communicate with each other, and by forming new networks of neurons – pathways – all of which promote obsessive repeated substance use. The addiction changes even cause neurons that are involved in the addictive process to become larger in size and more dominant. The brain essentially becomes physically geared toward substance use as its priority occupation.

Therefore, you can see that the neuroplastic changes that occur when the brain transitions to an addictive state are profound indeed. They are embedded in our DNA, the activity inside of our brain cells, the structure of brain cells, and the interconnections between brain cells. These changes alter how individuals react when exposed to addictive substances, usually forever. People in recovery can live normal lives, and be just like other people, but with one fundamental difference. Their brain's response to addictive substances will always be different than in non-addicts. So, while other people can have a beer after work, the addict in recovery cannot, lest the enduring addictive changes in the brain be triggered once again. I've seen this play out hundreds of times in my work in addiction, the same old story over and over – *I thought I could handle it this time*. Fortunately, just as neuroplasticity is involved in the development of addiction, so, too, can it be used to beat addiction.

As an example of the impressive therapeutic power of neuroplasticity, I'll illustrate using the scenario of a typical stroke victim. A stroke occurs when the blood supply to part of the brain gets cut off by a blockage of the artery that supplies that part of the brain. The affected brain tissue dies, rots away, and never grows back, actually leaving a vacant cavity in the brain. If the affected part of the brain is the part that controls the individual's left arm, then they'll be unable to move their left arm after the stroke. However, over the next eight months or so, with the proper therapy, the stroke victim can gain back function of their left arm, often just as well as before the stroke. *But how is that?* The part of their brain that controls the left arm is dead and rotted away. The answer is neuroplasticity. The stroke victim's brain – with the proper therapy – can adapt and form alternative pathways around the dead brain tissue to regain control the left arm. However, if the stroke victim had just sat around and not participated in therapy to develop new brain pathways, their arm would've ended up permanently paralyzed.

Just like stroke rehab programs, addiction treatment programs rely heavily on neuroplasticity to help addicts recover their life and functionality. Addicts are taught new ways of thinking, new ways of reacting to people and situations, and new behaviors that promote recovery and counter the addicted brain. We'll discuss this further in chapter 10.

*

People with brains that are more plastic (that is, more susceptible to changes) are most susceptible to these addiction-related brain changes when exposed to addictive substances. Sadly, that happens to be children, adolescents, and young adults, whose brains are still "under construction." The fact is that the brain doesn't finish maturing until about age 25, and until then it's super-plastic and exquisitely sensitive to drugs and alcohol.

Pathways that are laid down in the developing brain tend to become permanent, kind of like tracing a line in wet cement with your finger. This is because children and adolescents learn information and behaviors that they'll need to use for the rest of their life. Thus, people whose brain hasn't finished maturing can develop especially deeply imprinted mental pathways related to substance use. This is why early onset of substance use and addiction is especially ominous. Even the fetal brain develops pathways related to addiction when exposed to psychoactive substances due to maternal substance use, and the hapless child may be born with addiction pathways already embedded. This is, of course, a significant risk factor for the development of addiction later in life, often not so far in the future.

So, adolescents who use substances are more likely to develop the brain changes that cause addiction. To make matters worse, adolescents are also more prone to engaging in risky behaviors, including substance use. There are social and psychological reasons for adolescents' willingness for taking risky behaviors, such as peer pressure, boredom, a need to fit in with the crowd, and a need to show independence from parents and authority. However, it appears that the as yet un-matured brain also plays a role in their propensity for risky behaviors. Certainly, trying out new experiences and taking risks is more likely among teenagers than in other age groups. While this can have a number of benefits – such as making teens more likely to try out sports, be more courageous in social situations, and better able to make risky decisions such as choosing career paths – it can also result in some unwise decisions, such as trying out drugs and alcohol, engaging in unsafe sexual practices, and dangerous driving. To make matters worse, the pre-frontal cortex (PFC – the brain's "CEO") is among the last parts of the brain to finish maturing. As you will recall, the PFC is the seat of our ability to reason, exercise sound judgment, and make wise decisions.

Because of these brain factors, the earlier the age of onset of substance use, the higher the likelihood of developing problem substance use and addiction. For example, data from the U.S. National Survey on Drug Use and Health has shown us that when an individual begins using alcohol at age 12, the risk of developing an alcohol addiction is nearly double that of someone who begins drinking at age 21 (7.2% versus 3.7%). Similar findings have been made for other addictive substances, including marijuana. Moreover, earlier age of onset of substance use is a strong predictor of a more rapid onset and progression of addiction. Of course, other risk factors come into play, such as peer influences, parental involvement, availability of drugs and alcohol, genetics, and so on, but the fact is that the developing brain is exquisitely sensitive to the long-lasting deleterious effects of addictive substances.

Unfortunately, exposure to one addictive substance in individuals with a developing brain increases their risk of addiction for all substances. Even "vaping" (the so-called e-cigarettes) has been shown to create addictive brain changes, and increase the likelihood of developing addiction to other substances. The resulting elevated risk of addiction is not only during adolescence, but lasts into adulthood.

The adolescent brain also responds differently to addictive substances than do adults. Studies have suggested that adolescents feel more of a high and less sedation than do adults, particularly with alcohol. Because of this, they're less subdued than are adults, more energetic and aggressive, and more likely to engage in risky behaviors.

Research has established that alcohol and drug use in adolescence are associated with reduced brain volume, and disruptions to the connectivity and communication between brain regions. Notably, these disruptions appear to impair communication between the higher-level brain functions (i.e. the executive functions in the PFC) and the rest of the brain. These effects likely persist for life, and there's reason to believe that they impact the ability to succeed in education and career, as well as other important life functions.

Most of the research into the effects of drugs on the developing brain has been focused on alcohol and marijuana, because those are by far the most commonly used drugs in adolescence (besides nicotine). The fact that marijuana and alcohol are legalized may make people view them as "soft" drugs, but their effects on the brain can be significant and long-lasting. Both have been linked to problems with learning, memory, attention, and executive function. The risk increases with younger age of use, the frequency and amount of use, and the duration of use, but binging patterns of use – commonly seen among adolescents and young people – has been identified as a particularly nasty contributor to persistent structural and functional brain problems. People don't even have to develop addiction to experience these adverse brain effects.

Substance use during adolescence has also been associated with functional problems, such as externalizing disorders (such as attention-deficit hyperactivity disorder (ADHD), conduct disorder (CD), and oppositional defiant disorder (ODD)), other "heavier" substance use, difficulties in school, family conflict, and problems with social functioning. Substance use is one of the main contributors to accidents and injuries among adolescents. Of course, there's the question of the "chicken and the egg;" which causes which – the substance use or the social problems? Well, both go hand-in-hand. Social conflict and poor parental/family relations are a risk factor for substance use, and the behavioral problems brought on by substance use tend to cause social conflict, especially within the family. One thing is certain: regardless of which causes which, substance use among adolescents makes things worse, and causes other more enduring problems.

These are the ways that the developing brain responds to substance use in a unique way, and it's why I'm saddened every time I see young people vaping or engaging in substance use. The developing mind is a precious and sensitive treasure, hardly something to be permanently sullied with substance use.

*

We've discussed the effects of addictive substances on the two main brain systems that are involved in the development of addiction: the executive control system, and the learning system. However, neither of these two systems operates in isolation. All parts of the brain are linked together to provide a complex control mechanism for determining how we think and act.

Other parts of the brain also chip in to contribute to the obsessive, all-consuming substance use that occurs in addiction. For example, the part of our brain that's responsible for assigning our attention also becomes heavily involved. Although our brain is capable of remembering a lot of stuff and thinking about a wide variety of things, we have limited attentional resources; we can only really focus and pay attention to one thing at a time. As such, a part of our brain plays an important role in deciding what we pay attention to at any given time. The abnormally massive reward stimulation provided by addictive substances disrupts attention processing, so that undue attentional resources become focused on obtaining and consuming the addictive substance. The addicted mind's attention becomes stuck on one thing – obtaining and using the substance, and little or nothing can override that for long. This plays a significant role in the development of an obsession with the substance, as individuals become increasingly unable to focus on or concentrate on anything else. Soon, they lose interest in anything other than substance use, as their attentional resources become increasingly diverted to substance use.

The part of our brain that creates and regulates our emotions (the *limbic system*) is also involved in the addiction process. Our brain assigns emotional states to our motivations; we experience joy with the achievement of our goals, and disappointment, anger, and sadness with failures. When substance use becomes the brain's near-exclusive almighty motivation, the emotions that can accompany the highs and lows of addiction can be especially extreme. The neurotransmitter fluctuations caused in the limbic system by addictive substances are far above that which ordinarily occur. As such, it's hardly surprising that people in active addiction show especially volatile emotional states. Most loved ones can attest to the volcanic anger that's dished out when anyone comes between the addict and their drug. Extremes of emotional behavior, such as aggression and violence are not uncommon. The joy felt with any success in obtaining drugs or alcohol is so profound that even physical effects occur – such as rapid heartbeat, sweating, and goosebumps. The positive emotions experienced by obtaining the substance adds to the reward effect of substance use.

*

Have you ever noticed how some behaviors you do take a lot of concentration and focus, while others take none at all? For example, if you're baking cookies for the first time, a number of steps are involved. You have to read through the recipe, plan out your actions, and think about what you're doing. Only then will you get a proper batch of delicious cookies. However, making coffee – which takes a number of steps – is automatic for many people. They do it day after day, time after time, and the process becomes so ingrained into their brain that they can be totally distracted and thinking about something else and still make a perfect pot of coffee. The sequence of steps is so automatic that ten minutes later they might not even remember doing it. The difference between the two behaviors – following the new cookie recipe and making a pot of coffee – is that the coffee-making is a much-repeated behavior, so the brain has entered the sequence of steps and movements required into its memory banks. The brain does this so that we can be efficient and perform our routine behaviors without having to think our way through them every time. Imagine if you had to figure out and think your way through unlocking your car, adjusting your seat, and starting your car every morning. Thankfully, we don't have to do this because our brain has made the sequence of steps and body movements automatic for us, for the sake of efficiency.

Earlier we discussed "bottom-up" and "top-down" brain processes. Brain scientists refer to the brain processing that controls behaviors and actions that have become automatic for us as "bottom-up" processing, because the behaviors are remembered and controlled by the lower, more primitive, unthinking parts of our brain (the *brainstem*), which happen to be located at the bottom of our brain. Behaviors and actions that we have to put conscious thought into and think our way through are referred to as "top-down" behaviors, because they involve the higher level, thinking parts of our brain (the *cerebral cortex*) which are located at the top of the brain.

As addiction develops and the behaviors around obtaining and using substances become repeated over and over again, they, too, become automatic "bottom-up" behaviors; just like making coffee becomes a "bottom-up" behavior once we've repeated it enough times. When this happens to addiction-related behaviors, responses to cravings and cues become automatic, unthinking, and further removed from control of the thinking part of the brain (i.e. the executive control system). For example, I've spoken to one individual in recovery who used to go to the liquor store every day after work. While he was in active alcoholism, he went to the liquor store after work so many times that the complex set of behaviors involved in driving to the liquor store became automatic for him. One day about four years into recovery he was at work and became very stressed during a particularly tough day. He got in his car after work and his mind was focused completely on his problems and stressors. Next thing he knew, he was at the liquor store. He swears he didn't plan on going there; it was an automatic response to stress when his mind was distracted, left over from his long-passed addiction days. Fortunately, he dove away without going inside.

Because the behaviors that lead to obtaining and using substances are repeated so often during the course of addiction – often many times a day for months or years – they become deeply entrenched automatic, "bottom-up" behaviors, requiring no planning or thought. The effect is deepened by the abnormally high levels of motivational, emotional, and attentional resources assigned to substance use. As such, addiction becomes very much an automatic behavior or set of behaviors that propagates the substance use, even when it's no longer fun or enjoyable. Although I hate using the term "habit" when referring to addiction, addiction really does become a habit.

Disrupting these automatic behaviors and re-establishing "top-down" control of behavior is a major goal of addiction therapy. Despite the deep-seated nature of addiction-related learned habits and behaviors, this is surprisingly easy to do once a few principles have been adopted. Families of people in recovery can help immensely with this process. We'll discuss this in detail in chapter 11.

*

While we're on the subject of the brain, we should briefly discuss the phenomenon of "blackouts." Many families aren't sure what to believe when a substance user denies remembering certain things, so it helps to know about blackouts when you have an addict in your life. Although blackouts famously occur with alcohol, they can also occur with other drugs that act on the neurotransmitter known as *GABA*. This includes mostly drugs that are CNS depressants (such as alcohol, benzodiazepines, and barbiturates – see chapter 3). Most especially, the sedative-hypnotic class of drugs known as benzodiazepines (such as diazepam or lorazepam) are highly associated with blackouts, which is why they're often used as "date-rape" drugs.

Blackouts are a form of substance-induced amnesia. Specifically, blackouts induce *anterograde amnesia*, which simply means that the individual can remember everything before the onset of the drug effects, but nothing afterwards.

People don't have to be addicted to alcohol or drugs to experience blackouts. They can occur in anyone who binge drinks (i.e. has more than two or three drinks at a time), or takes even one dose of a CNS depressant drug, even if they only do so occasionally. Studies have shown that about 40% of college students have experienced blackouts during a binge-drinking episode at a party.

When people experience a blackout, their brain is incapable of forming memories, but is otherwise capable of performing purposeful tasks reasonably well. They can even have complete conversations, perform complex actions such as driving a vehicle, but later have no memory whatsoever of the time they were drunk or high. They don't forget what they've done, they just don't record any of it in memory. This is why, no matter how hard they try, they can't remember what they did during a blackout.

Blackouts appear to be caused by the speed at which blood alcohol/drug levels rise, rather than simply the amount of alcohol or drug used. Some people appear to be more predisposed to blackouts than others; anyone who's had one blackout is much more likely to have another, those who were exposed to alcohol *in utero* are predisposed, and there appears to be a genetic predisposition as well.

There are two types of substance-induced blackouts: 1) total blackouts (*en-bloc* blackouts), and 2) partial blackouts (*fragmentary* blackouts). En-bloc blackouts involve a total amnesia of the entire period of intoxication. Fragmentary blackouts (sometimes called brownouts or grayouts) involve missing pieces of memory from the period of intoxication, although the missing gaps in memory may be recalled when prompted. Fortunately, brownouts are probably much more common than are blackouts.

En bloc blackouts are total: the individual has no memories whatsoever of the intoxication period, and even when sobered up cannot recall any events, even when given an account of the events. When someone experiences a blackout and says they have no memory of the evening before, they're likely telling the truth. I've heard more than a few blackout drinkers tell me that the first thing they would do in the morning would be to go look out the window to see if their car was in the driveway. Some found their vehicle damaged, or parked across the neighbor's lawn, or not even there, with no idea whatsoever about what happened. Because alcohol (and other drugs) are associated with dis-inhibition and risky behavior, many people with no memory whatsoever of the event have faced serious consequences due to their actions while intoxicated, including killing someone while driving impaired, assaulting someone, or damaging property. I've spoken with many addicts who've woken up in jail with no idea how they got there or why they were there. Not a good feeling. Having no memory of the event, or being intoxicated at the time of a crime carries absolutely no weight in a court of law, nor does it excuse anyone of liability for damage.

Although individuals don't have to be addicts to experience blackouts, people who have blackouts are likely engaging in risky, problem substance use and should consider re-evaluating their drinking or drug practices.

Even when blackouts or brownouts don't occur, being in a state of intoxication affects perspective, attention, and memory formation, so many individuals have an incomplete or inaccurate memory of their doings while engaged in substance use. A very important part of addiction treatment includes the addict taking responsibility for their past actions. I encourage families of addicts in recovery to tell their loved ones of their past actions in order to fill in the blanks in case of memory impairments, so as to ensure the completeness of this therapeutic exercise.

*

During early recovery, the addicted brain enters a period of relative chaos. The brain has been trying its very best to correct for the repeated ultra-high spikes in reward-relevant neurotransmitters (primarily dopamine, glutamine, serotonin, and opioid peptides) for months or even years, so it has pushed its natural production of these important neurotransmitters way down. As well, the brain has reduced the number of receptors for these neurotransmitters, all in an effort to compensate for the insanely high levels created by substance use. When people stop using psychoactive substances, it takes a while for the brain to understand that this is more than just a temporary reprieve from the onslaught of drugs, and to start putting things back to normal. The brain takes time to recover after years of chemical abuse, so restoring the brain chemistry to physiologic levels doesn't happen overnight.

As such, there'll be a period where these feel-good neurotransmitters and their receptors are at rock-bottom levels. The result is that the individual feels the opposite of "high" – depressed, listless, unmotivated, and fatigued. This produces a state known as *anhedonia*, where the individual is unable to feel pleasure, even when engaged otherwise enjoyable activities. They may also experience anxiety and emotional volatility as the abused brain struggles to regain normal function. These effects are most pronounced during the immediate withdrawal period, while the body and brain detoxify themselves by clearing out all the drugs and their toxic metabolites, but the effect can last months. We'll talk about this more in chapter 10, when we discuss withdrawal and detoxification in more detail.

Of course, not every person experiences anhedonia for very long, and some will bounce back remarkably quickly. Some experience the opposite, where they feel high on life – an effect known as the "pink cloud effect" (again, we'll discuss this in chapter 10). Negative feelings, such as depression, anxiety, and anhedonia can worsen cravings for returning to substance use, so they're an important risk factor for relapse in early recovery. As such, individuals should be watched for any such symptoms, and these should be addressed promptly in order to optimize the addict's chances of success at recovery. Fortunately, medical science has a number of medications (most notably the anti-depressant/anti-anxiety medications known as *selective serotonin re-uptake inhibitors* (SSRIs)) that do an excellent job of helping the brain recover its neurotransmitter levels back to normal again, and sometimes a short course of such a medication may help addicts in recovery to improve their quality of life, reduce their difficult symptoms, and prevent relapse. Family members and friends can help make a difference by watching out for such symptoms in their loved one in early recovery.

*

Earlier in the book we discussed the reasons why addiction is widely considered to be a disease. As can be seen from our discussion on the brain in addiction, addictive substances produce pathological and enduring physical and physiological changes in the brain, resulting in the behaviors that we know of as the symptoms of addiction. These brain changes can be seen on brain imaging studies, such as MRI and PET scans, as well as under the microscope. This provides powerful support for the disease model of addiction. The overall message is that addiction is a matter of biology, not a matter of morality, or weakness of character. Despite the offensive and irresponsible behaviors and outbursts, it's important that we strive to separate the disease and its symptoms from the person if we wish to help an addict. It can be challenging sometimes – to say the least – but it's better for all involved when we take the high road by acting with compassion and love, even when we dish out "tough love."

As we'll see in the upcoming chapters, this doesn't mean that we let addicts off the hook for their antics, nor does it mean that we allow them to walk all over us and our property. Rather, acting with compassion and love also includes establishing boundaries, and being firm and urbane. By becoming knowledgeable about addiction and addicts, we can cut through the lies and deceit and protect ourselves and our loved ones as we set out to help the addict in a productive way... with our boundaries intact.

Although addiction is primarily a disease of the brain, we can't simply isolate brain function alone as being responsible for this disease. It's brain function, together with genetic make-up, environment and experiences, and the mind (our psychology) that all come together in the process of developing addiction. We must look at all those aspects together in order to understand an addict's mindset and experience, and what we can do to help. That's why this book covers all these inseparable topics all under one cover. In the next chapter we'll discuss the addicted mind – the psychology of addiction – and how the workings of the mind produce the thoughts and behaviors that make up addiction. *Wait, what? What's the difference between the brain and the mind?* Well, the brain is an organ, while the mind is not. The brain is a physical object that can be studied under a microscope, while the mind is all the intangible things that come from the brain. The mind is our consciousness, awareness, sense of self, imagination, creativity, and instinct. Now let's look at how it plays a role in addiction.

6

The Addicted Mind

The human brain is a complex organ with the wonderful power of enabling man to find reasons for continuing to believe whatever it is that he wants to believe.

– Voltaire

In the previous chapter, we discussed the effects of repeated use of addictive substances on the brain, and how these result in physical and physiological changes to the brain that create addiction and produce its typical symptoms. While the direct physical effects of substances on the brain explain many of the thoughts and behaviors of addiction, they don't explain everything. To fully understand the addict, we must also understand the effects of substance use on the mind.

As mentioned at the end of the previous chapter, the brain and mind are different things. While the mind comes from the brain, the brain is a physical thing – a body organ – and the mind is not. While it's the workings of the brain that somehow produce the mind, unlike the brain we cannot touch the mind, look at it under a microscope, or see it on imaging scans. Unlike the brain, the mind has no shape or form. The mind is all those things that surround our consciousness and awareness, our creativity, and imagination.

The brain and mind are certainly intertwined; when the brain is sick or damaged the mind is usually affected. In the last chapter we discussed how the substance-sickened brain causes addicts to think and act differently. In this chapter we'll examine the psychology of addiction; psychology is the science that studies the mind and its functions, and how the mind affects our behaviors. As such, we'll be looking at how social situations, feelings, perceptions, and self-awareness are affected by addiction and how these, in turn, affect normal thought processes and behaviors to produce the symptoms of addiction.

Although everyone is different and you can never generalize rules to all people, the psychological mindset and symptoms we'll be discussing in this chapter are generally applicable to the vast majority of people in addiction, particularly as their substance use progresses to the point where it's causing significant disruption to their life.

*

Addicts are excellent actors. They lead a double life, going to great lengths to present a false front, as if all's well. However, they're hurting inside, and their mind is consumed by constant invasive thoughts about substance use. They're wracked with worry and fear, and they carry tremendous guilt and shame. They present this false front in order to conceal their problem with substance use; they don't want anyone to interfere with their drinking or using, and they'll go to any lengths to protect it. Indeed, secretiveness and denial are among the cardinal symptoms of addiction.

As a result of this false front, it's very difficult to have a true appreciation of the depths of dysfunction that people in addiction live with. Although most addicts are able to maintain a reasonable level of function for a while – some people call them "functional" addicts or alcoholics – as the substance use becomes increasingly dominant, it pushes out all other aspects of normal life, and life becomes a moonscape of a single focus – substance use. By that point in their addiction, addicts may be able to carry out a relatively normal conversation with others – and even smile and laugh – but obtaining and using substances and avoiding withdrawal has become the sole focus of their thoughts and actions. It's a miserable way to live.

Before I experienced addiction myself, I had patients who I knew or suspected were "problem" substance users, but they always portrayed themselves as living a fairly normal life. When I began working in addictions, I encountered some of the people I had once seen as medical patients and I could see first-hand what their lives were *really* like. Many lived absolutely miserable, destitute lives while they were in active addiction. They sure had me fooled when I saw them as medical patients, because I had no idea what their life and mindset were really like. When I was in active addiction, I, too, put up a false front, and I was even able to continue practicing medicine for a while. I believe I fooled a lot of people. Inside, however, I was deeply hurting, and my life was in shambles.

The lesson here is that when we interact with someone who may be engaged in "problem" substance use, all may not be as it seems.

*

There are a handful of dysfunctional psychological processes that dominate the addicted mind. These are heavily involved in the progression of substance use to the point where it becomes an addiction, and they also drive many of the odd behaviors and thought processes that we see in addicts. We'll look at each of these in this chapter. They are:

- **The "dissonant self"** – this is the terrible feeling of guilt that people feel when their behavior deviates from how they believe that good people should behave,
- **Negative psychology** – this is a mindset that's dominated by negative feelings and thoughts, such as pessimism, self-loathing, and depression,
- **Loss of self-esteem, but elevated pride** – when self-esteem is low, the mind often tries to compensate by projecting an elevated false pride,
- **Dysfunctional coping** – rather than coping with stress through healthy de-stressing approaches (such as exercise, or recreation) or solving the problem causing the stress, dysfunctional coping involves avoiding problems, and attempting to escape from reality. This is known as *escape/avoidance coping*,
- **Cognitive bias** – this is the ability of the mind to make up and believe reasons to justify or rationalize behaviors that are harmful and unwise, even if those justifications are obviously untrue, and
- **An "external locus of control"** – this is where people feel like helpless victims of the world, and they come to believe that their fate is determined by outside forces or people, so that there's no point in trying to solve their problems or make their lives better.

Let's now look at each of these dysfunctional mental processes in our endeavor to understand a loved one who suffers from addiction. Learning about the dysfunctional addiction-related mindset enables us to understand and connect with an addict, and to be more effective at helping a loved one overcome addiction.

The Dissonant Self. Nobody grows up dreaming of one day becoming a drug addict or alcoholic. When it does happen, it can be a huge psychological disappointment in the self, to say the least, and that disappointment weighs painfully on the mind. Addiction is burdened with a sanctimonious social stigma, and addicts apply society's injurious stigma to themselves.

Humans have a fundamental need to feel good about themselves. We need to see ourselves as useful, competent, and needed. We also need to see ourselves as fundamentally good. By the time we reach our late teens, we all have a deeply established set of beliefs, standards, and values about what's right and wrong, and what makes a person good or bad. In order to feel good about ourselves, we need to see ourselves and our behavior as being consistent with these deep-set beliefs.

Fulfilling our beliefs and values is so important to our psyche that it becomes an important part of our self-identity. For example, a cherished part of most people's identity includes such things as being good at their job, being a loving parent, conducting themselves with honesty and integrity, and so on. People are comfortable with their self-identity when their behaviors are in accordance with their values. If they don't see themselves as good parents, good at their job, or honest they suffer considerable psychological pain, because their real self is dissonant (inconsistent) with their ideal self.

In chapter 4 we discussed the symptoms of addiction, and these can include some unlovely dissonant behaviors, such as blowing off responsibilities, lying and deceiving, impaired driving and other risky behaviors, neglecting one's own children, and even crime. Such behaviors represent a glaring deviation from people's beliefs, standards, and values, and creates a huge chasm between the ideal self and the actual self; in other words, it creates an enormously dissonant self. Addicts are already feeling badly about themselves because of the stigma attached to substance use, but the behaviors that accompany addiction give them even more reason to beat themselves up. Disapproval from family and friends over their substance use, failure to meet important responsibilities and obligations, censure and firing at work, loss of income and savings, and a feeling of lack of self-control add to the negative self-evaluation.

When people violate their personal beliefs, standards, and values (in other words, when they experience the dissonant self) they suffer considerable psychological distress. Addicts abandon self-defining roles, such as their work, parenting, and connections with other people. Their fundamental need to feel good about themselves is unfulfilled, and the distress from the dissonant self hangs over them day and night like a dark cloud. The distress is worsened when they see that their actions fall short of others' expectations, especially people who're important to them.

Just like other people don't understand why addicts can't just stop their drug or alcohol use when it's causing their life to crumble, addicts don't understand either. They see themselves as weak, immoral, and lacking in self-control. Addicts don't like what they've become, and it causes them great psychological discomfort. Guilt, remorse, shame, and self-loathing become the norm in the addicted mind, all a result of the dissonant self.

One of the fundamental models of human motivation is known as *cognitive dissonance* theory. We discussed cognitive dissonance earlier; cognitive dissonance theory states that the mind experiences great distress (this psychological distress is known as *cognitive dissonance*) when our behavior doesn't match our beliefs and values, so we're driven to seek to reduce or stop the offending behaviors that result in the dissonant self. In other words, we feel bad when we behave badly, so our mind pushes us to stop the bad behavior. This drive to correct the psychological discomfort created by the dissonant self is very powerful, and is one of the main reasons that people generally try to behave in a good and moral way.

There are two ways that we can stop the psychological pain when our behaviors don't match our beliefs about what's good and right: we can change the bad behaviors, or we can change our beliefs. For people in active addiction, neither of these options is viable; they can't stop their substance use, and it's too much of a stretch to try to believe that substance use and the related behaviors are good and right. As such, the only option left for resolving the psychological pain from the dissonant self for the addict is by avoidance and escape, which they try to accomplish by numbing their mind through substance use and isolating themselves from anything that reminds them of how bad their behavior is. That's why addicts really hate being lectured by family and friends about how bad their behavior is – they're already well aware of it, and they're trying to escape from it. When we remind them of it, it's like driving a stake through their already punctured heart.

Sadly, cognitive dissonance and substance use form a vicious circle that propels addiction to deeper, darker levels. The pain created by cognitive dissonance worsens the substance use, which worsens the cognitive dissonance, which further escalates the substance use, and so on. As such, addiction – regardless of how the substance use began – soon becomes a snowballing cycle of negative feelings and using substances to cope with the negative feelings. I consider cognitive dissonance to be one of the primary psychological drivers of addiction. Breaking this cycle is a major focus of addiction therapy.

Negative Psychology. "Positive psychology" is a fairly recent trend in psychology research – it's the study of what makes life most worth living. The concept is pretty cool: rather than the traditional focus on what makes people *un*well, positive psychology focuses on the thoughts, feelings, and behaviors that make people feel happy and fulfilled. People who's mind is in a state of positive psychology are happy, grateful, and have a positive outlook on life – in good times as well as bad. It's hardly surprising that positive psychology has been correlated with multiple measures of physical and mental health.

On the contrary, "negative psychology" describes a mindset that's gloomy and pessimistic. In most cases, the addicted mind exists in a state that's an extreme example of negative psychology. Addicts feel like victims of the world, they blame their situation on other people and situations (*you'd drink too if you had my spouse*), and it makes them angry and resentful. They're pessimistic, and ruminate on their misfortunes. They project the worst outcomes for their problems. They're consumed with guilt, shame, and remorse over their substance use and related behaviors, and they obsess about past events. Their self-identity is utterly conflicted and unfulfilled, and their self-esteem is at rock bottom. They feel helpless and hopeless about their life situation, and have an external locus of control (which we'll discuss shortly). They have no ability to cope with stress – other than their substance use and by running away. They experience significant fear and anxiety, as they believe that the world is a cruel and unfair place, and that their world can come crashing down on them at any minute. Remember this when your addict loved one tries to project an image that all is well; if they're far enough along in the addiction process, all is probably not at all well with their mind. These negative thoughts and feelings weigh constantly on their mind, making them deeply unhappy and providing impetus for further substance use and isolation from the world.

When the mind is filled with such negativity, people have very little capacity to handle new stressors. They're quick to anger, and get stressed and anxious over little things. They're completely robbed of any modicum of peace and happiness. They have no resilience or hardiness, and are vulnerable to the smallest of stressors. Negative psychology creates such uncomfortable thoughts and feelings that some people will turn to anything to get a break from the pain. Negative psychology is a common pathway to addiction, as well as a consequence of addiction. The painfully negative mindset makes vulnerable people ripe for addiction, as they turn to substance use – usually without any intention of becoming addicted – as a quick and easy way to numb the pain. For those whose substance use began for other reasons, negative psychology inevitably develops as they get sucked deeper into their substance use and life begins to tumble out of control. As such, negative psychology can be both cause and effect of addiction, and – as with cognitive dissonance – a vicious cycle of painful feelings and substance use develops. As with cognitive dissonance, breaking this cycle is a major focus of addiction therapy.

A history of trauma is a significant risk factor for addiction, and a common reason that people engage in repeated substance use. Recurrent, unwanted, painful, invasive thoughts of past traumas contribute significantly to a negative psychology, and these thoughts may be a source of pain for many people in addiction, on top of everything that we just discussed. Survivors of traumatic events may live with a chronic negative mindset, and may find substance use to be a welcome escape from the pain.

Of course, it's not difficult to understand how someone trapped in addiction could develop a negative mindset when their life is crashing down around them and they're troubled by self-destructive substance use that seems to be out of their control. However, there are also physical effects of addictive substances on the brain that make the brain feel inherently downcast and melancholy. Here's why.

As you may recall from the previous chapter, the "high" from addictive substances comes from the release of huge amounts of the "feel-good" chemicals (neurotransmitters) in the brain. The brain compensates by suppressing these excessively elevated neurotransmitters, with the result that they're at extremely low levels after the intoxication wears off. The ensuing depressed mood makes the addicted mind prone to a negative mindset, thus contributing the psychological factors. The result is a state of mind that's so negative and gloomy that it propels addicts to continue with their substance use, if only to obtain a temporary reprieve from their painful state of mind. This negative mindset presents a significant barrier to treatment, because individuals may feel that they can't handle life without their drug or drink. Family and friends of addicts are best placed to help addicts overcome this barrier to recovery, as we'll discuss in detail in chapter 9.

Low Self-Esteem and Elevated Pride. The dissonant self – the failure to live up to one's own standards, beliefs, and values – causes addicts to get heartlessly down on themselves. The additive effects of the disapproval of others, the stigma of addiction applied to the self, and a negative mindset pushes their self-esteem to morose depths. As we've discussed, the mind has a fundamental need to feel good about the self, so this low self-esteem creates yet another source of psychological discomfort. The mind tries to compensate for this low self-esteem by projecting a false and exaggerated pride.

Psychologists identify two types of pride: *authentic* (good) pride versus *hubristic* (bad) pride. Hubristic pride is the kind that's arrogant, boastful, self-absorbed, conceited, and narcissistic. Authentic pride is when we're proud of a legitimate accomplishment, but we aren't shoving it in everybody's face. The dysfunctional pride that rules the hour in the addicted mind is hubristic; it's an attempt to cover up for rock bottom self-esteem.

Good pride (authentic pride) isn't a bad thing; we're right to be proud of our accomplishments. In fact, authentic pride is a valid part of healthy self-esteem. Authentic pride can be a great motivator and a healthy part of our positive psychology.

The pride that's commonly seen in people in active addiction is driven by low self-esteem, and represents an instinctive mechanism to reduce the psychological discomfort that follows from their compromised values and beliefs. They compensate by projecting a fabricated positive view of themselves by inflated demonstrations of pride, and conversely by criticizing and nit-picking others. They become consumed by being "right" and can't acknowledge their own shortcomings. Small wonder others find them obnoxious and difficult to be around.

For most people, pride is a by-product of accomplishments and feelings of self-efficacy and self-worth. In other words, they have something to at least partly back up their pride, over-inflated as it may be. In people in active addiction, displays of pride are over-inflated and defensive in nature, with nothing to back it up.

When people rely on hubristic pride to compensate for low self-esteem, they become heavily dependent on validation from others to prop up their sense of self-worth. That's why a lot of people with low self-esteem overspend on expensive cars, houses, and other showy items; they want to be noticed and admired and praised in order to prop up their fragile ego.

Criticism cuts through their ego like a knife. So it is with addicts who rely on hubristic pride to compensate for their low self-esteem. They tend to be unwilling to admit that they have a problem, and even if they do they tend to insist that they don't need anybody's help. This presents a serious barrier to treatment because they may interpret efforts to point out their problem and help them as ego-threats. They view any suggestion that they may need help as a challenge to their pride, and become defensive – sometimes even aggressive or violent – at attempts to help them.

The projection of a façade of pride by addicts is done not only to fool others, but also to fool themselves, in an effort to reduce their psychological discomfort over their woeful life situation.

This masquerade of pride requires tremendous exertions. The effort required to maintain this fake pride and to try to sell it to others (and to themselves) can be exhausting. And it brings out some ugly behaviors. In order to maintain appearances they lie, cheat, and exaggerate. They're jealous of others. They're judgmental and look for fault in others, always trying to cut others down to elevate themselves. They become defensive and aggressive when anything or anyone challenges their delicate ego. When they don't get the praise and validation they seek from others they become angry and resentful. It's an ugly, dysfunctional coping mechanism that makes addicts difficult to be around.

This hubristic pride is a major barrier to addicts' ability to accept help, and a source of the negative and painful mindset that drives addiction. They see accepting help as an admission of defeat, which is intolerable to their naked ego. As such, the low self-esteem that generates this false pride is a major target of addiction therapy. Family and friends are well placed to initiate the removal of this barrier to recovery, as we'll discuss in chapter 9.

Dysfunctional Coping. Lots of people find psychoactive substances to be a relaxing escape from stress, which is why some will go out for a drink after a stressful day. Other people prefer exercise, or watching a movie, or meditation, or some other distracting activity as a preferred way to unwind. Most of us have some way that we wind down from stress and negative feelings; these are our *coping mechanisms.*

Some people who feel overwhelmed by stress or negative thoughts or feelings may turn to addictive substances regularly as an escape. They may find the euphoric feelings and the sedating, numbing, soothing effects of the high to be their only escape from tortured and invasive thoughts, stresses and worries, negative feelings and emotions, and mental illness symptoms. They may also find the feeling of detachment that they get from drugs or alcohol to be a welcome escape from an unkind world. This is the "escape/avoidance" coping that's already come up a few times in our exploration of addiction.

It's this escape from reality that draws a lot of people into the repeated substance use that brings about the brain changes that become addiction. However, even people whose addiction started for other reasons usually end up relying on substance use as a form of escape. Addiction is a progressive condition that inevitably causes a lot of problems and stresses, and people end up seeking relief from the world, other people's "nagging," and their own negative psychology through their substance use. It's an example of what the famous Swiss psychiatrist Dr. Carl Jung was talking about when he referred to addicts as: *people [who] will do anything, no matter how absurd, to avoid facing reality.*

Besides substance use, the other dysfunctional coping mechanism that characterizes addiction is social isolation. Individuals attempt to escape their problems by avoiding the world and its hardships (real or perceived), and the people who remind them of their problems (such as "nagging" family and friends). They prefer the company of other addicts, because other addicts' pathetic situation makes them feel better about their own pathetic situation, and the group effect reduces their feelings of guilt and cognitive dissonance. As such, "downward social comparison" is preferred, while "upward social comparison" – being around people who're healthy and thriving – is avoided because it magnifies their own terrible actions and situation. Social isolation and hanging out with a new group of friends are often one of the earliest symptoms of addiction noted by family and friends.

If people are to have any hope whatsoever of succeeding in recovery, they must learn to cope with life's highs and lows in a healthy way. Addicts are people whose go-to coping mechanism involves running away through social isolation and substance use, and they can easily return to the same behaviors and relapse if life again becomes stressful for them once they're in recovery. As such, learning to accept life's ups and downs as normal part of life and to handle these aspects of life in a healthy and functional way is a major focus of addiction treatment. For example, the Twelve Step program – which is what the majority of addiction treatment programs are based upon – isn't about not drinking or using drugs; rather, it's about learning to handle life on life's terms, so that the need to escape life through substance use falls away. And it works.

Cognitive Bias. A "cognitive bias" is a mental distortion that the human mind uses to protect its beliefs and what it wants to believe. Through these biases, the human mind manipulates information to fit with its pre-existing beliefs and attitudes. People see what they want to see. This doesn't just happen with addicts, it happens with everybody.

For example, let's say a guy named Michael takes art lessons and paints a portrait of his wife. Michael's very proud of his painting and all the hard work he put into it, and really believes (and wants to believe) that it's quite good. Because of cognitive bias, Michael's mind will have a tendency to ignore obvious mistakes or bad points in the painting, and his mind will focus more on the positives. He'll also have a tendency to de-emphasize comments from others that suggest that the painting isn't good, and place undue emphasis on information that suggests that it's very good. Although cognitive bias occurs to some degree in everyone (nobody's capable of being 100% objective), these mental distortions are pushed to extremes by the addicted mind.

Cognitive bias is a natural feature of the human mind that causes people to ignore information that refutes their beliefs (or what they want to believe) and place undue emphasis on information that supports their beliefs, even if that information is suspect. These biases occur largely on a subconscious level, although the bias can also occur purposely. These biases affect our decision-making and behaviors, as we act on faulty, biased assessments of available information.

The addicted mind uses cognitive bias to warp facts and reality to rationalize and substantiate what cannot be logically substantiated – their self-destructive substance use and related behaviors. The addicted mind also uses cognitive bias to try to reduce cognitive dissonance by making excuses for the substance use and other dissonant behaviors. However, such irrational and illogical behaviors as substance use cannot be truthfully rationalized, so the truth must be deconstructed or the facts greatly distorted in order to provide this substantiation. Cognitive bias is the mechanism by which the addicted mind attempts to accomplish this.

There are lots of different types of cognitive bias, but there are four main types that are especially relevant to the addicted mind:

1) **Attentional bias** – this is where the mind assigns excessive attentional resources to information and cues that are related to obtaining and using substances. If an addict enters a room where there's one tiny substance-related cue, they'll pick up on the cue and their mind will be laser-focused on it. For example, if an alcohol addict enters a room and there's a half-empty glass of wine sitting in a corner on a table, the alcoholic will quickly pick up on it and will be unable to concentrate on anything else because of attentional bias,

2) **Optimism bias** – in this type of bias, the addicted mind clings to the belief that the individual will have the ability control or stop their substance use on their own, despite multiple previous failed attempts. The optimism bias is somewhat paradoxical, given that the addicted mind is deeply pessimistic in nature. The optimism bias is profound in addiction and presents a significant barrier to treatment, because it makes individuals believe they don't need any outside help. It's also a major cause of relapse because people develop the belief that they can try drugs or alcohol again after a period of abstinence, and that *this* time they'll be able to control it, despite past experiences,

3) **Approach bias** – this is the tendency to choose behaviors that lead toward obtaining or using substances, even if those behaviors are harmful or unwise. The approach bias causes addicts to engage in unsafe or risky behaviors to get their drug or drink. Impaired driving, prostitution, and other crimes may be chosen and the risks ignored or rationalized. This is commonly seen in relapse situations, where

individuals choose small steps that lead back to substance use, substantiating the reason for each small step even though they're fully aware that they're headed toward a relapse situation, and

4) **Memory bias** – this is the tendency to recall information in a way that supports substance use. This bias is a significant cause of relapse, as people in recovery have a strong tendency to recall substance use as "fun," even though they were thoroughly miserable during their active addiction. The memory bias persists and even worsens as people progress in recovery. The further they are from their last drink or drug, the more likely they are to remember their substance use in a positive light. Combatting the memory bias is a major focus of relapse prevention.

Addiction treatment and relapse prevention programs address cognitive bias by making people aware of these dysfunctional mental distortions so that they can identify and challenge them as they occur. One of the significant values of attending recovery support group meetings is that they're an effective counter to cognitive biases that would otherwise creep up and trigger relapse. Families and friends of addicts in recovery can play a significant role in countering addiction-related cognitive biases by challenging the addict on their distorted thinking as it arises.

External Locus of Control. As addiction deepens and problems and consequences accumulate from substance use, people with addiction may feel overwhelmed by life and the world in general. They often begin to feel like victims of the world – like they're being picked on – a condition known to psychologists as *self-victimization.* Self-victimization has been identified by research as a significant cause of psychological pathology, such as emotional pain, depression, anxiety, substance use, and suicide.

Like any victim, addicts who perceive themselves as victims of the world become angry and resentful, with their anger directed at other people, institutions, and even God. Unfortunately, the people who bear the brunt of this anger and resentment are usually those who're closest to the addict, the ones who want to help them.

When people feel like victims of the world, they begin to believe that their problems and fate are outside of their own control, and that their own actions won't change anything. Psychologists refer to this mindset – where people feel that their own life situation is outside of their own control – as an *external locus of control.*

People with an external locus of control feel helpless and hopeless, and resign themselves to being passive observers of their own life. They begin to believe that any effort they would put into making their life better would be pointless. They give up on trying to deal with their problems and become withdrawn. Some will withdraw into avoidance and escape behaviors, such as substance use and social isolation.

It's a horrible thing to believe that you're a helpless victim of outside forces with no ability to influence your own situation. The anger, resentment, and self-pity that result fuel further substance use. This mindset also presents a significant barrier to recovery, because people with an external locus of control blame everybody and everything for their life situation – except for themselves. They can't accept that they played a role in their own demise and that they must take responsibility and take an active role in their recovery.

Addicts' external locus of control also impairs their self-efficacy beliefs – beliefs that they have the ability to accomplish a given task – so that they believe they're incapable of recovery. They may believe that there isn't any point to even trying to beat their addiction, so they won't even try. An external locus of control makes addicts believe that they drank or used because their spouse is such a tyrant, or because their finances had gotten so badly, or because they didn't get that great job they interviewed for. As long as they maintain these beliefs, every new stressor in recovery will be seen as another excuse to return to drink or drug.

In helping addicts to heal and achieve the mindset they need to succeed in recovery, this external locus of control and learned helplessness must be defeated. If recovering addicts continue to believe that whether or not they drink or use is determined by other people and things, they'll relapse as soon as the next life challenge appears.

*

Although the tangible brain and intangible mind are separate entities, they're intertwined and each contributes in its own way to determining our behaviors, including self-destructive substance use. As such, our study of the effects of repeated substance use on the brain (in the previous chapter) and on the mind (in this chapter) explains the symptoms of addiction, and gives us an understanding of why people who're caught in addiction behave the way they do. There's no other way to understand the behaviors that we know of as addiction, because they're so illogical as to defy understanding.

The study of the addicted mind demonstrates that recovery from addiction is not simply the absence of using drugs and alcohol. Rather, the underlying causes of the addiction and the psychological dysfunction must be addressed and healed, or relapse is almost certain. Until the dissonant self is corrected, the negative psychology is turned to positive, self-esteem is restored and fulfilled, healthy coping mechanisms are learned, and the dysfunctional and harmful thought processes are corrected, the addicted mind will persist, and any abstinence from substance use will be from sheer willpower. And we know how willpower works in the addicted mind… it doesn't. The Twelve Step program refers to recovery without healing as "white knuckling it," because it boils down to a daily battle with the mind to hold back from substance use. However, when care is taken to see to healing and restoring the addicted mind to proper function, the need and desire to drink or use falls away. It really does work like that.

As you can see, the addicted mind is a dark place. Although addicts are great actors and can put on airs that everything's fine, they're hurting inside. Their mindset, their negative thoughts and emotions, their non-stop obsession with substance use, and their crippling outlook on life amounts to a deeply troubled person. No one can be happy and at peace and have any chance at recovery unless these psychological burdens are nursed back to health. One of the reasons for the success of the Twelve Step program is that it directly addresses these issues, and provides the therapeutic and social supports necessary for a recovery to better health of mind and body. This is why the majority of addiction treatment and relapse prevention programs are Twelve Step-based.

Unfortunately, even with the best of therapy the addicted brain and mind are not cured, and they remain ever-present under the surface, ready to re-establish their dominance. As such, the need for ongoing care and maintenance of recovery through life-long recovery activities is critical to successful recovery.

In the next chapter, we'll examine an issue that applies to more than half of people who develop addiction: comorbidity – the co-occurrence of addiction and mental health disorders.

7

The Link Between Addiction and Mental Illness

If you could read my mind, you wouldn't be smiling.

– Tamara Ireland Stone, *Every Last Word*

Doctors seem to love coming up with complex words to describe simple things. True to form, they use the word *comorbidity* to describe a mental health disorder and addiction present at the same time in the same person. You may also hear this referred to as *concurrent disorders* or *dual diagnosis*. Although – technically – the term "comorbidity" can refer to any two diseases that occur together and affect each other (for example, drug addiction and HIV/AIDS are a comorbidity), in this chapter we'll be referring to comorbidity in the context of the co-occurrence of addiction and mental illness.

In the medical field, addiction is considered to be a mental health disorder. More properly, it may be thought of as a disease of the brain, but because it affects the mind and causes many psychiatric symptoms – i.e. disordered thinking and behaviors – it falls under the aegis of psychiatry. However, the line between psychiatric disorders (disorders of the mind) and neurological disorders (disorders of the brain) is blurred, because we now know the neurological basis of most psychiatric disorders. *Does it matter?* Well, I believe it sort of does, because the term "neurological disorder" tends to attract much less social stigma than does the term "psychiatric disorder," unfortunately.

Regardless of how you frame it, although addiction affects the mind, it's primarily a disease of the brain, so it can also be classified as a brain disease. To wit, the U.S. National Institute on Drug Abuse (NIDA) defines addiction as: *a complex brain disease characterized by compulsive, at times uncontrollable drug craving, seeking, and use despite devastating consequences— behaviors that stem from drug-induced changes in brain structure and function* (from their document *Comorbidity: Addiction and Other Mental Illnesses*).

Addiction and other mental illnesses overlap in many more ways than just semantics. We're already familiar with the brain and mind changes caused by the repeated use of addictive substances, as we've discussed them in the previous two chapters. These changes occur in some of the same brain areas and affect the same brain chemicals (neurotransmitters) that are responsible for other mental health disorders, such as depression, anxiety, or schizophrenia. It's therefore not really surprising that addiction and other mental health disorders tend to occur together.

When people suffer from a mental health disorder as well as addiction, both conditions are likely to have a worsened course. For example, compared with either condition occurring alone, comorbidity is associated with:

- More severe psychiatric symptoms,
- More dramatic adverse effects from substance use, including more blackouts,
- More physical health problems,
- Greater likelihood of financial problems and homelessness,
- Poorer management of personal affairs,
- More serious relationship problems, including with family,
- Greater likelihood of displaying verbal hostility, disruptive behavior, aggression, and being argumentative,
- Greater likelihood of ending up in jail,
- Lower likelihood of completing treatment or following a treatment plan,
- Increased experiences of social stigma, and
- Increased likelihood of suicidal thoughts and behaviors.

About half of the people who experience a mental disorder in their lifetime will also develop a substance addiction, and vice-versa. The rate is even higher among adolescents, about 60%.

*

So, what exactly defines a mental health disorder? After all, many (perhaps most) people have mental issues or symptoms that bother them from time to time, such as excessive worries, a little obsessive-compulsiveness, a bit of a low mood, or uncomfortable memories of past events. However, what makes such mental symptoms a mental health *disorder* is when these issues cause problems to the point of interfering with the ability to function in life. Since mental illnesses are conditions that affect our thinking, emotions, and behaviors, it's not hard to imagine how people with such afflictions could cross the line to where it affects their ability to function socially, at work, or with their family responsibilities.

We have names for these disorders of mental function: depression, anxiety disorders, schizophrenia, bipolar disorder, and anorexia are some among many. The definitions and diagnostic criteria of the various mental health disorders are standardized in an internationally accepted compendium known as the DSM 5 (*Diagnostic and Statistical Manual of Mental Disorders*, the fifth version of which is currently in use).

Addiction and other mental health disorders share lots of common features. So much so, that they overlap and can be difficult to separate from each other when trying to arrive at a diagnosis. Their commonalities include:

- Symptoms – as with other mental illnesses, addiction affects people's emotions, thoughts, and behaviors, as we've seen. Repeated substance use causes many of the same symptoms as those that are seen in other mental illnesses, such as depression, anxiety, psychotic disorders, and obsessive-compulsive disorder. There's so much overlap in symptoms that doctors are not supposed to diagnose a mental health disorder in anyone who's involved in substance use, lest a misdiagnosis be made,
- They cause each other – "self-medicating" the symptoms of a mental health disorder with addictive substances is a common cause of repeated substance use and addiction. Conversely, substance use can cause or precipitate mental health disorders,
- Similar genetics – many of the same genes that can make people more likely to become substance addicted can also make them more likely to develop a mental health disorder... and vice-versa,
- Similar risk factors – many of the risk factors for addiction are also risk factors for mental health disorders, and
- Similar brain defects and deficits – addiction and mental illnesses result from dysfunction in many of the same neurotransmitters, brain pathways, and brain structures.

*

Because addiction and mental illness overlap so much, it's absolutely crucial that they both be treated at the same time. It's very difficult to halt substance use in individuals who have untreated mental illness; conversely it's very hard to treat a mental illness when individuals are using psychoactive substances. As such, correctly identifying a comorbid mental health disorder in individuals with addiction is crucial, and their chances of success in recovery depend heavily upon getting it right.

For clinicians, the symptoms of comorbid mental health disorders and addiction can be so tangled up as to make diagnosis a serious challenge. However, the importance of treating both is such that extra care and caution must be taken to avoid missing cases of comorbidity. The high rate of co-occurrence of addiction and mental illness necessitates a high degree of suspicion when one condition is identified; individuals being treated for substance use should be carefully screened for psychiatric conditions, and vice versa.

The diagnosis of mental illness can be difficult, especially if there's also substance use involved. There are no blood tests or imaging studies to make the diagnosis; doctors rely on standardized questionnaires and a description of symptoms. However, even these screening tools are easily confounded by the overlap of symptoms. To make matters worse, people are reluctant to admit to substance use as well as mental illness symptoms. Even when properly diagnosed, someone in active alcohol or drug use is unlikely to seek or respond to treatment for a mental illness.

The stigma carried by mental illness and addiction – each in their own right – contributes to many people living in denial of their conditions, or with difficulty in finding the courage to come forward for help. People are understandably psychologically resistant to being diagnosed and taking on these new identities – labels – that are viewed as negative, even by friends, family, lovers, and employers. Affected individuals may be ashamed, in denial, or unwilling to reveal their symptoms. They may stonewall the doctor when questioned about their mental symptoms or substance use. I remember when I was seeing my doctor about my depression; she knew something was amiss, so she asked me a number of times about substance use: *do you use drugs?* My reply: *Nope. No way. I'm dead-set against drug use.* Half of the time I was high when I was talking to her. Likewise: *how much and how often do you drink alcohol?* My reply: *not at all. Not even socially. I'm an abstainer.* I doubt I was ever in her office without smelling of vodka.

The secretive and deceptive nature and denial that we see in people in active addiction is also often seen in mental health disorders. They convince themselves that they can best handle their problems on their own, and they may have an obsessive need to be in control. Handing their problem over to someone else's care may be insufferable to them.

As if these barriers to diagnosis and treatment of comorbidity weren't enough, yet another challenge to diagnosing mental health problems is that affected individuals may not realize they're suffering from one. Often, they've lived with the condition for so long that they've long forgotten what it's like to feel "normal." As well, many mental health disorders – including addiction – are characterized by a "lack of insight." You may recall from an earlier chapter that "lack of insight" means that affected people are unaware of the symptoms they're experiencing, sometimes even incapable of being aware. This is seen in bipolar disorder – where affected individuals are unaware of their symptoms but are able to accept the truth when confronted with enough evidence – and schizophrenia, where they remain completely oblivious to their symptoms, no matter how much they're told otherwise. This is a baffling thing to see in real-life, because their psychiatric symptoms are so obvious that it's hard to believe they're not aware. For the uninitiated, this impaired awareness of illness is difficult to comprehend. It may cause conflict because people will think those who lack insight are faking or trying to pull one over on them, and the affected people are defensive about the suggestion that there's something wrong with them. The main concern about people lacking insight into their illness is that they won't seek help, will resist help when offered, and may be unlikely to cooperate with treatment. They don't believe there's anything wrong, so why would they want treatment?

Because of all these difficulties with the diagnosis of comorbidity, clinicians rely heavily on family members to provide background information, their own observations of symptoms, and corroboration for the information given by the patient. The timeline is also crucial. One of the keys to confirming that a mental health disorder is present on top of the addiction is if the mental health symptoms pre-dated the substance use. For example, anxiety is a common symptom of substance use, but if the anxiety symptoms were observed prior to when the substance use began, then there's likely an anxiety disorder underlying the addiction. These kinds of temporal observations from family members are very helpful for doctors.

Good quality addiction treatment centers are experts at identifying comorbidity. They have psychiatrists on staff who're specially trained in sorting out comorbid disorders, and they have the advantage of observing patients closely in order to detect symptoms of a mental health disorder emerging following a period of abstinence from substance use. As well, by the time they're in treatment, most individuals are ready to let go of their secrets and be honest about their symptoms, which also makes diagnosis easier.

*

As you might expect, research has confirmed that treatment of one of the comorbid conditions makes treatment of the other more likely to succeed. Further, we know that treating both conditions together in an integrated approach achieves better outcomes for both conditions than does treating them separately. This is great, because most addiction treatment facilities have the appropriate staff and expertise to treat addiction and mental health disorders at the same time and in the same place. However, this isn't usually the case when people seek help at the community level.

Within many healthcare systems, addiction and mental illness are treated separately, by different professionals and at different clinics. Each is treated in geographically separate sites by a mix of health care professionals with different backgrounds. While the professionals in each field have an understanding of the other, neither side may have sufficiently broad expertise to address the full range of problems presented by comorbid patients. This poses a challenge for the diagnosis of comorbidity, and makes integrated treatment difficult or non-existent.

Sadly, there are further barriers to treatment that are faced by people who suffer from comorbidity. Most notably, comorbidity is disproportionately seen among those who are socioeconomically disadvantaged, and this population may lack access to proper help; those most affected are those with the least access to care. As well, people with comorbidity are more likely to end up in the criminal justice system, which can make matters much worse. Finally, the social stigma that people with addiction face are added to the stigma of mental illness, and this may make them more likely to socially isolate and add to their reluctance to come forward for help.

Although primary care doctors are generally well trained in mental health issues, medical training in addictions remains woefully inadequate. As such, people with comorbidity slip through the cracks at the primary care level. The presence of a mental health disorder should prompt a careful assessment for substance use, and vice-versa. If a clinician doesn't have the have the appropriate skills to rule out comorbidity, referral should be made for specialized assessment.

I've been saddened to see that there are some substance use treatment centers that refuse to allow their patients to use any medications, including those necessary to treat serious mental illness. Fortunately, such "alternative" treatment facilities are in the minority. As well, some treatment centers don't have on staff any professionals who're qualified to diagnose mental illness, prescribe medications, and monitor treatment outcomes. This bias against properly treating comorbid mental illness is counter-productive, as many addicts don't stand much of a chance against their addiction unless their mental illness is diagnosed and treated.

*

In chapter 5 we discussed the developing brain and its particular vulnerabilities to addiction. Although addiction can occur at any point in an individual's life, exposure to substance use typically first occurs during adolescence. This is also the period of time during which mental illness symptoms may first begin to emerge, so comorbidity is often already a factor by the teen years. Strong evidence has emerged showing that early exposure to substance use is a significant risk factor for the development of addiction, as well as the later development of other mental health disorders.

When adolescents experience symptoms of mental illness they may not recognize them as a treatable medical problem, and may see substance use as their only escape from the troubling symptoms. Even if they do realize they may have a mental health disorder, adolescents are likely to avoid coming forward for help for fear of stigma, social rejection by their peers, and being labeled as "crazy." As a result, adolescents are particularly prone to using drugs or alcohol to "self-medicate" mental health symptoms. This may explain the higher rate of comorbidity among teens than in the general population. This underlines the importance of identifying mental illness symptoms in young people, especially in those who're using addictive substances, and identifying substance use in young people with symptoms of mental illness.

I was recently involved in the care of a young man – Cory – who illustrates this point perfectly. This nineteen year-old came to see me because he wanted help breaking his addiction to marijuana. He couldn't get out of bed in the morning without smoking pot, and he smoked pot all through the day. In order to pay for his drug use, he had tried dealing, but some thugs had broken into his apartment and stole his drug supply at gunpoint. As a result, his supplier wanted the $20K that he was owed for the drugs, and our young friend was in deep trouble. Broke and in despair – and fearing for his life – he moved back into his parents' house.

When I interviewed Cory, I found that his addiction had sprung from an undiagnosed chronic anxiety disorder. Since he was very young – perhaps even before he was ten – he was bothered by worries and fears that he couldn't get out of his mind. He worried constantly about dying, or something happening to his parents, or just had an unshakeable feeling of impending doom. He was uncomfortable in social situations, always feeling like everyone else was sizing him up and judging him. His frequent panic attacks were unbearable for him. When he tried smoking pot with some friends when he was only 13, he suddenly felt comfortable in his skin, and he was no longer bothered by his worrisome thoughts. Cory then began smoking pot whenever he was facing a social situation, or his anxiety was bothering him. Soon, he was using it daily, convinced he couldn't function properly without it. As soon as the marijuana's effects wore off, the anxiety came back even stronger; he would literally crouch in a corner in fear until he could smoke his next joint.

When Cory was 15, his parents took him to see a doctor about his anxiety. For the next four years he saw a number of psychiatrists who attempted to treat his anxiety, but medications failed. When he was asked about substance use, Cory denied ever using alcohol or drugs.

Anxiety – even terrible anxiety – is usually very easily and successfully treated with low-dose, well-tolerated medications. I suspect that Cory didn't respond to any medications because his daily pot use was antagonizing and opposing the effects of the medications, which is why nothing seemed to work with him. Although Cory felt relief from his anxiety when he was intoxicated on marijuana, the rebound effect made his anxiety much worse afterwards. Of course, living in constant fear of a drug dealer trying to collect $20K from him (which he and his parents didn't have) would give anybody anxiety.

So, I sat down with Cory and his parents and we came up with a plan. We got him into a three-week addiction treatment program in a city that was several hours away, so as to remove him from the tense situation with his dealer. After discharge, we got him into a sober living house for six months in the same city as the treatment facility.

When I next saw Cory he was a completely different young man. He'd been off the drugs for nearly a year. He was back living with his parents again, slowly getting back on his feet. While he was in addiction treatment the staff psychiatrist had started him on a low-dose anti-anxiety medication (a selective serotonin re-uptake inhibitor (SSRI)), and – no longer opposed by the effects of the marijuana – the medication was working well for him. His anxiety disorder was now under good control and seldom bothered him. He no longer experienced panic attacks, and he was comfortable in social situations. He had a job that he enjoyed. His parents had made arrangements to come up with the money to pay Cory's drug dealer, and Cory was paying his parents back bit-by-bit from his paychecks. Cory was sober, happy, healthy, and functioning well. He was even planning to go to college. He was a far cry from the addicted nervous wreck with a ruined life that I'd met the year before. The secret to his success was that the treatment of his addiction and his anxiety required that both be treated together.

Cory's example demonstrates the importance of identifying and treating mental health symptoms in children and adolescents, identifying substance use in adolescents with mental illness symptoms, and the necessity of treating the addiction and mental illness at the same time. Cory's case also shows that even the most hopeless situations have a solution or at least a way to improve the situation when it comes to mental health and addiction. It all starts with the addict becoming ready to take a leap of faith, let go of their need for control, and accept help.

*

One specific type of mental health disorder deserves special mention because of its prevalence and association with addiction, and that's depression. Addiction and depression make the perfect marriage. They're so alike we can barely tell them apart, and it can be very difficult – sometimes impossible – to figure out which came first and brought the other one on. In this context, we're talking about "clinical depression," not merely a feeling of sadness or having "the blahs."

The medical term "depression" refers to a condition where a depressed mood occurs on most days, and is accompanied by vegetative symptoms. These are symptoms which make individuals "vegetate:" they lose interest in doing any kind of activity (including things that they normally find fun), sleep changes (usually excessive sleep, although the sleep may be poor in quality or involve simply lying awake), poor or overactive appetite, feelings of guilt (usually excessive and unwarranted), low energy, poor concentration, and inability to feel joy in anything (anhedonia). As well, there may be suicidal behavior (fantasizing about, planning, attempting, or completing suicide), and psychomotor agitation (physical jitteriness, and fidgeting).

As well, *psychosomatic* symptoms may occur in depressed individuals. These are physical symptoms without a pathological cause. Commonly, these involve pain (particularly in the joints and muscles), headaches, stomach upset, diarrhea, dizziness, fatigue, and just plain feeling unwell. Depression can also worsen the symptoms of just about any pre-existing physical symptoms. So, people with low back pain may notice an increase in their pain, people with abdominal disorders may notice their symptoms flare up, and so on. In other words, depression tends to cause physical as well as mental symptoms.

In medical jargon depression is known as a mood disorder; mood disorders also include anxiety disorders and bipolar disorder (sometimes referred to as manic depression). Mood disorders are caused by fluctuations in the same neurotransmitters that fluctuate wildly with addictive substance use, thus the close association between substance use and mood disorders.

Because depression is caused by low levels of certain neurotransmitters (most notably serotonin, norepinephrine, and dopamine), this mental health disorder can happen to anybody, including people whose life is going well. It can also be triggered by traumatic events, such as the death of a loved one, in which case it's known as *reactive depression*. However, it often happens to people who have nothing in particular to be sad about, who aren't particularly stressed, and whose life is going well. Of course, it's often triggered by the wild fluctuations in neurotransmitters produced by frequent substance use.

The statistics for mood disorders and substance use comorbidity are staggering. According to the National Institute on Drug Abuse (NIDA), the lifetime risk of having a mental disorder – of any kind – is 22.5%. The lifetime risk of alcoholism is 13.5% and 6.1% for other drug addiction. The lifetime rate for any mood disorder (depression or anxiety disorder) is 19.3%. Compared with people with no mood disorder, those with depression were approximately twice as likely, and those with bipolar disorder approximately seven times as likely, to have a substance use disorder. Substance use disorders were shockingly common among people with bipolar disorder: 56%.

The association between substance use disorders, mood disorders, and suicide is well-established. As we've discussed, intoxication causes people to lose their inhibitions, and impairs their judgment and ability to reason. It may magnify their depression and the feelings of despair and hopelessness that go with it. This creates the perfect storm for impulsive, poorly thought-out, and self-destructive acts – including suicide. Many addicts find themselves so desperate to escape their addiction that they see suicide as their only way out. This is especially so after multiple failed attempts to stop their substance use on their own.

In studies listed by the NIDA, two-thirds of people who successfully committed suicide had a substance use disorder. When comparing various psychiatric diagnoses, individuals with comorbid depression and substance use disorder are at the highest risk for suicide.

Mood disorders and substance use disorders mutually worsen each other and impair treatment outcomes and prognosis, so it follows that successful alleviation of one condition facilitates recovery from the other. Treating people's mood disorders will almost certainly reduce their substance cravings and improve their overall chances at sobriety.

Withdrawal from most addictive substances involves symptoms that mimic clinical depression, which may be misdiagnosed if the clinician isn't aware of the substance use. This occurs because all the feel-good neurotransmitters that were driven to ultra-high levels during the high crash down to levels well below normal when the drug is stopped, resulting depressive symptoms. Because of this effect, depression is a common problem in early recovery, and a common cause of relapse.

Depression is an excruciating illness, truly a form of suffering. The depressed person is miserable, low-functioning, and feels guilty, hopeless and alone. There was recently a TV ad for an anti-depressant medication that showed a woman lying across her unmade bed in her pajamas: disheveled, doleful, despairing, and down. It was full daylight – when she probably should have been at work or otherwise living her life – and she was just laying on her bed staring into space, tossing and turning. This image successfully personifies the experience of depression.

People who experience true clinical depression suffer the crushing weight of it on their ability to function. The lack of motivation, and the desire to just lay there and vegetate are so overwhelming that the individual will blow off even urgent chores, ignore the phone, and just lay there staring into space all day. Even showering is too much effort.

It's easy to see how people feeling this way, might find any brief reprieve from these horrible symptoms a relief – including that provided by substance use. Their desperation to have something – anything – make them feel good, if even only for a little, while is understandable. Naturally, alcohol and drugs provide only a brief and artificial escape from the suffering and, being depressants themselves, will actually worsen the symptoms and lower the depressed person's already diminished level of function.

*

Of considerable concern to those who live around people in active addiction are psychiatric symptoms that may cause violence. These are often due to substance-induced psychosis, agitation, and loss of inhibition. These dangerous symptoms may emerge during addiction in people who've never experienced them before.

Psychosis is caused by over-production of the neurotransmitter dopamine in certain parts of the brain. Given that many addictive substances (most notably marijuana, stimulants, and hallucinogens) stimulate over-production of dopamine in the same areas of the brain, it's not surprising that psychosis can be a prominent feature of the "high" produced by these drugs. Indeed, the use of these drugs has been known to cause permanent psychosis. I had a young patient who developed schizophrenia (a psychotic disorder) the very morning after he used the stimulant ecstasy (MDMA). He claims that it was the one and only time he had ever used the drug. It ruined his life. At the time he was in his third year of an economics degree, but because of his symptoms he had to abruptly drop out. He was unable to hold a job and ended up on welfare disability support, almost certainly for life.

People with psychosis usually can't tell that their hallucinations, paranoia, and other symptoms aren't real, so they may act on them. They truly believe that their psychotic experience is real, no matter how bizarre or unreal the experience may be. If they experience auditory hallucinations that involve voices giving them instructions, they may find it difficult to resist following the voices' instructions. When I was an intern I met one young man with stimulant-induced psychosis who had killed both of his parents in their home after repeatedly hearing voiced instructions in his head to do so. If someone with psychosis experiences paranoia they may act to defend themself. Just the other day I interviewed a binge-drinker who has experienced a number of psychotic episodes while coming off an alcohol binge, including one where he thought people were trying to attack him. He grabbed a kitchen knife and was swinging it around at his would-be attackers. Fortunately, none of his family were at home at the time, and the neighbors called the police when they saw him chasing around in his front yard yelling and screaming and brandishing a knife.

We discussed the hallucinations that can occur with alcohol withdrawal back in chapter 3. As well, intoxication with alcohol can cause mood instability, hostility, and agitation, which may result in angry or violent outbursts. Some people are "angry drunks" and prone to these episodes. Unfortunately, alcohol also famously reduces people's inhibitions, so they may act on their agitated impulses and cause scenes of conflict or even violence. They say that only a drunk can get in a fight at a yard sale.

Stimulants are heavily associated with psychosis, as well as dangerous and violent behaviors. This is especially likely to happen in individuals who're chronic, heavy users of stimulants. The psychosis that accompanies heavy cocaine use usually involves paranoid states that are accompanied by relatively intact reasoning. Cocaine-induced psychosis is usually not especially bizarre, and is typically temporary in duration. On the other hand, with methamphetamines these psychotic states are more bizarre, include delusions and paranoia, and may last for prolonged periods: weeks, months, or even years at a time. A common pattern seen with methamphetamine addicts – where they alternate between binges of amphetamines and alcohol binges – may appear like a cycling bipolar disorder, because the user alternates between a hyperactive, psychotic/manic stage during amphetamine binges, and sedate, depressed symptoms during alcohol binges.

I see examples of methamphetamine psychosis nearly daily near my place of work. There's one young man who lives in a nearby apartment who I see out back smoking his crystal meth pipe. He's especially prone to paranoia and delusions, and regularly walks through the area accusing random strangers of spying on him and trying to harm him. The police are at his apartment nearly daily, sometimes more than once a day, probably called by the addict's terrified neighbors. There's a pair of methamphetamine addicts who hang out at a strip mall near my place of work who similarly put on scary displays. It's a young guy and girl, who appear to be a homeless couple. The girl is pretty sedate, but the guy walks through the mall parking lot yelling and screaming at no one in particular; I'm not sure exactly what he's saying, but he's definitely agitated. It's a sad thing to see such young, otherwise capable minds so badly damaged by substance use.

Of course, hallucinogen drugs cause psychosis, as their name implies. The hallucinations tend to be mostly of the visual type. Besides the hallucinations, they also cause visual distortions, paranoia, and delusions. Some unfortunate hallucinogen users go on to develop prolonged or chronic, recurrent episodes of psychosis ("flashbacks") that may go on for some time after the last drug use. The hallucinogen known as PCP (phencyclidine) is especially likely to cause delusional psychosis symptoms that lead to violent behavior.

The association of marijuana with psychosis is less clear. For example, the finding that frequent marijuana use in adolescence can increase the risk of developing psychotic disorders in adulthood appears to mostly apply to individuals who carry certain gene variants (in the *catechol-O-methyltransferase* gene). However, the risk of psychosis with marijuana use does not appear to be limited to those with this specific genetic vulnerability. For example, recent research has shown that people who use marijuana daily are nearly five times more likely to develop psychosis than non-users. Age of first use, genetic vulnerabilities, and the amount used are likely all factors.

As with other cases of comorbidity, substance use and psychosis have a reciprocal relationship. Substance use can bring on psychosis, and psychotic disorders can beget substance use and addiction. For example, compared to the general population, people with schizophrenia carry about three times the risk of alcoholism and about five times the risk drug addiction.

*

Unfortunately, I see many individuals who're given excellent opportunities for addressing their addiction and/or mental illness by the health system, by their family, or even by the criminal justice system... but they squander the opportunity. *Why?* Because they're not mentally ready to accept help. Addicts invented stubborn, and when they're not ready to accept help, no amount of threatening, cajoling, bribing, or pushing will move them to make the deep commitment necessary to beat addiction.

In the next section of this book, we'll discuss the process by which addicts become ready to accept and commit to help, and how even the most reticent of addicts can be transformed to the readiness and commitment they need to find wellness and sobriety. We'll also focus on how you can play a significant role in helping your loved one become ready and willing to beat addiction, and how you can be an important part in helping them through the process of treatment and recovery.

Section Two – Helping an Addict

8

How to Talk to and Connect with a Loved One in Addiction

My son is not a marionette I can control with words or wishful thinking. My actions are not his actions. My pulling his strings isn't the same as him doing the work. What I've done is to give the addict wearing my son's face a stage for going through the motions. What I need to do is to clip the strings.

– Sandy Swenson, *The Joey Song*

We'll begin our "how-to" study for helping a loved one with addiction by making one thing clear: *you are not, and will not be your loved one's therapist.* Not now, not ever. Please don't try to be. By the time you finish this book you'll know more about addiction than most medical doctors and psychologists. You'll be familiar with how people become ready to seek and accept the help they need, you'll know all about the treatment/rehab process, and the relapse prevention programs. However, your highest value will be as a supporting character, not as the therapist.

Don't worry; I'm not saying this in order to condescend, or to say that you're not smart enough, or lack the credentials to be a therapist for your loved one. Rather, it's because you're too close to them. When we're too close to another individual, our ability to provide an objective opinion and advice is impaired by our history with that person. Even sponsors in the Twelve Step program don't sponsor people who're family members. In my own case, I currently have a family member who's having a terrible struggle with alcoholism, and he's at the point where he desperately wants to stop his drinking. Although I am an experienced A.A. sponsor – as well as a doctor and therapist – I'm too close to him for me to attempt to be his sponsor or therapist. Rather, I've taken him to A.A. meetings and introduced him to people who can help him, and I've given him the phone number to connect with qualified addictions professionals in our area. I let the professionals help him; I serve only to support him and to steer him to the right resources, as any family member should.

Doctors are among the most experienced folks around when it comes to helping people with problems, including medical, social, mental, and other issues. They do it for a living. Yet they're strictly forbidden from becoming involved in the medical care of family members, and can even lose their medical license for doing so. This is because doctors can have their judgment unduly influenced by personal feelings and emotions, and they lose all objectivity when dealing with loved ones. They're unlikely to ask the probing questions that they would ask other patients, and are unlikely to perform physical exams, especially of intimate body parts. Patients, too, feel uncomfortable having a family member as a doctor, and are unlikely to be truthful or forthcoming. They're also more likely to refuse treatment that's offered. A doctor who'd been in practice for over 30 years – and whom I greatly admired – told me this story when I was a medical intern:

> *When I was first in practice, I came home from a shift in the ER and my wife told me that our son was sick. He was only eight years old at the time. My wife asked me if I would check him out, so I went up and saw him in his bedroom. He was in bed and looked like he had a temperature. He looked sick. I asked him a few questions, and then told him he had the flu. I told his mom to give him some Tylenol and fluids, and that he'd be OK in a few days.*
>
> *During the night the boy was moaning and crying, and I went in to see him. I told him to suck it up and to stop being such a baby. My wife wanted to take him to the ER but I said no, he's fine, he just needs to stop being such a baby. So, I told my wife to give him some more Tylenol, and we went back to bed.*
>
> *First thing the next morning, my wife called me to our son's bedroom. The poor little guy was so sick that we couldn't rouse him and he was drenched in sweat. My wife opened his pajamas to wipe him down with a washcloth, and there it was: a meningitis rash. We rushed him to the ER, where he was resuscitated and then admitted to hospital for treatment of his brain infection. He survived, but he nearly died.*
>
> *Because he was my son, I didn't take a complete history from him and his mother, and I didn't examine him. Because of that, I missed the obvious telltale signs of meningitis, and the boy nearly died for it. If a*

stranger would have brought me a sick eight year-old child in the ER I never would have treated him like I did my son, and I certainly wouldn't have told him to suck it up and stop being a baby. The lesson: only a fool treats a family member.

I never forgot his advice. It's the same when we're trying to help a family member in addiction. Even if we have some expertise in the issue – as you will when you've completed reading this book – we cannot be our loved one's therapist. As long as we know that and respect it from the start, we'll avoid a potential disaster. So, what can we do to help our loved one, then?

Our role as family members and friends involves some important functions:

- Ensuring that our loved one knows that there's effective help available whenever they're ready to accept it, and that we can put them in touch with the right people who can help them,
- Being approachable, which means that we don't place ourselves in a position of conflict, or "nagging," and that we demonstrate a knowledge of addiction and a willingness to listen and learn,
- Making our loved one aware that we understand that addiction doesn't define them, and that we hate the disease but love the person,
- Providing accurate information when asked,
- Setting boundaries, employing "loving detachment," avoiding becoming an enabler, and being tough and firm when the loved one attempts to manipulate us,
- Ceasing to participate in the chaos, which means we stop being part of the addiction, and
- Engaging in self-care, so that we're healthy, happy, and whole. We can't help anyone when we're a nervous wreck participating in chaos.

Over the rest of this book we'll discuss exactly how to accomplish these functions. To begin our discussion, there are some seminal don'ts that I suggest to people who're dealing with an active addict. **Don't**:

- Lecture, threaten, preach, moralize, or make emotional appeals to addicts about their substance use. They're already very well aware that what they're doing isn't right, and they're already wracked with guilt about it, even if their pride won't allow them to show it outwardly. Increasing that guilt further propels substance use and drives a pointless wedge between you and the addict. Your lecturing won't make them stop,
- Try to deal with them while they're intoxicated,

- Hand over control of conversations to an addict. It will inevitably turn into a non-productive argument that you cannot win. Arguing with an addicted mind is an exercise in futility,
- Lie, make excuses, or cover for the addict's behavior, or otherwise try to protect them from the consequences of their substance use,
- Take over an addict's responsibilities, except when absolutely necessary (such as caring for the addict's children when the addict cannot safely do so). Protecting addicts from the consequences of their behavior enables their substance use,
- Give an addict money, no matter what they say it's for,
- Feel guilty or responsible for an addict's substance use and behavior. Addicts will engage their "blamethrower" and try to blame everybody but themselves. It helps reduce their own feelings of guilt and is an effective manipulation tool. Avoiding feelings of guilt may be easier said than done, and we'll discuss it in more detail in section 3, and
- Surrender control of your happiness and peace of mind to an addict. Again, this is easier said than done, but we'll nail down exactly how to do this in section 3.

*

Helping an addict begins with stopping the fighting. As we'll discuss in later chapters, this is also the first step in extricating yourself from the chaos of the addict's life to regain your sanity. The relationship between an individual in active addiction and family members is almost always adversarial. Both sides are involved in creating this relationship. The addict shirks responsibility, does terrible selfish things, lies and deceives, and becomes defensive and aggressive every time they're confronted. Money is wasted, opportunities are lost, there's often trouble with the law, and the obsession with substance use is incomprehensible. The addict's loved ones are offended and frustrated by the repeated bad behavior and sloughing of responsibilities, and react in the way people naturally react when someone's behavior is repeatedly and purposely unacceptable: with anger and frustration.

Although this adversarial relationship is to be expected, it's counter-productive to helping a loved one find their way out of addiction, and it's counter-productive to your happiness and peace of mind. I suggest that people take a different approach when dealing with a loved one in addiction. I suggest taking the high road, and letting go of the natural response to the symptoms of addiction. This doesn't mean letting your loved one off the hook for all the destruction and crappy behaviors, not at all. Part of the healing process in addiction treatment and recovery involves owning up for past behaviors, resolving to correct the behaviors and thought processes that led to these behaviors, and making amends to those who were harmed. However, in the meantime, chastising someone in active addiction is unlikely to result in any such contrition and restitution. Rather, it just serves to get a defensive and angry response from the addict, and creates an angry barrier between you and your loved one.

As we discussed in chapter 4, addicts have an elevated pride to compensate for a low self-esteem, and this false pride requires constant validation from others. Their pride makes them need to be "right" in every situation. As well, addicts usually feel like victims, as they spray their "blamethrower" around, blaming their woes and their behaviors on everyone but themselves. Anger and resentment are nearly universal in this group. So, basically, we have someone who's definitely not going to respond to criticism or a scolding by accepting responsibility and apologizing. Rather, we'll get nothing but anger, denial, and defensiveness thrown back at us, and an even bigger barrier between ourselves and the addict. One day – if the addict makes it into recovery – they will have to own up for their past behaviors and the consequences of their actions, but not now, not in their present sick state of mind.

Scolding and berating someone for bad actions and behaviors – even if it's well-deserved – is a form of punishment, designed to make the perpetrator feel bad, with the hope that the bad feelings will keep them from re-offending. Well, I can tell you that addicts already feel bad about themselves and their actions. In fact, the guilt, remorse, self-loathing, and regret that they carry on their shoulders every day is tremendous, and escaping these dark feelings and emotions is a major reason that they keep on with their substance use. They already feel terrible about what they're doing, even if their addict's pride won't allow them to show you that. One more scolding to add to that negative feeling – no matter how well deserved the scolding – isn't going to help. If feeling bad about their substance use and related behaviors were an effective way to get addicts to stop, they would've stopped long ago.

There's no point to lecturing addicts about all the damage they're causing, how they're ruining their life and their health, how they can die from addiction, and how they're hurting other people. They already know all that. It weighs very heavily on them. If you believe that presenting enough evidence of the harms of addiction will make an addict stop their substance use, then think again. All you accomplish is to drive the addict further away from you.

When we lash out at or scold a loved one in addiction we're showing them that we don't understand what they're going through. They come to see that we don't understand at all the obsessions and compulsions that are driving their behavior, so they come to see us as "naggers" who don't understand, and therefore unapproachable. *Why talk to someone about your problem if they don't understand it at all and they'll just nag you?* Nobody wants to come clean and lay their heart out in front of someone who'll be judgmental and critical.

I suggest that you show your addict loved one that you're making an effort to understand what they're going through, why they're behaving as they are, and that these are symptoms of substance use, not indications that they're a bad person. I want to emphasize here – once again – that substance use doesn't *excuse* bad actions or behaviors; rather substance effects on the brain and mind *puts these actions and behaviors in context.* So, I suggest letting your loved one know that you understand the context of their behaviors, including the substance use.

When we back away from the situation, addicts are surprised by our understanding, and relieved by our restraint from pushing them toward something they're not ready for. We can't will or push these people into recovery, but we can try to understand them and gain their trust. That's how we open the door to realistically helping them become ready to accept help.

*

Just because we seek a non-adversarial relationship with an addict doesn't mean that we turn a blind eye to the terrible things that they do. Rather, we stay firm, but keep confrontations from degenerating into an angry exchange. Here's how to go about doing that. It may take some practice:

Choose your battles. Don't waste a confrontation on every bit of crappy behavior that occurs, just the ones where there's a specific message and a point to it. For example, one super-common confrontation with no point to it is when a family member finds an addict's stash of drugs or alcohol. The family member will freak out, confront the addict angrily, and make a show of flushing the drugs or pouring out the alcohol. Naturally, the addict freaks out in kind. That's an example of a pointless confrontation. You're only proving that you outsmarted your loved one, and that the substance use is wrong. It's a hollow victory. *So what?* Even if your loved one denies substance use, simply letting them know that they're not fooling anyone is enough to make your point, which should be done with or without finding a stash. Sure, if you find a stash, destroy it. But is there a point to turning it into a big confrontation? When your addict loved one finds out that you destroyed the stash, they may or may not confront you about it. I suggest avoiding an argument about it, and saying something firm and with a point, such as: *if you bring drugs/alcohol into this house it will be destroyed. It puts us all at risk.* You've made your point, now end the conversation. Walk away from it if you must, but don't get drawn into an emotional back-and-forth with no point.

Let's discuss an example of a worthwhile confrontation with a point. Let's say you find out that your addict loved one took $50 from your wallet to buy drugs. A confrontation on the matter is worthwhile because it allows you to set boundaries and make a point that matters. For example: *I know that you took $50 from my wallet, and I know you used it to buy drugs. In the future we'll make sure that no one leaves money lying around the house, since your behavior has come to this. I will be keeping track of the money you took, because you will pay me back one day.* You made your point, now end the conversation, lest it degenerate into a pointless bitter argument of denials and vitriol. You could also take advantage of the situation to add other boundaries, such as advising the addict that they'll have to move out of the house if there's any more theft, if you choose to take that approach.

The scenario just described is also a perfect opportunity to let your loved one know that you understand what they're going through. For example, consider adding: *I know that you took the money because you're desperate for drugs. I believe you're addicted, and I know that people are driven to desperation by addiction* [if the individual denies drug use at this point, just continue with your statement]. *I want you to know that I understand that you're not a bad person, but that you need help. I have some information about how to get help, and I want you to know that everybody is capable of beating addiction. If you ever decide that you've had enough, I can put you in touch with the right people.*

So, this confrontation had a point: establishing a boundary (*theft will not be tolerated*), accountability (*you will pay me back one day*), and showing the addict that you understand and are approachable. Allowing the confrontation to degenerate into an argument or emotional exchange will destroy your point, and your point will be forgotten. When you feel the anger welling up inside because the addict is pushing your buttons, before you get sucked into an argument ask yourself: *is it worth it? Do I have a point to make here, or am I just going to "nag" and lecture and lash out?* As we'll discuss in upcoming chapters, part of regaining our sanity when dealing with an addict is extricating ourselves from the addict's circle of chaos, and that begins by refusing to get dragged into pointless arguments.

Avoid emotional outbursts. It takes practice to avoid being drawn into an emotional exchange, especially over such an emotional issue as watching a loved one destroy their life with substance use, and seemingly doing their level best to destroy yours at the same time. You can expect the addict to respond to your confrontations with emotion, defensiveness, and perhaps even aggression. However, *you* must be the one to keep your emotions in check, to avoid responding to emotion with emotion, and to end the confrontation when your point is made, before the encounter degenerates.

This can be really hard to do. You must exercise a high degree of self-control and take the high road when an errant addict is pushing your buttons and acting like a goon. All that pent-up frustration inside you can explode outward, using an argument as an outlet. Be sure that you take some time to calm down prior to initiating a confrontation; if you're already angry going into the conversation, then you're more likely to be suckered into a fight.

We'll talk in section 3 about how to get the anger, resentment, frustration, and pain – as justified as it all is – off your shoulders in a healthy way, so that you aren't easily drawn into pointless emotional exchanges.

Control the conversation. Confrontations degenerate when *you* lose control of them. The addict may try to draw you into a fight, but you must be the one to make sure that you don't allow your emotions to become involved and be drawn in. Do your best to make your point, and then get out. If you can't make your point, end the conversation and try again at a more opportune time.

Addicts are hurting, and the addicted mind seeks to make other people hurt. Addicts love to draw other people into the chaos of their life and to unleash their anger on those who're close to them. It's up to you to control the conversation by keeping your emotions in check, and not allowing it to degenerate. The addict has a sickness of the mind; it's up to you to take the high road. If you ever feel that you've lost control of the conversation and you've been sucked into another battle, extricate yourself. Repeat in your mind: *I will not participate in the chaos. I will not be a part of my loved one's addiction.*

Never make a threat that you don't intend to keep. Addicts are master manipulators; it's part of their disease. They seek out enablers that they can manipulate, and those who care about them are the ripest targets. If you give them an inch, they'll take a mile, so to speak. If you threaten a sanction and you don't follow through on it, the addict will know that you're malleable and easily manipulated. I suggest that you carefully consider each boundary and consequence, exactly when they will apply, and how you will apply them before you communicate them to the addict. Now is not the time for empty threats. Manipulators can smell empty threats from a mile away, and addicts are expert manipulators.

*

By ending the unwinnable arguments and battles, it becomes possible to begin breaking down the barrier between you and the addict. The goal is to get to a point where the addict feels comfortable reaching out to you to talk about their struggles. This requires the addict being 100% certain that sharing and coming clean with you will not result in an emotional eruption. This requires that you make it known that you've learned about addiction but want to listen and learn more, that you aren't judgmental, that you can respect confidentiality, and that you aren't going to be punitive.

An important part of establishing an environment where the addict feels comfortable talking to you involves taking a compassionate mind-set rather than a punitive or correctional one. This can be really hard to do when someone's doing terrible things to themselves and others, and generally acts like a jerk. However, the disease model of addiction helps us to separate the sickness from the person. It's important to remember that you're dealing with an unwell person who's showing symptoms of a sickness. Hate the disease, but try to remain compassionate for the person.

It's OK to be firm with your addict loved one, to call them out on their lies, and to stick by your rules and boundaries. Even taking tough sanctions such as kicking the addict out of your house is fair game, if it's part of your plan to enforce your boundaries and to stop enabling the substance use. However, I suggest that when you do have to enforce boundaries you do so in a non-judgmental, non-emotional, non-condescending way, and always in the context that your reaction was not out of anger, but because you will not tolerate your boundaries being crossed.

The emotions that we're hit with when a loved in is in active addiction are tremendous and overwhelming. Many people may never before have experienced such raw and conflicting emotions of such magnitude. Frustration and confusion emerge from watching someone we care about engage in self-destructive behaviors that don't make any sense. Sadness and dismay appear in the mix because the person we once knew and loved seems to be completely changed. A feeling of betrayal burns because the addict is choosing substance use over family, children, work, and everything of value. Guilt runs deeply because we somehow partly blame ourselves for the addiction and for not being able to help the addict. These and the many other emotions that come out of the experience share a few things in common: they're all negative, they're prolonged, they're intense, and they rob us of our peace of mind and happiness.

We'll talk in chapter 14 about how to deal with these emotions and release their grip from our psyche in a healthy way. In the meantime, it's important to recognize these feelings, and to endeavor to keep them out of our interactions with the addict. This means understanding addiction and the addicted mind, and preparing ourselves in advance for any conversations of importance. After a while, practice makes this easier. But it's never easy to keep emotions out of such an emotionally charged life-changing event. However, if you let your negative emotions into your conversations – especially anger and frustration – you'll lose control of interactions and you'll impair your ability to help the addict. Allowing these emotions to speak for you just draws you back into the chaos.

Empathy – our ability to put ourselves in another's shoes – goes a long way to helping us to be compassionate in our approach to an addict. Healthcare workers are trained to deal with difficult people (although sometimes it doesn't seem like some of them are very good at it), and empathy is a key tool for doing so. It's so much easier to feel empathy for someone you know and love as opposed to a stranger. However, sometimes we can be extra hard on people who're close to use, so we must watch for that.

Try putting yourself into the shoes of your addict loved one. Imagine that you feel physically and mentally sick most of the time because of the substance use. The last thing you think of before you go to sleep (or pass out) is your substance, and the first thing you think of when you wake up (or come to) is your substance. Imagine being in a state of mind where you can't concentrate on or concern yourself with anything but your substance use. Imagine feeling constant anxiety over how you will ensure an ongoing supply of your drug. It's like addicts live in a cruel prison, surrounded by four walls that are the physical and mental "need" for their substance, and their mind can't penetrate those walls.

There's more. Imagine living where you're constantly disappointed in yourself. You've repeatedly let everyone down: at work, at home, your friends, and even your own kids. You're constantly under an overwhelming load of guilt, remorse, shame, and self-loathing. Your self-esteem is in your boots. Worst of all, you feel hopeless and helpless, like there's no way out. You feel you're too addicted, too messed up in the head, and have messed up too much of your life to ever get out. You think about suicide every day.

Remember: people aren't usually very far along in their addiction when they reach the point where their substance use is no longer fun, and they'd do anything to stop. The addict's pride and the constant conflict with you may keep the addict from letting on, but they're not at all enjoying their situation. They're miserable, and they don't like who they've become any more than you do. They aren't choosing substance use over you, or their job, or their kids. They have long ago passed the point where their substance use is a choice; otherwise they would "just stop."

So, a little exercise in reflecting on what it's like to be the addict goes a long way to helping us to be patient, tolerant, and compassionate when dealing with them, and to leave our anger and frustration out of it. Best to walk away when that becomes difficult, calm down, and try again later. As soon as our emotions take over, we're no longer in control of the interaction. Showing compassion for someone doesn't mean that we let them walk all over us. We can – and should – still set and enforce boundaries, maintain control of interactions, and be firm in our resolve. Showing compassion means that regardless of the nature of our interaction – even if we're kicking someone out of the house – we do so with respect, with fairness, and without allowing emotions to drive our speech or actions. Compassion is about separating the sickness from the person, even during moments of tough love.

*

In order to be a part of the solution to your loved one's addiction, there are certain messages that I suggest that you get across. The best way to do this is to make sure that you repeatedly include this information in all your serious interactions, so that your loved one hears the message over and over, and the message penetrates that inward-focused addict brain. These messages serve three purposes: 1) they help reduce and prevent conflict, 2) they help the addict move toward a willingness and readiness to seek and accept help, and 3) they let the addict know that you're a safe resource to talk to, and even a first point of contact when they're ready to accept help.

When your loved one gets and understands these messages, you'll ruin their substance use for them, because these messages will resonate in their mind every time they drink or use. Their substance use will never be the same again; they'll always think about your message, and they may begin believing that there's a way out. They may begin ruminating on the possibility of life after addiction.

When we get these messages across, addicts begin to see that we understand – or at least we're trying to understand – their experience, and they see that we're not judgmental and condemning. It lays the foundation for the addict to see us as a first resource to reach out to when they become ready to talk and ready to at least consider accepting help.

Here are the messages that I suggest you make sure you get across to your loved one:

It's OK to acknowledge your addiction. As we've discussed in previous chapters, the addicted mind is fixated on denial and covering up problems. Due to cognitive dissonance and the impaired function of the brain's executive functions, people can deny their problem to others as well as themselves, even when they're deep into their addiction.

Nobody can deal with or even discuss a problem that they don't believe or won't admit they have, so in order to get anywhere addicts *must* acknowledge their addiction. Indeed, the very first of the Twelve Steps is admitting that there's a problem. However, it's important not to try to force this on an addict. It can be hard for someone to admit that they have an addiction, even though it's obvious to everyone around them. Cognitive dissonance, impaired insight, and good old addict's pride are huge psychological barriers for an addict to admit there's a problem. As we'll discuss in the next chapter, there's a psychological process involved, and it takes time for some people. Family and friends are in the very best position to help addicts move along in this process.

You can be a huge part of the addict's acceptance process simply by providing a safe, non-judgmental, and understanding venue for your loved one to begin discussing that there's a problem. I suggest that you don't demand this acknowledgment of the problem. Trying to force the acceptance of the problem on an addict by shoving the facts in their face creates barriers and doesn't help the problem at all. I suggest simply communicating to your loved one the reasons that you believe they have a problem with substance use (you can describe the symptomatology that we discussed in chapter 4), and that it's OK to admit that there's a problem. Then walk away; let it sink in. Don't push. Don't allow it to turn into a debate. Eventually, they'll likely be ready to admit the problem to you or to someone else, and it will be helped along because you took an understanding, non-judgmental, and non-punitive approach.

Besides cognitive dissonance, one of the main reasons that the addicted mind refuses to admit to a substance use problem is fear: fear of being exposed, fear of getting in trouble, fear of being judged, and even fear of arrest. The biggest fear, though, is that someone will try to interfere with their substance use. If the addict believes you'll throw a tantrum and try to lock them down and babysit them to stop the substance use, or that you'll try to force them into treatment, they're not going to admit anything to you. By communicating your understanding of the disease model of addiction and taking a non-judgmental, non-punitive, and non-pushy approach, you can do much to allay the fear as well as the cognitive dissonance.

You are an unwell person who needs to get well, not a bad person who needs to become good. Just as we need to separate the disease from the person, so does the addict. This, too, goes a long way to reducing cognitive dissonance and fear as barriers to recovery. Understanding that they're experiencing the symptoms of a brain-dominating disease helps addicts in three ways: 1) it reduces their cognitive dissonance, allowing them to accept that they have a problem, 2) it helps them to give themselves a break, so that they can believe that they're worthy of recovery and a good life, and 3) it helps them to realize that theirs is a treatable disease and there's a viable way out.

This may be the single-most effective message for transitioning the addict from seeing you as an authoritarian nagger to seeing you as someone safe to approach to share their struggles with. Once the arguments and battles have stopped and you've stepped outside the addict's circle of chaos, this message positions you as an objective, open-minded source for support.

Every person is capable of a full and permanent recovery from addiction. Most people in active addiction feel like recovery is way out of reach for them. Their self-confidence is understandably low after multiple failed attempts to control or stop their substance use. Getting through detoxification is especially daunting for them; even though that only constitutes a week or so of their life, they're usually terrified of it, and may doubt their ability to get through it. This lack of belief in their ability to beat addiction is a serious barrier to recovery.

Psychologists define *self-efficacy* as the belief that one has the ability to accomplish a desired result. Self-efficacy is a mediator and predictor of success in a number of domains of life, and an especially important predictor of outcome in addiction recovery. Recovery from addiction requires significant commitment: a willingness to give up a lifestyle that has been *the* source of comfort for a prolonged period of time, a willingness to face a world and its problems after living in avoidance, involvement in daily recovery activities, confronting and taking responsibility for ugly and shameful past actions, and abandoning well-worn thought patterns, behaviors, and an approach to life. If individuals don't believe they're capable of recovery, then they're unlikely to render the commitment and exertions required for recovery. After all: *why waste the effort if recovery is unachievable?* As such, a lack of self-efficacy can be a serious barrier to people seeking or accepting help, and can make relapse a self-fulfilling prophecy.

Strong self-efficacy beliefs lead to realistic goal setting and expectancy of success, which in turn determines subsequent behavior. Individuals who possess a high sense of self-efficacy for a particular goal visualize success scenarios that provide motivation to put in the effort needed to succeed. Self-efficacy is known to be a determinant of changed behavior, which is exactly what we seek when we help someone overcome addiction. Those who doubt their self-efficacy visualize failure scenarios and dwell on what can go wrong. It's difficult to achieve success while fighting self-doubt; those who doubt their self-efficacy become erratic in their analytic thinking, lower their aspirations, and the quality of their performance deteriorates. This can have serious ramifications in recovery from addiction, where effort and motivation must remain high in order to achieve such a difficult goal.

Self-efficacy has been found to be a strong predictor of performance across a number of important life aspects (academic, vocational, athletic, social, and health), ability to cope with life, and perseverance in the face of difficult problems. Of particular note, self-efficacy predicts future performance independently of and better than past performance. This is an important factor given that most people with addiction have tried multiple previous times to control or stop their substance use, and many are coming back from relapse. Instilling a sense of self-efficacy helps them to start fresh with renewed focus, despite past performances.

However, self-efficacy must be realistic, and addicts must be brought to the realization and acceptance that ending their addiction is within their grasp. The self-efficacy that enables recovery can be brought about and bolstered by reminding your loved one often and in no uncertain terms that every individual – no matter how addicted, how messed up in the head, and how much life is messed up – is capable of a full and lasting recovery and return to good function and happiness. However, the proof is in the pudding, and you can offer your addict loved one irrefutable evidence that what you say is true. This can be accomplished through a therapeutic technique known as *vicarious experience*. Allow me to illustrate through a story from my own addiction experience.

When I was in active addiction I was miserable. Miserable. I tried everything – or so I thought – but I couldn't stop. I was at the point where I was living the addict's paradox: I couldn't live without drug and drink, but I couldn't go on living that way. I had come to believe that I was incapable of beating addiction – in other words, my self-efficacy was low – so I resigned myself to death. I was planning my own death, as I saw it as the only way out of an unbearable existence.

Then, some friends came to my house and found me passed out on the floor. They took me to the local detox center. I went willingly. I had no expectations of recovery, but I thought it would be good to go a few days without drinking or using to feel better physically, and I liked the idea of hiding out at the detox center where nobody could find me. While I was there, some guys from A.A. and N.A. (Narcotics Anonymous) came in twice a day to put on Twelve Step meetings. I listened to their stories and found that they had all been as bad or worst than me in their addiction, yet here they all were

– in recovery and living normal, happy lives again. They gave me a copy of the A.A. book (*Alcoholics Anonymous*, also known as "the Big Book"), and I read stories from other people who had been hard-core addicts and alcoholics like me and similarly found life and happiness again in recovery. Suddenly, a light went off in my head, and I knew that I could do recovery just like they did; in other words, I suddenly developed high self-efficacy. The effect was powerful; I went from being a dead man walking – someone who accepted that he had to die – to someone who knew that life and happiness were possible again. It's like I was a convict on death row pulled from the electric chair at the last second by the Governor's pardon. And I haven't taken a drink or a drug since that moment. *That* is the power of self-efficacy.

You will notice that my self-efficacy came from vicarious experience – hearing and reading the stories of other people who were in my same situation (or worse) and successfully beat addiction. If you wish to engage your loved one through such vicarious experiences, you may wish to contact a local Twelve Step group (they all have a website); reaching out and telling their stories is part of their creed. However, make sure your loved one is ready for that first, otherwise it may not help. Ambushing your loved one with an unexpected visit from a Twelve Step member probably won't go well. In the meantime, you can do much to provide your addict loved one with self-efficacy simply by getting the message across that you have information that demonstrates that everybody is capable of a full and lasting recovery and a return to better health and function, no matter how addicted they are.

I'm angry at drugs/alcohol and addiction, not at you. Although you may be really, really angry with your addict loved one, I'm hoping I can talk you into separating the disease from the person, and trying to direct your anger more at the addiction, and less so at the person. If you want to show your loved one that you understand what they're going through and why, and you want your loved one to see you as approachable and understanding, then I suggest that you communicate that addiction does not define them.

As we've discussed in previous chapters, people in active addiction get very down on themselves, and their self-esteem is low. Their life and mind have been so completely taken over by their substance use that they usually begin to believe that their addiction defines them. Society's stigmatized view of addicts bolsters this self-defeating attitude. Helping your loved one to break this stigma and to separate the disease from the person is immensely helpful for regaining some vestiges of feelings of self-worth and – importantly – self-efficacy. Both are powerful factors for influencing readiness to take the leap and commit to accepting help.

I suggest letting your loved one know that you will always love the person inside, and that you want that person back. Let your loved one know that you're angry at the disease of addiction for what it's doing to them, for how it's taking your loved one away from you. If you don't define your loved one by addiction, then they're less likely to define themself by it as well. Until they're in recovery, they may not get that message from anyone or anywhere else. Getting this message across is a big step forward in helping the addict to win back the self-esteem that gives confidence and self-efficacy for recovery. It also sets the tone for the next important message.

You are worthy of recovery, and you deserve to be happy and healthy. This is important for showing that your love is unconditional, even if you've had to resort to some tough love. Addicts are very disappointed in themselves and they tend to beat themselves up mercilessly. Psychologists refer to this as the *inner self-critic*, and it's very destructive. It's OK to examine our mistakes and to learn lessons that we can apply to make ourselves better, but the inner self-critic involves ruminating on one's failings and shortcomings to the point where it breaks down self-esteem and causes a deeply negative mindset.

Even if they put forward an outward appearance of arrogance and self-righteousness, deep inside addicts are very down on themselves. Many believe that they aren't even worthy of recovery or deserving of a happy life. It presents yet another barrier to recovery.

This message is important for helping addicts to give themselves a break, and to begin seeing recovery as something they deserve. Allowing this message to come out in your interactions with your addict loved one helps them to regain the self-esteem and self-efficacy necessary to make the decision to accept help.

Low self-esteem has been associated with low levels of self-efficacy, and also the use of dysfunctional coping mechanisms, both of which must be overcome in order to sustain recovery from addiction. Studies have demonstrated that self-esteem has a close relationship with resilience, self-efficacy, and self-control among people recovering from addiction. You can be the first link in the chain to recovery by helping your loved one to have unconditional love for themself and to regain some sense of self-worth. You don't have to flatter them or smother them with adulation; you just have to get across the message that inside the hard addict exterior is a person who's loved and needed and wanted. Like you, they should be coached to remember that even if they hate what they've become, they should love the person trapped inside the addiction.

I'm not going to be your enabler. Although your love may be unconditional, you should avoid the pitfall of allowing an addict to leverage your love to help them with their substance use. Enabling is a form of accommodation that makes it easier for the addict to obtain and use drugs or alcohol, protects them from fully experiencing the consequences of their substance use, or helps them to avoid facing up to their problem and getting help. By being an enabler you are actually participating in the addiction, even though you're trying to help, with the best of intentions. Sadly, my experience has been that most families and friends don't even fully realize it when they've been drawn into enabling an addict.

Addicts are master manipulators, and they naturally gravitate to people they can exploit. Their usual focus is on obtaining money, or something they can sell or trade for drugs or alcohol. Those who love them most are the prime targets, because the addict can leverage their love and desperation to help. Addicts will make emotional appeals for money, with the saddest of stories to back up their demands – often accompanied by tears and promises to stop drinking or using. They know your soft spots and they know what you want to hear.

We'll talk in depth about how to cease being an enabler in chapter 13. In the meantime, getting the message across that the enabling will stop and that you will not be manipulated helps remove you from the addict's circle of chaos, and helps you to stop participating in the addiction. By the time you finish this book, you'll be an expert non-enabler.

I see it time and again when I talk with the families and friends of addicts. The families are torn because they would do *anything* to help their addicted loved one, so the addict uses that emotional connection to convince them that giving the addict money is the best way to help. As a rule, I suggest that you never give an addict money. The drive to obtain their next drink or drug is so profound that they will always use the money for substance use, regardless of what the money was intended for. That's why they'll spend their rent and grocery money on obtaining their chemical crutch.

I know this guy who's an alcoholic, of the binge-drinking type. He'll go two or three months without a drink, and then – *bam!* – he binges on alcohol for four or five days and becomes transformed. He's a dedicated family man, with a wife and three young kids. Under ordinary circumstances, he'd do anything for his kids. They're not a family that has much money, and they barely scrape by paycheck to paycheck. However, his wife had managed to put away $1,000 for buying nice birthday and Christmas presents for their kids. On his most recent binge, this guy tore apart the house until he found where his wife had hidden the $1,000, and took off with it on a drunken binge. Three days later, there was nothing left of the money. When he sobered up, he was ashamed of what he had done to his kids, and couldn't believe he had stooped so low to get drinking money. However, such is the nature of addiction. It doesn't matter what the money is intended for; when an active addict gets ahold of it, it *will* go to substance use.

So, if your loved one makes emotional appeals for money for food, or rent, or medical bills, or whatever, know that the money will almost certainly go entirely to substance use. Addiction is a disease of the "here-and-now," and consequences don't matter when it comes to getting that drug or drink. To addicts, getting evicted in a few weeks is a problem they can worry about when it happens, so getting the drug or drink *now* is all that matters. If you recall, this happens because the part of the brain that's responsible for thinking, planning, and evaluating consequences (the prefrontal cortex, or PFC) is rendered virtually inert by addictive substances.

When it comes to tough love, you must be firm, even in the face of heartbreaking emotional appeals. You must be consistent. You must make sure the rest of the family is on board and firm and consistent as well, or the addict will pick on the weakest member of the family. When you set boundaries and rules you must stick by them, no matter how tough it may be. If you give a little, you will be pushed twice as hard. Remember: this isn't about punishing the addict; it's about not being an enabler. More on that in chapter 13.

I'm willing to support you in your recovery. By "support," we're not talking about financial support, unless that's something you choose to do. A major barrier to addicts becoming ready to seek and accept help is the fact that they usually feel overwhelmed by life. During their addiction they may have gotten into trouble with work, school, family, and the law. They've avoided and run away from their problems, and they've burned bridges. They feel overwhelmed by the thought of having to let go of their escape/avoidance behavior (substance use and social isolation) and face up to life and its problems. Many even say that they don't want to get sober because their life sucks too much.

When people feel overwhelmed it's immensely helpful for them to know that someone's in their corner, no matter what. Letting an addict know that you'll be there to provide love and encouragement does much to break down fear as a barrier to recovery. To them, life is a scary and threatening place where bad things happen to them. Knowing they won't have to face life alone is immensely reassuring.

Some people who've cut an addict from their life and have no more contact with them may wish to consider getting this message to the addict, if they can. Again, it's a matter of personal choice that each person can only make on their own based on their own situation, but some people allow recovering addicts back into their life as long as the addict is taking care of recovery and participating in recovery activities.

By telling your loved one that you will support their recovery, you're providing an anchor from which they can build life again. When we let an addict know that we'll be there to support recovery, it does two important things: 1) it lets the addict know that they don't have to face life alone, and 2) it lets them know that they're worth it. Starting the journey of recovery is far less daunting when you know you'll be doing it with someone who understands.

There is life after recovery. People in active addiction believe that their situation is an impossible quagmire, and that their life is too messed up to be fixed. However, I've seen countless times where even low-bottom addicts bounce back remarkably well in recovery, as long as they take care of one thing: their recovery. In fact, remarkable come-backs are the norm.

Addicts are stricken with a negative psychology, so they're pessimistic and brooding. They usually believe that life is too messed up to bear, and there's no way out. However, there is life after recovery, and all of life's problems suddenly seem tolerable once they're finally confronted head on with a clear mind. When addicts in recovery confront their problems they remove a dark burden from their shoulders, as the burden of an un-faced problem is always greater than the actual problem itself.

As the addicted mind clears from the toxic effects of substance use, the tendency to ruminate and blow problems out of proportion begins to evaporate. As well, in addiction treatment addicts learn to take their problems one day at a time, so that their problems aren't so overwhelming. We'll talk more about this approach to breaking down life's problems into bite-sized chunks when we talk about self-care in chapter 14.

By reassuring an addict that you have information that addicts are able to thrive again in recovery – no matter how much chaos their life is in right now – you're providing a point of focus for finding the motivation they need to commit to recovery. They'll begin thinking about what you said, and they'll begin finding reasons that recovery is worth the effort.

*

This chapter was focused on communication with an addict, but a recurring theme was communicating without being drawn into the addict's circle of chaos, and without participating in the cycle of addiction. I've made some suggestions about maintaining control of conversations and interactions with an addict, and much of this involves changing how we think (i.e. having attitude changes) about addiction, the addict, and what exactly our role is in helping an addict. In section 3 we're going to talk about attitude changes, establishing and maintaining boundaries, using "loving detachment," and asserting self-care into the equation. Communication with an addict becomes much easier once these skills have been learned and engaged, so fear not: if accomplishing what we've discussed in this chapter seems daunting, by the time you finish this book you'll be much better equipped to do so.

In the meantime, let's continue our discussion about how to help the addict. In the next chapter, we'll discuss the mental process that occurs as addicts move from denial and refusal of help to readiness to admit to their problem, let go of their need for control, and commit to treatment and recovery. Family and friends are in the very best place to help and even guide addicts along in this mental process. This is one area where you can have the greatest impact on your addict loved one's future. Let's get to it.

9

How to Help a Loved One Become Ready and Willing to Accept Help

<u>Addiction</u> - When you can give up something any time, as long as it's next Tuesday.

– Nikki Sixx

Have you ever thought to yourself about an addict: *why won't they let me help them?* If you share this frustration, you're not alone; it's one of the most common sentiments that I hear from families and other loved ones of people caught in addiction. The answer to that question is one of the odd features of addiction, and one that we rarely see with other diseases.

Usually, when people are suffering from an illness that causes them discomfort or worry, they go to their doctor at the earliest moment and eagerly accept treatment. Yet when addiction is wrecking individuals' lives and making them miserable, they refuse to get help. It's a bizarre aspect of addiction, and a source of great frustration for people who're watching an addicted loved one endure a tortured existence.

Most people who find themselves drinking or using drugs are able to walk away from it without too much difficulty once they realize it's becoming a problem. However, those who cross the line into addiction – where their brain and mind have undergone the changes we've discussed in the previous section – this turns out to be something that they just can't pull off. However, even some of the most hard-core addicts will reach a point where they finally let go of the need for control and seek and accept help, and do whatever it takes to beat their addiction. I've met many hundreds of low-bottom alcohol and drug addicts who've successfully returned to good health and function in complete abstinence from any substance use. Crack addicts, meth-heads, gutter-alcoholics... with or without mental health problems, it doesn't matter. I've met all types who're now living normal, productive, drug-free lives. So, how do we get the addict in *your* life to become one of those millions of addicts who've managed to leave their substance use in the past?

In my work and research I've noticed that people with addictions follow a strikingly similar path as they go from obstinate denial and refusal of help to full and complete readiness to give themselves honestly and wholeheartedly over to the help they need. Of course, every individual is different, and some will seek help much sooner than others. Nonetheless, I've observed four different stages of mental readiness for recovery. These are:

Stage 1 – addiction begins taking its toll. This begins when individuals realize that their substance use has become abnormally frequent, and they're seeing the beginnings of adverse effects from their substance use on their health, family, finances, job, and well-being. They start having arguments at home over their drinking or using and their behaviors while intoxicated or hung over (i.e. in withdrawal). They begin covering up for their substance-related misbehaviors or neglected responsibilities. They begin calling in sick at work or missing school or other responsibilities more than usual. People who're not addicts will usually stop or significantly cut back their substance use by this point.

At this stage, they're not willing or wanting to stop their drinking or using, even if they could. They become annoyed and defensive when people talk about their drinking or using. They try to get "naggers" off their back by hiding their substance use and promising that they'll stop, even though they have no serious intention of doing so. They become good at making excuses for their substance use (*I'm just going through a rough time*), and for their behaviors while intoxicated or hung over (*I was feeling sick, I think I'm coming down with the flu*).

They're already starting to choose their substance over people and things, and are willing to endure frayed relationships, sagging job performance, loss of hobbies and activities, and material loss for their substance use. They're developing tolerance to their substance of choice, and are drinking or using larger amounts and perhaps more often. They may begin experimenting with other substances as they "chase the high." They begin to change their friends and hangouts in favor of other people and places that support their substance use.

They're getting physically sick from their substance use. Cognitive dissonance is getting noticeably uncomfortable. Their daily thoughts are becoming increasingly focused on substance use and worry over how to make sure they have an adequate supply. They sense that they're somehow becoming a different person, doing things they previously would've considered selfish and stupid. They may not understand what's happening to them.

Stage 2 – full-out addiction. This stage begins when addicts reach the point where they do want to stop, but they stubbornly insist that they can do so on their own. *I got this*, and *I can stop: I've done it before*, and *as of Monday I'll stop* becomes their oft-repeated mantra to concerned family and friends. They sincerely mean it and believe it when they say they'll stop. They believe that their willpower and determination will do it. Everything becomes "tomorrow." *Tomorrow* is when they'll deal with the bank problem, fix the broken garage door, have that talk with their boss, or take the kids to the movies. And they believe it every time they say it.

Even though addicts in this stage are going to great lengths to conceal their alcohol or drug use, they aren't fooling anyone. Family and friends are worried sick, and are repeatedly trying to get them to talk to a doctor, go to rehab, go to A.A., but the addicts come up with every reason, every excuse not to. Their denial is in full swing, and they try to downplay the extent of their problem to their family and friends, their doctor, and anyone else who tries to help. They need to be in control. They want to stop, but they still don't believe they need any help. If they do accept help, it'll only be bits and pieces of their choosing, and they won't fully commit. They may even pretend to seek help to get the "naggers" off their back.

Their false pride and substance-disordered thinking are in full swing. All the behaviors and thought processes that we discussed in the previous section are present. They're angry, resentful, self-pitying, selfish, and blameful.

At this point they're probably trying – over and over and over again – to control or stop their drinking or using. But it always has to be *their* way: on their own with them in control. They're seeking what the Twelve Step program refers to as "the easier, softer way:" *I'll just use on weekends*, or: *I'll switch to beer, or weed*, or: *I won't drink or use until after work*, are the plan, but it never works out. They may attempt the famous "geographical cure" by moving to a new city to escape their problems, but this never works; they may have many problems in a certain place, but the place isn't the problem.

Each new low (an impaired driving charge, ending up in jail, losing their job, etc.) makes them swear off the drugs or alcohol, and they mean it. Sometimes they do stop. It will last a day or two, sometimes a week or more, but they always end up right back where they started because nothing has changed in their substance-soaked mind. Despite all their failures, they still cling to the belief that they can stop on their own. They're not ready to fully commit to what it takes to beat addiction.

They're seeing some serious losses from their substance use: marriage, job, money, house, drivers' license, access to their children, their health. If they don't get out of this "not yet ready" stage they'll end up homeless, edging toward jails, institutions, and death. They're having serious health problems. They're sick all the time. But the substance use continues, and accelerates.

Stage 3 – readiness to surrender. Those lucky enough will enter this stage of readiness before they've lost too much, including life itself. This is the stage where they're finally desperate enough to seek and accept help. This is what's referred to in the Twelve Step program as "hitting their bottom." This is when the essential ingredient for recovery comes into play: a complete willingness to give up their need for control and to do what they need to do to beat their addiction. This means giving up on the need to do things their way; after all, their best thinking and doing things their way has gotten them into this mess. They're ready to "surrender" their need for control and secrecy, and their need to keep a pathway back to their substance use open "just in case."

At this point they may express a sense of relief that all the lying, deception, and running around are finally over. They may become much more honest about things, and begin revealing the true extent of their substance use and what they were doing to obtain their substance. The details may be shocking, even to those who thought they knew what the addict was up to.

Stage 4 – terminal addiction. This stage only happens to those who never reach stage 3, or who did, but relapsed and gave up trying. They may have tried rehab and other programs numerous times but have always found themselves back drowning in their substance use. Some of these people may have honestly tried in their recovery efforts, others may not have fully committed. In most cases, these are people who didn't continue with recovery activities after attending treatment, which they may have done multiple times.

This stage begins when addicts finally give up, and accept that they'll ride their addiction to the end. This is where we find serious physical and mental consequences of chronic substance use (such as Wernicke-Korsakoff syndrome, advanced liver cirrhosis, and/or alcoholic cardiomyopathy in alcohol users).

People in this stage usually live on the fringes of society, and look and act like outcasts. This stage of addiction will almost certainly be fatal. However, there are still those who escape the grave and find sobriety if they finally become willing to commit to recovery, as in stage 3.

Our goal when we're attempting to help addicts is to get them to stage three of readiness for recovery. As you may have noticed, readiness for making a full and lasting commitment to recovery is entirely mental. It has nothing to do with how long or how much or what kind of substance use has been going on; it's all based on the state of mind of the addict. So, our job is to plant the seed in the addict's mind that'll get them mentally ready for recovery. We do so by using the information that we obtained in part 1 of this book, and breaking down the barriers to recovery one by [...] away at the barriers to recovery, the information and at[...] convey to the addict will weigh on their mind and will be [...] thoughts. We ruin their substance use for them, because they [...] what we said every time they use. Every time addicts th[...] miserable they are they'll think of the information and attit[...] imparted. So, let's talk about how we can help a loved one move to stage 3.

*

The first thing to remember here is something we talked about in the last chapter: you are not your loved one's therapist. You are not the one who will fix the addict. Your job here is as a facilitator; to help your addict loved make the mental shift to move to stage 3 and full readiness to do whatever it takes to beat addiction… and then connect your loved one to the professionals who will help them. That may not sound like much, but getting an addict to the point of readiness is a huge, life-saving accomplishment. Of course, you also have a huge role to play while your loved one is in treatment, and for relapse prevention when they're in recovery – if you choose to do so. Those aspects of the addiction and recovery process will be covered in the next two chapters.

Becoming ready to accept and commit to help is an entirely mental process for addicts, so helping them to make this transition involves breaking down the significant mental barriers that block their way to recovery. In the previous chapter, we discussed how you can plant the seed in the addict's mind that will provide the basis for the transition. These messages are designed to help break down the mental barriers to recovery. Just to remind you, these messages are:

- You are an unwell person who needs to get well, not a bad person who needs to become good,
- I'm angry at drugs/alcohol and addiction, not at you,
- Every person is capable of a full and permanent recovery from addiction,
- You are worthy of recovery, and you deserve to be happy and healthy,
- I'm not going to be your enabler,
- I'm willing to support you in your recovery, and
- With recovery comes a return to life.

By including these messages – subtly, or overtly – in your conversations, you're helping to erode the mental barriers to recovery. However, in this chapter we'll look at the mental barriers to recovery in a little more detail in order to find out how to further break them down and allow your loved one to make the inferences and conclusions necessary to move to a mental readiness for recovery.

Before we start, let's be sure to put our role as helpers into perspective. Remember the Chinese finger trap? Some problems require more strategy and brains than they do raw muscle power, and addiction is one such problem. So... easy does it. I would imagine that if you're reading this book you're tired, exasperated, and anxious about your loved one's addiction, and you want them to be better *tomorrow*. However, by pushing too hard you risk coming across as a nagger and alienating yourself from the addict. You want to get the message across that you've learned about addiction and want to listen and learn more, and that you're a safe resource for talking about the addict's struggles in a non-judgmental, non-punitive, and confidential way. You want to get the message across that there is a solution, and that millions of people who were deep into addiction have beaten it. You want your loved one to know that you can be part of that solution by putting them in touch with the right people who can help – when they're ready – but that it doesn't necessarily have to be through you that they get help. You want your loved one to know that your informed and understanding hand is extended, and that it's just a matter of taking your hand when ready.

*

Let's look at each of the mental barriers to readiness for recovery, beginning with fear. We've already encountered many of these concepts in our examination of the addicted mind; now we'll look at these aspects of addiction psychology that keep addicts out of treatment and how we can help to methodically break down these barriers.

Fear. The addicted mind is constantly consumed with fear and anxiety. This is due to fears around what will happen to them as their problems mount and life continues to fall apart, but it's also due to the effects of addictive substances on the brain. As we discussed in chapter 5, addictive substances push the "feel-good" chemicals (neurotransmitters) in the brain up to super-high levels, and when the drugs wear off these chemicals rebound down to abnormally low levels. The resulting ultra-low levels result in depressive symptoms – including pessimism and a negative outlook – as well as anxiety. As such, when they're not intoxicated, addicts tend to be ridden with feelings of impending doom, excessive worry, and anxiety. To make matters worse, the brain also responds to the effects of the addictive substances by engaging its stress and panic mechanism (the *hypothalamic-pituitary-adrenal stress axis*), which results in the release of high levels of stress hormones (especially cortisol and adrenaline). The overall result is a constant state of fear and arousal in the brain that's only worsened by a perilous life situation.

Many of the fears that plague the addicted mind cause addicts to fear recovery, and drive them to avoid anybody or anything that tries to come between them and their drug. The specific fears that present a barrier to readiness for recovery include:

- Fear of withdrawal and detoxification,
- Fear of living life without their crutch (*how will I deal with life without drugs or alcohol?*),
- Fear of the unknown (*what's going to happen to me in treatment?*),
- Fear of giving up control and giving themselves over to the care of others (*what if treatment is too hard and I need a drink or drug?*),
- Fear that their life is such a train-wreck that life in recovery will suck,
- Fear of failure at recovery,
- Fear of being exposed as an addict and being branded by stigma, and
- Fear of arrest, and otherwise having to take responsibility for their past actions.

Telling someone our fears has a remarkable calming effect, especially if that person is someone who cares. When you've taken care to establish yourself in your addict loved one's eyes as someone who's safe and understanding to talk to, they may decide to come to you to unload. That's a huge step forward, and you can help it along by letting the addict know that yours is an understanding ear.

I suggest making it known that you've done some reading and research and have an understanding of addiction and what addicts go through, and that you have knowledge about addiction detox and recovery programs. People nowadays – especially young people – place a lot of emphasis on facts and valid information. This book will give you some facts and information that will ring true for the addict. However, it's best to make sure that you say that you understand and are willing to listen and learn, not that you know what they're going through. Addicts always say: *only an addict understands an addict*, and they tend to be offended when non-addicts say: *I know what you're going through*. When I was in active addiction, my mother used to say that she understood what I was going through, because she had the same problem with peaches; when she bought a basket of peaches she couldn't stop eating them. Needless to say, it didn't make me want to talk to her about my struggles.

The idea here is to get the addict talking, not to come across as a know-it-all. *I know how you feel*, or *I know what you're going through* will probably not be well received. Try something more like: *I've done some reading about addiction and I'm trying to understand what you're experiencing. I'd really like to hear about what's on your mind and what your struggles are*. The idea is to project that you're open-minded, non-judgmental, and truly wanting to understand. I suggest putting that information out there so that the addict is aware of your attitude, and leave it at that. I suggest not inviting the addict to talk, because that might be perceived as being pushy. They'll come to you when and if they're ready; trying to push won't speed that up. They must come to you with an open heart, ready to be honest and forthright, and that can only be done when they're ready. Again, we're playing with the Chinese finger trap, right?

Getting the addict talking and beginning to see you as a safe and helpful go-to resource is our goal here. Telling addicts what they're experiencing doesn't open the door to two-way communication; asking them to help you to understand does. The addict may not take you up on your offer right away, but the thought will be there and they'll likely come to you at some point, when ready. Try not to push, just extend your hand and leave it at that. The addict will take your hand when ready.

I've learned through my own experience with addiction and through my interviews with addicts that the fears that keep addicts from recovery are largely unfounded. That means that when we work on allaying their fears in order to help them we don't have to lie to them or exaggerate; we have the truth on our side. Treatment and the Twelve Step program are designed to help addicts with a train-wrecked life to ease their way back into life and handle their problems one day at a time. And it works very well. I've heard many addicts in recovery say that their worst day in recovery was way better than their best day in active addiction – even though in recovery they've had to face their fears.

When addicts are facing criminal charges, debts to others, and the shame of having treated other people badly, remaining in social and mental isolation by hiding out with their substance use is their security blanket against the fear that these significant predicaments impart. However, when they've had a chance to clear their substance-soaked minds, finally facing up to these issues lifts a tremendous load off their shoulders. The tools for facing life's ups and downs that they learn in treatment, and the support of their recovery sponsor and – most importantly – from family and friends provides them with enormous comfort and the strength they need to face their problems and put things right.

My experience and the experience of hundreds of addicts in recovery whom I've interviewed has been that judges, debtors, landlords, and other authorities greatly respect recovery, and they're tremendously pleased when someone in recovery has the courage to come forward and own up to their responsibilities. They're always predisposed to give them a break. It might not save someone from jail time or other consequences, but it always makes a difference. Owning up to past wrongdoings – even if it means going to jail for a while – is a powerful and necessary aspect of healing from addiction. Debtors are almost always predisposed to cut addicts in recovery some slack and arrange a reasonable repayment schedule. Judges and debtors are so accustomed to addicts running away from their responsibilities that they greatly respect one who comes forward – sober – wishing to put things right.

A powerful way of allaying addicts' fears is through vicarious experience. We've already discussed vicarious experience in the previous chapter, but just to remind you this term refers to the positive influence of hearing the stories of other people that one identifies with. In the case of addiction, vicarious experience involves allowing addicts to hear the stories of fellow addicts who were as bad – or worse – than they were in addiction and have beat their disease and found happy and healthy life again. Because it's someone who's shared their experience, addicts can identify with the person sharing the story and visualize themselves succeeding as well. I would suggest – when your loved one agrees to it – arranging for someone who's in recovery to come and speak to your loved one. The easiest way to do this is by contacting the local Twelve Step people. Helping out others is how Twelve Step members stay sober, so there's always a number of individuals who're very eager to come and talk to you and your loved one. They know what they're doing; they won't shove recovery, or the Twelve Step program, or anything else down an addict's throat. They'll tell their story, answer questions, and let the addict know that help is available if they want it. And they'll leave it at that, so that the addict can reach out when ready, if they wish to. Meanwhile, the addict will begin realizing that recovery is attainable, and that the fears around recovery are unfounded.

Optimism bias. We spoke in chapter 6 about "cognitive bias," which is the tendency of the human mind to distort facts and selectively pay attention to information that supports what the mind believes or wants to believe. As we discussed, this biased thinking is greatly magnified in the addicted mind. One of these biases is referred to as the "optimism bias." It's quite bizarre that the addicted mind – which is characterized by pathological pessimism – would be capable of excess optimism, but it does so in only one area: the persistent belief that addicts hold that one day they will be able to control or stop their substance use on their own, in their own way. What's especially bizarre about this belief is that addicts cling to it despite multiple failed attempts to stop or control their substance use in the past.

The optimism bias is pretty much universal among addicts. In fact, the Twelve Step program has even given this bizarre thinking a name: "the insanity of addiction," based on the adage (that's often falsely attributed to Einstein): *insanity is doing the same thing over and over again and expecting a different result.* This unfortunate cognitive bias is a factor in active addiction, where people believe that they can stop their substance use on their own, and it's also a factor in recovery, where people begin to believe that they can try drinking or drugging again and that *this* time they'll be able to control it.

I find that the best way to help addicts to overcome the optimism bias is through a powerful behavior-changing technique that psychologists refer to as *metacognition*. "Metacognition" is just a big word for a simple concept: making individuals aware of something they're doing but not aware of. Much of the optimism bias occurs automatically, as the mind warps facts to align with what it wants to believe. Simply by making people aware that this is a common symptom of the addicted mind, they can identify and challenge the flawed and dysfunctional thinking when it occurs. Addicts may be reluctant to accept this information, but if it's presented to them matter-of-factly they may begin to accept it, because they'll see it happening in themselves.

I run into this "insanity of addiction" a lot in my work with people in active addiction. When I explain this flawed thinking process and how it makes them continue refusing help in order to try one more time to quit on their own, I usually get resistance, because they really want to believe that they can do it on their own, and they don't want to give up control. It's seldom an "a-ha moment," where they snap out of it. However, once they're aware of this fact, it gnaws away at them and they begin to question the insanity of trying to quit their own way over and over again.

It should be the same with your loved one. Don't expect an immediate cessation to the: *I got this, **this** time I'm going to quit* attitude, but you can begin the process by putting the seed in their mind. I suggest being non-confrontational about it, and not demanding action based on the information you pass along. I suggest being matter-of-fact and non-judgmental, and then leaving it to sink in. Don't allow it to become a debate. You should put this information forward whenever you can, the most opportune time being when your loved one makes yet another promise to quit. I would suggest saying something along the lines of: *you know, I've read that a common symptom of problem substance use is a continuing belief that you can stop your substance use on your own, without any help. Think about it: how has doing it your way worked out for you so far? Your own best thinking has gotten you into this horrible mess. Perhaps you should consider talking to someone about how they can help you finally get control of this."*

Reduced self-efficacy. We discussed the concept of self-efficacy in the previous chapter; it's the belief that one has the ability to achieve a desired outcome. Despite the "optimism bias," when people in active addiction get to the point where they finally concede that they need help, they're often beset by doubts that they have the ability to live without drugs or drink, even with help.

Extensive research has shown that when people have low expectancies about their ability to achieve a desired outcome (such as beating addiction), their beliefs become a self-fulfilling prophecy. This is because they're unwilling to expend much effort on something that they believe is futile. Psychologists are well aware that self-efficacy beliefs play a huge role in determining behavior, especially changed behavior. Positive self-efficacy beliefs are a predictor of outcome for any goal, and an especially important predictor of success in addiction recovery.

Beating addiction requires an "all-in" commitment, daily effort, and ongoing determination from addicts; it's a difficult thing to beat. When addicts don't believe they're capable of recovery, they aren't going to put forward the commitment and effort required; in fact, they probably won't even seriously try. After all, why waste the effort on something so hard if the outcome is unachievable?

Again, we can apply the principles of metacognition. This involves pointing out that negative self-efficacy beliefs are a normal part of addiction, because recovery and life can seem overwhelming. This information should then be coupled with the fact that every individual – no matter how addicted, how messed up their life is, and how messed up they are in the head – is fully capable of a full and lasting recovery and a return to a good and productive life… with the proper help and commitment.

The other way to boost self-efficacy is – once again – through vicarious experience. As I explained earlier, hearing about how other people beat addiction was the turning point for my recovery.

Pride. In chapter 4 we talked about the bizarre pride of addiction, where individuals try to compensate for their rock bottom self-esteem by projecting a false, exaggerated pride. In this state of mind, people are exquisitely sensitive to "ego-threat;" that is, they become defensive and even aggressive at any suggestion of their shortcomings. They may view offers of help as a serious challenge to their ego, and this alone can be a significant barrier to admitting that they have a problem, and accepting help.

When people in active addiction "reach their bottom," they become willing to let go of their need for validation of their pride, and they're finally willing to do whatever it takes to get healthy. They're so thoroughly fed up and done with the misery of their addiction that they're finally willing to let go of all of it: their pride, their need for control, their denial, and their need to keep the pathway to their substance use open. Until that time, this odd pride born of low self-esteem presents a significant barrier to treatment.

This barrier to recovery can be easily overcome by communicating to your loved one that addiction doesn't define the person, that it can (and often does) happen to anyone, and – like any other sickness – people need help to beat it and get healthy again. I suggest projecting a non-judgmental demeanor, and reassuring your loved one that addiction doesn't happen because of weakness, or lack of willpower, or because someone is a bad person. Your loved one may or may not be ready to buy into the disease model of addiction, but I suggest communicating that addiction is a matter of biology – a result of physical changes in the brain – and not a matter of morality or weakness. In other words, by helping an addict to separate the disease from the person, we can change the focus to defeating the disease rather than defeating the person.

The approach here isn't to break down the addict's pride or need for validation. Rather, our goal is to separate addiction from the addict's sense of self-worth and self-identity.

Secretiveness and denial. In the previous section we discussed the secretive nature of the addicted mind. Addicts lie, conceal, and deceive in their efforts to hide their substance use and the extent of their problems. When addicts are in treatment, they're guided to overcome this obsessive need for secrecy because they must get all their secrets out in order to confront their demons and heal. To wit, the Twelve Step program refers to itself as a program of "rigorous honesty" because of the need for full disclosure for healing. Secrecy is how addicts try to maintain control of their situation; they're afraid if others know the extent of their substance use and what they're up to that they'll try to stop the substance use. Therefore, clinging to secrecy indicates that an addict hasn't yet reached their bottom.

I hear it over and over again from addicts who finally become ready to be honest and give up on the secrecy and lies: it's a tremendous relief for them. It takes considerable effort to remember one's lies and to constantly try to weave a web of deceit. They feel immense relief at ending the constant games and lies. When they get their secrets off their chest, it lifts a tremendous weight from their shoulders, as it's the beginning of the end for all the guilt, self-loathing, remorse, and cognitive dissonance.

Even in recovery, ongoing rigorous honesty is an absolute necessity. When addicts begin hiding their issues and problems and keeping secrets it's usually the beginning of the "relapse cascade." In other words, the secretiveness, lying, and deceit must end to beat addiction and to maintain recovery. As the Twelve Step program says: *we're only as sick as our secrets.*

You should not endeavor to get your loved one to become "rigorously honest" with you; that's not your place. If your loved one decides to come to you and unload their secrets, that's fine, but I'd advise against pushing for that. You are not their therapist. The professionals at treatment facilities and the people in the Twelve Step program are the ones who have the correct background and detachment to do that. However, you can begin the process of getting your loved one to understand that it's OK to let go of the secrets and the lies. This can be done by providing a safe, non-judgmental, and non-punitive place where your loved one can tell you what they need to tell you and admit that they have a problem and need help. As well, you can get the message across that the shameful behaviors fall under the umbrella of addiction symptoms, and don't define the person. Just because addicts lie doesn't mean they're liars. You can also get across the message that ending the lies and secrecy and games is always a huge relief. As this message sinks in, the addict may begin getting used to the idea that it's OK to unload their secrets, and that it'll be a huge relief to do so, whether it be done with you or with someone else.

If your loved one does begin to share with you, you should be prepared to be shocked. You may find that you had no idea of the extent of the substance use and unlovely behaviors. Resisting the urge to react with emotion and anger is imperative. You don't want your loved one to decide that it was a mistake coming to you and coming clean. That would set them back considerably. If you don't think you can handle the conversation, then I would suggest that when the addict comes to you, you make an appointment for your loved one with a doctor or counselor who's knowledgeable about addiction.

One mistake that I see in lots of families of addicts is that they try to entrap their loved one in "gotcha" moments by catching them in their lies. They become detectives who try to expose their addict loved one's lies, and then confront them about the lie. For example: finding an alcoholic's hidden empty liquor bottles, or finding a meth pipe, and then making a scene out of it. I suggest avoiding such moments unless there's a specific point to it. Simply proving over and over again that your loved one has a substance use problem and is being deceitful is a hollow victory at best, and just further drives a wedge between you. It does the opposite of creating a safe space where your loved one feels comfortable coming forward to share their struggles and fears with you.

I would suggest confronting your loved one about a lie only when there's a specific point to it. For example, if dangerous behaviors occur – such as impaired driving – letting it slide is never wise because other people's lives are at risk. However, as always, when you confront an addict don't allow it to become a back-and-forth argument. Go in, present your evidence, make your point, and then get out. Getting drawn into an argument or debate over the matter is an exercise in futility and the confrontation loses its impact. Remember, addicts are prideful, defensive, in denial, and blameful of everyone but themselves about everything; arguing with them is an exercise in futility and a sure recipe for wearing away at your own sanity.

Fear of detox and withdrawal. I've found that among people in active addiction fear of detoxification and withdrawal is a huge barrier to even attempting recovery; most of them are terrified of it. This is especially so among opioid addicts and meth addicts, because of the notoriously difficult withdrawal symptoms associated with these types of drugs. Although we've already discussed fear as a barrier to recovery, this particular fear deserves special consideration.

I've spoken to many active addicts who say that they were long ago ready to stop their substance use and commit to treatment, but fear of withdrawal was their sole remaining barrier, or at least the biggest one. In virtually all these cases, the individuals had tried self-detoxing by tapering themselves off their drug, but this never works; self-tapering requires an ability to control their drug use.

However, surprisingly few addicts realize that detox and withdrawal can be made much safer and more comfortable by taking advantage of medically assisted withdrawal. In order to do so, they must let go of their need for control and secrecy and either check into a detox center for 5-7 days, or go see an addictions doctor if they plan on detoxing at home. We'll discuss this in more detail in the next chapter. In the meantime, you can help break down this significant barrier to recovery by telling your loved one something along the lines of: *you know, I've looked into it and detoxing and withdrawing doesn't have to be difficult. The medical people can help you so that you have few if any withdrawal symptoms, and you are much more comfortable while your body detoxes. If you ever want to know more about it, come talk to me, and we can get you to talk to the right people about how they can help you.*

*

It's of the utmost importance to understand the feelings and mindset of anyone we try to help, especially when we're trying to help an addict. Addiction is such an illogical and reason-defying problem, that most people don't understand the mindset of the addict when they try to help, and that has much to do with their frustrations and their inability to make a connection. We discussed the addicted mind and brain in section 1, which provides a sound basis for understanding who we're dealing with. In the initial stage of addiction (our stage 1 that we discussed at the beginning of this chapter), the individual starts out enjoying the substance use, is still living a fairly functional life, and may even enjoy the rebellious lifestyle, especially if the individual is a young person. People in this early stage of addiction usually don't realize (or choose to ignore) the ramifications of staying on the road they're following, and the utter destruction that it will cause them if they continue. They usually don't want to stop their substance use at this point, so any efforts to convince them to stop, be honest, or seek help may hit a brick wall. They usually resent addiction-related advice from anyone at this point as nagging. The attitude of: *I won't let that happen to me*, and: *I'm just having some fun and letting off steam* prevails. This is the point where the breakdown in communication and attachment between the addict and the family and friends usually begins and the walls come up. Taking a less aggressive approach at this point in your loved one's unfortunate journey may be appropriate.

Once problems begin to add up, most people are able to back off or stop their substance use. However, for those who can't or don't and addiction develops, the mindset begins to change once their substance use and behaviors enter stage 2. As their substance use becomes less "fun" and more of an obligation, they begin to feel mentally and physically sick more often, serious consequences of their substance use begin arising, and their mentality changes. Once they've tried a few times to cut back or quit and couldn't they begin to realize that they're trapped and not in control of their substance use. At that point their mindset usually involves feeling utterly overwhelmed. They may feel a crushing weight on their back, and feel overwhelmed by life and life's problems, the feelings of helplessness, and also by the guilt, shame, fear, self-loathing, and anger that develop as the pathological mindset of addiction takes hold. At that point, they become much more amenable to suggestions of information that may help them to move toward a readiness to admit their problem and seek and accept help. That's when the suggestions from this chapter can be most effectively applied.

It's important that your approach to helping the addict is one of providing information, and letting them know that help is available when they're ready.

Extend a hand and then leave it at that. It's important not to corner addicts and preach or proselytize. I suggest that you avoid becoming a nagger, for the sake of your own sanity as well as in the interest of avoiding building walls between you and the addict. Trying to talk addicts into accepting help, or trying to bribe them with promises of rewards if they go for treatment are counter-productive, even if done with the best of intentions. Addiction is a difficult beast to beat, and requires a profound personal commitment and determination. Only true, intrinsic motivation – a deep internal desire and drive to beat addiction – on the part of the addict will propel them to the daily commitment and effort needed to beat addiction. Moving them to the point where that intrinsic motivation exists is how that's accomplished, not by bribing, nagging, threatening, or cajoling them. Next, we'll talk about the specifics of motivation that leads to success, and the disasters that can occur when addicts are pushed into treatment.

*

As we discussed in chapter 5, addictive substances work by super-charging the brain's reward system, making substance use the number one motivation. Once the mind has reached the addicted state, the motivation to obtain and use substances trumps all other motivations. That includes even basic motivations, such as the drive to eat, and avoid danger. As well, the drive to use or drink even overtakes some deeply emotionally held motivations, such as the desire to take care of loved ones, build financial security, and achieve goals. That's why even addicts who were once excellent, loving parents may neglect their children, spend all their savings, and sacrifice their goals in their efforts to propagate their substance use. So, the motivation to continue with substance use is very powerful – *overpowering* – and in order to help someone become ready to accept help and commit to recovery we must help them to find motivation that overpowers the choke-hold that substances hold on the brain's motivation system.

This is an obvious requirement for recovery, so a lot of people go to tremendous lengths to help give their addicted loved one the necessary motivation for recovery. Unfortunately, this is one instance where common sense does not prevail, and people may be doing more harm than good when trying to motivate an addict. Let me explain.

Psychological studies have long shown that if people are given external rewards for changing their behavior, they may perceive that they're participating in the activity for the reward, not because they enjoy or want the new behavior. Similarly, if there's external pressure, then the individual is also inclined to conclude that the activity is being done to answer to the pressure, rather than for self-fulfillment. In other words, people are more likely to succeed at difficult behavioral changes – such as overcoming addiction – based on *intrinsic motivation* (motivation that they find within themselves), rather than *extrinsic motivations* (such as bribes or threats), because they perceive that the outcome of the task is meaningful and fulfilling for them. Given the significant motivation that addictive substances provide, it takes genuine intrinsic motivation to have the best chance to succeed.

Psychologists refer to this negative effect of extrinsic rewards on motivation as the *overjustification effect*. When activities provide their own inherent rewards, motivation for these activities or behaviors no longer depend upon external rewards. However, the overjustification effect may occur if extrinsic rewards are introduced and supplant intrinsic rewards. Even when people are truly motivated by intrinsic motivation – i.e. they want recovery for recovery's sake – adding extrinsic rewards may actually be harmful, due to the overjustification effect. In other words, even introducing extrinsic rewards when an addict is properly motivated for recovery may reduce the addict's chances of success. This effect occurs with all tangible and expected rewards, including rewards that are offered to go into treatment, or to complete treatment, or to go a certain period of time without using or drinking. Extrinsic motivations may come from actual positive rewards – such as cash prizes for completing treatment – or they may come from avoiding a negative penalty – such as to get a nagging loved one off their back by going to treatment. Neither the carrot nor the stick is going to save the addict.

The impact of external versus internal motivators is especially conspicuous in addiction treatment. For example, an individual I interviewed in a detox center illustrates this point famously. This was a very bright and likeable young man – his name was Gerald – who was in the detox center on a court order. Gerald had resorted to doing burglaries and dealing drugs to support his substance use, and he had been caught by the police with a lot of drugs and stolen property. It was not his first time in court, so he was facing a significant prison term, but the judge agreed to suspend the sentence if he attended detox, a four-week residential treatment program, and then participated in an aftercare program. So, here he was in the detox center – an easy choice over prison, *right?* I asked Gerald if the court order was the only reason he was there, and he said no, because he had been wanting to get sober for a long time. However, when we were talking he recounted a lot of substance use-related stories in a positive light, as if they were fond memories; I sensed he really was not there because he was ready to get sober. When I went back to talk to him the next day, he was gone. He had suddenly and abruptly left, even leaving his possessions behind, and there was therefore a warrant for his arrest. A very powerful extrinsic motivation – avoiding a lengthy prison term – had failed to provide this young man with the necessary motivation to succeed in treatment; a perfect example of the overjustification effect.

The galvanizing power of intrinsic motivation is so important to recovery that it's common to see addiction counselors telling addicts that they must be doing recovery for themselves, not for their family, or their children, or to get their job back, or any other extrinsic reason. In my own work, I've seen that this is sage counsel; people who're attempting recovery for extrinsic reasons tend to fail. This is counter-intuitive, so a lot of people find this concept difficult to buy into. After all, what can be more motivating than to quit substance use for your children? However, if addicts could have stopped their substance use for their children they would've done so long ago. People in active addiction "choose" their substance use over their children time and again, I did it myself when I was in active addiction. No, people must do recovery for themselves: because they want to be happy and healthy again, because they want to end the misery and madness, because they want their life back. Their chances of success in recovery depend on it. Sure, getting their children back, saving their marriage, and getting their job back are all benefits of recovery that addicts can acknowledge... however, their first and foremost motivation must be because they want it for *themselves*, not for their children, not for their job, not for their marriage. After all, the motivation to use drugs or alcohol was stronger than their motivation to save their job, or their marriage, or to be there for their kids many times in the past. When push comes to shove, and they're facing powerful cravings and the drive to return to their substance use they will once again choose the drugs or drink over their marriage, job, or kids. They *must* be doing recovery for themselves.

This may sound like we're asking addicts to be selfish, but we're not. We know from research and from experience that people who're in treatment and recovery for themselves – intrinsic motivation – stand a far better chance of success than those who're there for someone else – extrinsic motivation. All those other people and things – the kids, spouse, family, friends, job, and so on – directly benefit when the addict succeeds in recovery. Since the very best chance of success in recovery comes from intrinsic motivation – doing recovery for themselves – it's not selfishness at all. It's the best way to end the chaos and become a productive and loving parent, spouse, employee, and friend again.

I've seen many, many cases where loved ones of addicts – who're acting out of the deepest of love and with the best of intentions – actually reduce their loved ones' chances of success in recovery by introducing financial incentives for attending treatment, or for recovery. This is most commonly seen in the parental-adolescent groups, where parents offer a young person a new car, or a cash prize for attending and completing rehab. Similarly, I see lots of loved ones encouraging addicts to: *do it for your kids*, or addicts who're offered by their employer to keep their job if they get sober. Recovery from addiction is a serious, life-and-death undertaking that requires deep commitment and determination, and such extrinsic motivators are not going to induce the commitment needed to overcome the motivation of substance use. Besides, once the reward is paid out, then the serious business of maintaining sobriety for the long term remains, and if the motivation wasn't intrinsic, then it'll just dry up when the carrot is no longer being dangled.

When a young person shows up for addiction treatment and tells me their parents are buying them a car for completing treatment I immediately think to myself: *I wish they hadn't done that!* The parents mean well, but by providing an extrinsic motivation – the new car – they're introducing the overjustification effect and reducing their child's chances of success in recovery. Ironically, I know one young man who got a brand-new Dodge Charger from his parents as a reward for completing treatment, and he ended up selling the car to finance his relapse less than a month after completing treatment.

Individuals who're attending addiction treatment and recovering from addiction should be guided to make sure that they're there for themselves, not for someone or something else. Certainly, they can use their children, or their job, or other extrinsic factors as reasons that sobriety will benefit them, but they must be primarily doing their recovery for themselves. Again, while this sounds selfish, it's not. Their best chance of success is if they're doing recovery for themselves, and all other people and things in their life will benefit from their success at recovery. Extrinsic motivators can and should be acknowledged, but they must not be allowed to supplant intrinsic motivations.

One individual I knew well from many clinical encounters was admitted to a detox center nineteen (yes, nineteen) times, desperate to break free from his addiction to opioids and alcohol. He was in his 40s, but he had a younger wife and two children under five. He told me that he once had a well-paying job and lived with his wife and children in a very nice home. However, as his addiction developed and his behavior worsened his wife became fed up with his constant promises to stop his substance use, and she finally left with the kids to go live with her family. His addiction progressed, and he soon lost his job as well as his house, and ended up living on the street. Every time he was in the detox center he insisted that he was ready to get sober so that he could get his wife and children back, and get his job and house back again. Those are certainly legitimate and worthy reasons to want to get sober. Each time I interviewed him he was in tears because he missed his wife and kids so much. He resisted the idea that he must get sober for himself and focus on himself in order to get his family back, because he stubbornly believed that his family would be the stronger motivator. However, he never succeeded. Sadly, he died of an overdose shortly after discharge from his nineteenth bout in the detox center. This man appeared to genuinely want to get sober, but we're left to wonder if he may perhaps have succeeded if he hadn't so stubbornly clung to his extrinsic motivations and instead followed our advice to orient his motivation to be intrinsic.

One type of extrinsic motivator that *does* help is positive feedback and encouragement, because it has been shown in studies to enhance intrinsic motivation. The overjustification effect occurs only with rewards that are perceived as exerting control over one's behaviors, and not rewards that provide information on how one is doing, as is the case with positive feedback. Indeed, as we'll discuss in the next chapter, I encourage families and friends of addicts to be active cheerleaders throughout the treatment and recovery process.

Intrinsic motivation has other known effects that are relevant to addiction treatment. Intrinsic motivation has been positively correlated with persistence in difficult training programs (such as intensive training for athletes), positive learning outcomes (such as reduced school drop-out), and an increased interest in seeking information. All these virtues of intrinsic motivation are of great value as addicts set out on the steep learning curve of treatment and recovery.

Of course, when people enter recovery and experience healing, many extrinsic rewards follow. As life normalizes, they begin to realize extrinsic rewards, such as an income, the return of loved ones in their lives, kudos for their recovery, happiness, and stability. However, these are bonuses, rewards of the fruits of their intrinsically motivated recovery, and not a carrot that's dangled in front of their eyes to draw them into recovery. Intrinsic motivation is a crucial aspect of the mentality required to succeed in treatment and recovery, given the short-term costs of early recovery – struggling with withdrawal and cravings, facing a return to normal life, participating in treatment and recovery activities, resisting urges, etc. So, if you're thinking of offering the addict in your life a reward for attending treatment, or if you've been making threats or using cajoling to get the addict into treatment, or trying to appeal to the addict to stop the substance use for the sake of the kids, or to save the job, or whatever, repeat the following to yourself ten times: *neither the carrot nor the stick will save the addict.*

*

In your zeal to see the addict in your life move forward and get help, it can be tempting to apply a lot of pressure. After all, when we want something with all our heart we can push with all our heart. When we haven't experienced addiction ourselves, we don't understand that addiction isn't simply a matter of "just stopping," and our lack of understanding can make us push even harder, because it seems simple to us. However, by this point in your reading you can see that addiction is a serious brain disease with a powerful hold, and it may take some time before your loved one comes around – if ever. It would be nice if we could make a few calls and take a loved one to where the right help is available. However, it just won't work that way, and pushing or attempting to do so is counter-productive.

I suggest that you never push or press the issue with your addict loved one. Rather, I recommend that you take the attitude that you're there to "plant the seed" in the addict's mind, and then allow the seed to grow. You should incorporate the information that we've discussed into your conversations, and make it known that you've done some research and have some information. I suggest creating a safe space, where the addict knows that coming to you to talk is not going to be met with a judgmental, angry, or punitive attitude, and I suggest making it known that you're learning about addiction, but that you wish to listen and learn. Coming across as a nagger or someone who pushes the addict at every opportunity to go to treatment, or someone who's constantly reminding them of how bad their behavior is accomplishes nothing but pushing the addict further away from you and your proffered help.

In an upcoming chapter, we'll talk specifically about healthy boundaries that you should have in place to ensure your sanity and to ensure that you aren't manipulated into being an enabler. One of the principles that we'll discuss is that we should never do for addicts what they can do for themselves, and this applies especially to guiding addicts toward treatment and recovery. If we make all their arrangements for them, they lose their feeling of intrinsic motivation, and they feel that they're doing something for us. I suggest that you look into what resources are available to help addicts in your area and how to access those resources, but that you allow the addict to make the arrangement and follow through on them. *Help* the addict, but don't *do it* for them.

For example, I'm often asked by people to talk to a family member who's struggling with addiction and wants help. I explain to addicts what help is available, how it works, and what's required of them, and I give them the contact information. Then, I allow them to make the calls themselves, and to follow through on the arrangements that they make. If they need a ride to an appointment or a Twelve Step meeting, I'll offer to pick them up and take them, but I don't make the appointment for them or insist on picking them up to make sure they go. They have to be doing recovery for themselves, not because I'm pushing them along.

In the next chapter, we'll discuss the options that are available to addicts who reach the point where they're ready to seek and accept help, and what role loved ones can and should play in the treatment process and early recovery.

10

What Happens in Addiction Treatment, and How You Can Help

We cripple people who are capable of walking by choosing to carry them.

– Anon

The most important thing to know about beating addiction is that recovery isn't simply the absence of using drugs or alcohol; otherwise we could treat addiction by locking addicts in a room without access to substances for a period of time. Obsessive substance use is – in the end – a symptom of greater problems with the brain and mind that result from repeated substance use, as well as the problems that led to the repeated substance use. We discussed in section 1 the many brain and mind issues that are both cause and effect of chronic substance use, and if those issues aren't addressed then successful abstinence from substance use is highly unlikely. Perhaps more importantly, individuals who haven't had these brain and mind issues addressed will still have difficulty in coping with life, and will continue to live with a tortured addict's mind. In that frame of mind, the go-to way to handle life's challenges is by escape/avoidance coping rather than by facing life on life's terms. Sooner or later, social isolation and substance use will re-emerge.

Another important point about recovery is that – for most individuals – their recovery will require abstinence from any kind of addictive substance to maintain recovery. There are two models of recovery from addiction: one is abstinence from using any addictive substances, and the other is "harm reduction," which involves controlled use of addictive substances. I'm a firm believer that the only way for people who're truly addicts to recover and get back to good health and function is through abstinence from all addictive substances. After all, one of the defining characteristics of addiction is the inability to control or stop substance use despite obvious negative consequences from the substance use. People who can control their substance use are not truly addicts, or they would've done so long before drug or alcohol use ruined their life. For those who cannot control their drinking or using, abstinence is the only way to ensure that they don't slip right back into old ways.

As we discussed in chapter 5, the brain undergoes fundamental changes in structure and function when individuals cross the line into addiction, and these changes become deeply embedded in the brain. Entirely new neural pathways are created, and brain cells (neurons) undergo changes in their DNA expression and chemical messaging that change how they respond when exposed to psychoactive substances. Overwhelming research evidence and decades of documented experience have shown that these changes are time-stable, usually lasting a lifetime. That means that once the addicted brain develops, that person will never again respond normally when exposed to addictive substances, even after decades of abstinence. Future exposures to addictive substances re-activate the addicted brain, so that even one drink or drug will almost certainly result in a relapse to the same old obsessive substance use and behaviors. Even after years of working with people in addiction and recovery, I'm still always amazed at how quickly individuals in recovery revert to the addicted brain's thought processes and behaviors after even a single exposure to drink or drug.

The psychology of the addicted mind includes a penchant for finding the "easier, softer way" to beat their addiction (a phrase taken from the Twelve Step program). That means that if there's a way to beat addiction without having to go through detox, participate in treatment, and put in the effort of recovery activities, and – best of all – not have to give up their substance use, then addicts are all for it. Naturally, right? When addicts hear of "harm reduction," they therefore immediately like the sound of the concept: *you mean I can keep drinking and using? Sign me up!* However, research science and an abundance of clinical experience have shown that this seldom works. By definition, addicts cannot control their substance use, harm reduction or otherwise.

"Harm reduction" – a return to substance use in a "controlled" fashion – is flawed is several fundamental ways. We've already discussed how neuroscience, clinical experience, and the fundamental nature of addiction don't support this type of harm reduction. Besides that, harm reduction depends on self-control in a group of people who have a serious impairment of their self-awareness and self-control brain circuitry as soon as they're exposed to addictive substances, and it relies on accountability that depends on self-reporting in people who have in the past been completely deceitful and dishonest about their substance use. There's no way to verify when or how much substance use is occurring, as even our best drug testing cannot give us that information. Besides, what's the definition of "controlled" or "acceptable" substance use? How many lines of cocaine are "acceptable" and how many times a week of smoking meth is considered "controlled?" How much potentially fentanyl-laced heroin can people put in their arm that "reduces harm?" What's the line between acceptable intoxication and unacceptable drunkenness? How do you keep alcohol intake from creeping up, as it has in the past, and how do you monitor and enforce it?

Earlier today I ran into a guy I know who's in recovery from heroin and alcohol addiction. I met him when he was in our local detox center, and I've run into him a number of times at A.A. meetings and around town. He was doing well in recovery – he had married his longtime girlfriend (who was also in recovery), he had his son back in his life, and he had a decent job. Then, about a year and a half into recovery he told me he was thinking of smoking pot. I told him I thought it was a bad idea, and why. He did it anyway; his addict's mind rationalized it: *it's a harmless drug, it's legal, I've never had a problem with pot, everybody does pot*, and so on. Before long every time I saw him he was stoned. He even made a fool of himself at a couple of A.A. meetings because he was so stoned, and once even had to be escorted out. It turns out that his wife left him because they were fighting over his pot use, and because they were broke. He had lost his job (I'm sure it had something to do with him being stoned all the time), and he was spending their rent and grocery money on pot. It's sad to see someone who was doing so well in recovery give it all up because he made himself think he could safely use drugs again. It's the "insanity of addiction:" he convinced himself that *this* time doing drugs would be different.

Maybe there are addicts out there who can return to "responsible" substance use again, but personally I doubt it. As for me, you couldn't pay me to even try; there's no way I'm going to risk sacrificing everything that's important to me and going back to that horrible, miserable life in addiction. I've seen too many friends and patients in recovery fall again after talking themselves into having a few drinks, or doing a hit at a party, or taking up a "soft" drug, and I've seen too many of them die from it.

The Twelve Step program is abstinence-based, and they explain why in their literature: *the idea that somehow, someday [they] will control and enjoy [their] drinking is the great obsession of every abnormal drinker. The persistence of this illusion is astonishing. Many pursue it into the gates of insanity or death* (*Alcoholics Anonymous*, page 30). Although they're talking about alcohol, the same applies even more so to drug use. I'm not at all a fan of an upstart addiction recovery program known as "SMART Recovery" simply because it teaches "recovery" based on self-controlled use. It's not at all based on science and clinical experience, and its website cites shoddy and unsupportable statistics about its success. Many addicts who're grasping at straws to find substantiation for continuing their substance use are attracted to this program simply because it tells them that a harm reduction approach is valid. It provides addicts with what they're looking for: an "easier, softer way." For those who can control their substance use, all the power to them; but they're not really addicts by the very definition of addiction.

Anyway, enough said about abstinence-based recovery versus harm-reduction-based recovery. It should be noted that the term "harm reduction" is also used in other contexts that shouldn't be confused with what we're talking about here. Specifically, "harm reduction" also refers to the practice of providing safe injection sites and needle exchange and disposal sites for people who are in active addiction, so as to reduce overdose deaths and HIV/Hepatitis transmission rates. That type of harm reduction has nothing to do with recovery and nothing to do with our discussion here.

*

When it comes to addiction treatment, rehab, or therapy – whatever term we use, they all mean the same thing – we're talking about a therapeutic program that identifies and addresses any special issues that addicts suffer from (such as past traumatic experiences, social issues, and mental illness), the causes and effects of the addiction, and provides addicts with the "tools" they need to return to normal, healthy, functional living. Relapse prevention is also a big part of any such program that's worth its salt. There are a number of options available, and we'll go through each of them. No person is "one-size-fits-all," and addiction treatment programs aren't either.

I've always thought that the term "addiction treatment" is a bit misleading. After all, it's not like what we traditionally think of as "treatment," such as when you take an antibiotic as a treatment for an ear infection and it's all over. Nobody walks out of a treatment program cured of addiction; recovery from addiction is a lifelong commitment that requires ongoing care and attention. Successful recovery depends upon remaining mindful of the potential for relapse, and maintaining measures to prevent relapse. Even people with years of recovery must use the tools they learned in treatment to prevent relapse, particularly in moments of stress or other times of vulnerability. As such, I liken addiction to other illnesses that can be controlled but not cured. Like those illnesses, addiction recovery requires ongoing care. Diabetes is the perfect example. Undiagnosed or untreated, diabetes can cause many health problems and even premature death. However, when properly treated and controlled, people with diabetes are at no higher risk than anybody else for health problems, and can live a normal and long life. Like addiction, diabetes can't be cured, but it can be managed with daily care. So, to stay healthy, diabetics must take daily care to manage their disease. If they don't, their disease can flare up and cause them health problems and even death. So it is with addiction; addiction should be viewed as a condition that's *managed*, rather than *cured*.

A frequent problem that I see in addicts who attend a treatment facility is when they complete the program and return home with no plan for their ongoing recovery. This is a common problem with non-Twelve Step-based treatment programs (the majority of treatment programs are Twelve Step-based). Many people just "parachute" back into their old life again and carry on as if nothing had ever happened, with no plan or resources in place to continue to support their recovery. Some of these facilities have "aftercare" programs that involve a weekly meeting for 6-12 months at the facility. However, the dropout rate is high. Usually the problem is that too much travel is involved to get to the weekly meetings unless the individual happens to live near the treatment facility. Another problem is that as the weeks pass, individuals see fewer and fewer of their friends from the same treatment cohort, so the social aspect of the meetings falls away and they lose interest. And 6-12 months of aftercare isn't nearly enough; recovery activities must be in place for a lifetime. Addicts who come home from treatment with no plan for ongoing recovery activities are treating their addiction as if it was cured. They often find out the hard way that it wasn't.

Just as I'm not a huge fan of the term "treatment," I'm also disappointed by the word "rehab." The term is a bit loaded, with implications that an individual is being rehabilitated or corrected after misbehaving, as if they were in prison. However, both terms are in general use and widely understood, so we should simply understand them in the correct context – that treatment/rehab programs are therapy whereby individuals recover from the physical and mental devastation of addiction and learn healthy and functional life skills to prevent relapse.

The addiction rehab/treatment process occurs in several phases:

1) Assessment,
2) Detoxification,
3) Treatment/rehab, and
4) Aftercare/relapse prevention.

Let's look at each of these.

*

Assessment. The treatment process relies heavily on a detailed intake assessment, because there's a huge variety of factors that directly affect treatment planning, such as: history of past trauma, risk factors, current social situation, types and amounts and duration of substance use, social support situation, and presence of mental illness. Families and loved ones are an important part of this process, because pre-treatment addicts may still be somewhat secretive and suspicious of addictions workers, and they may lack insight or be in denial into the extent of their problems and symptoms. As such corroborating information from people who know the addict well is especially helpful.

Depending on the condition of the addict at the time of assessment, family members or others who know the addict well may be relied upon as the main source of information. Some addicts are in very hard shape – physically and mentally – when they arrive for treatment. The kind of information that will be asked during the assessment includes:

- Past medical and surgical history,
- Past history of mental health and substance use problems,
- Current medications,
- Family history of physical and mental health problems and addiction,
- Substance use history,
- Legal history (past and current troubles with the law),
- Social history (current place of residence, living conditions, employment and income, financial resources, insurance coverage, social support system), and
- Plans for after discharge from treatment.

Family members should be prepared to provide this information to the treatment facility. But don't worry if you're not sure about the extent of your loved one's substance use or symptoms; during the treatment process, the staff at the facility are very adept at picking up on undiagnosed mental illness and finding out more about each individual's substance use and health history, so that good treatment facilities seldom allow problems to slip through the cracks.

*

Detoxification. To begin the process of recovery and healing from substance use, addicts must first go through *detoxification* (or "detox"), the process of allowing the brain and body to rid themselves of the substances and their toxic metabolites. As the body clears these noxious substances, the unpleasant experience of withdrawal occurs.

Some treatment programs provide detox care, while others require that individuals have already completed detox before they arrive at the facility, and may require negative drug tests prior to admission. If detox must be completed prior to attending the program, I strongly recommend attending a detox facility, or at the very least consulting a doctor who's experienced in managing drug detox if the individual will be detoxing at home. Cravings during detox can be intense, and the drive to use to stop the withdrawal symptoms puts individuals at very high risk for relapse during the detox period.

Attending a detox center is a much safer option in case of complications from detoxing, and improves the chances of success because it offers:

- A safe and isolated place to detox away from temptations, distractions, triggers, and access to substances,
- Knowledgeable and qualified staff who can provide management of symptoms,
- Access to opioid replacement therapy, if appropriate and desired, for individuals who were opioid users,
- Immediate help if complications occur,
- The ability to connect and share the experience with other motivated addicts in recovery,
- The ability to connect with addiction counselors,
- A chance to work out an individualized plan for treatment and recovery,
- Access to proper information and facts about addiction, and
- The chance for addicts to show family and friends that they mean business by taking action (agreeing to attend the detox facility), rather than just making more empty promises. Actions speak much louder than words when it comes to addicts.

Most detox programs last about five to seven days, although they may allow people to stay longer if difficulties arise. It's very important to understand that a week at a detox facility does **not** constitute addiction treatment; rather, it's the prelude to treatment. While detoxing, addicts' minds are clouded as their brain withdraws from habitual substance use, and they're distracted by their withdrawal symptoms, so very little or no time is spent on addiction therapy during detox. Rather, the focus is on getting individuals safely and comfortably through their withdrawals. However, while in detox, addicts are often introduced to recovery groups such as the Twelve Step program, and counselors usually work with them to come up with a plan for treatment and recovery.

The exact symptoms and duration of withdrawal will depend on the type of substances used, the duration and amount of use, and the biological characteristics of each individual. We discussed the specifics of withdrawal from each of the various types of drugs in chapter 3. Individuals who were using more than one type of drug (i.e. polysubstance use) may experience overlapping withdrawal symptoms from the different drugs. It should be noted that withdrawal from alcohol or benzodiazepines can be dangerous and should therefore always be done under proper medical supervision, and never at home alone.

As we've already discussed, withdrawal is a dreaded and feared hurdle for addicts, and a significant barrier to treatment. Many individuals who've reached the point where they desperately want to stop their substance find the fear of withdrawal to be their most significant deterrent from attempting recovery. By taking a leap of faith and placing their trust in a detox program, addicts may feel a great sense of relief and empowerment. A detox facility is a great way to commit to getting better. It's a safe place to ride out the withdrawal symptoms, escape from all the worries of the world for the week, focus on recapturing life, and come up with a viable plan of action for recovery.

Families and loved ones can play a very important supportive role during detox. The idea is to show the addict that taking action – rather than just making more empty promises – results in support and enthusiasm from loved ones. Most detox centers allow patients to make and receive calls, and I suggest getting a number of individuals who are important to the addict to call to show support. Hearing from people daily is helpful. Most detox centers also have short visiting hours once or twice a day, and I suggest that someone visit the addict daily. Much of my work with addicts has been in detox centers, and I can say that receiving a supportive visit from family and friends is deeply meaningful for individuals who're detoxing. Remember: the act of giving up control and committing themselves to an inpatient detox center to face withdrawal is a major leap of faith and a huge step for addicts; it's a deeply significant experience for them, and they need and deserve validation for it. Phone calls, visitation, and shows of support from family and friends allow addicts to form associations between taking action toward recovery and positive outcomes. Bringing them a card, or their favorite food, or other tokens of appreciation and support is also significantly helpful. You can make important associations during this one week that will influence your loved one's entire recovery.

*

Addiction treatment. To break the cycle of dysfunctional thoughts, behaviors, and substance use, the underlying factors that led to the development of addiction must be identified and addressed in each individual, and the effects of substance use on the brain and mind must likewise be addressed. This is the basis of addiction treatment programs.

As we've discussed in previous chapters, addiction results from significant disruptions in thought processes (cognition) that result in dysfunctional and harmful behaviors. As such, *cognitive-behavioral therapy* (CBT) – or a variant of CBT – forms the basis of most addiction therapy programs. CBT refers to a wide variety of counseling approaches that focus on changing how individuals think about and respond to their environment. You may hear of a number of other therapeutic approaches, but they all boil down to some form of therapy designed to teach addicts to challenge and change maladaptive and self-destructive thinking (cognition) and behaviors.

The best data about addiction treatment centers are available from the U.S. These data show that the majority of addiction treatment centers are Twelve Step-based, which research has shown to be the most effective approach to addiction treatment and recovery. Some treatment centers are not Twelve Step-based, which doesn't necessarily mean they lack validity. However, not all addiction treatment programs are created equally, and there are many addiction treatment programs available that are absolute nonsense and lack any validity whatsoever. Sadly, many of these make outlandish claims of success on their websites, citing success rates that have no basis in reality. Frankly, I've been appalled by some of the nonsensical addiction treatment programs that prey on unknowing victims. For example, I was involved in the care of one young man in a detox center who had just been to one such treatment program. It was a "hydrotherapy-based" treatment facility; I investigated this place and found that their treatment was based on spending hours per day in a sauna followed by drinking large amounts of water, and a bizarre "therapeutic" technique that they referred to as "constitutional hydrotherapy." This involved alternating hot and cold water packs on the abdomen accompanied by "sine waves" from a machine. The website posted outlandish claims of success rates that far exceeded standard treatment approaches. Their entire staff was utterly unqualified to be treating people with addiction. This young man's parents paid a tremendous amount of money out of pocket to send their son to this treatment facility (well above the national average fees for addiction treatment) because they bought into the claims of a near 100% success rate. Unfortunately, this young man relapsed on the flight home from his three weeks at this facility; he got drunk on the flight and went on a methamphetamine binge that same day. Fortunately, most addiction treatment centers aren't nearly as scammy as this one, but caution is advised when choosing a treatment program, particularly if it isn't Twelve Step-based.

Why the emphasis on Twelve Step-based programs? Considerable evidence has shown that the Twelve Step approach to treatment and recovery is – by far – the most effective therapeutic intervention in terms of success at recovery and psychological healing. The Twelve Step program gets right at the root of the problem: the causes of addiction and the effects of the traumatic experience of addiction on the brain and psychology. To wit, the program isn't about "saying no to drugs or drink;" rather, it's about learning to live "life on life's terms" and accepting and handling life's ups and downs without having to resort to dysfunctional ways to cope. The process of the Twelve Steps is remarkably effective at clearing away the mental carnage of months or years of substance use and related behaviors, and correcting the dysfunctional attitudes and thought processes that brought about the obsessive substance use in the first place.

As a doctor and research scientist I'm absolutely impressed by the Twelve Step program for two main reasons: 1) even though the program was developed in the 1930s, it's entirely consistent with the current science of addiction, and 2) it amounts to an extremely effective form of CBT, even though it predates the invention of CBT by nearly 50 years. As a therapist I'm amazed by the Twelve Step program's methodical yet simple approach to converting the addicted mind from a state of extreme negative psychology to one of well above average positive psychology. Indeed, studies have shown that people who've completed the Twelve Steps score higher on measures of positive psychology than do normal, high-functioning non-addict individuals. I find the Twelve Step program to be especially potent at helping people who've long suffered from the psychological effects of past traumas to come to terms with their past and to finally find an end to traumatic events as an ongoing source of unhappiness and mental torment.

As well, the Twelve Step program provides an extensive system of social support and recovery activities for ongoing recovery support and relapse prevention for a lifetime, and is widely available. As a doctor and therapist, I recognize it as a complete package. Best of all, it's free; anyone can attend the meetings and participate.

Resistance to the Twelve Step program – which is largely misguided – lies with the criticism of it being a "religious" program. This misunderstanding of the program derives from the fact that the Twelve Step literature often uses the word "God." However, I've interviewed many agnostics and atheists who've found sobriety and health through the Twelve Step program, and they're entirely comfortable with how the program fits with and respects their beliefs. Personally, I am not a religious person, and I find that I don't have to sacrifice any of my beliefs to participate in the program. I don't want to spend too much time on the issue, but the Twelve Step program is intended for and respects people of all cultures, beliefs (or non-beliefs), languages, race, and background. Anyone who's interested in learning more about this fantastic program may wish to check out my book *A Trip Through the 12 Steps with a Doctor and Therapist*, which is available on amazon and from other booksellers.

*

Addiction therapy follows a philosophy known as the "biopsychosocial" model of care. This is a paradigm of care that acknowledges that disease affects people in many domains of their life: biologically, psychologically, socially, and spiritually. This is the model of care that's used for all healthcare today, not just addiction treatment. It acknowledges that good health isn't simply the absence of disease; rather, health is determined by all aspects of an individual's life. This includes their socioeconomic situation, their psychological well-being, their social support and connections, and their spiritual health – as well as their biological health. Those things all come together to determine an individual's level of health and well-being, and – conversely – disease adversely affects all those things. As such, healthcare has abandoned the age-old practice of treating the cause of a disease as the sole approach to restoring people to health, and now focuses on addressing all aspects of what determines an individual's health. This is the biopsychosocial model of care, and – properly administered – it has remarkably improved outcomes in treating all types of disease. Few diseases demand the biopsychosocial model of care more than does addiction.

There's no question that addiction wrecks people's biological health in the brain and virtually everywhere else in the body. They tend to be poorly nourished, deconditioned, and may have significant organ disease from the toxic substances. Similarly, addiction affects people mentally and emotionally, as we've talked about in section 1 of this book. Addiction also makes people "socially sick." As people are drawn further and further into their addiction and related behaviors, they become increasingly socially isolated. They end up rejected by friends and family, who become tired of the irresponsible behaviors, the lies and deceit, and all the other anti-social behaviors. Addicts gladly push their family and friends away anyway, as they tire of the constant "nagging" about their addiction. As job, school, healthy relationships and other normal social activities fall away, addicts become socially isolated to the point where their primary social contacts are limited to the closed world of their fellow addicts.

The spiritual dimension is probably the least understood of the four factors of the biopsychosocial model. Most people equate spirituality and religion, but this is incorrect. Spirituality is about connections outside ourselves, such as connections with other people, the world in general, and – for some – some kind of a higher power. An overwhelming volume of research has shown that these connections are a powerfully therapeutic aspect of addiction recovery. PhD psychologist and noted addictions researcher Wayne Skinner provides a good explanation of the spirituality dimension of recovery: *when people find connection to a larger frame of meaning that allows self-transcendence and meaningful engagement in recovery practices and social re-engagement, they are more likely to change from addictive preoccupation to increased behavioral self-control, mindfulness and reconnection with others in ways that are meaningful for the person* (Skinner, pages 2-3).

*

Counseling in addiction treatment is heavily focused on "metacognition," which we've already encountered in earlier chapters. Metacognition is the ability to recognize and gain insight into one's own dysfunctional thought patterns. Metacognition training allows addicts to recognize and challenge the dysfunctional thought processes that have led to their past behaviors.

You may recall that much of the dysfunctional thoughts and behaviors that constitute addiction are due to "bottom-up" processes of the brain. This means that they become automatic, occurring without involving any prior thought or consideration. In other words, once addiction gets going, the brain's executive control system (our ability to think, plan, consider consequences, and make sound decisions) is removed from the loop. Metacognition is a key technique for re-asserting the executive control part of the brain after it has been disabled by repeated substance use. As the brain recovers its ability to function properly following detoxification, metacognition allows individuals to use their thinking abilities to overcome what had been automatic reactions and behaviors during their active addiction. Quite literally, addicts go from the infant brain to the adult brain.

Metacognition enables this transition back to allowing addicts to use their brain for something other than just keeping their ears apart by teaching them to recognize dysfunctional addiction-related thinking ("stinking thinking"), to challenge this dysfunctional thinking when it occurs, and to apply properly ordered thinking so that the addiction-related thinking no longer translates into addiction-related behaviors. It's a very potent and very effective technique for recovery.

Counseling also addresses the various causes and effects of addiction, encompassing all aspects of health (i.e. the biopsychosocial approach to healing). Specifically, some of the areas addressed include:

- Coming to terms with past traumas,
- Self-esteem,
- Insight into cues and triggers,
- Developing healthy ways to cope with life, and
- Interpersonal relationships.

Most addiction treatment programs employ a variety of therapeutic activities, such as:

- Group and individual counseling,
- Diagnosis and management of comorbid mental health disorders,
- Medication management,
- Recreational therapy,
- Health care and self-care,
- Family therapy,
- Healthy living (returning to proper diet, exercise, and sleep habits), and
- Aftercare planning and relapse prevention.

There are a whole bunch of types of addiction treatment programs available, based on the level of care provided and whether or not the individual stays at the facility during treatment. For each type of treatment available, there are many further options in terms of cost and location. Sometimes a local facility may be the obvious choice, or a particular facility that's covered by your health insurance, or perhaps one that's been recommended by a friend or a health professional. Some individuals purposely choose a facility that's geographically distant because they want to "get away," although I feel that there's enough isolation provided by local facilities, and staying local allows for more contact with the addict's support system.

The general types of addiction treatment programs are:

- Inpatient,
- Residential,
- Partial hospitalization programs (PHPs),
- Outpatient,
- Intensive outpatient programs (IOPs), and
- Long-term rehab.

I strongly recommend that loved ones become involved in the decision-making process when choosing a type of treatment and a specific treatment facility. As we know, the addicted mind typically includes a profound need for control, and addicts have a tendency to seek a treatment type that gives them the most freedom. People in active addiction or early recovery tend to be evasive of help, and pick-and-choose what help they will accept and what help they will forego. They tend to underestimate the amount of help they need, and may make poor decisions about treatment. As the Twelve Step program suggests, they may seek the "easier, softer way." As such, addicts should be open to guidance from family, friends, and healthcare providers when choosing treatment options. Addiction is a serious, life-threatening disease, and deserves a serious approach to treatment. Taking the easier, softer way often reduces the chances of success. Better to do it right, and get it right.

Fortunately, many areas have a local intake and assessment service that helps take the guesswork out of deciding which treatment program is right for your loved one. These services interview addicts and their families, perform an assessment of the addict, and provide recommendations from qualified addictions professionals about the type of treatment that would best suit that particular individual. They can also provide referrals to the appropriate treatment program, and provide information about financing options, insurance coverage, and public assistance programs.

The primary decision is whether a residential program or an outpatient option would be more suitable. Inpatient and residential programs offer some advantages over outpatient programs, such as:

- Removing addicts from an environment where they'll be exposed to cues and triggers and access to substances,
- Removing addicts from toxic environments and relationships (if applicable),
- Allowing for more intensive and focused treatment,
- Allowing for undivided attention on the treatment program,
- Providing a social environment with other people who're focused on recovery (i.e. a "culture of recovery"),

- Ensuring some solid recovery time prior to re-integrating into life and society at home, and
- Allowing access to allied services (such as a psychiatrist, social worker, and a recreational therapist, etc.) under one roof.

Let's now look at each of the different types of treatment programs.

Inpatient rehab. This is the most restrictive type of program, and involves staying on a ward in a hospital or treatment facility for the entire duration of the program. These patients remain under 24-hour supervision, and are usually not permitted to leave the ward. Inpatient rehab differs from residential rehab in that it's more intensive, involves closer supervision, and involves less freedom of movement. This type of program is often used on an emergency or involuntary basis (such as after an overdose or following a suicide attempt), or for incarcerated individuals.

Residential Rehab. This is the mainstay of addiction treatment, and most addicts will attend a residential program. Addicts live at the facility during the entire time of their treatment program, although they may be granted more freedoms, such as going for walks outside, or using recreational facilities in the evenings. Many programs will grant day or weekend passes as individuals progress through the program. Residential rehab involves a longer stay (usually three to six weeks) than does inpatient rehab, and is done outside of the hospital system.

Partial Hospitalization Program (PHP). PHPs are sometimes offered as a hybrid of residential and inpatient programs. Addicts are housed on-site and have access to staff on a 24/7 basis, but the daily routine is less regimented and they have more personal freedom. It may be used as a step-down treatment following discharge from the more intensive inpatient rehab.

Outpatient Programs. This approach to treatment involves addicts living at home or at a sober living house and attending treatment activities during the day. There are a wide variety of outpatient programs available, all differing in intensity and duration. Outpatient programs are generally a less preferable and lower level of treatment compared to residential programs, but offer a less expensive and more flexible alternative.

People who consider choosing an outpatient program should be highly motivated, due to the higher level of freedom involved. In some cases, people who have attended more intensive residential programs but have relapsed or require additional therapy may also be good candidates if they're sufficiently motivated. I suggest that certain features should be in place prior to considering outpatient treatment:

- A healthcare professional knowledgeable about addiction should be aware of the addict's substance use history and agree to the outpatient program,
- Individuals should be detoxed and free of significant withdrawal symptoms prior to starting,
- The substance use should have been less intense and of shorter duration,
- Individuals should have a safe place to live, free from influences to use substances,
- They should not live alone,
- There should be a good social support system in place, and the supporters should be aware of the addict's substance use history, red flags to watch for, and agree to supporting the addict's recovery, and
- There should be no untreated comorbid mental health disorders.

Overall, outpatient programs are appropriate for individuals who are motivated to beat their addiction, have more insight into their situation, and have a good outside support system in place.

Intensive Outpatient Program (IOP). This type of program is meant as a step-down following completion of an inpatient or partial hospitalization program. As with other outpatient programs, individuals attending an IOP live at home or at a sober living house and attend sessions during the day. The IOP is designed to support the transition from a program with restricted freedom to community-based care. The IOP is also often recommended for individuals who may require continued counseling, such as those with comorbid mental health disorders, or those who suffer from deeper issues, or frequent relapsers.

Long-Term Rehab. These are residential treatment programs that last 3-12 months. These long-term programs are intended for individuals with a particularly complicated addiction, such as those who've struggled with repeated relapses despite attending residential treatment programs. Long-term programs are often based on a special therapeutic approach known as "therapeutic communities." This type of therapy is directed at re-socializing individuals who've had difficulties adjusting to integration into society. This approach is appropriate for people with a particularly severe course of addiction, those who've been homeless, have a history of criminal behavior, adolescents, and people with serious or complicated comorbid mental health disorders.

*

So, what will your loved one learn in rehab? The goal of addiction treatment is to identify and address the causes of the addiction in each individual – which is usually one of the causes we listed back in chapter 1 – and to undo the horrible psychological effects of months and years of substance use and related behaviors – all that stuff we talked about in chapter 6. The biopsychosocial model of care is widely used, meaning that care is put into helping addicts to heal biologically, socially, psychologically, and spiritually.

Addiction is – at its heart – a dysfunctional coping mechanism. In treatment, individuals are taught to cope with life on life's terms. They're taught acceptance – that life is always going to have ups and downs no matter who you are, and that's just how life is. Acceptance of life's events – whether good or bad – helps addicts to stop seeing themselves as victims of the world, and represents a big step toward stopping the anger and resentment that plays a central role in driving addiction.

Addicts are also taught a simple technique to overcome the feeling of being overwhelmed by life and recovery. As we've previously discussed, the addicted mind has a tendency to ruminate – to obsess about the past and to terrify itself by projecting all life's problems into the future, dreaming up worst-case scenarios. Addicts cause themselves such anxiety that they drink or use to calm themselves and to mentally "check out" from their dreamt-up "reality." This rumination is counter-productive, as it consumes much of their brain capacity and accomplishes nothing except to scare them. In treatment, addicts are taught to take life one day at a time; wasting time ruminating about the past and what should have or could have been is a waste of time and brain-power. Rather, they're taught to accept the past as something that has happened and they can't change. Similarly, they're taught that projecting their problems into the future is also a waste of time and brain-power. Worrying about things that haven't happened (and probably never will) is simply a cause of unnecessary stress. Rather, they're taught to focus on today, and the things about their life that they can change. They're taught that the best way to handle life's problems and to accomplish goals is to concentrate on doing what they can do on *this* day to make their life better and to accomplish their goals, and to allow tomorrow to take care of itself. They can still plan for the future, but they don't plan the outcome of future events or ruminate about how things might turn out. It sounds simple, but this remarkable approach to life gives many people – addict or not – a piece of mind that they may have never before known.

Addicts can find recovery itself overwhelming. After all, the thought of living the rest of their life without the drug or drink that's been their comfort and their crutch for months or years can be terrifying. Many doubt their ability to do so. Even the thought of a month in recovery can be overwhelming for them. As such, they're encouraged to take their recovery – just like they take life – one day at a time. It's much less overwhelming if they just focus on staying sober today, rather than worrying about months, years, or a lifetime. After all, anybody can stay sober for one day, *right?* They learn to just concern themselves with today: to do the things they need to do to stay sober today, and then let tomorrow look after itself. If they're struggling, they can just focus on one hour at a time. Even people who've been in recovery for years – who long ago stopped having cravings or even thoughts about drinking or using – still take life and their recovery one day at a time.

Addiction treatment is also heavily focused on addressing the painful and addiction-driving symptoms of cognitive dissonance. You may recall from our discussion about cognitive dissonance back in chapter 6 that this is the psychological pain that people feel when their behaviors don't line up with their beliefs about how a good person behaves. Resolving cognitive dissonance is usually accomplished in several ways. First of all, addicts are taught about the disease model of addiction, and that they were suffering from the symptoms of a disease. While this does not excuse the terrible behaviors that they displayed during their addiction, it puts it into context. They thereby learn that they are unwell people who need to heal, not bad people who need to become good, that their addiction does not define them, and that addiction is a matter of biology, not a matter of morality, bad character, or lack of caring.

The most effective technique for relieving the troubled mind from dissonance involves the Twelve Step process, which is a simple and methodical way to allow individuals to put past behaviors right, and to prevent any further dissonance by correcting future behaviors such that the ideal self and the actual self are brought in line. Addicts are asked to list and discuss their past wrongdoings, as well as their resentments in order to get those things off their chest. Next, they're asked to identify the "character defects" that made then behave in such a loathsome way, and to commit to correcting these negative aspects of their behavior. These include such tendencies as lying, and being selfish, impatient, intolerant, angry, and so on. Finally, the addicts make a list of all the people they've wronged or harmed by their behaviors, and then undertake making amends to all those people. This process has a powerful effect on self-forgiveness and dissonance reduction, and imbues individuals with a positive psychology. They begin feeling good about themselves and their behaviors for the first time in years. It frees them from the negative and painful guilt, remorse, self-loathing, and regret that had plagued their substance-soaked minds for so long and had driven their ongoing substance use. It also provides a template for pro-social behaviors that allow them to re-engage with family and friends and to re-integrate into society in a functional way.

These therapeutic processes contribute to the overall goal of restoring key psychological constructs: healthy self-esteem, a positive self-identity, high self-efficacy for recovery and for life, and a positive psychology. Some of the various counseling techniques have different names (such as *dialectical behavioral therapy* (DBT), *rational emotive behavioral therapy* (REBT), *motivational interviewing*, and *psychodynamic therapy* (PT), for example), but they all boil down to targeting cognition (how people think), and behaviors (how people act and react). As we've discussed, virtually all of them use techniques derived from the Twelve Step program to accomplish this, regardless of the specific style of counseling used.

One approach to metacognition that's commonly used in addiction treatment is known as "mindfulness." In my own practice, I advise the use of mindfulness in the sense of awareness of one's own thoughts and motivations and behaviors; in other words paying attention to one's own thoughts and actions as if one were an outside observer. However, in many addiction treatment centers they teach "mindfulness" in the sense of a specific meditation discipline that comes from Japan. I have a couple of issues with "mindfulness" in terms of the specific meditation doctrine. First of all, this discipline of meditation teaches that one should be mindful of one's thoughts (which is good), but be totally non-judgmental of one's thoughts and feelings, as these are neither right nor wrong, nor good or bad. It teaches that we should be acting as an accepting observer of our thoughts rather than challenging dysfunctional thoughts. I disagree with that concept because the addicted mind is filled with thoughts that are outright wrong and harmful – thoughts that lead back to substance use. I teach people to actively challenge and root out thoughts that are dysfunctional and harmful. After all, addicts have long been plagued by thoughts that are definitely harmful and wrong, and have led to these individuals' spectacular demise, and could potentially kill them if they go unchallenged. The other issue that I have with the specific doctrine of mindfulness meditation is that it's a doctrine, and has rules, rituals, and practices that must be learned and practiced. I believe that spending precious time in treatment teaching people weird meditation rules is a waste of time, and that people are unlikely to continue on with complicated practices once they're out on their own. As such, when I refer to "mindfulness," I mean simply being aware of one's thoughts, and challenging thoughts that are dysfunctional and would lead back to a negative mindset and substance use. In other words, mindfulness is the same as metacognition.

I commonly hear from addicts in recovery that following treatment they found that they have life skills that are much better than they've ever had before, even before they ever started drinking or using drugs. In order to end the feelings of self-pity and self-victimization that are typical of the addicted mind, they learn about acceptance. That means acceptance of their life situation – the good and the bad. After all, acceptance of one's life situation frees people from constant dissatisfaction with what they have and an obsessive focus on what they don't have. Such a mentality is toxic. With such a mind-set, even when people get something they wanted they find it strangely unsatisfying because they immediately start pining for the next thing. People who ruminate on such things are stricken with anger and resentment because they feel they're being short-changed in life, and they waste brain-power by focusing on what they don't have and envying those that they perceive as better off than themselves. They take on the identity of self-pitying victims of the world. All these negative emotions are what make people unhappy, and in the past have led these people to substance use to cope. Acceptance is key to happiness, and lack of acceptance is a route to negative feelings of anger, resentment, self-pity, and envy.

In addiction therapy, individuals learn to take action when there's something within their power to control to improve their life, and to accept the things they cannot change, rather than roil with anger, resentment, and self-pity. They learn to identify the positive things in their life and to have gratitude for those things. Happiness is a matter of perspective; I've met wealthy, materially successful people who're deeply unhappy, and I've met people who barely get by but are truly happy. It's all based on their perspective on life, and not on their material success. The key to a perspective of life that makes one happy is acceptance and gratitude. These are what make people happy, and these are the kinds of life skills and attitudes that are taught in addiction treatment. The goal is to end the negative, pessimistic, self-pitying, and angry mindset that belies addiction.

This is far from a complete review of the various techniques and practices that constitute addiction treatment, as that subject alone would fill a book. However, the overall process involves converting addicts from an extreme negative psychology to a positive psychology, teaching them metacognition, re-learning pro-social behaviors, and teaching them how to handle life on life's terms without having to resort to social isolation and substance use to cope. Relapse prevention and aftercare planning are also a crucial part of addiction treatment, and we'll discuss that topic in the next chapter.

*

A commonly heard catchword associated with addiction treatment is "neuroplasticity." We've already run into this term in chapter 5, but let's quickly review, because it's an important concept in addiction recovery. The term "plasticity" refers to the ability of our body tissues to adapt to our needs. The brain is among the most plastic of tissues in our body, as it's geared to make rapid changes to its structure and function so that we can learn new things and adapt to new challenges. For example, when we start a new job we quickly learn new information, such as the names of co-workers, the layout and routine of the workplace, and even new skills that we need to do our new job. Our brain rapidly makes changes to its structure in order to incorporate these things into memory so that we're able to adapt to our new job. This occurs because of neuroplasticity – brain plasticity.

People who come to recovery could be considered to be in a state of negative brain plasticity. If they've been in active drug or alcohol use long enough, their life activities may have degenerated to the point where they aren't using their brain very much, and certainly aren't challenging it. For those who've gone far enough down the path of addiction, their attention and focus has been on substance use and little else for some time. They haven't been engaged in learning, problem-solving, and otherwise using the types of brain activity that promote growth and strengthening of the brain's abilities; the brain has become a flabby couch-potato.

Addiction treatment involves a turn-around for the addict's brain; individuals are constantly challenging their brain and setting new demands on it, learning and adopting new habits, new ideas, and new ways of thinking. They're learning about addiction and what it has done to them, and how to recover control over their lives. The learning curve is steep and it pushes their brain plasticity to new, healthy levels. New brain pathways are being formed that allow old, dysfunctional addiction-related pathways to be by-passed. In other words, neuroplasticity is allowing them to adjust their brain from a weak, unhealthy one that's geared to substance use to one that's strong, active, and geared toward approaching life in a robust and healthy way.

Although the brain changes that caused addiction will remain for life and can be re-activated at any time with future exposure to addictive substances, neuroplasticity allows addicts in treatment to learn new ways of thinking, new behaviors, and new habits that lay down new pathways that by-pass the addiction-related brain pathways that made addiction behaviors automatic.

This positive neuroplasticity can be enhanced by another aspect of addiction treatment, something I refer to as "brain hygiene." Brain hygiene is a where we use the brain's plasticity to enhance its performance for improved physical, mental, emotional, social, and spiritual well-being. It's more than just forming new neural pathways that allow addicts to use their brain for recovery rather than for scheming about how to obtain and use substances; it's also about getting the brain healthy again. After months or years of inadequate diet, poor and irregular sleep, lack of exercise, and repeated exposure to toxic substances, the brain is an unhealthy organ. The rest of the body is pretty unhealthy, too, and it takes a healthy body to house a healthy mind. When addicts enter therapy and are exposed to regular physical activity, yoga, deep breathing, quality sleep, relaxation, socialization, positive thinking, hobbies, a healthy diet, sports, listening to music, meditation, reading, and mindfulness, they're participating in activities that boost the health of the body and brain – brain hygiene. This is why most addiction treatment programs involve a wide range of activities.

*

It must be pointed out that attending a formal addiction treatment program is not necessarily the only path to recovery. While accredited treatment programs – particularly those that are Twelve Step-based – generally offer the best chance of success, they may not be feasible or practicable for some people. I must confess that I myself never attended an addiction treatment facility. My treatment program consisted entirely of the Twelve Step program. It worked very well for me, exactly as it's meant to work. However, I had certain features in place that made it work for me. First of all, I had a safe place to live, where I lived with other people who knew my situation and were supportive, and I lived far away from immediate temptations of drugs or alcohol. I didn't have a dealer living next door, and there was no alcohol kept in my house. I didn't have a group of friends dropping by with a case of beer or a bag of heroin. Additionally, I was very strongly motivated toward recovery. I was doing it for myself, not to please someone else or to get a job back or other extrinsic motivators. Finally, I delved into the Twelve Step program wholeheartedly and enthusiastically, with both feet in the program. I didn't pick and choose which parts of the program that I would do and which I wouldn't. I gave myself over to do everything the program asked of me and what my sponsor suggested; I surrendered my need for control.

That means that I got myself a sponsor and connected with him regularly, I did the Steps (oddly enough, the Twelve Steps only work if you do them, which some people don't), I read the A.A. book every day, I went to meetings (in fact, I went to two meetings a day for the first three months of my recovery), and I connected with other people in recovery every day.

In my research, I've conducted interviews with hundreds of people who beat addiction through the Twelve Step program, and I've found that those who succeed are the ones who likewise do what the program asks. The vast majority of people who didn't succeed are those who didn't complete the Steps, and didn't have a full commitment to the program. Working through the Steps is where the self-discovery and healing occurs, where the relapse prevention mindset is established, and where recovery skills are learned. The research literature has also found that completing the Twelve Steps is a tremendous predictor of success in recovery.

While using the Twelve Step program as my addiction treatment worked very well for me, it might not work for everyone. It was not my plan to only use the local Twelve Step program; I was planning on attending a three-week addiction rehab program. However, by the time a bed came open for me I had been sober for almost five months, and had completed the Steps, and was fully engaged in the Twelve Step program for my ongoing recovery. I had experienced remarkable healing and revitalization (mentally, physically, socially, and spiritually) through my vigorous involvement in the Twelve Step program so – after much discussion with my family and my sponsor – I decided that the rehab program would be redundant, so I continued on with what I was doing.

There are a number of different types of Twelve Step groups available, such as Alcoholics Anonymous, Narcotics Anonymous, Cocaine Anonymous, Marijuana Anonymous, and so on. There are differences between them that some individuals may wish to explore. For example, I began by attending Narcotics Anonymous, on the recommendation from my doctor. However, there were some things about that particular program that didn't work for me, so I tried Alcoholics Anonymous, and I found my home there. Addicts don't have to have a problem with alcohol to attend Alcoholics Anonymous.

Indeed, many A.A. members are meth addicts, or cocaine addicts, or heroin addicts who've never had a problem with alcohol. They – like me – just find the A.A. groups to be more therapeutic for them. I know some A.A. members who don't even have any kind of addiction, alcohol or otherwise. I've met dozens of people who attend A.A. because they have mental illness and attending A.A. helps them function better, and I've met some people who have had significant trauma in their past who also find A.A. helps them to cope better even though they've never had a problem with substance use.

The Twelve Step program is an ingenious and excellent avenue for learning to heal from any kind of life dysfunction, learning to cope better in life, and simply to find peace of mind and happiness in life. There are Twelve Step groups for many types of dysfunctional coping, such as Gamblers Anonymous, Sex Addicts Anonymous, and Overeaters Anonymous. There's also an impressive Twelve Step group for helping people to recover from the adverse effects of other people's substance use, known as Al-Anon and Alateen (we'll talk a bit more about Al-Anon in section 3). As well, the Twelve Step program is taught by business consultants and life coaches to senior executives and other people of all walks of life around the world. Not because they have any kind of addiction, but so that they can learn the potent life principles that are part of the program, which translate well into business and leadership skills. To wit, use of the Twelve Step program for general business and life coaching has been licensed to more than 300 organizations worldwide, none of which have anything to do with addiction.

Every person and their situation is different, and there's no one-size-fits-all addiction treatment plan. What clicks for one individual may not click for another. However, it's fair to say that most people with a serious addiction require residential treatment to break the cycle of substance use and begin healing. This may be especially true if there are complicating factors such as:

- A comorbid mental health disorder or suspicion of one,
- Previous failed attempts at recovery with lesser interventions,
- Polysubstance use, and
- An unsupportive or unsafe home environment.

*

Your role in your loved one's addiction treatment is that of cheerleader, but that's a much bigger role of much more importance than you may think. Having interviewed hundreds of addicts who've been through the experience, I can tell you that the treatment process is deeply important to those who go through it, and to have important people in their life acknowledge and support their treatment is hugely important to them. In other words, even a little encouragement goes a long way to boosting their motivation; a lot of encouragement – to include tokens of encouragement, such as visits, calls, a card, and shows of enthusiasm and interest – goes a very long way.

I also strongly advocate that families and friends become involved in making decisions about which avenue to take for addiction treatment, as I mentioned earlier in this chapter. The addicted mind has impaired decision-making circuitry, and the nature of addiction includes underestimating one's need for help, and seeking the "easier softer way" to beat addiction, often at the cost of success. As such, addicts may lack the objectivity to recognize that they require a higher level of care, such as a residential treatment program. It's never a bad idea to involve the advice of others when making the decision about treatment program types. The choice of type of treatment should be a group decision, based on what will afford the addict the best opportunity for healing and success in recovery. All other considerations – including important things like family, job, and responsibilities – should be secondary. After all, without successful recovery, none of those things will benefit. Taking three or four weeks out of life to attend treatment is a small price to pay for getting life and all the things that matter back again. Remember: we're dealing with a serious, potentially fatal disease that robs people of meaningful life.

*

People in addiction treatment are moving from a mindset of negativity – pessimism, anxiety, fear, self-victimization, low self-esteem, and tremendous guilt – to one of hope, optimism, and burgeoning confidence. They're learning all about why their life crashed down around them and why they behaved for so long in a way that made them hate what they had become. They're getting answers to the questions that have haunted them for months or years. And they're finding out that they're not bad people because of it. They're learning the skills they need to confront and handle life's problems and stressors after living in fear of life. They're learning gratitude for what they have and beginning to enjoy some of life's simplest pleasures again. They're anxious to show off their recovery to their family and friends, and to show their true selves to the world again. Treatment and early recovery is a deeply meaningful and important thing to them. When family members show the same enthusiasm and an interest in hearing about what the addict is learning, it validates the process and embosses the motivation needed for beating addiction. Ambivalent or hands-off family or friends is deeply hurtful to addicts in treatment.

Loved ones often get caught up in their desire to help the addict by taking over the addict's responsibilities and protecting the addict from life. Although done with the purest of intentions, this is a form of enabling, and it's counter-productive. As well, families should avoid providing rewards for completing treatment – remember our discussion of the negative effects of extrinsic rewards on motivation. It's OK to sit back and allow the treatment process to take its course, and to allow the addict in recovery to take responsibility for life on their own, using the life skills they learned in treatment. Providing moral support and being a cheerleader is by far the best contribution that families and friends can provide, and it's more than enough. No need to feel guilt for doing nothing more than this. Now, let's move on and talk about what happens after treatment and during the short- and long-term in recovery, and the important role that you can play in recovery and relapse prevention.

11

Recovery and Relapse Prevention, and How You Can Help

Whether you think you can or you think you can't, you're right.

– Henry Ford

Once your loved one has completed treatment your role changes somewhat. You can still have a significant impact simply by acknowledging and validating your loved one's recovery. Addicts feel deeply proud of their recovery – as they should – and it's hurtful for them to see family and friends acting flippant or dismissive about their recovery and their efforts. In order to provide motivation-boosting moral support, the first thing that families must understand is that attending rehab is not a cure for addiction whereby addicts return home and carry on with life as if nothing had happened.

When addicts come home from treatment, they're still new to recovery, and some may not yet even be a month out from their last drink or drug. They've absorbed a tremendous amount of information and have (hopefully) undergone tremendous healing. However, they still have much work to do. We'll discuss in this chapter what that recovery work is, and where you can fit into it. In the meantime, it's important to understand that addicts returning home after treatment are somewhat fragile mentally and emotionally, still wracked by cravings and thoughts of drinking or using, and still unused to life without the one thing that was the dominant force in their lives for so long:

substance use. Maintaining their motivation and self-efficacy remains a priority, and an enthusiastic and understanding support system is tremendously important. Indeed, numerous research studies have shown time and again that an intact and active support system is a potent predictor of success in recovery.

Besides offering moral support, perhaps the most useful contribution that families can make is by becoming knowledgeable about addiction and recovery; exactly what you're doing by reading this book. However, family and friends who're knowledgeable about recovery must be careful about how they use this knowledge. Let me explain.

With the know-how about addiction, recovery, and relapse prevention that you'll come away with after reading this book, it can be easy to begin making "suggestions" to your addict loved one. As we've previously discussed, you must always remember that you are not your loved one's therapist, nor are you their recovery sponsor; you're too close to them for that. Your advice and suggestions will likely soon be perceived as nagging and pushing, and this can drive a wedge between you and your loved one. As well, it can make your loved one feel that you're being judgmental about the adequacy of their recovery efforts and know-how. It's the Chinese finger trap again. Easy does it.

If you notice that your loved one isn't doing recovery activities as you think they should, I suggest you avoid trying to push them into attending meetings, or doing their recovery reading, or talking to their sponsor. Although you're doing it out of love and laudable concern, it's counter-productive. Just like you can't push an active addict into readiness for recovery, so too can you not push an addict into recovery maintenance. By doing so, you're adding an extrinsic motivation – making them do their recovery activities to appease you rather than due to their own intrinsic motivations. If you feel that your loved one is neglecting their recovery activities, I suggest two options for intervening. First, you can have a brief chat with the recovering addict and voice your concerns and why you believe your concerns are valid, and then leave it at that. However, statements like: *I think you should go to a meeting tonight*, or asking: *have you talked to your sponsor today?* are probably going to be perceived as pushy and judgmental, and your loved one will likely get their hackles up. You can't do recovery for your loved one and you shouldn't try to.

The other way that I suggest expressing your concerns is to call your loved one's recovery sponsor or addiction counselor and discuss your concerns. Sponsors and counselors are experienced at handling such issues, and they're in the proper place to have frank discussions with addicts without the perception of nagging or interference. Unlike you, they have the necessary distance and detachment for having frank conversations with the addict.

Likewise, you shouldn't try to solve your loved one's life problems for them or otherwise do for them what they could – and should – be doing for themself. Part of their recovery involves learning to take responsibility for their past actions, and to handle life on life's terms. By taking on their responsibilities for them, you're helping them to avoid/escape life, and we know how that approach to life has worked out for them in the past.

Let's start off by looking at how relapse happens and how addiction counselors teach relapse prevention, and then we'll look at how you can be a part of your loved one's early and ongoing recovery success in a helpful way.

*

I've met, interviewed, and heard the stories of hundreds of people coming back from relapse, and I've noticed some common threads that seem to bind many of them together. My observations agree with the findings in the addictions research literature, as well as written testimonials that I've read from people who've relapsed, going back decades.

Understanding how relapse happens is important, so that recovering addicts can recognize the process in themselves and engage their relapse prevention "tools" when they see themselves headed that way. Likewise, understanding relapse is important for people who're close to recovering addicts so that they can intervene if necessary. My recovery sponsor is an older guy – in his 70s – with many years of sobriety and a lot of experience in helping newcomers. He amazes me by how he can almost smell relapse in people. Many times he's whispered in my ear at a meeting: *see that guy over there? He's going to relapse in the next couple of weeks.* Honestly, I've never known him to be wrong about it. Some people can really sense when someone is on the path to relapse. And that brings up the most important point about relapse: relapse is almost always a process, not a spontaneous event.

One study found that relapse usually develops over a period of at least three weeks, often longer. So, teaching addicts in recovery to recognize and arrest the process of relapse before it plays out is a cornerstone of relapse prevention. We'll discuss exactly how to do that, and how these actions can be planned out and practiced in advance as part of an effective relapse prevention strategy. The relapse process has been broken down into three distinct stages in the research literature:

- **Stage 1 – Emotional relapse** – at this stage, addicts aren't thinking about going back to substance use, and they don't want to relapse. However, their emotions and behaviors are funneling them toward relapse. During treatment, addicts are taught to self-monitor for the red flags for emotional relapse; these are represented by the acronym HALT (hungry, angry, lonely, tired), so that they can recognize trouble brewing and engage their recovery tools. The emotional relapse stage can be recognized when recovering addicts begin:

    o   Engaging in denial,

- Bottling up emotions,
- Not attending recovery meetings, and not sharing at meetings,
- Self-isolating,
- Neglecting self-care,
- Feeling restless, irritable, and discontent, and
- Experiencing thoughts of substance use to escape tension and bottled-up negative feelings.

- **Stage 2 – Mental relapse** – in this stage, motivation for recovery and efforts at recovery activities erode and the addict becomes increasingly attracted to the idea of returning to substance use. This stage of relapse is characterized by:

    - Bargaining (thinking up scenarios where substance use would be OK, rationalizing going to high-risk environments (such as parties with old drinking/using buddies), rationalizing relapse by committing to only "occasional" substance use, or by switching to a different addictive substance),
    - Cravings and pervasive thoughts about substance use,
    - Glamorizing or engaging in fond memories of past substance use,
    - Rationalizing connecting with people, places, and things associated with past substance use,
    - Downplaying the consequences of using,
    - Lying (this is a major red flag),
    - Convincing oneself of the viability of ways to control substance use, contrary to past experiences,
    - Seeking out opportunities where relapse would be possible, and
    - Full-out planning a relapse.

Occasional thoughts of drinking or using in recovery are common, and aren't in themselves an indication of mental relapse. You'll notice that the word "rationalizing" appears several times in the description of mental relapse, as well as the word "bargaining." In chapter 6 we discussed "cognitive bias" as a feature of the addicted mind, where the mind will bend the truth, warp facts, and ignore contradictory information in order to support what it wants to believe. This begins happening in mental relapse, as individuals ignore facts about the peril of relapse and convince themselves that: **this** *time it'll be different,* **this** *time I'll be careful,* **this** *time I'll control it.* Rationalizing substance use and downplaying the consequences indicates that an individual is well on the road to relapse.

- **Stage 3 – Physical relapse** – this is where addicts begin using substances again, in lapses and/or relapses. They usually engage in physical relapse after they've had the time to convince themselves that it's OK to drink or use again during mental relapse, and they've had some time to get used to the idea. They often plan ahead for the exact moment they'll relapse, usually during a window of opportunity during which they believe they won't get caught. I've seen lots of people carry on the charade that they're still in recovery long after they've physically relapsed. Often they'll even continue going to recovery support group meetings, but they seldom fool anybody for long.

During treatment, addicts are taught the stages of relapse and provided with an action plan to interrupt the process as soon as they find themselves on the path to trouble. The earlier on in the relapse cascade that individuals recognize and take action to interrupt the process, the higher the likelihood of averting disaster. We'll discuss these relapse action plans shortly, but often all it takes is a simple phone call to a sponsor or another addict in recovery and a little bit of honesty to derail the entire relapse cascade. Sadly, many people returning from relapse report that they recognized very clearly that they were in the process of relapsing, but did nothing to interrupt it, even though they knew better.

There are certain indicators that allow addicts to recognize that they may be vulnerable to relapse, or on the road to relapse. These should flag addicts to engage their relapse prevention tools:

- Feeling hungry, angry, lonely, and/or tired (HALT): We've already discussed the HALT acronym as an indicator of emotional relapse, stage 1 of the relapse process. The purpose of HALT is to allow addicts in recovery to recognize these feelings when they occur, and act on them lest they become a trigger for relapse. These are all self-care issues, so HALT should cue individuals to HALT what they're doing and take a moment to take care of themselves. Friends and family members can also alert their loved one if they notice self-care is needed. The HALT acronym represents being **H**ungry (not eating properly), **A**ngry (irritable, edgy, mood swings, defensiveness), **L**onely (self-isolating, being secretive, making excuses not to socialize, not asking for help), or **T**ired (not getting enough rest, overworking),
- Handling stress poorly, elevated stress reactions,
- Experiencing mental illness symptoms,
- Not participating in a recovery program, bad-mouthing recovery activities, showing contempt for recovery, denying a need for recovery activities, or feeling over-confident in recovery. These indicate a change in attitude and motivation for recovery,

- Reactivation of denial,
- Reactivation of avoidance,
- Irresponsible behavior (such as skipping school or work),
- Changes in routine,
- Lying, deceiving, becoming defensive,
- Re-engaging with or even thinking about dubious people, places, and things related to past substance use, and
- Glamorizing, thinking positively about, or talking about substance use.

Some people can just "sense" when something isn't right with the recovering addict. I find that family members, friends, and other people who're close to a recovering addict are really good at that. They just know that something is "off," and they have concerns. If you're feeling that way about the recovering addict in your life, you're probably right; my experience has been that family and friends are usually spot-on. If you sense that something isn't right and you fear that relapse may be developing, there are a couple of things you can do as your action plan.

Depending on your level of involvement with your loved one's recovery, you can either intervene yourself, or notify the right person who can intervene. Intervening yourself can be problematic, because addicts are more likely to be defensive with people close to them than with outsiders. If you approach your loved one with your concerns yourself, I suggest that you do so directly and honestly, explaining your concerns, why you feel that way, and that you think they should talk to their sponsor or counselor about it, or go to a meeting. This is most appropriate if you've been involved in your loved one's recovery and it's been agreed that you'll be part of their "red flag team."

The other option is to contact your loved one's sponsor or addiction counselor directly. Twelve Step sponsors and addiction counselors are experts in dealing with this kind of situation, so that you can step back and allow someone with the appropriate distance and background handle it. I strongly encourage loved ones of people in recovery to get permission from the addict at the very beginning of recovery to contact the sponsor or counselor when needed and to keep that contact line open. Now is the time to use that privilege.

Many detox facilities have a relapse prevention program, where addicts in recovery who fear they may relapse can be admitted for a few days to remove themselves from their situation, get some time with a counselor, and re-invigorate their recovery. I've seen a lot of recovering addicts check themselves in for relapse prevention during a moment of vulnerability or a crisis, always with good effect. Even just going to a recovery group meeting and opening up about their concerns is usually enough to derail relapse. In my experience, an addict in recovery who's in trouble ends up avoiding relapsing if they simply tell someone about it – either a sponsor, counselor, trusted friend, someone else in recovery, or a family member. Even a phone call will do it. If the addict cares enough to come forward and be honest about their thoughts of relapse, they care enough to respond to help. That's all it takes.

Some addicts in recovery cross a line where they've made up their mind that they're going to relapse, and there's nothing that'll stop them. They'll be defensive, aggressive, and remove themselves from help. They'll run away when confronted, not answer the phone when their sponsor tries to contact them, and disappear so that anyone who tries to help can't find them. When this happens, the old laser-focused addicted mind has taken over just like in their using days, and there's nothing that'll stop them from relapse. In a case like that you may have no choice but to let go and hope that your loved one comes back to recovery before too long, still in one piece. Remember, it takes some addicts several tries (or more) before they make it in long-term sobriety. Some relapses are brief, others are not. Sometimes it takes a relapse to shake up an addict to a deeper commitment in recovery. After all, even a brief relapse causes untold misery in addicts. I've worked with hundreds of addicts who've just come back from relapse and they're a miserable lot, even if their relapse only lasted a few days. Never once have I seen somebody come back from relapse saying: *that was awesome!*

*

Having an action plan is quite simple for addicts who feel their recovery may be in jeopardy. The number one action they can take is to reach out, and not keep it inside. I've observed two factors that seem to propel recovering addicts to keep their concerns about relapse to themselves, even though they know better: feelings of guilt, and a latent desire to relapse. Similar to their behavior during active addiction, addicts on the path to relapse may put on an outward appearance that all is well, even while they're roiling inside. I've seen people continue this charade even after they've started drinking and using again, pretending to be in recovery.

The most effective way for addicts to reach out when they're on the path to relapse is by calling their sponsor, or another addict in recovery. As well, going to a meeting and sharing is a fantastic way to halt the relapse process. When individuals come clean with another addict in recovery or go to a meeting, it's highly unlikely they'll relapse that day, and it'll most likely stop the relapse process cold. Coming clean about their struggles and their thoughts stops the secrecy (remember: *addicts are only as sick as their secrets*), and allows for the engagement of the resources needed to halt the relapse cascade and correct what's wrong. Sponsors and other members of recovery support groups are experts at this. Just getting it off their chest and letting someone else in has a remarkable effect on addicts who're struggling. Calling their addiction counselor is another excellent option, although – unlike a sponsor – counselors are usually only available during office hours, and it may take some time to be able to speak with one. My experience has been that once an addict on the path to relapse finally reaches out and comes clean about it, the relapse doesn't happen. A phone call can literally save their recovery.

Besides the two mainstays of relapse prevention – picking up the phone and/or going to a meeting – counselors teach addicts "The Big Three" relapse prevention tools for when they recognize that they're in the relapse process. These tools – all three are borrowed from the Twelve Step program – are designed to interrupt the dysfunctional thinking that drives the progression from vulnerability to relapse to the actual relapse. When the addict's brain starts making its owner believe that drinking or using is a good idea, these tools are effective for taking back control. They're simple, but they work:

1) **Remember when** – when the addicted mind starts trying to convince the addict that drinking or using was fun and a great escape from reality, addicts are encouraged to pause and think back to all the misery, sickness, pain, loss, and regret that their substance use caused them, how badly they wanted to stop, and how difficult it was to stop. Remembering specific situations that were especially painful during their active substance use is helpful. Most addicts have a few specific situations from their past that they use for their "remember when,"

2) **Follow the tape through to the end** – when the addicted mind becomes obsessed with relapse, it just focuses on "the party." "Playing the tape through to the end" is a mental cue that addicts are taught that reminds them to follow through in their mind and think about what happens after the party, the next day. They think about the guilt, shame, disappointment in themselves, sickness, and renewed obsession with substance use that will inevitably follow "the party." I always remind addicts that nobody ever comes back from even a brief relapse saying: *that was awesome!*, and

3) **Actively avoid high-risk situations** – it's true of any temptation that it's much easier to say no at the beginning than it is at the end. Addicts are taught to cut off high-risk situations as soon as they recognize them developing, rather than waiting and allowing situations to progress to where getting themselves out will be difficult. Many of the relapse situations that I've seen occurred after addicts allowed themselves to get into a situation that they knew damn well was high-risk, and they knew perfectly well that they shouldn't be there... but they did it anyway. Recognizing and actively avoiding these situations is a must-do relapse prevention technique.

*

One of the most important aspects of maintaining recovery – as well as ensuring that recovering addicts are able to live with a happy and serene mindset and function well in life – is learning to cope with stress. We must remember that addicts are people who, in the past, had escape and avoidance as their go-to reaction to stress. In other words, when times got tough, their reaction was social isolation and substance use. If they don't learn to handle life's stressors properly, they can easily revert to old ways. This is why stress is such a common cause of relapse, and why proper stress coping skills are so effective for relapse prevention. Remember, too, that there are other forms of escape/avoidance coping that should be watched for, lest recovering addicts who aren't coping well with stress switch to these. These can include such dysfunctional practices as "process addictions" (such as compulsive gambling, compulsive shopping, and sex or porn addiction), involvement in co-dependent relationships, and even such as activities as isolating themselves and watching movies or reading to escape reality. All are dysfunctional ways of shutting out the world in response to stress.

The various addiction counseling techniques all include teaching addicts skills for coping with life, all of which are drawn from the Twelve Step program and all of which have been validated by research. They include:

- Accepting that life may not always go well or as planned; ups and downs and surprises are simply a normal part of life,
- Learning to stop ruminating and obsessing over the past or blowing problems out of proportion by projecting them into the future (both of which are common habits of the addicted mind),
- Correcting low self-esteem by bringing together the ideal and actual self,
- Self-forgiveness, thereby ending the constant self-loathing that haunts the addicted mind, and ending the guilt, regret, remorse, and self-criticism that create constant low-grade stress,
- Establishing self-efficacy for recovery and life in general through vicarious experiences,
- Establishing a recovery support system through meetings, connecting with others in recovery, getting a recovery sponsor, and maintaining a social support system of family and friends,
- Self-care, including diet, physical activity, proper sleep, and proper medical and psychiatric care,
- Developing a self-identity as a person in recovery,
- Altruism,
- Anger management, and
- Becoming a helpful and productive member of the family unit and society.

One of the reasons that most addiction treatment programs are Twelve Step-based is because it provides an excellent framework for each of the above recovery skills. The fellowship that exists within the Twelve Step program provides an excellent recovery-based social support system, even for individuals who don't have other family or friends in their life. The fellowship provides a "culture of recovery" whereby members take on recovery as part of their self-identity, a key ingredient for success in recovery. Members are each encouraged to link up with a sponsor, which is an individual with years of experience in recovery who can take the addict under their wing and take them through the Steps and mentor them in life in recovery. Continued long-term participation in the program after discharge from a treatment center is therefore of significant proven benefit to the success of recovery and the ability to return to life with a high level of function.

*

So, what makes people relapse after all the work they've done to get through detox and withdrawal and a treatment program? Surveys of people who've relapsed showed the following common reasons: stress, negative mood, anxiety, drug-related cues, temptations, boredom, and lack of positive supports (e.g., job, family relationships, and responsibilities).

Making addicts aware of the common dangers of relapse has been shown to be an effective measure for relapse prevention, and is therefore a technique used by addiction counselors. The U.S. National Institute on Drug Abuse (NIDA) lists the ten most common dangers that lead to relapse:

1) Being around familiar drugs, drug users, or drug-related settings,
2) Experiencing negative feelings,
3) Celebrating positive feelings,
4) Experiencing boredom,
5) Getting high on *any* mood-altering substance,
6) Experiencing physical pain,
7) Focusing on getting high,
8) Having a lot of money all of a sudden,
9) Taking prescription medications that cause a high, and
10) Believing that occasional drug use is possible.

These are generalities, and some may be more of a danger than others for specific people. As well, there are other factors that can trigger relapse, such as feeling lonely, experiencing stress, and untreated mental health symptoms. Each person in recovery should reflect on what their own triggers are, and this is usually done together with a counselor in treatment. This allows addicts to take measures as part of their relapse prevention plan to avoid their specific triggers. For example, my big triggers are stress, and feeling bored. This meant that I needed to take measures to ensure that these factors were minimized in my life in recovery. Fortunately, the Twelve Step process – which I completed in early recovery – gave me the ability to handle stress in a much better and healthier way than I ever previously could, and this has been very effective in protecting me from returning to old ways to cope with what may sometimes otherwise amount to unbearable stress. I also took a graduated approach to returning to work and life in general, rather than rushing back into a full-stress routine in early recovery. *Easy does it* guided my early sobriety, and I still repeat that to myself if life gets a bit testy for me. As well, since boredom is a relapse trigger for me, I make sure that I always have a list of things on hand that I can do in moments when I'm alone with nothing going on. I've started a couple of hobbies, I always have a reading list that I'm working through, I take courses, and I have workout goals. That ensures that I always have something to do rather than sit idle and get into trouble. If I don't feel like doing one activity, there are always others on hand. Other factors aren't really triggers for me, so I haven't had to worry about addressing them. For example, celebrating a success or having positive feelings aren't really triggers for me, nor is having money in my bank account (which happens occasionally). However, for some people those are triggers, and if so they're well advised to take care in advance to ensure that they have measures in place to counter the effects should they arise.

*

Not all relapses occur on the same scale. Some individuals are able to re-establish their recovery early after a relapse, while others may continue with their renewed substance use for months or years. To this end, the medical literature makes distinctions about a return to substance use based on how it plays out:

- **Lapse** – the return to substance use is brief and not at the previous levels; this is usually in the context of the addict drinking or using again and instantly regretting the decision and returning to recovery, and
- **Relapse** – re-activation of the addiction; a return to previous levels of use and behaviors.

I've heard a lot of addicts refer to a "lapse" as a "slip." I generally don't use the terms "lapse" or "slip" for a couple of reasons. First of all, I don't like minimizing the impact of a return to substance use on any scale. The risk of overdose death is very high during relapse, and death often occurs during a "lapse." This is primarily because addicts in recovery commonly return to the same high doses that they were using during their addiction, and their tolerance may be lower so that their previous dosing levels may now be fatal for them. As well, even a single use of drugs is dangerous because nowadays addicts have no way of knowing exactly what's in the drugs they buy; the fiendish presence of the ultra-high potency opioids (such as fentanyl) that now adulterate drugs has become the norm.

The other reason that I don't use the terms "lapse" or "slip" is because regardless of how long the return to substance use lasted, there was still a mental process to get there and obviously something is going wrong with the individual's recovery. As such, I don't like making it appear like it was but a momentary lapse in judgment. Something went wrong in recovery that caused the individual to go to a place where there are drugs or alcohol, and put the toxic life-wrecking substance in their body. To write it off as a "slip" is to squander an opportunity to correct something that's not right. Rather, I use the term "brief relapse" if the relapse was... well... brief.

I've seen quite a few cases where a relapse was brief. This usually happens with alcohol; I haven't seen it happen quite so much with opioids and stimulants. I recently interviewed a guy who was three years into recovery from drugs and alcohol, but had experienced a brief relapse. He had gotten into a bitter argument, and immediately marched down to the bar. He ordered a beer, and took a few sips, immediately regretted it, and then walked away. I know he was being truthful, because I see him regularly and I know that he hadn't been out on a full-out relapse. Brief relapses (or "lapses") do occur.

One thing that stands out about relapse is how incredibly rapidly people with even years of recovery return to their previous levels of substance use, the same behaviors, and the same mental state when they relapse. It's often a matter of a day or two before they're right back to where they were before.

Another guy I interviewed – Tyler – wrecked his six years of recovery with a three-day drinking binge that started after agreeing to go out for "a beer" with a friend. That "a beer" triggered an immediate full-out relapse that, fortunately, only lasted three days before he checked himself into a detox facility. The evening that Tyler went out for "a beer," he went home drunk and his wife did the: *I'm not going through this again!* thing (and rightfully so) and kicked him out. He had very little money with him, and his wife (wisely) called the bank to shut down his bank card and credit card so he quickly ran out of cash and ended up drinking mouthwash by the third day of his relapse. He was sleeping on a park bench because he didn't have enough money to rent a room. When I saw him in the detox facility he looked trashed, and he was deeply ashamed and disappointed in himself (his breath smelled great, though). He definitely wasn't saying: *that relapse was awesome!*

Tyler's case illustrates how quickly a "slip" or "lapse" ("go out for a beer") can progress to a full-blast relapse, but it also illustrates a couple of other points that are important to understanding relapse. This guy had been sober for more than six years when he relapsed. When I asked him why he thought he relapsed, he immediately answered that it was because he had stopped all his recovery activities. About eight or ten months earlier, he had stopped going to meetings, ceased contact with his sponsor, and had given up on his other recovery practices. *Why?* I asked him. *Life got busy*, he said. *Besides, I was six years sober so I thought I was good.* Without his recovery activities, life began getting to him, and he lost touch with the recovery frame of mind. In hindsight, he said that he was getting quicker to anger, wasn't as good at handling stress, and began thinking about drinking again. He believed that "going out for a beer" would be harmless, because he'd limit himself to one or two and then go straight home. Famous last words. Unfortunately, his story is far from uncommon. So, as we can see from Tyler's story, the relapse process often begins with the decision – conscious or unconscious – to let go of recovery activities, especially ongoing participation in a recovery support group. It's very common to see relapse occur in individuals who drift away from doing the things they need to do to remain in recovery, as Tyler did.

The other important point that Tyler's story illustrates is how quickly the old addiction brain circuitry can be re-activated following exposure to even one episode of substance use. In Tyler's case, with the intent of having "one or two beers" this guy went from normal middle-aged responsible family man, six years sober, to drinking mouthwash and sleeping on a park bench and looking and feeling like hell in a matter of a couple of days.

Let's look at another story just to further illustrate. This guy – Liam – was a low-bottom cocaine and alcohol addict, nearly ten years into abstinent recovery when he relapsed. During his initial addiction he was using $1,200 a day in cocaine, and went broke despite having considerable financial resources. After ten years in recovery he had again done well for himself financially. When he was only a few weeks from what would have been ten years in recovery Liam was travelling through Italy with his girlfriend. They had stopped for the night in a little Italian town and were having dinner at the *locanda* (inn) where they were staying. In that town there was a specific traditional liqueur that had been made locally since the 19th century, and the innkeeper came to Liam's table and offered Liam and his girlfriend a shot of this special liqueur on the house. Liam declined, of course, but the innkeeper appeared nettled by the refusal to partake, so Liam's girlfriend pressed him to take it. *It's just one shot, Liam!* She knew he was an addict, but she didn't know him back in his drinking and using days, and she didn't understand the nature of addiction. So, Liam acquiesced and took the innocuous-looking little one-ounce shot. After all, *what harm could it do? He had been in recovery ten years, right?* Liam had stopped participating in his recovery activities over a year before, and that kind of thinking was seeping back into his addict's mind.

For the next three days, as Liam and his girlfriend toured Italy, Liam was completely rocked by an obsession with that one innocent little shot of alcohol; he could think of nothing else. No matter what they did or saw, Liam could only think of that shot of liqueur. On day three after the drink, on the plane to go home he got so drunk that he had to be helped off the plane in a wheelchair when they landed. So started an eight-month bender of alcohol and $1,000 a day cocaine use that again took him to his bottom. Fortunately, Liam is back in recovery again, with his life back on track.

Liam's story once again shows the power of a "lapse" – in this case a one-ounce shot of liqueur – to explode into a full-blown relapse. Even at ten years in recovery that one tiny drink was enough to re-engage the addiction circuitry in his brain, and his mind was completely consumed by an obsession to drink and use again. Even the arresting beauty of touring Italy couldn't get his mind off substance use.

Liam's story again illustrates the power of relapse. When Liam stopped doing the things he needed to do to stay sober – his recovery activities – he began a process that ended in relapse. Despite his ten years of sobriety, within a year of stopping doing what he needed to do to stay sober he had a lapse that became a full-blown relapse.

*

It's often said that relapse is a normal part of recovery, and I've heard addiction counselors say that. I believe that the reason behind this odd statement is the desire to attempt to encourage individuals to come back to recovery after a relapse, by reassuring them that relapse is "normal." Fair enough. After all, the shame involved in relapsing keeps many individuals from coming back to their recovery support groups or being truthful about their relapse, and it's good to help reduce that shame to help them find the courage to come back. However, I've never really liked the idea of teaching addicts that relapse is "normal."

This view of relapse as normal can actually end up enabling alcohol and drug use by suggesting that everybody relapses in recovery. Part of the relapse process involves cognitive biases that search for any reason to substantiate a bad decision, and this view of relapse as being "normal" can be fodder for the addicted mind. When the addicted mind is trying to talk an individual into relapsing, a little voice will say, over and over again: *come on, it's a normal part of recovery.*

I believe that it's more appropriate to look at it this way: *relapse may happen and often does, but doesn't have to happen.* It should be everyone's goal in recovery to never relapse. Personally, I've never said to any addict that relapse is a normal part of recovery.

However, if relapse does happen, it's important for the addict to be reminded that relapse is not the end of recovery. Relapse does not mean that treatment isn't working, the person isn't trying, or the person will never be able to succeed at recovery. Families and friends of addicts are usually in the best position to intervene and help the addict back into recovery following relapse, because they're usually the first ones to recognize the relapse, and addicts may be too ashamed to contact anyone outside their immediate circle of family and friends.

Some people relapse many times before they finally get recovery, and some individuals go to treatment a number of times. What's important is to never give up. Addiction is a virtually uniformly fatal disease, and ruins the lives of those who're still alive. I've met a number of people with a long and healthy recovery who were in treatment three or four times (or more) before they finally "got" recovery. Every individual is worth another effort. **Relapse must never be allowed to be the final defeat.**

As the first point of contact following relapse, those who are closest to addicts (such as family and friends) can be instrumental in talking them down from their shame so that they find the courage to return to their recovery support group, or return to a detox facility if need be, and to be honest about what happened. Pointing out that we can't change the past, that we must accept what happened and move forward in a positive way is helpful. Addicts should be reminded that even relapse can have a silver lining if they learn from the experience in order to make their recovery stronger moving forward. They should also be reminded that many people in their recovery support group (perhaps even their sponsor) have relapsed in the past, but they all came back to pick up their recovery.

Relapse can really shake and terrify those who care about the addict. Loved ones often throw up their arms and declare: *I give up!* And their frustration is absolutely valid. However, families, too, must remember that relapse must never be allowed to be the final defeat. Unfortunately, because of the significant mortality rate associated with relapse, sometimes it is the final defeat for some addicts. However, for those who survive relapse, families who want to help must adopt the attitude: *OK, it happened... let's accept that and move forward and get back on track*, and pass that attitude on to the relapsed addict.

When addicts relapse, it may be some time before they're ready to come back to recovery. In Tyler's case, he checked himself in – of his own accord – after three days of a full-blown relapse. In Liam's case, it was after eight months. I've seen many addicts come back to recovery after a "lapse" – a few sips of beer, or taking some pills, or doing a line of powder cocaine at a party. That seems to happen a lot. Some have to go through the same mental process to become ready to accept help as they did the first time around, but I've observed that they tend to do so much more quickly than before; probably because they already know that recovery is possible (i.e. they have self-efficacy) and they know how it works and what to do.

The impact of relapse on family and friends can be tremendous. The last time I saw Tyler, his wife still hadn't allowed him to come back, two years after his relapse. I'm sure there may have been other underlying problems in that marriage, but the relapse seems to have been the final straw for her. One person I know well – his name is Harmeet – is a crack addict who has been in recovery for many years, but has relapsed a couple of times. On his most recent relapse he just disappeared. He's very close to his parents and lives in an apartment in their house, but they had no idea what happened to him, where he was, or even if he was alive. They had the police out looking for him. I suspected he had relapsed, so I asked around, and ended up finding out that he was at a crack house on a binge. He'd been missing three weeks before I located him, though, and his parents were nervous wrecks. Fortunately, Harmeet survived the ordeal and found his way back to recovery, but his parents are still devastated by the experience. We'll talk in an upcoming chapter about how best to maintain your own health and sanity if a loved one relapses.

*

One recurrent theme about relapse that emerges from Tyler's and Liam's stories is that the gradual progression to relapse often begins when people let go of their recovery activities, even if they have significant recovery time under their belt. Let's talk about that for a moment.

Certainly, not every individual needs to participate in ongoing, long-term, recovery activities to maintain abstinence. There are addicts who've participated in recovery-based activities for a while, and then never again and never relapsed. However, it's very common to see people who've given up their recovery activities revert to old ways, and begin the downward mental spiral to relapse. I see it a lot. I suggest that to abandon recovery activities is to tempt fate with a potentially fatal disease.

As we've previously discussed, people don't walk out of an addiction treatment facility cured of their addiction. To cure addiction would require putting the brain back to its pre-addiction state, with all the substance-induced brain changes restored to normal. However, as we discussed in chapter 5, that just doesn't happen, as these brain changes persist for a lifetime. As well, there are psychological factors, such as a tendency to revert to escape/avoidance coping when life becomes overwhelming. No, addiction cannot be cured, but it can be maintained in remission. Addiction can be managed so that addicts can enjoy a full, happy, and productive life, but it can't be cured. The fact is that relapse rates are high, and the same conditions that originally brought on the addiction can easily arise again without proper care. This is why successful recovery requires ongoing care and attention, with what I refer to as "recovery activities," or "doing the things one needs to do to stay in recovery." Addiction isn't unique in this respect; a number of other diseases can be managed with proper daily care, but not cured, such as diabetes, asthma, and hypertension.

So, what are these "recovery activities?" Well, the primary and most important recovery activity is continuing active involvement with a recovery support group, which includes regular attendance at meetings. Other activities include reading recovery literature, learning about addiction and recovery, maintaining contact with other people in recovery, regular contact with a sponsor, and practicing healthy coping skills. I make no secret of my support for Twelve Step groups as the absolute best choice for recovery support. The Twelve Step program is heavily supported by independent research studies that show it to be – by far – the most effective pathway to long-term sobriety, and it's a complete package, providing members with the framework and support for all the recovery activities needed for recovery. Indeed, involvement in the Twelve Step program has been convincingly shown by research to be a significant a predictor of short- and long-term success in recovery.

I've observed in my research that ongoing participation in recovery support groups and other contact with people in recovery allows recovering addicts to keep their head in the game, to remember who they are in terms of their addiction. Healing from addiction and maintaining recovery gives addicts the privilege to live and function among normal (i.e. non-addict) people, but they must always remember that they're not quite the same as everybody else. They are people who have fundamental changes to their brain that cause them to react differently to psychoactive substances than do normal people. So, while other people may be able to go out for a drink after work – or perhaps do a line of powder cocaine, or smoke a joint – they cannot, lest they ruin their lives once again. Participation in a recovery group, doing their recovery reading and learning about themselves and addiction, and maintaining contact with other people in recovery allows them to remember who they are: addicts in remission.

As well, ongoing participation in a recovery support group allows them to belong to a "culture of recovery" that values abstinence and maintains vigilance against factors that promote relapse.

By continuing with their recovery activities, addicts are able to maintain their newfound life coping skills, and they're coached along the way. Having a sponsor and other individuals in recovery to talk to when life becomes tough allows them to avert mental crises that could otherwise get them into trouble.

The cost is too high when addicts wander away from their recovery activities. Based on Liam's and Tyler's experience – which is far from unique – I suggest that addicts in recovery commit to a lifetime of recovery activities. Of course, as addicts progress in their recovery they usually require less and less time for these activities, but they should always keep in touch with them. For example, in early recovery individuals require a lot of meetings, and a lot of contact with their sponsor, but the need reduces as they progress in their healing and build a pattern of success in recovery.

Attendance at recovery support group meetings is extremely important for the short- and long-term, and is especially vital in the initial stages of recovery. In fact, many addiction counselors recommend that addicts attend ninety meetings in their first ninety days after treatment. When the counselors in detox told me that, I thought they were crazy: *no way can I go to ninety meetings in ninety days!* I ended up doing 172 meetings in my first ninety days. Why? Because I absolutely loved the meetings. After being sick and miserable for so long, I could sense that the way out would be among these other people in recovery, and I loved the healing that I was experiencing through my Step-work. I was learning about myself, and I was learning how to be healthy and to never go back to that miserable existence. I loved the meetings. My family began to trust me again, because they saw me going to meetings and doing my work. After years of hearing my repeated empty promises, my words were meaningless to them, but my actions meant something.

It would surprise the non-addict to see how many people who attend recovery groups have been in recovery for significant periods of time. My impression of Twelve Step groups before I saw them for myself was that they were a bunch of drunks and junkies sitting in a circle whining to each other about how they can't get sober. However, the meetings are nothing like that. They consist of large numbers of people with significant sobriety – many with decades of abstinent recovery – who're there to help others as well as themselves. There's a rich air of positivity, and an altruistic attitude whereby they'll go well out of their way to help another addict in need. Their main focus is on newcomers.

The Twelve Step program works best – of course – when individuals actually do the Steps. Indeed, the recovery success rate skyrockets in people who do the Steps. That's because the Steps are a remarkable process that involves healing and relapse prevention – unparalleled in my opinion and according to the research literature. Although most addiction treatment facilities are Twelve Step-based, many only guide addicts through the first three Steps, meaning that graduates of these programs must pick up on the Step-work after they get back home. The meat of the healing occurs in Steps four through nine, and much of the relapse prevention skills are derived from Steps ten through twelve. Addicts who only do the first three Steps miss out on all that healing and growth.

As was mentioned in our discussion about the addicted mind, addiction involves an especially severe cognitive distortion known as the memory bias. This causes addicts in recovery to begin remembering their substance use as a positive experience, even though they were thoroughly miserable and desperate to stop. As well, the optimism bias is notoriously severe in the addicted mind, causing individuals in recovery to begin believing that enough time has passed so that they can begin safely drinking or using again. Recovery activities are the key defense against these cognitive biases that drive relapse. These activities help keep the addicted mind on track rather than distorted by cognitive bias.

Twelve Step-based rehab programs have the advantage that addicts are already familiar with the Twelve Step program when they graduate from treatment, and are therefore equipped to continue participating in the Twelve Step fellowship after discharge and – ideally – for the rest of their life.

Another useful approach to relapse prevention in early recovery involves the use of sober living houses. Returning to an unsafe place to live – i.e. an environment with easy access to drugs or alcohol, and many cues and triggers around – just makes maintaining sobriety that much more difficult. For example, for those who live in a home where other people are still using substances, or their dealer lives nearby, or other cues and triggers are omnipresent, the risk of relapse will be elevated. Sober living homes offer a chance to re-integrate safely into society, and to engage in a structured lifestyle of healthy living and recovery activities. It gives addicts time to get into a routine consistent with ongoing recovery success, and to arrange for safer accommodations after the sober living home. Most sober living homes offer inexpensive accommodations for up to a year, and provide programs for relapse prevention, such as support groups, on-site counselors, medication support, and relapse prevention training. Many individuals who attend outpatient addiction treatment programs live in a sober living home while they participate in the treatment program, and for a while afterwards as they adjust to recovery. My experience with sober living homes is that they're well liked by the individuals who live in them, and they provide an excellent start to a lifetime of recovery. I highly recommend sober living homes for early recovery.

*

As you're well aware by this point in your reading, addiction and mental illness are closely – even intimately – associated. Well, it's the same with relapse. Relapse of mental health symptoms can precipitate relapse into substance use, and vice-versa. As such, it's helpful when people close to an addict in recovery watch for signs of mental illness, particularly in early recovery.

Depressive disorders are especially common in early recovery and are associated with an increased risk of relapse. This association with relapse is likely because the low mood reduces motivation for recovery, and may push individuals to return to old ways by self-medicating their low mood. As well as depression, two common depression-related symptoms that should be watched for are the "pink cloud effect" and "anhedonia," which we'll discuss shortly. Let's look at why mood disorders happen in recovery, how to recognize them, and what to do if you recognize these symptoms in your loved one.

As we've previously discussed, addictive substances affect the brain by artificially causing massive over-production of "feel-good" neurotransmitters in the brain's reward center. In order to try to counter these abnormally high levels, the brain dials down its natural production of these feel-good chemicals. (Actually, it reduces production of the chemicals, lowers the number of receptors, and increases breakdown of the chemicals.) After addicts stop their substance use, the dialed-down neurotransmitter levels can take a while to correct back to normal levels. Until that happens, addicts go from having abnormally high levels of their feel-good brain chemicals to having abnormally low levels. The result is the opposite of feeling good – feeling listless, down, and depressed.

The good news is that the depression that may happen in early recovery is usually temporary – lasting 4-8 months at most – and is generally very easy to treat. Most cases are successfully treated with a low-dose once a day medication that's well tolerated. The impact of alleviating the suffering of depression is profound for the individual and for recovery. Some cases are tougher to treat than others, and medication doses may have to be titrated, or other medications used. Psychotherapy, particularly Cognitive Behavioral Therapy (CBT), has a role in treating depression, although it's very time-consuming and expensive to properly pursue. It's crucial for recovering addicts to recognize and seek help for depression, as untreated depression is a major risk factor for relapse. We know that treating depression can decrease cravings and improve a number of recovery-related outcomes.

Depression in early recovery can be masked by the *pink cloud effect*. The pink cloud effect, first described by Alcoholics Anonymous in the 1930s, is a psychological phenomenon commonly seen in early addiction recovery. It's a state of unusually elevated happiness and grandiosity in spite of difficult life circumstances. Most of the psychology literature views it as being undesirable and a negative influence on recovery, despite the positive feelings it entails. It's great to feel happy in early recovery, but the pink cloud effect is a state of delusional elation, to the point where it causes an inability to accept and meet life circumstances. It's dangerous to recovery because individuals can lose sight of and ignore problems, and become over-confident and complacent in their recovery. This may lead them to stray from their plan of action for recovery, and bring on the feeling that it's OK to drink or use again. As well, the pink cloud effect doesn't last forever – it seldom lasts longer than three to six months – and when individuals "fall off the cloud," they can fall hard.

It's important to distinguish between the pink cloud effect and the normal elation that people naturally feel from their newfound freedom from addiction. They're finally free from this horrible, life-consuming compulsion that had stolen their happiness. For the first time their mind is clear. Their time, energy, and thoughts are their own again, no longer sacrificed to fulfilling an obsession with obtaining and using their poison potion. Every one of their senses is alert and alive – they feel re-born. Long forgotten emotions awaken. They can live again, connect with people, and do things. Yes, they may have many problems to clean up, but they've learned how to tackle their problems one day at a time, so they're no longer overwhelmed. They've learned to stop allowing their problems to "own" them. They're learning to forgive themselves and even feel good about themselves, for once. They're feeling good physically and mentally, people and things they've lost are coming back, and they're slowly regaining the trust of themselves and others. So it's only natural that they're going to feel a little high on life in early recovery.

So how do we know if someone's riding this dangerous pink cloud? The pink cloud effect likely occurs because addicts' emotions have been anesthetized by drugs and alcohol for so long that the sudden awakening of normal feelings can be intense. There's a fine line between the normal elation of early sobriety, and the pink cloud effect. There's no blood test, no set way to determine if someone's too high on life, but it's usually clear pretty clear when things aren't right. The line is crossed when people have lost touch with reality, their emotions aren't adjusting to reflect their real-life situation, and they're in denial about their problems and challenges. Over-confidence in their recovery is noticeable and concerning.

If someone in recovery is experiencing the pink cloud effect, it's not really a disaster. They just need to be watched to make sure that they remain in touch with reality and don't get so cocky about recovery that they stop doing their recovery activities. As well, individuals who're "riding the pink cloud" should be watched for a crash when the euphoric effect wears off. This usually occurs about 3-6 months into recovery, and if the brain's neurotransmitters haven't yet normalized, the result can be a crash where individuals go from an extremely elevated mood to an extremely low mood, in a matter of hours. This sudden drop can knock them off their feet and cause a depression that will keep them off their feet. Obviously, this isn't only a terrible outcome in itself, but it's also a major risk for relapse.

Even people whose neurotransmitter system has normalized by the time the pink cloud wears off can run into problems. They may feel boredom after the high emotions give way to more modest feelings and stop doing the things they need to do to stay sober. They may feel despondent, fearing that something's wrong, and they may question if recovery is worthwhile – or even necessary.

It's proper for recovering addicts to be happy in sobriety and to be proud of their accomplishment, but when it gets to the point of distraction from real life and the necessary efforts for recovery, then it becomes dysfunctional and should be addressed. There's no magic way to directly address this, other than an awareness of the problem so that we can watch for it. Often people don't recognize they're "clouding," and might not be amenable to the suggestion. Gentle persistence and nurturing are probably the best approach. Once people accept that they're on a pink cloud, they can't be talked off it, but they can be talked through it. Discussing their immediate life issues and a plan for addressing them helps them face reality. As well, it's helpful to explain what the pink cloud is and how it works. They must understand that the high emotions are temporary and will end, so they can be mentally prepared. Close contact with friends in the know or a recovery sponsor is crucial, so that help is there for the fall from the cloud. Isolation is characteristic of a low mood, so this should be watched for. Missing meetings and losing contact with recovery friends and sponsor are also concerning symptoms.

Another mood-related phenomenon commonly seen in early recovery is *anhedonia*, which is simply the inability to experience pleasure. It's a common feature of withdrawal from substance use, and also a common feature of a number of mental illnesses, such as mood disorders (depression, bipolar disorder, anxiety disorders, dysthymia, etc.), schizophrenia, and PTSD. Anhedonia is another example of the overlap between mental illness and addiction.

Anhedonia is a common symptom in the immediate detox and abstinence period, but may become chronic, lasting months or longer. Although it can happen with any drug or alcohol, it's especially prevalent in methamphetamine withdrawal, due to that drug's especially harsh and long-lasting effects on brain chemistry. As with other depressive symptoms in early recovery, anhedonia results from the abnormally low levels of "feel-good" neurotransmitters following cessation of substance use.

Anhedonia is almost always accompanied by other symptoms, caused by the same low neurotransmitter levels. These are sometimes referred to as vegetative symptoms. These include low energy, lack of desire to even try doing things that are usually pleasurable, and a depressed mood. Because of the overlap in symptoms, there's a fine line between anhedonia and clinical depression. These symptoms are sometimes so severe as to make the person unable to function normally. Living that way is very difficult, and there's a natural tendency to want to relapse to resolve these symptoms, even if only temporarily. Some people end up experiencing the pink cloud effect, which masks these depression symptoms very well for a while, but some don't. If the brain chemistry hasn't returned to normal by the time the "pink cloud" wears off, the person can fall hard, and very abruptly.

Anhedonia is strongly associated with increased craving and intensity of withdrawal symptoms. Therefore, treating anhedonia could be critical in terms of relapse prevention strategies. We know that untreated mental illness is a very strong risk factor for substance use, and this seems to be in large part due to the anhedonia seen in many mental illnesses. Different therapies have been developed to treat anhedonia. In general, there are two main approaches: psychotherapy, and low-dose antidepressant medications that correct the abnormal brain chemistry.

Often a short course of a once-a-day, non-addictive antidepressant medication called an SSRI (selective serotonin re-uptake inhibitor) is appropriate, as it returns the brain chemistry to healthy levels. Usually only about 4 months of this medication may be required, maybe longer in former meth users. A medication closely related to SSRIs – called bupropion – has proven particularly effective for anhedonia associated with withdrawal. It's used as an antidepressant medication, and is known as an "energizing" antidepressant, because it tends to be particularly helpful with low energy levels.

Interestingly, research has shown that recovery support groups that involve face-to-face meetings also have a significant effect on reducing anhedonia.

It's good to encourage recovering addicts at any stage of their recovery to visit with their doctor if they're experiencing any mood disorder symptoms, such as depression, anhedonia, and anxiety. Trying to tough out depression results in needless suffering and an increased risk of relapse.

*

You may have heard of *medication-assisted therapy* (MAT). Let's talk about MAT because it may come up in your loved one's treatment and recovery plan.

Medications are available to reduce withdrawal symptoms and to help with relapse prevention for people with addiction to opioids (like heroin, codeine, and oxycodone, for example), or to alcohol. There are no such medications currently approved for use for treating stimulants or other types of addictive substances.

For individuals with opioid addiction, there are currently three opioid withdrawal and/or relapse prevention medications approved by the FDA:

- Methadone – opioid replacement,
- Buprenorphine – opioid replacement, and
- Extended-release naltrexone – blocks opioid effects.

Methadone and buphrenorphine (available under a number of trade names, such as Suboxone®, Bunavail®, and Subutex®) are known as "opioid replacement therapies." They're used to relieve withdrawal symptoms, and reduce cravings in people who're in recovery from opioid addiction, allowing them to better focus on treatment for their addiction. Then, once treatment has been completed, the dose of these drugs is reduced by a slow, controlled taper until the individual is opioid-free. At least, that's how they're *supposed* to be used.

Methadone and buphrenorphine work because they're long-acting opioids that bind to opioid receptors in the brain and block them, without making the individuals feel as high (euphoric) or sedated. They also prevent individuals from getting high if they try using other opioids, such as heroin, although this effect can be overcome if individuals use really high doses. Because the opioid replacement therapy drugs remain attached to the opioid receptors in the brain for an extended period, withdrawal symptoms don't occur, or are greatly reduced, as are cravings.

Methadone is usually given to addicts in the form of a powder that's dissolved in liquid to produce a fruit-flavored drink that's given once a day. If you drive by a pharmacy that dispenses methadone first thing in the morning, you'll probably see the addicts lined up to receive their daily dose of methadone. They must drink it in front of the pharmacist and then open their mouth to prove that they swallowed it. I've personally seen addicts outside pharmacies spit out their methadone – which they somehow managed to pocket in their cheek – and then get on the phone to sell their methadone or trade it for heroin. This just demonstrates that you can't force individuals into recovery. If they want to use drugs or alcohol, they will; they'll always find a way.

For individuals who've proven that they can be trusted, the prescribing physician will often arrange for them to have "carries," which are pre-packaged take-home doses of methadone, so that individuals can take their dose every morning without having to line up at the pharmacy.

Buprenorphine is – like methadone – a long-acting opioid used for opioid replacement therapy. However, it has some advantages over methadone:

- It's less sedating,
- Individuals can be tapered off it more quickly than with methadone,
- It's longer lasting, so it can be dosed every other day or even twice a week (rather than daily, as with methadone), and
- It's available combined with naloxone (which we'll discuss shortly) to prevent abuse.

Buprenorphine also has a better side effect profile than methadone, but it's a much more expensive option.

The drug naloxone isn't an opioid, but it's an opioid blocker, which means that it binds to opioid receptors in the brain so strongly that it removes bound opioids and prevents any newly consumed opioids from binding. Because of this property, it's used to reverse the effects of opioid use, which has made it a life-saving medication for treating opioid overdose. Naloxone doesn't work when taken orally. That's why when individuals take a buprenorphine-naloxone combination pill (such as Suboxone®) orally like they're supposed to, the naloxone doesn't affect them. However, if they try to abuse the pill by crushing it up and snorting it or injecting it, the naloxone will block the opioid receptors so that they don't get high. This is designed to prevent people from abusing buprenorphine.

Opioid replacement therapy – using the opioids methadone or buprenorphine to support recovery – is an often misunderstood option in addiction treatment. It was originally intended for short-term use (maximum of six weeks) to taper individuals off opioids in order to minimize withdrawal symptoms and reduce cravings. However, this treatment approach has taken on a life of its own, with many individuals remaining on these opioids for years.

I don't wish to disparage the utility of opioid replacement therapy for those who struggle with opioid addiction, but I have some concerns with it. First of all, opioid replacement therapy has become something of an industry. The drug companies that produce these drugs make tremendous amounts of money from them, so they encourage the long-term use of these drugs. As well, prescribing these drugs can be a lucrative endeavor, especially if they're not prescribed carefully and well. Before each visit with the prescriber, addicts are supposed to be urine-tested to confirm that they have no other drugs in their system – i.e. that they're complying with treatment – and they should be interviewed to check for side effects, symptoms, and how recovery is going. I have first-hand knowledge of a number of methadone/buprenorphine clinics that do none of that, not even drug testing. Rather, they crank addicts through like a sausage factory, often without addicts even meeting the prescriber. Essentially, clinics like that amount to a legalized "pill-mill." The prescribers make a ton of money, but they probably do just as much harm as good.

Another concern I have is the duration of therapy. In my research, I've conducted interviews with a number of recovering addicts who're on opioid replacement therapy. One recurring theme is how they end up remaining on the drug for extended periods of time despite feeling that they no longer need – or want – the treatment. I've heard from many individuals that their requests for their prescriber to taper down and stop their opioid replacement therapy were declined by the prescriber. I'm talking people who've successfully completed treatment, have good recovery and supports in place, and have years in recovery. One individual told me that he's been on methadone for nine and a half years(!), has had his requests to get off methadone declined by his prescriber multiple times, and feels that he's traded in one drug dependence for another.

Perhaps my most serious concern with opioid replacement therapy is that many individuals perceive it as some sort of a cure or standalone treatment for opioid addiction. Opioid replacement therapy should be used – at best – as a part of an overall treatment plan to reduce the risk of relapse in early recovery while the addiction is treated. However, in practicality, it's often used as the sole basis of treatment. I've interviewed a number of individuals who've never been to treatment, don't participate in any kind of recovery groups or activities, but who're on opioid replacement therapy. In fact, many of them admit that they're not in recovery. They may have switched to other drugs that aren't blocked by methadone and buprenorphine, such as stimulants or alcohol, or they find they just have to use higher doses of heroin to get the effect they seek. The rationale for prescribing opioid replacement to these individuals is harm reduction – reducing their opioid use. That's fine, if it works for them. However, for individuals who truly wish to beat their addiction, opioid replacement should never be viewed as a standalone treatment.

I want to be careful, however, not to disparage the value of opioid replacement therapy for the right individuals when prescribed in a careful and responsible way. Opioid replacement therapy has been shown to improve retention of opioid addicts in treatment programs, reduce the severity of withdrawal symptoms, and reduce opioid use (although it has been shown to increase stimulant use), mortality, criminal activity, and drug-use-related HIV infection. However, most of the studies that examined the benefits of opioid replacement therapy were short-term, and involved individuals who were actively involved in recovery programs. The benefits are less clear in those who remain on replacement therapy for longer than 6-12 months, or who're not in recovery.

Unfortunately, opioid replacement therapy remains poorly available in the U.S., where one study found that only about 12.5% of people in recovery from opioid addiction used these medications, largely due to accessibility issues.

The other medication that's approved for treating opioid addiction is extended-release naltrexone. Naltrexone is a non-opioid medication, so it's not opioid replacement therapy. It's similar to naloxone, which we discussed in an earlier paragraph. It helps with recovery by reducing cravings by blocking opioid receptors in the brain. If the recipient relapses and uses opioids the naltrexone will block the effects of the drug. Unfortunately, the recipient must already be detoxed before starting this medication, so it doesn't help with the immediate withdrawal period. Naltrexone's purpose is to discourage relapse, rather than relieve withdrawal symptoms. Treatment with naltrexone is often initiated after the individual has tapered off opioid replacement therapy.

The Internet is loaded with "alternative treatments" for withdrawal and addiction. Buyer beware; the vast majority are absolute scams, designed to prey on desperate people in the full knowledge that addicts are always looking for the "easier, softer way" out of their addiction. I would highly recommend discussing any purported addiction therapy potion with a healthcare professional knowledgeable about addiction prior to purchase. One such potion that deserves mention due to its recent rapid rise in popularity is *ibogaine*.

Ibogaine is a drug that has been getting a lot of attention lately because of its purported usefulness in helping people to detox from active drug use. The drug is derived from the iboga plant (*Tabernanthe iboga*), a shrub that grows wild in the rainforests of western central Africa. The roots and bark of this plant contain a number of psychoactive compounds, one of which is ibogaine. Ibogaine is a psychedelic and hallucinogen (like LSD, magic mushrooms, or Salvia – see chapter 3).

Ibogaine is used legally in some countries as an aid for withdrawing from drug use. It's banned in many countries, including the U.S., but is commonly sold on the illicit drug market. According to a recent BBC report, many Americans with addictions are going to Mexico to access ibogaine. While researching this drug, I found numerous websites selling what they purported to be ibogaine, accompanied by outlandish claims of its effectiveness.

At the present time ibogaine is the subject of intense interest – and controversy – because of anecdotal reports of its effectiveness in reducing withdrawal symptoms and cravings in people withdrawing from opioid addiction.

The controversy around the use of ibogaine as a treatment for addiction is based on four main factors:

1) The drug is somewhat dangerous, and a number of deaths have been attributed to its use,
2) The drug is illegal in the U.S. and many other countries,
3) As a hallucinogen ibogaine itself has potential for abuse and addiction, and

4) The drug has not been properly studied for use in treating addiction.

The ibogaine controversy requires proper research to settle the issue of whether or not it should be embraced as a mainstream part of treating addiction. However, there are a couple of barriers to getting this research done. First of all, nobody can patent ibogaine, so there's no financial incentive for big pharma companies to spend millions of dollars in researching the drug. Second, the drug's legal status is an impediment. Third, because of the multiple side effects of the drug, it may be difficult to get approval to study it in humans. The U.S. National Institutes of Health tried to initiate a research program for ibogaine in the mid-1990s, but the program got bogged down in licensing and commercial rights arguments and never got off the ground. The current position of the U.S. National Institutes of Health and the National Institute on Drug Abuse, who hold the purse strings for ibogaine research, is that the iboga plant compounds are neurotoxic and therefore unsafe for study in humans.

However, ibogaine supporters can take heart: researchers published findings in 2019 showing that they've worked out how ibogaine works on the brain, and that a version of ibogaine with all the therapeutic properties but without the hallucinogenic and other dangerous side effects is likely on the horizon.

While the research data on ibogaine use for detoxification for drug use has been spotty and generally of low quality, a recent small but well-designed clinical trial demonstrated "substantive" effects of ibogaine on opioid withdrawal symptoms and drug use. The study subjects were all people who had been unsuccessful with previous treatment attempts (not involving ibogaine). The study participants were followed at regular intervals for their first 12 months in recovery, and ibogaine appeared to help some of the study participants.

Although the focus of ibogaine use for addiction has mostly been for opioid addiction, there are indications that single-dose ibogaine may be useful for other substance addictions as well; specifically:

- Cocaine,
- Alcohol,
- Amphetamines, and
- Nicotine.

Ibogaine has not passed through the usual safety and efficacy trials required by the FDA and other health regulators, so users should beware of the uncertainty and risks involved. Indeed, there are some serious concerns about the safety of ibogaine use, including the risk of:

- Persistent psychosis – induction of symptoms similar to schizophrenia, which may be permanent,

- Hallucinogen Persisting Perception Disorder (HPDD) – random, unexpected recurrences of "drug trips," and
- Death – there have been at least 30 fatalities attributed to ibogaine use, but there may have been more, given that it's an illicit drug and is used covertly.

In the absence of FDA and other health regulator approval and all the research evidence that goes with it, there appears to be overwhelming anecdotal evidence that single-dose ibogaine does reduce withdrawal symptoms – including cravings – for various drugs of addiction. However, there are also some serious safety concerns about the drug. As well, since the drug is unregulated, there's no way of knowing exactly what's contained in ibogaine preparations purchased illicitly.

At best, single-dose ibogaine may be a small piece of the answer for addiction, helping people get through the withdrawal and detox part of recovery. Like other drugs it does nothing to take care of the underlying causes of addiction and the mental and physical damage that are caused by active addiction.

The reason that I've spent so much time here discussing ibogaine – which is far from being a mainstream addiction therapy – is because I've noticed that within the substance-using community there's considerable buzz around this drug, and I know that many individuals obtain and use it. My experience so far has been that it tends to be used by heroin addicts who use it to reduce withdrawal symptoms between doses of their heroin.

Earlier, I mentioned that there are medications available for treating addiction to opioids and alcohol. We've discussed the opioid medications, now let's take a quick look at the medications approved for use in treating alcohol addiction, of which there are three currently approved by the FDA:

1) Naltrexone – this is the same drug that we discussed above, which blocks opioid receptors. Well, like opioids, alcohol also activates opioid receptors, so it's believed that naltrexone may reduce the rewarding effects of alcohol and reduce cravings in some individuals,
2) Acamprosate (Campral®) – generally reserved for use in individuals with a more severe alcohol addiction, this drug may reduce symptoms of prolonged withdrawal, such as anhedonia, insomnia, anxiety, and restlessness, and
3) Disulfiram (Antabuse®) – this drug makes people very sick if they consume alcohol, so it's used to deter people from drinking. Even using alcohol-based hand sanitizer can result in terrible sickness. Obviously, it's only for use in motivated individuals, but even then compliance is an issue, so it works best if it's given on a supervised basis to make sure it's taken properly.

I advise that people should beware of the "Sinclair Method," a proprietary regimen invented by a physician based on principles and questionable research that are over half a century old. The Sinclair Method involves taking naltrexone before drinking alcohol in order to reduce the desire for more drinks. The idea is to help problem drinkers to continue with their alcohol use, but consume less. The Sinclair Method website claims a "78% success rate," but the statistic is meaningless because it doesn't define what "success" is, over what period of time this "success" occurs, nor where this statistic comes from. Although there aren't many studies examining the use of naltrexone in treating alcohol addiction, the existing research literature – all short-term studies of 3 months or less – found that taking naltrexone as in the Sinclair Method will help one out of nine people reduce or stop their alcohol use in the short-term – hardly a "78% success rate."

It must be remembered that methadone, buprenorphine, ibogaine, naltrexone, disulfiram – or any other drug – is not the complete answer to substance addiction. At best, drugs may help with withdrawal and may help curb cravings for a period of time. These drugs do nothing to address the underlying causes and effects of addiction. As such, any drug used for treating addiction must be viewed as only a small piece of the overall approach to bringing the affected individuals back to a healthy and productive life in long-term recovery. Unfortunately, I've seen many people put off addiction treatment because they place their forlorn hopes in the next new drug that "cures" addiction.

*

Now, let's talk about relapse prevention techniques that are taught by professional addiction counselors, the so-called recovery "tools" that addicts learn in treatment and in recovery support programs. Relapse prevention is one of my research interests, so it's an area I'm passionate about. It's truly heart-warming to see addicts in recovery getting their life, their family, their priorities, and even their personality back, so I feel that relapse prevention is of paramount importance, lest these people lose everything they've worked so hard to get back.

Fortunately, we have lots of recovery "tools" that work very well... *if individuals use them.* For people who've been through treatment and/or a recovery program such as the Twelve Steps, relapse almost always occurs after doing something they know they shouldn't have done, and when they ignore their tools. As we've discussed, relapse is a process, and often occurs because individuals made up their mind long beforehand that they were going to relapse. We can lay effective tools at an addict's feet, but the addict must pick them up for them to work.

The meat and potatoes of relapse prevention – or "recovery maintenance" – is teaching addicts actionable stuff that they can easily incorporate into their daily routine and use on a day-to-day basis to avoid relapse. After a while, these things become automatic, but – like any good habit – must be practiced conscientiously in order to be properly picked up. So... how do addiction counselors teach addicts to avoid relapse? Let's look at that now.

*

There are some basic relapse prevention principles that are common to the various counseling techniques and recovery support groups. These may be considered to be the "rules of recovery," and include:

- Committing oneself to recovery,
- Seeking healing by completing treatment, completing the Twelve Steps, and engaging in ongoing recovery activities,
- Understanding that relapse is a process, recognizing that process when it occurs, and interrupting the process as soon as it's recognized,
- Changing things in one's life that favor relapse (such as avoiding people, places, and things associated with substance use),
- Becoming completely honest with oneself and others,
- Asking for help when facing struggles,
- Adhering to the rules of recovery, and
- Practicing self-care.

There are a few types of counseling approaches in use by addiction treatment programs. Although they have different names (The Daley and Marlatt technique, Gorski's Developmental Model of Recovery (DMR), and Marlatt and Gordon's Relapse-Prevention (RP) Model) they're all very similar and operate off the very same principles that we've discussed in this chapter. The basic underlying approach is the same: helping addicts to see relapse as a process, become more self-aware, identify high-risk situations, develop coping strategies, be aware of cues that can set off cravings, develop a balanced lifestyle, and develop a lapse/relapse plan.

*

So how about a relapse plan? I advise a simple action plan, very simple. When addicts feel they may be on the path to relapse they should do all of the following, in order:

- Get to a safe place away from the relapse opportunity or trigger,
- Call their sponsor, or another addict in recovery, or their addiction counselor, or a family member or friend, *and be honest,*

- Practice "The Big Three" (we discussed these earlier: remember when, play the tape through to the end, and avoid high-risk situations), and
- Go to a meeting *and be honest.*

If they don't have a sponsor or belong to a recovery support group, then now's the time to do so, when times are good, before relapse occurs. In the meantime, if they don't have that and they feel they may be relapsing they should express their concerns to someone who knows about their addiction and understands – that may be you if you've established that kind of a relationship. Many detox facilities have a relapse prevention program, where they allow addicts who fear they may be on the path to relapse to stay for a few days, talk with the counselors, attend meetings, and stabilize their situation. So, joining a recovery support group, finding a sponsor, getting some phone numbers of other people in recovery, and finding out about local relapse "emergency admission" programs can all be part of an addict's overall relapse prevention action plan.

Once addicts have relapsed, they should check into a detox center to make sure they withdraw safely, and to stabilize their situation to stop the relapse. Once there, the counselors can help them decide what to do, based on their particular situation and the circumstances of the relapse. They may recommend a return to treatment for individuals who've had a full-out relapse, or close follow-up and improvements to their recovery activities for others. Certainly, the factors that led to the relapse should be identified and addressed. For example, if it was poor stress-coping, then perhaps doing the Twelve Steps may help, or closer contact with a sponsor, or taking a break from the stressful situation (such as taking some sick leave from work, perhaps). For addicts who relapsed because they don't have a safe substance-free home and environment to live in, or who lack a proper healthy routine, then perhaps a stay at a sober living home may be in order.

I've seen a pattern over and over again, where addicts relapse, and then don't listen to anyone's advice or opinion, and refuse all help. They stop drinking or using, but nothing changes. Once again, it's the stubborn addict's mind at work: *I can do it myself*, or: *I know what went wrong [then they state some simple reason], I'll just fix that next time*, or: *it was just a slip, I'm good.* Once again, it's the know-it-all addict's mind looking for the easier softer way out, and trying to maintain control. I've seen time after time people with that attitude going through multiple relapses until they finally let go and accept the help they need and open their mind to suggestions to improve their recovery.

When addicts come back from relapse and just want to pick up life exactly like it was before, they're doing little or nothing to address the problems that led to relapse. I always remind them: *addiction is a serious, uniformly fatal chronic disease; you can't just go back to life as normal and pretend that nothing happened.* Yet, many do, and I've seen many of them die before they finally "get it." When relapse occurs, it's because something's wrong; if that something isn't identified and corrected, another relapse is only a matter of time. Relapse should always be taken seriously, and never just brushed off.

*

So far we've talked all about recovery maintenance – i.e. relapse prevention – so let's now talk about your role in your loved one's recovery. In general, I would make the following suggestions:

- Give your loved one space to do their recovery; don't try to control the addict's recovery or do it for them, and don't try to impose your idea of recovery on your loved one. Addicts are responsible for their own recovery,
- Let your addict loved one know that you've read about addiction and recovery, and want to listen and learn. Create a relationship where your loved one feels comfortable coming to you to discuss struggles and concerns, knowing that you'll be open-minded, non-judgmental, and understanding,
- Adopt the role of recovery facilitator and cheer-leader, *not* recovery police and enforcer,
- Always remember that you are not your loved one's addiction counselor or sponsor,
- Take action (which we'll discuss shortly) if you sense relapse brewing or if you believe relapse has occurred... then step back; you can't control addicts who've made up their mind to relapse any more than you can control addicts in active addiction,
- Although regrettable, relapse is common in addiction, and may be a learning experience that allows addicts to do better next time; never regard relapse as the final defeat, and
- Do not blame yourself for an addict's relapse; addicts are responsible for their own behaviors and their own recovery.

*

After everything you've been through with your loved one's addiction, you're undoubtedly filled with profound longing for them to succeed in recovery. That's understandable; no one wants a repeat of that chaos and nonsense, and to watch a loved one train-wreck again. That's fine, but you must resist the urge to try to do recovery for your loved one.

I commonly see those close to addicts adopt the role of recovery director or recovery police. Although it's always done out of love and caring, it actually does more harm than good. If your loved one lacks motivation for recovery or to engage in recovery activities, then your pushing won't increase their motivation. Addicts need to be doing recovery for themselves, not to please anyone else (remember we talked about the negative effects of extrinsic motivators in the previous chapter?).

I suggest that loved ones resist the urge to become overly involved in addicts' recovery; it's proper to allow addicts to find their own way, for better or for worse. If addicts are going to make mistakes, they'll make mistakes, and hopefully they'll learn from them. It would be nice to hold their strings and manage their recovery for them, but that just doesn't work. Those who're supporting addicts in recovery should do just that: support their loved one. They should see themselves as cheerleaders and facilitators, rather than enforcers and supervisors. Once addicts have (finally!) accepted help, now's the time for family and friends to throw their support openly behind them. They're much more likely to embrace recovery when they see how it gains the approval of those who're important to them, and whose trust they want to regain.

I suggest keeping conversations about recovery light – addicts are often far from ready to discuss their situation. Allow the recovering addict to set the pace. They definitely won't discuss their situation with someone they believe doesn't or can't understand their experience. They're still learning to be open and honest about everything, including painful and embarrassing matters, but you may have to do some work to earn that level of trust. We've already discussed how to do that, but don't be pushy about it. Easy does it; remember the Chinese finger trap.

If you feel that your loved one isn't serious enough about recovery, or isn't doing enough recovery activities, then I suggest calling their sponsor or counselor. They know how to handle these situations and – unlike you – they have the detachment necessary to handle concerns with the addict. Once you've done so, I suggest letting it go and allowing the process to do its thing; your part is done.

I also suggest that families be careful to avoid placing expectations upon a recovering addict. Many people view treatment as a magic cure for addiction, and expect to get their loved one back in a pre-addiction state. However, addicts have been through a deeply traumatic experience, and they've brutalized their brain, mind, and body for a long time. Many individuals are only introduced to the healing process while in treatment, with the expectation that they will complete the healing and growth afterwards. Addicts may need some time and understanding to accomplish this. Many workplaces give their employees time off after addiction treatment, just like they would someone who's coming back from having surgery. It's healing time.

We discussed the addicted mind in chapter 6, and you've undoubtedly suffered under its cruel effects yourself, *ad nauseum*. Until proper healing has occurred you may again encounter some of the negative mental effects of addiction, such as inflated pride, a need to be right, and defensiveness. You may have to put up with these and other behaviors in early recovery, particularly if your loved one hasn't completed the Twelve Steps. However, you can expect to see a whole new person once they've completed the Steps under the tutelage of a good sponsor.

To avoid placing too much expectation on addicts in recovery, people must understand and accept that treatment doesn't necessarily make all the problems from the addiction suddenly evaporate. Indeed, addicts in early recovery may face a barrage of difficulties related to their past actions, such as pending criminal charges, the inability to drive due to impaired driving charges, significant financial debt, unemployment, custody issues for their children, and health problems that could be profound, such as HIV or hepatitis infection from past high-risk behaviors. Addicts already feel tremendous pressure to clear up the damage of their past and put their life together, and having family and friends put undue pressure and expectations on them serves only to create additional stress. Easy does it.

In addition to refraining from placing expectations, friends and family should avoid trying to solve addicts' problems for them. Offer help when asked – within your set boundaries – but allow addicts to paddle their own canoe. Avoid doing for an addict what they can do for themself, and avoid shielding them from the consequences of their substance use. Addicts must learn to take responsibility for the mess they've made, and find their own way to make things right; it's part of the therapeutic process. Besides, it's unfair to you to take on responsibilities and problems that aren't yours to bear (we'll talk more about that in section 3).

As recovery and healing progress, addicts become increasingly adept at handling their problems. As their mind emerges from the fog of substance use, they begin regaining their ability to think, plan, and organize. Whereas their days were once completely occupied by obtaining, using, or recovering from addictive substances, they now find time in the day to turn their attention to real-life issues. Patience should be liberally applied, but take heart: I'm always amazed at how incredibly well addicts in recovery are able to put together a happy and well-functioning life once again.

*

Honesty and forthrightness are important to an addict's recovery, as keeping secrets is a major path to relapse. To this end, I suggest creating a relationship where the addict can be honest and forthcoming with you about life and recovery. If addicts are hurting inside, or struggling with cravings or obsessive thoughts about drinking or using, or otherwise not well, we don't want them putting on an outward appearance that all's well. Better that they reach out to someone and get it off their chest; they're taught to do so in treatment. Often those who're close to them are the people addicts are least likely to be honest with. If addicts believe their loved ones are judgmental, or don't understand their experience, they're unlikely to reach out or be honest with them. If they think their loved ones expect everything to be lollipops and rainbows now that treatment's finished, that's the impression they'll always project. They don't want to risk angering or disappointing family and friends by admitting that they're experiencing struggles.

I suggest that the best way to foster a trusting environment where addicts will feel comfortable honestly sharing their struggles with you is to project the attitude that you're working very hard to understand their experience and struggles, and that you want to learn more. For example: *I've done a lot of reading about addiction and recovery so I can learn about what your experience is like. I could never fully understand because I've never been there myself, but I want to listen to you and learn.*

When you make yourself a point of communication with a recovering addict you have to be in the right frame of mind to do so. You must be able to listen without reacting with criticism, shock, anger, or being judgmental. That means you must be prepared to hear some things you won't like, or that may even shock you. You can choose how to respond to information: you can react with disappointment, or you can act with patience, understanding (or a desire to learn if you don't understand), compassion, and love. Or... just listen. You don't have to react or say anything. You don't have to have all the answers. I suggest always thanking addicts for their honesty and courage in sharing their thoughts and feelings with honesty. I always do, because when they have the courage to be honest it goes far to keep them from relapsing, and it shows that they're really trying. It takes great courage to be honest and forthright about unlovely things, especially for a previously secretive addict. That courage should be acknowledged and praised.

*

I encourage families to provide a substance-free environment. Removing drug or alcohol paraphernalia, and – of course – drugs and alcohol from the home is a matter of courtesy toward the addict's efforts to beat addiction. In early recovery it's much easier for addicts if they live in home without immediate temptations. They don't need to have their resolve tested unnecessarily. Now isn't a good time to keep a stocked bar, your pot stash, or even a bottle of wine around. I've been in recovery a long time, and cravings and desire to drink or use have long ago stopped for me, but my family still keeps my home drug- and alcohol-free. They do it out of respect for my recovery, and just to make sure that in a moment of vulnerability my home is a safe place. Although I'm not tempted to drink or use and I feel very strong in my recovery, I must always remember that I'm an addict and alcoholic and that I'm not bullet-proof. I'm just much more comfortable in a substance-free home.

The question always arises about addicts going to events where alcohol or even drugs will be present. I suggest that in early recovery addicts should avoid all such situations, full-stop. Later on, going to such events is acceptable, but I suggest that for the rest of their life addicts go to events where alcohol is present only if they have a good reason to be there. For example, I recently went to my niece's wedding, where there was an open bar. I had a good reason to be there. However, I was recently invited to a pub with some friends to grab some hot-wings, and I declined. I just don't put myself in those situations unless I have a compelling reason to be there. As far as parties or places where there will be drug use, I believe that all people – addict or not – should not put themselves into situations where they'll be around drug use. Certainly, for an addict to be at a party where there's cocaine about or people are smoking meth is an absolute non-starter.

*

So, what if relapse occurs? Well, it could very well happen. According to the U.S. National Institute on Drug Abuse (NIDA) the relapse rate for substance use disorders is 40-60%. However, I would like to qualify that statistic. That number encompasses all addicts, regardless of what their recovery looks like. My experience has been that the relapse rates are much lower in individuals who are intrinsically motivated for recovery (i.e. they attend treatment willingly, are enthusiastic about recovery, and are engaged in the treatment and recovery process) versus those who are there for extrinsic motivations (i.e. because of a court order, to please a family member, or to keep their job). As well, those who engage in recovery activities (attend meetings, complete the Twelve Steps, maintain regular contact with a sponsor, etc.) have a far better chance of success than those who carry on in recovery without those crucial supports in place. As well, other factors further lower the risk of relapse, such as getting proper medical care for co-occurring mental illness, and having a social support system in place. Even among people who participate in a Twelve Step program after discharge from treatment, my experience has been that those who complete the Steps do much better in recovery than do those who just attend meetings. So, as scary as the 40-60% relapse rate sounds, it cannot be applied to every individual. The rate will be much lower for those who're motivated to maintain recovery and who engage in doing the things they need to do to stay sober.

Hopefully your loved one won't relapse, but if it does happen it may be the learning experience that was needed to take recovery more seriously. Some addicts relapse several times or more before they finally get recovery right. I watched a friend of mine progressively destroy his life with cocaine and alcohol as he repeatedly failed in his attempts to get sober. He would check into a detox center and get a few months of sobriety under his belt, but would then relapse. I watched as he cycled through this process at least a dozen times, but I always held out hope for him. During his short bouts of sobriety he would attend Twelve Step meetings and say all the right things, but then he would drop off and disappear. Finally, he "got it." At one point something clicked in his mind, and rather than simply attending meetings he got himself a good sponsor, did the Twelve Steps (for the first time), and applied himself to all the Twelve Step program has to offer. I'm pleased to say that he recently celebrated three years of strong and stable recovery, his family is back together again, and he's a happy and productive member of society again. In fact, he has helped many other people struggling with addiction find their way to recovery. He's a perfect example that relapse – even multiple relapses – isn't necessarily the end of the story.

You'll probably notice early on that something isn't right with your loved one once the relapse process has begun. Addicts who are relapsing usually begin to act differently, such as becoming more socially isolated, more sullen, and more irritable. They begin to cut back on their recovery activities, and may even stop doing things that they enjoy, such as hobbies or fitness. Self-care may begin to drop. They may start hanging around with old drinking/using buddies again, and start going out on prolonged unexplained outings. You may even notice signs of intoxication and withdrawal. Addicts who're relapsing begin doing things that you and they know aren't good for recovery, but they rationalize and get defensive when you ask about it. The addict's brain is kicking in again.

When you recognize that something isn't right, I suggest that you approach your addict loved one and express your concerns in a firm, matter-of-fact way. As always, I suggest a non-judgmental approach without criticism and anger. As always, if it begins degenerating into an argument, end the conversation and walk away. You're there to express your concerns and suggest action, not to be drawn into a pointless argument. As you've learned in the past, arguing with an addicted mind is an exercise in futility.

If you confront an addict about your concern, I suggest that you ask the addict to contact their sponsor and/or counselor, and go to a meeting. I also suggest putting a call in to your loved one's sponsor or counselor to express your concerns. If your loved one wishes to discuss this further, then do so, but again stay in control so that it doesn't turn into a rationalization session or a debate. The addicted mind focused on relapse is just as good at deception, rationalization, and manipulation as it was during active addiction.

If your loved one avoids talking to you, I suggest not pushing the issue. As when your loved one was in active addiction, pushing is interpreted as nagging and serves to cause arguments without accomplishing anything. And it contributes to your own frustration. I don't suggest trying to control the addict's movements or otherwise trying to constrain them to prevent them from substance use. You can make suggestions and voice concerns, but you cannot control the addict who's decided to relapse any more than you can control the addict in active addiction.

It's devastating for families and friends when an addict relapses. *Here we go again!* The death rate is high in relapse, and the individual – who may seem to have been doing so well with treatment and recovery – suddenly reverts to the same old selfish, hurtful, uncaring know-it-all again. As tough as it sounds, a certain amount of acceptance and detachment is necessary to preserve your sanity; we'll discuss that in detail in the next section.

I suggest that loved ones of addicts who relapse keep in mind a few things: 1) addiction is a disease with a high relapse rate, 2) relapse often provides addicts with the lesson they need to succeed next time around, and 3) relapse must never be allowed to be the final defeat. As well, your loved one's relapse does not mean that you have failed. Too many family members and friends take their loved one's relapse upon themselves: *what did I do wrong?* or: *I should have made him go to meetings*, or: *I stressed her out too much,* or: *I pushed her too hard*, or: *it's my fault for kicking him out of the house.* Of course, that's all nonsense; addicts are responsible for their own actions, including relapse. They relapsed because they have a disease, and it wasn't being adequately managed. The addict is responsible for managing their disease, just as diabetics are responsible for managing theirs. Nobody poured the drink down their throat or put the needle in their arm. To beat oneself up over a loved one's relapse is wasted brain-power, and counterproductive. Addicts need healthy, high functioning family members, not nervous wrecks wracked by guilt and self-blame.

*

One of the themes of this book is that addiction is a family disease, and those who're hurt most by it are usually those who're closest to the addict. Many of those who care about addicts are left with significant issues as a result of the trauma of caring about someone who doesn't care about themself. Unfortunately, all the focus is on getting the addicts help, but addicts definitely shouldn't be the sole focus. We'll discuss *your* needs and *your* healing in the next section, but for now, let's talk about how the negative effects of someone else's substance use may affect your ability to be a positive part of that person's recovery.

Unresolved anger and resentment due to weeks, months, and even years of aggravation, worry, and frustration can result in even the strongest of us being somewhat quick to anger, and excessively sensitive to certain issues. Conflict in the home isn't good for anyone, including the addict, as the extra stress can precipitate relapse. As well, this kind of conflict threatens your ability to be a useful and safe contact for the addict. You want the addict to come to you in times of distress or struggle rather than keeping secrets out of fear of an angry response. That's why taking care of yourself, and recognizing and addressing the effects of someone else's substance use on you is important for the addict's recovery, as well as your own sanity.

In the next section, we're going to talk about self-care, and maintaining your health, sanity, and peace of mind despite someone else's substance use, no matter how tragic the situation may be. I've seen too many nice people whose caring resulted in them being driven into the ground by the selfish, wasteful, manipulative, and incomprehensible actions of an addict. It's as if they've handed power over their sanity over to an addict, who's insane themself. We'll talk about how to take back that power from the addict and how you can become even more effective at helping your loved one by doing so.

Section 3 – Staying Healthy and Sane While Helping an Addict

12

Challenging and Changing Your Attitude

For every minute you are angry you lose sixty seconds of happiness.

– Ralph Waldo Emerson

    You may be wondering why I saved the section about taking care of yourself for the last part of the book. It's not because the addict is the one with the problem, or because the addict is the one who needs help. No. One of the themes of this book is that addiction is a family disease. Unfortunately, all the focus tends to be on the addict, and the addict's problems, and what help the addict needs. Family, friends, and others who care about the addict are deeply affected and suffer from the effects of the disease of addiction. Many have their health, happiness, finances, needs, and mental health disrupted, and nobody seems to notice. Everything's about the poor addict.

    Not to worry, I didn't save your health for last because I believe that the addict is more important than you, or that taking care of the addict should come first. Not at all. Rather, it's because many of the ideas that we use to help addicts can be turned around and used to help you cope and take back your life and your sanity in the face of the chaos of dealing with someone else's substance use. Also, the foundation of self-care while helping an addict lies in having some attitude changes about addiction and your role in helping an addict, and these attitude changes are based on the knowledge that you've earned by reading the previous two sections of this book.

As I explained way back in the introduction, addiction is a family disease. I'm sure anybody who has an addict in their life understands this fully. So far we've talked about how addiction sicken the addicts, but now we're going to focus on how it affects those who care about an addict. Addiction rips apart the life and mind of addicts, but the ordeal of trying to help someone who doesn't want to be helped also tears through the life and mind of those who care about the addicts. Addiction affects addicts' family and friends physically, mentally, socially, financially, vocationally, emotionally and spiritually just like it does to the addicts. Addicts suck the people around them into a vortex of frustration, anger, self-doubt, and guilt, and makes them into people who do and say things that may make them not like themselves very much. I call it the addict's circle of chaos. Step into that circle – as people inevitably do when they try to help an addict – and calamity ensues.

I'll tell you what I've observed among the many families and close friends of addicts that I've been involved with, and you can see if any of it applies to you. I've seen those who genuinely care about someone in addiction become angry, frustrated, hurting, worrying, controlling, and nerve-wracked. I've seen them stricken with guilt, blaming themselves for someone else's substance use, actually believing that they somehow caused the addiction, or believing that the addict failed to overcome it because of their lack of caring or parenting or involvement. I've seen them so ashamed of their loved one's substance use and behavior that they socially isolate, avoiding friends and anyone else who may know about their "family secret." They put on a façade of normalcy, and trust nobody enough to reach out to share their struggles; if they do reach out, family and friends offer advice but don't understand the situation. They tire of useless (albeit well-meaning) advice from people who don't understand. Overall, I've seen tremendous frustration because they just don't understand why their loved one is throwing everything away over something that makes them miserable: *why don't they just stop?!?* However, most of all, I've seen the pain and hurt they endure as they watch someone they care about slowly self-destruct and seemingly turn into an unlikeable, antithetical person.

I've also seen loved ones of addicts get tired – really tired – of the constant chaos, the lies and deceit, the worry, the conflict, the constant asking for money, and the behavior that seems to get worse every week. I've seen them wracked with emotions as they struggle to find the right approach to dealing with the addict: *should I help them, or should I be done with them?* They want to help, but they just don't know how; nothing seems to work. I've seen people whose job, finances, and marriage have suffered because of someone else's substance use. I've seen people whose sanity is being whittled away because they have absolutely no boundaries. Mostly, I've just seen heartbroken, frustrated, and tired family and friends who understand the meaning of the terms "caregiver burnout" and "compassion fatigue."

It's natural to believe that once the problem goes away – i.e. the addict is in abstinent recovery – that all will be well again, including with those who've just survived the ordeal of dealing with the incessant nonsense of the addict. However, that's seldom the case. Dealing with an active addict – which often occurs over a period of months or years – is deeply traumatic and leaves scars and hang-ups that affect those who endured the effects of the addiction long after their loved one's last drink or drug. As well, life with an addict in recovery isn't necessarily all rainbows and unicorns; there may be a monstrous mess to clean up in the addict's life – financial ruin, joblessness, criminal charges, and so on – and the constant fear that the addict will relapse can be haunting. Fear, anxiety, worry, even paranoia may haunt the loved ones of an addict in recovery for a long time. The self-blame can endure as well. The attitude that: *I'll be fine if only they stop their drug use* is a troubling red flag, because it indicates that individuals haven't recognized the effects of the addiction on themselves, and that they've assigned their happiness to someone else's behavior.

When I become involved in the care of an addict, it's not just the addict who's my patient, it's also those around the addict who care and have been trying their utmost to help. So, one of the first things I try to accomplish in these individuals is a change in their attitude toward addiction and their role in helping the addict. Let's talk about a healthy attitude change, for your sake and for the better of those around you.

So, the next three chapters are about *you*; *your* recovery from the effects of someone else's addiction, and regaining *your* sanity and *your* life. The funny thing is that taking care of yourself and healing from and protecting yourself from the effects of addiction is far from selfish; in fact, when you're healthy, happy, at peace, and fulfilled, you're much better equipped to help the addict. We'll look at three pieces of the puzzle in terms of helping you to reclaim your sanity from someone else's substance use: adopting the proper attitudes, setting boundaries, and self-care. In this chapter, we'll talk about adopting attitudes that will help you stay sane and healthy, and better able to help an addict.

*

When I speak of "attitude," I'm referring to our perspective about something, our understanding of it and how it works. Changing our attitude about a problem allows us to use our newfound understanding to re-orient ourselves toward the problem and change how we view the problem, how we go about solving the problem, and how the problem affects us. When we change our attitude about these things, we can see that we have alternatives – choices – that we can make about how we react to the problem. In this case, the problem is someone else's substance use and how we help them. By changing our attitude about this problem, we can see that we have other choices than simply reacting to the addict's behaviors and being drawn into the addict's circle of chaos.

There are three attitudes that I'd like to discuss in this chapter, based on the information that we've discussed in the previous sections of this book. The three attitudes are:

1) Our attitude about the nature of addiction,
2) Our attitude about addicts, and
3) Our attitude about our role and how we go about helping an addict.

The attitude change that enables those who wish to help an addict reclaim their sanity and better help their addict loved one involves understanding and accepting certain facts:

- Addiction is a brain disease, caused by the toxic effects of repeated substance use on the brain; addiction isn't caused by you,
- Addiction is a progressive disease,
- Addicts can't control their substance use, and you can't control an addict's substance use either,
- Addiction can't be cured, but it can be successfully managed,
- If you're not happy, healthy, taking care of yourself, and functioning well, then you're not much good to yourself, to other people who need you, and to the addict you're trying to help,
- We are responsible for our own behaviors, not anyone else's,
- Covering for addicts, making excuses for their behavior, shielding them from the consequences of their actions, and taking over their responsibilities (except for the most essential ones, such as child care) amounts to participating in and enabling the addiction, and is unfair to you,
- Allowing another individual to decide whether you're happy or having a good day is giving away way too much power over yourself to that individual, and is especially foolhardy when that other individual is an addict of unsound mind. You deserve contentment, happiness, and peace of mind, whether the addict is drinking or using or not,
- The key to maintaining your sanity is to step outside the addict's circle of chaos and to stop participating in the addiction,
- Our sanity is best preserved by stopping our focus on the addict's behavior – something we can't control – and instead focusing on ourselves and how we react to the addict – something we can control,
- Addicts cannot be pushed into treatment and recovery; to succeed they must be ready, willing, and motivated,
- The responsibility to overcome addiction is the addict's, not yours, and
- You cannot do treatment and recovery for an addict; they must do it themself.

Before you decide to change your attitude, it's helpful to take a step back and examine your current attitude. The best way to do this is to look at how you react to the addict in your life. In particular, how has your life changed because of someone else's substance use, and how much of the chaos of the addict's life has spilled over into yours? Have you been taking the consequences of someone else's substance use upon yourself? It's true that when we take care of ourselves, we have much more to bring to other people we wish to help. So, have you been taking care of yourself? Are you filled with frustration, anger, resentment, and do you bring that to your relationships with other people? Based on your reading so far, has your approach to helping the addict been smart and informed?

Addicts are people with dysfunctional coping mechanisms, but how are *your* coping mechanisms? How are you handling the stress of dealing with an addict? Are you able to lay your head down at the end of the day and fall asleep with your mind at peace? Have you been "dealing with" this unusually intense stress by not dealing with it at all?

Some addicts have traumatic events in their past that have made them unhappy people, and may have contributed to their substance use. How about you? Do you have unhappy or traumatic memories that are unresolved in your mind, and continue to be a daily source of unhappiness for you? Are past traumatic events still dictating how you react to people and things in the present? Is the trauma of dealing with an addict affecting how you react to other people and situations?

People who're close to addicts often believe that once their loved one is sober and in stable recovery, life will be rosy again and they'll be happy and at peace. Many are surprised to find that they're still nervous wrecks. That's because they've been through an unnatural, prolonged, traumatic event, and the effects don't go away just because the event has ended. Addicts go to rehab to get their psychological issues addressed, but family members don't. I suggest that those who care for people in addiction take measures to get themselves well and take their life and sanity back, whether or not their loved one is in recovery. The time is now to get well and to stop being a victim of someone else's substance use; don't wait until the addict is in recovery.

For those who've been affected by someone else's substance use, I suggest that they start out by taking a step back and looking at how they react to their loved one's substance use, and how it has affected their life. I see many family and friends of addicts get sucked into a vortex of anger, unhappiness, anxiety, and dysfunction, yet they're so focused on the addict that they don't even fully realize how badly they themselves have been affected.

Try reflecting on a few questions for a little while, and answer them as truthfully as you can. Perhaps ask someone who's close to you what they think your answer should be. The questions:

- Have you been suppressing your emotions or feelings, and hiding them from others?
- Do you put on a false front in public?
- Are you in denial of the addict's problem; do you accept the addict's repeated promises because you want so badly for them to be true?
- Are you always on edge, suspicious, anxious, and alert about what the addict is doing?
- Are you able to work, spend time relaxing, and enjoy yourself without the addict's behavior being on your mind?
- Is the addict in your life placing expectations upon you that you're not comfortable with?
- Are you helping the addict with their problems, or are you taking their problems upon yourself?
- Do you take time for self-care? Do you do nice things for yourself? Are you able to enjoy yourself? Do you feel guilty when you do nice things for yourself?
- Do you get in arguments with or lie to other people because you're defending the addict's unacceptable behavior?
- Are you happy? Do you have peace of mind?

Now, ask yourself one overall question: *have you surrendered control of your happiness and peace of mind to an addict?*

*

By this point in our overview of addiction, you've (hopefully, if I've done my job right) learned a lot about the science and experience of addiction. During much of my fifteen years in practice as a doctor I was involved in medical education at two universities, and I can say with certainty that by this point in your reading, and from your own experiences with an addict, you know more about the science and nature of addiction – much more – than the vast majority of doctors. So, let's take that knowledge and look at how it can change your attitude toward addiction, addicts, and your role in helping an addict. Then, we'll take that attitude and look at how it opens new options for dealing with an addict.

The first attitude that's important to adopt is that: *you did not cause your loved one's addiction.* As we've previously discussed, the addicted mind characteristically sees itself as a victim of other people, the world, and life in general: *why is this happening to me?* Because their behavior is so far removed from their beliefs about how a good person should act, addicts feel tremendous guilt about their substance use and related behaviors (remember our discussion about cognitive dissonance in chapter 6). In order to lessen this self-guilt, the addicted mind seeks to blame others for the substance use and all the antics. Unfortunately, addicts' favorite target for their blamethrower is usually the people closest to them: *you'd drink, too, if you had my wife*, or: *I'm like this because of how you treat me*.

Addicts are masters of manipulation, and they seek enablers. A great way to lasso an enabler for their substance use is to use guilt, by making the other person feel like they're responsible for the addiction. When they hit on something that bothers you or you feel guilty about, they'll push it. When you hear such accusations they may get inside your head and you may even begin believing them. If the addict in your life happens to hit a raw nerve – something you already felt guilty about – then all the better. However, as you now know, people obsessively drink or use drugs because they have a disease, not because anyone caused it. Even in the beginning, before the addiction developed, using substances to deal with problems is dysfunctional and is caused by how individuals choose to deal with what bothers them. There's always another way to handle problems than by picking up that first drink or drug. Many people in this world have serious problems, afflictions, past or present traumas, and family conflict, but most do not use substances to deal with their problems. Addiction occurs as a result of brain changes from repeated exposure to toxic addictive substances, not because of any particular person or thing.

Feeling guilt about another person's addiction is a major cause of enabling behaviors, and a major tool of manipulation employed by the addicted mind. And it's utter nonsense. We'll talk more about blaming ourselves for someone else's addiction shortly. Addicts may also manipulate you by making false promises that play on your guilt: *give me some money for my rent, and I promise I'll go get help*. They have no intention of getting help, or else they wouldn't be making it conditional on your largesse. Rather, they know you'll feel guilty and blame yourself if you don't hand over the cash. Shedding ourselves of guilt for something that isn't our fault (addiction) and isn't our responsibility (the addict accepting help) is a major step to ending being an enabler, and to getting our peace of mind back.

Another fact to add to a proper attitude toward addiction is that: *you cannot control someone else' substance use*. The addict can't control it, and neither can you. Trying to control or stop addicts' substance use by scolding, arguing, reasoning, pleading, exposing their stashes, catching them in lies, following them around, snooping their phone, or locking them down and babysitting them won't stop their substance use, and won't solve the problem. Believe me, an addict who's determined to drink or use will find a way, no matter what. Such Herculean efforts at stopping the addict's substance use play a huge role in robbing us of our peace of mind and happiness, and it does zero to help end the addiction. It just draws us into the chaos. We're surrendering our sanity to the control of the addict, all for nothing. We're dealing with an incurable disease, and even locking addicts into a padded room won't address the root of the problem. As you well know by now, the only way to arrest addiction is by the willing participation of an addict in a treatment program that addresses the causes and effects of substance use on the brain and mind.

Addicts are unable to control or stop their substance use – otherwise it's not an addiction. That's in the medical definition of addiction (i.e. "substance use disorder") – an inability to control substance use. We, too, must accept that we can't control an addict's substance use, either. As long as anyone clings to the delusion that they can control their loved one's substance use, cure the addiction, or "fix" the addict, then they'll continue to fight a battle they cannot win. They succeed only in expending tremendous energy at the expense of their own needs and their sanity. In the process, such efforts create an ever-widening barrier between the addict and the loved one that further impairs their ability to help the addict. As we've discussed in the previous sections of this book, it's much better to act smarter rather than act harder. Now's the time for brains, not brawn. Easy does it.

Most people who try to help an addict try too hard. Just like Chinese finger trap teaches us, sometimes obeying our instincts to struggle harder and harder is the wrong way to solve a problem. Sometimes problems are best solved by going against our instincts and not trying to battle our way out of a problem. Helping an addict is like that. Like the Chinese finger trap, addiction is not solved by pushing harder and harder.

Addicts become so obsessed with obtaining and using their drug that they can't think about anything else, and the same thing can happen to those who care about them. When people really care about an addict, their caring causes them to become so preoccupied with whether or not the addict is using, what the addict is doing, and how to get the addict to stop that they have trouble focusing on anything else. It becomes an obsession, of sorts. While these efforts are all done with the best of intentions, the anxiety related to caring about an addict can cause poor sleep, appetite changes, difficulty concentrating, and anhedonia (yes, the same inability to feel pleasure that addicts experience). Work suffers, things that need attention go undone, money and time are wasted, and self-care and health suffer. Marriages and relationships are strained. An attitude change and making new choices is needed, or something will snap.

As an outsider looking in, it breaks my heart to see families and friends of addicts self-destructing over their escalating and intensifying exertions at getting their loved one sober. However, as you've learned by now, these exertions are not only futile, but actually harmful to the goal of getting an addict into recovery. In other words, people are driving themselves to insanity and dysfunction, and worsening the problem while they do so. They're pulling too hard on the Chinese finger trap, and it's getting really tight on their fingers, even cutting off the blood supply.

Putting an end to the otherwise endless battle of trying to control the addict and the substance use starts by changing our attitude about how we can help the addict. If your past approach to helping the addict in your life has drawn your own life into the addict's circle of chaos, you may have suffered unfairly from the consequences of the addict's actions, and it may have cost you much. That would be an acceptable sacrifice – perhaps – if it were actually helping the addict, but it's not; it's actually alienating the addict and enabling the addiction. If so, perhaps you may consider having an attitude change about your role in helping the addict in your life.

By adopting the attitude that the best way to help an addict is not by attempting to control the substance use – by babysitting, searching for stashes, following, locking down, going through their phone, or pleading, arguing, or reasoning – people can get their own life back. Letting go of the preoccupation with what the addict is doing and how to stop them allows people to attend to their own needs and life. We do this by adopting the attitude that: *I cannot control someone else's substance use, and I shouldn't try to.*

Another attitude change involves understanding who's responsible for the consequences of the addict's substance use. If you've ever asked yourself: *why am I always the one who always has to solve all the problems,* you're absolutely correct. So, I'll ask you a similar question: *why are you always trying to solve other people's problems?* You may have been taking so many of the addict's problems upon yourself that you're exhausting yourself. It's fine to care about an addict, and to be hurt by watching what they're doing to themself, and to want with all our heart to see them get help and get better, but taking their problems upon ourselves isn't the way to accomplish that.

During active addiction, addicts behave irresponsibly, and don't seem to worry at all about their dropped obligations and the people who're affected. So, those around the addicts do the addicts' worrying for them and pick up their responsibilities for them. This serves to further enable the substance use and irresponsible behavior, and makes addicts even more dependent on and manipulative of their loved ones. People begin to believe that they must cover for the addict in their life, that protecting the addict is an act of love, just like when they protect anyone else they love. Those who try to cover for addicts and protect addicts from the consequences of their actions take on the headaches and pressures associated with those responsibilities, in addition to their own stressors and obligations.

Soon, the addict is pulling your strings; they become demanding, they place expectations on you, and act as if they're some kind of an entitled pasha. They've successfully pulled someone else into their circle of chaos, and found an enabler. They may have used guilt to get you there, or taken advantage of your kind and loving disposition, or made you feel obliged because of your relationship, but they've got you there. You're protecting the addict and taking responsibility for the consequences of their substance use, and thereby enabling the substance use and participating in the addiction. If you adopt the attitude that: *I am not responsible for someone else's substance use, and I'm not responsible for the consequences of someone else's substance use,* you can see that you have a choice in the matter.

In order to stop the enabling and to stop sheltering the addict from the consequences of their actions – and to take their own life back – people who care about an addict must set boundaries, and take back the ability to say "no." Not because they don't care anymore, but because they do care and want to stop the enabling. They want to stop being part of the addiction and start being part of the solution. We all have a right to take back our sanity from a manipulative substance user. It's finally time for boundaries. Setting boundaries is the subject of the next chapter, so we'll nail down boundaries then.

Part of the process of healing from addiction requires that addicts take responsibility for their past actions and put things right. Trying absolve addicts of responsibility for their actions or take on their responsibilities for them interferes with this process. That means that family members should let go of their protective instincts, where they wish to shield addicts by lying for them, covering for them, and making excuses for their behaviors and shortcomings. Other people usually know what's going on anyway, so these attempts are probably futile. Loved ones of addicts should carry on with their own life, and stop allowing the addict to interfere with their plans.

Likewise, the responsibility to overcome addiction is the addict's, not yours. The substance use won't stop until addicts are mentally ready – meaning that they have the willingness to seek and accept help and the motivation to put in the effort required to do the things they need to do to beat addiction. The responsibility to do this belongs to addicts, not to the people who love them. Of course, family members have a responsibility to help one of their own who's in trouble. If family members wish to pursue this responsibility, then they should consider doing the things I suggest in this book – learn about addiction and recovery, and make sure their loved one knows that they're there to put the addict in touch with the people who can provide help when help is wanted. Family and friends can extend the hand of help, but the responsibility to take that hand and accept help lies with the addict.

The substance use that causes an individual to become addicted occurs because they put a drink to their mouth or a needle in their arm, it doesn't occur because of what you've done or said. There are risk factors for addiction – such as genetics, past traumas, and so forth – but these are not causes. Many people with unbearable stress and horrible life situations never turn to substance use to cope. Likewise, many people with terrible family relationships never become addicted. The turning point for my addiction was the stress of my divorce; that was when I began using drink and drugs to cope with stress, and my addiction developed from that. But that's on me, it's not the fault of my divorce, or the judge, or my ex-wife. Lots of people get divorced and go through horribly tough times without turning to drink or drugs. However, when I was in active addiction and my addict's blamethrower was in full swing, I blamed my substance use on everybody but myself. It's what addicts do. Don't fall for it.

Misplaced self-blame and guilt propel addicts' loved ones into an obsessive, guilt-ridden, endless cycle of trying to take the problem upon themselves, and they make themselves sick with guilt when they find they cannot solve the problem they believe they created. This path of self-destruction helps no one. Letting go of useless and misplaced self-blame and guilt allows us to accept that outside help is needed; addiction isn't something we can fix ourselves. We didn't create addiction, and we can't stop it either. We're dealing with a serious pathological medical condition that requires professional treatment; it's not something that we can "straighten out" on our own.

Anyone who wishes to help an addict should come to an acceptance that none of us is all-powerful, and that there are things in life that are beyond our control. There are many problems in life where we need outside help. A loved one's addiction is one such problem. This is a serious, life-threatening disease that requires the intervention of trained professionals to treat. Your efforts at interdicting your loved one's substance use, or babysitting them, or screaming at them, or lying awake all night worrying are not going to solve the addiction. They're not even going to make a dent in it. Your loved one's addiction isn't out of control because you didn't try hard enough or do enough. It's out of control because addiction is a rapidly and uniformly progressive disease.

This brings us to another attitude change: *you cannot beat addiction or do recovery for your loved one.* Your loved one must become ready to accept the help needed and willing to put in the considerable effort required, and you cannot do that for the addict. As we've discussed earlier in this book, you can – if you choose to – help move the addict toward readiness to do so, but you cannot do it for them and you cannot push or force them into it, nor should you try to. You are not and cannot be their addiction counselor or therapist, just like I cannot be the addiction counselor or therapist for someone I'm close to. Addiction is one of those problems in life where outside help is needed – period, full-stop.

*

One of the keys to healthy attitude change is acceptance. While "acceptance" sounds simple enough, it's not always simple when it comes to hard truths. The fact that we can't just reach out and stop a loved one from destroying their life is a hard truth, difficult to accept. Hard truths are especially hard to accept when they don't make sense. When addicts are self-destructing for reasons that are beyond all logic, acceptance is hard, because we can't understand the logic of it. That's why having a knowledge of addiction helps us to accept the situation so that we can stop banging our head against the wall trying to control our loved one's substance use. We can take a more intelligent, ordered approach, so that we know that we're doing our very best to help in an impossible situation. Accepting that we can't "fix" the addict on our own, and that helping an addict is best done by pushing less and working smart helps us to back off a bit and try another approach, just like when we try to get our fingers out of a Chinese finger trap. It also helps us to regain our own sanity by extricating ourself from participating in all the chaos.

There are some things in life that we must accept, whether we like them or not, because we cannot control or change them. We're humans, and not perfect, and certainly not capable of solving every problem. When we can't change something that's going on in our life, we can drive ourselves crazy by obsessing over how we wish it were different, or by complaining about it. But what's the point of wasting brain-power over something we can't change? Rather, it makes much more sense to focus on what we can change. Acceptance is about not wasting time and energy fretting over things that are beyond our control. We can't control an addict's substance use or behavior; what we can control is how we respond to the addict's behavior. We'll talk shortly about how having a proper attitude about addiction and your role in helping an addict opens up choices for how you respond to the addict's behavior. You can choose to stop *reacting* to the behavior, and instead *act* in a consistent way that preserves your sanity and better helps the addict. That way your actions and your peace of mind are consistent and according to plan, not entirely dependent on what the addict happens to be up to today. For now, let's talk a little more about acceptance and your attitude toward addiction.

When a person has lung cancer, their loved ones don't run themselves ragged trying to "fix" the lung cancer. Why? Because they've accepted that fixing the cancer is beyond their control. Having accepted that they can't fix the lung cancer, the family provide what support they can, and do their best to make sure that their loved one gets to see the people who can treat the cancer. Everybody knows and understands that the average person can't fix lung cancer so acceptance comes easy, and there's no guilt involved. But the average person doesn't understand that the same applies to addiction, so acceptance is harder and there tends to be guilt involved. However, by this point in your reading, I'm hoping that you can see that addicts need professional help to overcome their disease, so acceptance should come easier for you. Like the lung cancer victim's family, families of addicts should accept that outside help is needed, and their efforts at "fixing" the addict are futile. Like the lung cancer family, they should do their best to get their loved one into the hands of the professionals who can help. As we discussed in chapter 9, this won't happen until the addict is mentally ready to accept help. You know what, though? Many of the lung cancer victims that I saw in my medical practice also refused treatment, and some didn't even want to know the diagnosis. They weren't ready to commit to the efforts required to go through treatment, or they were in denial, or they were just happy with life as it was. Many ended up becoming mentally ready and then went on to get treatment, but many others died without ever doing anything to address their cancer even though the opportunity was there. You see, addiction isn't so different from other diseases.

I'm not suggesting that you stop caring, or stop trying to help, or stop wanting to see your addict loved one get over the addiction. Not at all. What I am suggesting is that you use your knowledge about addiction to stop making futile efforts at controlling the addict, and instead take a more centered approach at helping the addict, based on what science and experience tell us. Until addicts are mentally ready to accept help, throwing money at them, arguing with them, cajoling them, babysitting them, locking them down, following them, reasoning with them, and forcing them into treatment will do no good. It's unfortunate, but you may have to accept it for the time being as something you cannot change with a snap of your fingers. In section 2 we set out a process by which you can help an addict become ready for accepting help, and if you decide to participate in this process then that's something that you can control: your efforts at properly helping your loved one. What you can't control is when or if your loved one comes around and becomes ready for help. So, I suggest that you accept what you cannot change and focus on what you can change. We'll talk more about how to do this in chapter 14.

People may find it helpful to let go of a problem that's beyond their control by handing it over to God (if they are people of a faith), or to fate, or to providence, or to mother nature, or to whatever power that they believe presides over life. Or, it also works if they just take their worries and throw them up in the sky. That means surrendering their worries over things they can't do anything about. That sounds easier said than done when your loved one is involved in using substances that can be fatal, or engaging in high-risk behaviors, but worrying has never made a problem better or improved the outcome. Nobody has ever worried a problem away, or made a situation better by tossing and turning all night. However, when your loved one is slowly self-destructing with potentially fatal substance use, stopping the concern is impossible; but... stopping the pointless rumination and worry is possible. I suggest taking your concerns, sharing them with someone to get them off your chest, and then handing your concerns over to God or to whatever. Write all your worries and concerns down in a letter to yourself, and then burn the letter. Whatever it takes to get them off your shoulders and out of your head. And then let go of these things that are beyond your control anyway. Love and concern have their place, but we should never sacrifice our sanity for them, so that they dominate our thoughts and live in our head rent-free. We'll talk much more about putting pain and worry in their proper place in chapter 14.

Once you've taken a look at how you respond to the actions of the addict in your life, and you take on a realistic and healthy attitude toward addiction, the addict, and your role in helping the addict, you can see that you have choices. One of the themes of this book is that people's natural reaction to an addict – as it would be with anyone else in distress – is to go full-blast trying to help and protect that individual, but that's not necessarily the best way to help an addict. Addiction isn't like other problems that you run into in life. If you saw a loved one drowning in a lake you would probably run as fast as you could, and throw yourself into the water to help save them from drowning. That's great for helping someone drowning in water, but it's not the best approach to helping someone who's drowning in addiction. At first, they don't want your help, and they'll manipulate you to turn your desire to help into a way to enable their substance use, and they'll draw you into their circle of chaos at the expense of your own sanity and ability to function. Even when addicts finally do reach the point where they want help, the best way to help them still isn't to go full-blast into rescuing them; rather it's to put them in touch with the right people and then back off and let the system work, and allow the addict take responsibility for getting sober and working recovery.

Often, our knee-jerk reaction when things aren't going right is to try even harder to make them go our way, especially if we feel guilty because we think perhaps we're not doing enough. But when we push harder against things that we have no ability to change, the end result is even more frustration, anxiety, and sense of failure. Some people have great difficulty in stepping back and letting a problem play out, even though they really can't do anything about it. They feel they must do something – anything – and they push harder. Just like the Chinese finger trap, applying more pressure just makes some problems worse. So it is when we face addiction.

We discussed in section 2 how you can best help a loved one. If you're someone who must do something, *anything*, and push harder, try changing your attitude to see addiction as a problem that requires brains, not brawn. Make up your plan for helping the addict just like we laid out in section 2, and stick with it. Get your family on board. A gentler approach is much more productive, and makes the situation much more bearable, allowing you the time to take care of your own life, and the ability to reclaim your happiness and peace of mind. You may have to deal with addiction for a long time one way or another; are you willing to run yourself ragged and sacrifice your sanity for years on end? We'll discuss how best to reclaim your sanity in the next two chapters, but it all begins with an attitude change.

It can be difficult to let go of our instinct to act when we see a loved one suffering and circling down the drain. That can be especially so if the addict is one of our children. However, it's a simple life lesson: we aren't responsible for other people's behavior, no matter who they are, nor are we responsible for cleaning up the mess caused by their behavior. We do that for toddlers, not for adolescents and adults. We need to learn to accept that we're responsible for our own behaviors. Like us, they, too, need to learn that important life lesson, because recovery from addiction requires that addicts take responsibility for their past actions so that they can make amends, correct their behaviors, and free themselves from the burden of guilt, shame, and self-loathing.

*

In order to stop ourselves from being drawn into the chaotic action-reaction cycle – where the addict acts and we react – we can employ the simple technique of detachment. This involves detaching ourselves from the addict's actions (we'll discuss detachment in more detail in the next chapter) so that we no longer see ourselves as somehow obliged to be attentive to the addict's actions and participate in the resulting chaos. Detachment allows us to remove ourselves emotionally, physically, and mentally from the chaos created by the addict, so that we no longer see the addict's every mishap as our own crisis or disaster.

Detachment isn't about being cold-hearted; we're detaching ourselves from the addiction, not from the person. We hate the disease, and we separate ourselves from the disease and all the chaos it entails, but we love the person, and we're available to help the person when the person wants help. However, when our help amounts to participating in the addiction by protecting the addict from the consequences of their substance use and enabling the substance use, we're not helping anyone, and we sacrifice our own life and sanity.

It's not that we don't care anymore; we just choose to stop participating in the chaos. We choose to stop allowing the addict's behaviors to determine whether or not we're happy today, whether or not we can sleep tonight, and whether or not we can take care of our own needs today.

Detachment might be a new approach for some people, and they may feel guilty about it. Anyone finding it difficult to become a detached observer – but a caring observer, to be sure – of the addict's behavior, can ask themself a few questions: *has reacting to the addict's actions in the past stopped the substance use, or helped my loved one overcome addiction? Has reacting to the addict's actions brought peace and calm to me and my home, or has it caused chaos and conflict? Is reacting to the addict's behavior going to help solve the problem?*

Depending on your answer to these questions, perhaps you can answer this question: *is it worth surrendering my happiness and peace of mind to the addict by reacting to their actions?* When we're happy, healthy, and at peace we're much better able to be a supportive and helpful friend, family member, and co-worker, and we're much better able to see through the nonsense and help the addict we care about.

I remember back in my days of active addiction, when I would come home drunk, or my wife would find my alcohol or drug stash, she would explode with anger, and a huge fight would ensue. Arguing with a drunk or high addict never accomplishes anything. While my wife's anger was 100% justified, and I definitely deserved the dressing down that I got, my poor wife was driving herself crazy. She would be fuming mad for hours, would barely get any sleep that night, and would be totally unfocused the next day. It created considerable conflict and tension in the house with the rest of the family, and wouldn't accomplish anything, except maybe making me sneakier the next time. I was drawing her into the chaos of my life. The tension didn't make me stop drinking or using; rather, it just made me do what addicts do when they're stressed: more drinking and drug use. In hindsight, if she would've accepted that I was a drunk and junkie and that yelling at me wouldn't fix anything, she could've applied some detachment, living her life and taking care of herself and our family regardless of what I was up to. She could've stopped defining whether or not she was having a good day by whether or not I was drinking or using. She could've made it known to me that she would help me find help if I wanted it, and leave it at that. She could've applied boundaries (we'll discuss boundaries in the next chapter) to protect her sanity, perhaps even by kicking me out of the house and out of her life. However, she was reacting to my actions, and was bringing the chaos of my life into her own life, at the cost of her own happiness, peace of mind, and ability to function properly. And it did nothing to help my substance use problem or to "straighten me out."

When we become drawn into the considerable chaos created by the addict, we do so at great cost to ourselves, without solving anything. By allowing others to make their own choices and decisions – even if those choices and decisions are impaired by the disease of addiction – and to deal with the consequences of their own actions, we free ourselves from being drawn into burdens that were never ours to bear.

*

One of the barriers to detaching ourselves from the chaos is our vulnerability to being drawn into an argument. Addicts are angry, resentful, blameful people, so they love to argue. They feel miserable, and they love to spread the misery around. They're know-it-alls who think their predicament is everyone else's fault, so they love lashing out. We easily get sucked into arguments – often without even realizing it at the time – because it gives us a chance to let go and lash out at the addict, who's been a great source of frustration for us. By arguing, the addict finds an outlet for their anger and resentment and frustrations, and we find an outlet for ours. Meanwhile, nothing gets accomplished, and both parties come away from the argument feeling worse than when they went into it. It makes the addict want to go use or drink, and it makes us unhappy and robs us of any modicum of peace of mind.

It's only natural to get drawn into the action-reaction pattern with an addict by being drawn into arguing. Arguing is how addicts try to make us feel guilty and make themselves feel better. They try to rationalize their substance use based on our supposed shortcomings. They want to hurt us because they're hurting, and they'll say nasty things. Arguing with an addict is like trying to nail Jell-O to the wall – an exercise in frustration. How can you reason with a mind that's lost its ability to reason due to the effects of drugs on the brain's executive functions? How can anyone "win" an argument with an addict? Addicts are know-it-alls with a pathological need to be "right." They'll never bow down and admit that you're right and they're wrong, no matter what you say or how right you are. Arguments with addicts are a pointless, futile waste of time that draw you back into the addict's circle of chaos. The only outcome will be more of a distance between you and the addict, and the loss of your happiness and peace of mind.

We discussed in chapter 8 how people who deal with an addict should maintain control of conversations by stating their point, and then getting out before it inevitably turns into an argument. This takes practice and presence of mind, especially when the addict tries to bait you into an argument. However, with an attitude change about how we interact with an addict, we can choose to stop being dragged into pointless arguments, rather than just reacting to what the addict says. This takes practice, but avoiding arguments is a must-do for protecting our happiness and sanity, and detaching ourselves from the chaos.

*

The best and most loving and caring thing you can do for the addict, for all the people you interact with, and for yourself is to take care of your health and happiness – and to take those things back again if you've not been good at self-care. Paying attention to your own needs, establishing barriers, and doing some self-care is far from selfish – it's best for all involved, including the addict you wish to help. It's about having an attitude change about addiction, addicts, and how we go about interacting with an addict, and seeing that we have choices, rather than continuing to participate in the destructive action-reaction cycle. It's about taking a more effective approach to helping the addict, and no longer assigning our happiness over to the care of an addict. It's about accepting the things we cannot change (such as whether or not our loved one uses substances today), and taking the right action to change the things we can (such as how we react to the addict's actions). It's about acknowledging that we're most useful and able to help the addict and others when we're healthy, happy, and with peace of mind. When we treat ourselves with kindness and compassion, we become capable of treating other people with kindness and compassion. If we don't take care of our anger and resentments, we'll treat other people with anger and resentment.

Changing your attitude toward addiction may have already happened now that you've read about the science of addiction. The disease model of addiction helps us to separate the person from the disease, so that we don't see the addict as a bad person making bad decisions every day (which is how I used to perceive them); rather we see someone who's deeply hurting and caught up in something that's destroying their health and their life, but they have no control over. Believe me, the cocky, know-it-all, arrogant exterior is just a show; these people are hurting inside. To this end, changing our attitude toward addiction and addicts allows us to feel compassion for the addicts. As well, by learning the proper way to help addicts – as we've discussed in this book – we can adopt a changed attitude toward our role and responsibility when it comes to helping someone we care about with their addiction. We see that not going at it full-blast, trying desperately and in every way to control their behavior and change them doesn't mean we don't care; rather, it means we're applying our understanding of addiction and the addicted mind to provide care and support in the most effective way we can. It means that we choose to act smart rather than reacting, and we choose to stop our old ways of helping, which only bred conflict and distance with the addict, and drew us into participating in the addiction. So, while these attitude changes may – to the uninitiated – appear like withdrawal and selfishness, they're not. Rather, we're applying our knowledge of addiction to be much more effective in helping the addict while also remaining functional, happy, effective people in life.

I'd like to end the chapter by once again listing the facts that inform a healthy and productive attitude change about addiction, addicts, and our role in helping an addict:

- Addiction is a brain disease, caused by the toxic effects of repeated substance use on the brain; addiction isn't caused by you,
- Addiction is a progressive disease,
- Addicts can't control their substance use, and you can't control an addict's substance use either,
- Addiction can't be cured, but it can be successfully managed,
- If you're not happy, healthy, taking care of yourself, and functioning well, then you're not much good to yourself, to other people who need you, and to the addict you're trying to help,
- We are responsible for our own behaviors, not anyone else's,
- Covering for addicts, making excuses for their behavior, shielding them from the consequences of their actions, and taking over their responsibilities (except for the most essential ones, such as child care) amounts to participating in and enabling the addiction, and is unfair to you,
- Allowing another individual to decide whether you're happy or having a good day is giving away way too much power over yourself to that individual, and is especially foolhardy when that other individual is an addict of unsound mind. You deserve contentment, happiness, and peace of mind, whether the addict is drinking or using or not,
- The key to maintaining your sanity is to step outside the addict's circle of chaos and to stop participating in the addiction,
- Your sanity is best preserved by stopping your focus on the addict's behavior – something you can't control – and instead focusing on yourself and how you react to the addict – something you can control,

- Addicts cannot be pushed into treatment and recovery; to succeed they must be ready, willing, and motivated,
- The responsibility to overcome addiction is the addict's, not yours, and
- You cannot do treatment and recovery for an addict; they must do it themself.

The beginnings of taking back our happiness, peace of mind, and sanity when we're dealing with an addict lies in our attitude. Perhaps taking a moment to examine your own attitude toward how you will approach the addict in your life would be in order at this point. Then, we'll move on and talk about the next part of separating ourselves from the chaos, which is through setting boundaries, the subject of the next chapter.

13

Boundaries

"No" is a complete sentence.

– Annie Lamott

In the previous chapter, we talked about changing our attitudes toward addiction, addicts, and our role in helping an addict. Many people who have an addict in their life simply react to the addict's actions, which creates chaos because addicts' actions are chaotic. When people react to addicts' actions, they participate in the chaos, and it can draw their own life into disarray, and may rob them of their happiness and peace of mind. Sadly, usually such sacrifices don't even pay off, as the action-reaction cycle usually ends up creating conflict between loved ones and the addict, and never seems to bring about any kind of solution. If people who wish to help an addict adopt some attitude changes about how to help the addict, they can see that they have other choices besides continuing with the insane action-reaction routine.

Once they've changed their attitude about their role in helping the addict, loved ones can see that they have choices about how they interact with the addict in their life, and they can begin *acting* according to their new role rather than simply *reacting* to what the addict does. This is accomplished by setting boundaries. In this chapter, we're going to talk about boundaries, and how they can help you take back your sanity in an insane situation.

Boundaries are the rules and limits that we set on how others can behave around us and interact with us, and how we respond when people violate our limits. Boundaries have been described as: *a life enhancing system of "yes "and "no's"* (Black & Enns). Boundaries are what separate us from others, and help us to establish and define our self-identity. They're also about safety, and ensuring that we're treated with the respect that we deserve. Boundaries play a surprisingly decisive role in our happiness and well-being; setting and enforcing personal boundaries has been identified by research as a crucial part of mental and emotional well-being. Having boundaries is just as much a component of self-care and self-compassion as is brushing our teeth and eating healthy.

All relationships need boundaries. The path to healthy relationships of all kinds is to communicate our boundaries openly. Boundaries are about defining what our limits are, letting other people know what's acceptable and what's not when they interact with us. Without boundaries, people can take advantage of us. This is especially true when the other person is an addict; the addicted mind is manipulative, selfish, and always seeking an enabler. Indeed, boundaries are seldom more important than when the individual we're dealing with is an addict. Without boundaries, we're drawn into the chaos of an addict's chaotic life, at the expense of our own life and well-being.

Not having boundaries can affect all aspects of our life. It can cause us to overextend ourselves financially, physically, at work, and in our relationships, and it can create stress and anger that burns us out. It's hardly surprising that having unhealthy boundaries has been associated with co-dependency, depression, anxiety, and stress-related physical health problems.

Boundaries protect us from having other people's responsibilities piled on us. Boundaries allow us to establish what we will and will not be held responsible for. Inadequate boundaries can result in accepting more responsibility than we can handle, and this can lead to burnout. When I was a new doctor, I found that I had to establish and enforce boundaries around what responsibilities that I would accept. I was always being asked to work a little extra, and I had trouble saying "no." I found that agreeing to extra shifts, or staying late, as well as agreeing to other responsibilities led very quickly to me feeling exhausted. I had no time for myself, and I wasn't even getting enough sleep. I started saying "no" to all the extra stuff, and my life improved almost instantly. In other words, I set and enforced boundaries, simply by using the word "no."

Boundaries that protect us from taking on responsibilities that aren't rightfully placed on us are especially important when dealing with an addict. People who try to help an addict struggle to find that fine line between helping the addict, and enabling the substance use and participating in the chaos. Finding the right balance begins with adopting the attitude that we are not responsible for another person's substance use, we are not responsible for the consequences of their substance use, and we are not responsible for their recovery. Addicts run away from their responsibilities, no matter how important they may be. Loved ones typically then feel obliged to pick up the responsibilities themselves, and the addicts encourage it and use guilt to manipulate them to do it.

Some dropped responsibilities must be picked up, such as care of an addict's children if there's neglect. However, when we pick up other responsibilities that the addict has dropped, it becomes enabling, and it takes away from our own plans and activities, and creates chaos in our life. I'm talking about such things as paying their bills for them, calling their workplace to make excuses for them, or hiring a lawyer for them and bailing them out when they land in jail. Protecting an addict from the consequences of their substance use amounts to enabling the addiction, and it isn't fair to us. Why should we have to suffer the consequences of someone else's substance use, especially if it's doing nothing to help solve the overall problem? Having boundaries means not allowing the addict – or ourselves – to place those unrealistic responsibilities upon us. Boundaries allow us to stop enabling the substance use and participating in the chaos, and instead stick to our plan based on our informed attitude toward how we can properly help an addict. We can choose to extend a hand to help them find the help they need, and the addict is welcome to take that hand when ready, but we stop trying to do everything for them. In other words, we agree to be part of the solution, but we refuse to be part of the problem. When the addict is in tears asking for help (remember: addicts are master manipulators), it may tear your heart out, but just repeat the following to yourself: *I will help when it's part of the solution, but I refuse to help when it's part of the problem.*

*

It's not hard to tell when there's a boundary missing in our life. When people offend us because we haven't established and enforced how they may behave toward us, we become affronted, leaving us angry, and resentful. Feeling anger is an important indicator that a boundary has been crossed. Boundaries save us from a lot of unnecessary negative emotions and feelings. Boundaries allow us to stop people who seek to be hurtful toward us and make us uncomfortable. This is especially relevant to dealing with an addict. Addicts feel that they're victims, and they seek to lay blame and guilt on others. They're hurting, and it somehow makes them feel better to spread around the hurt. Those closest to them bear the brunt of this unacceptable behavior, and anyone who's lacking proper boundaries will be victimized. Boundaries protect us from having blame and guilt that don't belong to us shoved in our face.

My experience as a therapist has been that people are generally bad (*really* bad) at setting boundaries, and even worse at enforcing them. I've noticed that some women in particular struggle with boundaries, presumably because of their nurturing and giving nature. I've noticed that people who have low self-esteem and those who're people-pleasers are usually not good at boundaries either. While it's admirable when someone is willing to accept self-sacrifice in order to help others, constantly sacrificing our boundaries so as to avoid conflict or for fear of offending others or because we try to take on everybody else's problems isn't healthy.

Some individuals are good with some boundaries, but they still find themselves feeling disrespected, upset and disempowered in certain situations. This indicates that they may need to re-examine their boundaries.

There are various reasons that people don't set and enforce boundaries. In many cases, it's because they've never learned about boundaries, usually because they were never taught about such things as children, and they weren't given a voice as children. Often, they believed as children that not doing what others wanted to do would result in rejection or abandonment. Others allow themselves to be treated in uncomfortable ways because they fear confrontation. Others feel guilty about enforcing boundaries, because they believe they must always put others' wants before their own needs. Others just try to keep everybody happy by sacrificing their own needs – in other words, people-pleasing (the so-called "disease to please").

Many people allow their boundaries to be violated because they want to avoid conflict. They allow people to make them uncomfortable or even hurt them in the interest of "keeping the peace" with those individuals. They may even go so far as to repeatedly adjust their personal boundaries in response to how others mistreat them, and continually justify other people's disrespect. They "keep the peace" at the expense of their inner peace.

However, some won't enforce their boundaries because of legitimate fear, because they're dealing with someone who's violent or threatening, and avoiding conflict becomes a matter of safety. In such cases, attempting to set or enforce boundaries may be unsafe. Anyone in that unacceptable situation should contact their local family safety organization for advice, and to create a safety and escape plan. Physical violence and the threat of physical violence must never be tolerated or excused.

People who lack boundaries are often described as "shy" or "pliable" or "agreeable." They're people-pleasers, often at the expense of their own pleasure. They back down in times of conflicting opinions or they don't express their opinion. They do what other people want to do even if – deep down – they don't want to, and they don't speak up to say what they want to do. They're people who never say "no." They can't stand letting other people down, and will sacrifice their own plans to avoid disappointing others. They may feel responsible for keeping other people happy, and feel guilty over the smallest of things. What might appear to be love and sacrifice is really just a need to be liked. They may need everyone else's approval, and they may prioritize other people's perception of them over all else. They see others' needs as their own. They don't see that each individual is responsible for their own happiness. Often, they spend so much time doing what others want to do that they have trouble making decisions for themselves. When they do make decisions they feel anxious and question themselves. People who lack boundaries often fear rejection or abandonment. Unfortunately, people without boundaries often attract controlling people, and therefore may end up in abusive relationships.

Unfortunately, people who lack boundaries are also prime targets for addicts. As we've discussed in previous chapters, the addicted mind is manipulative, as it seeks any leverage to enable the substance use. Addicts can sense "weakness" – which is how some people describe lacking boundaries – and will employ guilt, pity, and otherwise take advantage of a loving and caring heart in order to get what they need. What they need is one thing – access to drugs or alcohol. They love to place blame on others for their misery and misfortune, and someone who feels responsible for their happiness due to poor boundaries is the perfect target. After a while, the addict's target may even start believing what they're being told and feel guilty about trying to establish boundaries.

Living without healthy boundaries has been likened to leaving the door to your home unlocked; anyone can enter anytime they want and do anything they want. Your privacy and well-being are at the mercy of the will of whoever happens to decide to enter. Making a conscious decision to create and enforce limits on how others may treat us is wonderfully empowering. It may seem scary or daunting at first, but the effect on self-esteem, self-respect, and inner peace is tremendous. It's worth the effort to get used to using healthy boundaries. If you have an addict in your life, boundaries are a must-do for extricating yourself from the addict's circle of chaos, and to stop participating in the addiction. It's how you take back your life and sanity.

*

Boundaries require some practice, as well as balance and finesse. They can be under-used, but they can also be over-used. To wit, some individuals have too many boundaries because of being hurt in the past. Rather than "boundaries," these may be thought of as "barriers," because they block out other people so as to avoid being hurt again. These people often feel they can't trust anyone, they avoid speaking or expressing their opinion because they feel it protects them from being hurt by someone disagreeing with them, they ignore other people's hurtful actions toward them, and they don't let anyone get close. They may even dissociate themselves from their feelings when they feel they're being violated, rather than speaking up for themselves. People with such excessive social boundaries can lower these barriers by adopting healthy boundaries. Balance involves allowing ourselves to get close to others, but asserting ourselves when others violate our feelings or limitations. Healthy boundaries protect us from being hurt or abused much better than does blocking everyone out or trying to ignore hurt or abuse when it happens.

Having healthy boundaries means that we don't feel guilty about seeing to our own needs, even if we must say "no" to someone else's needs. Good, kind, and loving people can be selfless and still say "no" when others cross their boundaries. Again, it's about balance; it's fine to give of ourselves for others, to compromise, and to sacrifice our needs in certain times. However, we should find the balance so that we're not always doing that, nor should we only look after ourselves. Giving up our own needs to help someone else with theirs should feel good, not make us feel angry or used. Boundaries are about self-care, being ourselves, and spreading our wings as individuals. So, if we spend money on ourselves, or take some time to do activities on our own, it doesn't mean that we don't care about our family or enjoy family activities. On the contrary, it's better for the family to have a healthy and fulfilled family member. It's about balance; being giving to family and friends, without giving all of ourselves away. Everyone should take opportunities to explore their own passions, hobbies, and outlets and grow as an individual, even if they're a member of a close family unit... *especially* if they're a member of a close family unit.

Setting boundaries shouldn't be difficult for anyone. After all, the world is full of boundaries, and people are used to respecting boundaries – whether they like it or not. We're not supposed to cut flowers out of our neighbor's garden, or spit on the floor at a restaurant, or drive on the wrong side of the road. People follow these boundaries without a word, because they've been in place a long time, everyone knows what they are, and there are consequences if they're violated. Some boundaries are implied; you don't need to explicitly verbalize them or explain them, because they're obvious. For example, physical violence of any kind is a boundary violation that must be protected absolutely in every instance, and never needs to be explained or explicitly set in advance.

When we first set and enforce boundaries, we usually get resistance from some people, while other people will recognize what we're doing and respect our boundaries. After a while people get used to them, and they become respected. However, it may take some conflict to establish them, which takes some courage and fortitude. Stick by your guns.

Those who're offended or become angry when we set boundaries are probably the ones we most need to set boundaries for. People will try to talk us into bending our boundaries in order to satisfy their own selfish desires; this is especially true of addicts. Addicts will inevitably chafe and resist when we set boundaries, and will constantly push at them until they see we're unwilling to bend. The addicted mind is a superb manipulator, so addicts tend to test barriers, and constantly push against them in their efforts to seek an enabler.

If people don't set boundaries in a healthy way – by speaking up for themselves when someone crosses their boundary – then they'll set boundaries in an unhealthy way. Often, they'll remain silent when their boundaries are crossed multiple times, until finally their frustration and anger build up to the point where they snap the next time someone crosses them. Rather than view the outburst as an attempt to set a boundary, others will see it as a tantrum, and go on violating our limits. Better to establish proper boundaries and correct people than to allow anger to guide our reactions.

People should not explain their boundaries, nor should they have to. Every person has the right to decide what their boundaries are. You can explain the reasons for your boundary if it helps you to establish the boundary, but I suggest not over-explaining or allowing it to turn into a debate or an argument if the other person resists – which is likely to happen with addicts. Boundaries require a resolute and firm attitude, or don't even bother trying. Allowing someone to talk you out of it when you attempt to set a boundary is going to make the next attempt even harder.

*

In many cases that I've been involved with, I've observed a complete breakdown in boundaries in individuals who're desperately trying to help an addict. In such cases, the focus had become completely on the addict – *did they drink/use yesterday? What are they doing? Did they go to work today? What kind of mood are they in?* – so that the caregiver lost sight of their own wants, needs, and self-care. In such cases, people spend tremendous amounts of time pandering to the addict in their life, caring for them when they're sick, covering for them, bailing them out of trouble, reacting to their temperaments and moods, and trying to figure out how to help them. But the addiction goes on and on.

Many loved ones who try to help an addict cancel their own plans because they feel obliged to stay home out of fear the addict will drink or use if left alone, or they spend their nights sleepless and worrying about and waiting up for the addict. People can easily cease living their own life when their preoccupation becomes the life of the addict.

Establishing boundaries with an addict is about taking our life back and reclaiming who we are. It's about ending the enabling. Establishing these boundaries is possible when we have an attitude change about addiction, addicts, and how best to help them. Establishing boundaries is how we implement our new attitude about how we will help the addict, and how we will live our own life while doing so. Boundaries are about not stopping or surrendering our life because someone else is tangled in addiction. Even though we care and need to help, boundaries are how we set about not trying to help in a desperate and dysfunctional way.

Setting boundaries can involve sitting down with the addict and spelling out exactly what our boundaries are. These can be general: *I am not taking responsibility for your substance use or for your recovery. Those things are your responsibility, and I'm not going to babysit you, try to control you, or try to push you into getting help*, or another example: *I'm not responsible for your substance use, and I'm not taking responsibility for the consequences of your substance use. If you miss work, you take it up with your boss, I'm not calling and making excuses for you. If you use up all your money, I'm not giving you any more money. If you get arrested for impaired driving, I'm not bailing you out and you can deal with the charges yourself.* Boundaries can also be specific, such as: *if you steal from me, I will no longer allow you to live in this house*, or: *if you are abusive toward me, you are out of this house and I will call the police.* Often boundaries are simply defined and established just by saying "no" without any accompanying explanations.

Let's compare the boundaries that I typically observe in addicts, versus the boundaries that I often see in loved ones who're trying to help an addict. Addicts tend to have what psychologists refer to as excessively *rigid boundaries*: they shun intimacy and close relationships, they're extraordinarily secretive about personal information, they reject and even become defensive at efforts to offer them help or discuss their situation, and they keep all others at a distance. On the other hand, those who're close to addicts and want to help them often have excessively *porous boundaries*: they have trouble saying "no," they become overly involved in the addict's problems, they tolerate disrespect and abuse, they allow the addict to invade their private space and disrupt their happiness and peace of mind.

You can see that the boundaries that typically occur between addicts and those who try to help them can be incongruent and polar opposites: addicts tend to have rigid boundaries, while those who care about them have porous boundaries. Indeed, addicts and their loved ones usually present extreme examples of rigidity and porousness in their boundaries when they interact with each other. Both are dysfunctional. The addicts' ultra-rigid boundaries prevent them from letting other people in to help them, prevent them from being honest and truthful enough to confront their problems, and alienate them from anyone who's not a fellow addict. These boundaries must change in order for addicts to accept help and engage in the cooperative and honest attitude they need to succeed in treatment and recovery. On the other hand, loved ones who try to help addicts must change their dysfunctional boundaries if they are to regain their sanity, and live with the happiness and peace of mind they deserve. Many families deal with addiction for years and years in one form or another; that's a long time to live with no boundaries in place to protect them from chaos and dysfunction.

*

There are different types of personal boundaries, all of which are relevant to establishing a balanced relationship with an addict. By "balanced," I mean doing all we can to help the addict, while maintaining proper limits that protect us and our sanity. Let's look at the different types of boundaries:

Physical boundaries – these include how people physically touch us and our personal space. A zero-tolerance boundary around physical violence and unwanted physical touch is an absolute. Physical boundaries can be violated when someone else touches us in a way or when we don't want them to, as well as when someone invades our personal space, such as going through our dresser drawers or rifling through our purse or wallet.

Physical boundaries are often implied, and don't have to be specifically laid out to be understood; people know they're doing something wrong when they violate someone's physical boundaries. For example, I recently spoke with a woman whose brother has developed a terrible meth addiction. They were always close, so he had a key to her house. One night, he used his key to get into her house in the middle of the night while everyone was asleep, and he made off with her family's TV, which he sold for drug money. Even though she had never specifically established entering her house in the middle of the night and taking items as a boundary, this was a significant violation of her physical boundaries, and her brother – as well as anyone else – would be well aware of this as an unspoken boundary. Similarly, physical violence of any kind is an unspoken boundary that applies to and is understood by every person.

Physical boundary violations are a safety issue. If physical boundaries are being violated they tend to worsen if they're tolerated. Involving the police and/or family trauma authorities and making an escape plan should be considered early.

Emotional boundaries – these boundaries are about our right to not suffer emotional abuse, such as belittling, undue criticism, mocking, or name-calling. Emotional boundaries are also being crossed when we find ourselves being guilted or shamed into doing things we don't want to do.

Like physical boundaries, emotional boundaries should be understood in advance without having to be spoken. Narcissistic and manipulative people rely heavily on emotional manipulation to get what they want, as do addicts. Boundaries are our defense against such disrespectful behavior.

Emotional boundaries are what separate our feelings from other people's feelings, moods, and actions. These boundaries enable us to help others without taking their problems or negative emotions upon ourselves. Allowing other people's moods – or substance use – to dictate our own mood or level of happiness is an example of what can happen with inadequate emotional boundaries. Many people who're trying to help an addict loved one are completely lacking in emotional boundaries.

Similarly, when we find that we base how we feel about ourselves on how others treat us, this may indicate a lack of healthy emotional boundaries. We should seek to find happiness within ourselves, and not allow people outside ourselves to determine whether or not we're happy. Healthy emotional boundaries help us to do this. It involves becoming used to using detachment: we feel for other people and try to help them, but we maintain detachment between their emotions and our own. Likewise, we value other people's opinions of us, but we detach ourselves from their words and actions. Our self-esteem and self-worth are to be found within ourselves, not in the opinions and words of those around us. We'll discuss healthy detachment in more detail shortly.

Because addicts like to spread around their misery, they often use those who're closest to them as emotional punching bags. Addicts are also manipulative, and if they see that their emotional abuse has an effect on their loved one – either by hurting the loved one, making them feel guilty, or getting the loved one to do what the addict wants – then the emotional abuse will certainly continue. Addicts have a radar for finding enablers, and violating emotional boundaries is one of their favorite tools.

I suggest that people immediately terminate the conversation when emotional abuse occurs, and remove themselves from the situation (or remove the addict from the situation). This is always a boundary violation, and allowing it to play out guarantees that it will happen again. I suggest never giving in to an addict's (or anyone else's) demands when those are accompanied by emotional abuse.

Material boundaries – these are our boundaries relating to our money and possessions. Addicts will push these boundaries to the limits, so I suggest establishing these boundaries very early on, especially as they pertain to money, use of your vehicle, and theft of your money or possessions. As we've discussed in earlier chapters, addicts' drive for obtaining the next drug or drink is so powerful that they'll be driven to extreme measures, especially after they've used up their own financial resources. I've seen multiple examples of otherwise kind, loving, giving, and self-sacrificing people who became predatory monsters in active addiction, even stealing from their own children, committing significant crimes, and resorting to prostitution. Family members and friends are the easiest and safest target, so addicts always push the material boundaries with their loved ones before they resort to other more desperate measures to obtain money for their substance use.

Material boundaries are also violated when someone pressures us to lend them money or an item, won't take "no" for an answer, or damages our property, especially if they don't replace or repair the damage. As with physical and emotional boundaries, material boundaries are usually implied and understood by all. When we talk about material boundaries with someone, it's usually because that person has violated our boundary, and we're confronting them to warn against future violations and to lay out consequences.

Time boundaries – this is an important and often unrecognized boundary that usually gets trampled by an addict. Think of all the time you've spent trying to figure out what the addict is up to, cleaning up the addict's messes, covering for the addict, wasting time at work because you can't concentrate, and lying awake at night tormented with worry. That's essentially wasted time, because it did nothing to help the addict and end the addiction, and much of it may have actually enabled the addiction… not to mention that it robbed you of your own time and peace of mind. With our attitude change about addiction, addicts, and our role in helping an addicted loved one, we may see that our time boundaries were being thoroughly violated. As we've seen, there's a big difference between helping someone and enabling someone; that's true of anyone we wish to help, but it's especially true when we're dealing with an addict.

The greatest casualty when someone violates our time boundaries is usually our free time, our time for leisure, rest, relaxation, and self-care. That's a high price to pay for someone else's substance use.

Time boundaries are about making sure our energy and resources are going towards truly helping someone, not enabling someone who's complacently taking advantage of our kindness. People – especially addicts – will selfishly stake a claim on our time but time boundaries ensure that we take care of ourselves as well. We're responsible for ourselves first; if we don't take care of our own happiness and peace of mind, no one is going to do it for us.

Sexual boundaries – these could be considered as a type of physical and emotional boundary, but they relate specifically to matters of intimacy. Sexual boundaries are violated by unwanted physical touch, pressure to engage in intimate acts, sexual comments, and even leering.

Sexual boundaries are often violated by people – whether they're addicts or not – who're intoxicated, particularly by stimulants or alcohol. Intoxication with these substances makes people uninhibited, and they may act impulsively. This is one of the reasons that I suggest that people avoid trying to deal with or interact with anyone who's acutely intoxicated.

Most addictive substances impair sexual function and desires, and may even render the addict impotent. In such cases, crossing sexual boundaries may represent an attempt to belittle, humiliate, control, or establish dominance, rather than an effort at sexual gratification.

Crossing sexual boundaries is an absolute, and should never be tolerated in the least. The sexual integrity and security of all people is critically important to their well-being and their ability to move through life as whole person. Violations of sexual boundaries can have profound damaging and lasting effects.

Intellectual boundaries – many people view these boundaries as unimportant, but they're of great significance in dealing with addicts. Intellectual boundaries are violated when someone else belittles our ideas, thoughts, or opinions. It's OK for others to disagree with us, but to be dismissive or to lie to refute our opinions crosses a boundary. Addicts do this by acting like know-it-alls, and dismissing the opinion of anyone who tries to correctly point out their situation.

I suggest that establishing intellectual boundaries is very important when dealing with an addict you wish to help. It's important to make an addict aware that you've taken the time to learn about the nature and science of addiction, and that – while you can never fully understand the experience because you've never been through it – you do know the facts about addiction. If the addict tries to argue – as know-it-alls will do – I suggest ending the conversation. This lets the addict know that you will not be suckered by BS excuses and explanations. This establishes you as someone the addict can talk to about addiction, when they're ready, but also as someone who will not be hoodwinked.

Intellectual boundaries are also what protect us from sacrificing our own plans, goals, and dreams in order to please others. It's fine to compromise on our goals in order to set common goals with someone else, but sacrificing what's important to us in order to keep the peace with someone is a violation of intellectual boundaries.

Allowing others to make decisions for us because we don't feel empowered to express our own wants and needs is another manifestation of inadequate intellectual boundaries. Everyone should take responsibility for their own life and happiness. Every individual has a right to and should protect their autonomy and uniqueness. It's what makes us interesting people, and what allows us to be fulfilled and complete. Being the way we are rather than what people want us to be sometimes requires asserting our intellectual boundaries.

*

Many people have lived their entire life with few boundaries, or without healthy boundaries. While they may have gotten by just fine living that way in the past, they may find that such an approach doesn't work well anymore once they have an active addict in their life. They may have found that the people in their life are respectful, and that they didn't really need to worry too much about boundaries. However, once a manipulative, selfish, enabler-seeking addict begins operating within their bounds, they're suddenly being sucked into participating in the addiction and the chaos at the expense of their own life and sanity.

Even people who've always been good at boundaries may find that they've never before had their boundaries pushed and tested like they do once they have an addict in their life, and they may find that they need a boundary tune-up to preserve their own health and well-being. For most people, yet another attitude change may be in order for them to set the proper dynamic when dealing with an addict.

Changing our attitude about boundaries involves no longer seeing placing limitations on other people's behaviors toward us as a selfish act or something to feel guilty about, and beginning to see limitations as a necessary self-care measure for our own well-being, and for ensuring that our relationships with others are healthy and functional. In other words, adopting an attitude that: *setting and enforcing healthy boundaries is a matter of ensuring that our rights are no longer violated, and that we receive the same basic respect that every person is entitled to, and is not a matter of selfishness or something to feel guilty about.*

We can add to that attitude when we're dealing with an addict: *establishing and enforcing boundaries is necessary to stop being an enabler, and to stop participating in the addiction and the chaos*. With this new attitude, having healthy boundaries is no longer an excuse to feel guilty, or to be manipulated and used by others.

Here are some principles to consider when you examine your attitude toward boundaries:

- You have the right to say "no" without having to explain or feel guilty,
- Your needs are as important as other people's needs,
- You have the right to be treated with respect in every situation, including in situations of conflict,
- You have the right to be free of unreasonable expectations placed on you by other people, or taken upon yourself because you feel obliged,
- You have the right to express your opinions and feelings without being ridiculed or belittled,
- You have the right to speak up when someone is making you uncomfortable or violates your limits, and
- Being sick with addiction does not give anybody the right to treat you with disrespect.

There may be some other principles that you feel are important to you, based on your own values and needs. Feel free to add to my list.

No one should apologize for, feel obliged to justify, or argue over their boundaries; doing so sends a mixed message. We may feel guilty or selfish about saying "no" and asserting ourselves, but learning to overcome such misplaced feelings and not allowing them to prevent us from having boundaries is a necessary life skill, just as brushing our teeth and other self-care skills are necessary for our health and well-being. By adopting a healthy attitude toward boundaries, we see that we have a choice to say "no," regardless of what our past practices were. With practice, any guilt or feelings of being selfish go away. Boundaries are necessary for our health and happiness, and result in respectful relationships. We have a right to be treated with respect, and it's not right to give up that right so that someone else can indulge in improper behavior – addict or not. Courage and determination may be needed the first few times that anyone asserts their boundaries, but with practice, it becomes easier. Soon, people know and accept your boundaries and you seldom have to say anything more about it.

Remember that boundaries are only necessary because other people are choosing to treat us in a way that compromises our physical, mental, and emotional well-being. All people have a right to be treated with respect, regardless of the other person's circumstances. Handing over the right to treat us with a lack of basic respect is not helping anyone. People who become used to trampling other people's boundaries and rights end up as ugly, unlikeable people. If children grow up seeing their parents allowing others to trample their boundaries and treat them without proper decorum and respect, they may grow up to do the same. We teach our children as much through our actions and principles as we do through our words.

In the end, we're all responsible for our own happiness and peace of mind; relying on other people to determine or control our happiness is a recipe for unhappiness. We take responsibility for our own happiness and peace of mind by keeping our boundaries. Similarly, we're not responsible for other people's happiness. Trying to keep the peace and make others happy by allowing them the to treat us as they wish is the basis of a dysfunctional relationship. You're way too awesome to be someone else's emotional punching bag. We all are.

*

Setting proper boundaries takes time. Often the right time to set a boundary is when someone offends us or pushes us and we feel angry or used. In such a case, someone just handed us an opportunity to announce and uphold our boundary, which we can do simply by saying "no" followed by stating that it crosses our boundary. If the way someone treats us, or speaks to us, or demands something of us makes us feel angry, manipulated, used, or controlled, then there's probably a boundary that needs to be established. Our instincts tell us when someone is crossing our boundaries, and that's the right time to speak up.

I suggest setting boundaries calmly and without expressing emotion – even though you may be angry. If we state and assert our boundary with anger and emotion, it may seem that we're just lashing out in anger, and our boundary may not be taken seriously. Rather, I suggest a calm but firm tone. Using "I" statements helps with assertiveness. For example: *I don't like it when you raise your voice at me, and I won't tolerate it. I need you to speak to me in a normal tone of voice or I will end the conversation.* Compare that boundary assertion to this one: *Stop yelling at me!*

Saying "no" is itself a boundary assertion, and "no" never needs to be explained. However, sometimes qualifying the "no" helps. For example, look at this boundary assertion: *No. I won't do that for you. I feel overwhelmed when you ask me to take care of your problems. I need time to take care of my own business, and I need you to take responsibility for yours,* and compare it to this one: *no!* We don't owe anyone an explanation for saying no, but the first time we say "no" it may help the other individual understand our boundary if we provide a framework. Then, next time the individual asks us to take on a responsibility that isn't ours and we don't wish to, we can simply say "no!" and it will be understood.

For people who have an addict in their life, I usually suggest considering some extra boundary "safeguards" that are specific to the addict. These include such measures as:

- Locking away valuables and private items,
- Safeguarding and frequently changing the password to online access to bank accounts, lines of credit, and other assets,
- Putting purses, wallets, and keys in a secure place when at home,
- Not leaving your cell phone laying around unattended,
- Securing items that could be pawned or sold easily, such as laptops, tablets, and jewelry,
- Not keeping addictive substances in the home, and
- Locking away prescription medications, regardless of what they are.

I also suggest discussing boundaries that apply specifically to the addict with other family members so that they can apply the same boundaries. If an addict finds a weak link in the family, they will push on that person.

For those who really struggle with setting and upholding boundaries – especially those who've had some issues from their past that seem to make it harder – making an appointment with a therapist, counselor, or even a life coach may be helpful. Sometimes we need a little help to get over some hang-ups, fears, and anxieties, and asserting oneself can be a real departure from the norm for some among us. There's nothing at all wrong with asking for a little help when we need to; I've certainly done so myself. Boundaries are such an important prerequisite for health, happiness, and peace of mind that it's worth the effort to make sure that we succeed.

Sometimes, people who grew up in boundary-less environments or who're surrounded by toxic or dysfunctional situations, may come to believe that this is the normal way of relationships, and they may try to hold on to what they know. I've found that many individuals don't really know what a life with healthy boundaries looks like, because they've never known respectful relationships. In such cases, time spent with a counselor may be particularly helpful.

*

For people who aren't used to having boundaries and holding those around them to respecting their limits, there may be some reluctance to changing their ways. However, an attitude change may be helpful. Realizing and acknowledging that happiness and peace of mind depend heavily on ending the frustration, anger, and insult that come with tolerating other people's disrespect may provide the motivation to step out and start establishing boundaries. This is something that we do for ourselves, because no one else is responsible for our happiness and peace of mind. We don't have to passively accept what other people bring to us. If anyone wants to do *one thing* for themself that will make a difference in their life this year, I suggest considering putting some attention and effort into establishing healthy boundaries as that one thing.

While we're talking about attitude changes, let's include the attitude that establishing boundaries that are specific to the addict is not selfishness, nor is it unkind. When we live our life to please everyone else, we live our life feeling frustrated and powerless. This is because what others want may not be good for us, and may even be detrimental to our own well-being. We're not being selfish or mean when we say "no" to unreasonable demands or when we express our opinions, ideas, wants, and feelings, even if they differ from those of others. When we live our life trying to please an addict, it's a guaranteed recipe for chaos and insanity. We're placing a target on our back for the manipulative addict, who's searching for enablers. By establishing boundaries with an addict, we may initially have to use some tough love – because there will be resistance – but it's not unkind or selfish. They may be sick with addiction and come across as pathetic, but it's better for them, it's better for us, and it must be done if we want to be part of the solution rather than part of the problem. You're reading this book because you want to help an addict and keep your sanity, and healthy boundaries are a lynchpin for both goals.

As we begin to establish boundaries and make our limits and standards known to others, it becomes easier to assert ourselves, and it takes less effort because our boundaries become known to others. Before long, our boundaries are known and accepted, and everyone becomes used to them. When we notice someone doing something toxic the first time, we shouldn't wait for the second time before we address it or cut them off. When we live by the "wait and see" tactic, we only leave ourselves vulnerable to a second attack. As our boundaries get stronger, the wait time gets shorter. Better to feel bad for a moment by saying "no" – and stop it – than to continue tolerating unacceptable behavior and feel bad all the time.

Manipulators are difficult to escape from, and when we start saying "no" they'll start with the head games and attempts at emotional blackmail. They'll accuse us of being selfish. They're happy when we give in to their demands and do things their way at our own expense, and they don't like it when we finally draw a line for our own sanity and well-being. It's those people who're being selfish, not us, and they're the reason we need boundaries.

When we surrender our own happiness and peace of mind in attempts to please others, we're creating a dysfunctional relationship. Manipulators are never satisfied by what we give, and the next demand is accompanied by an expectation that we'll once again surrender our will. Insecure people tend to let go of boundaries out of fear of angering the other person or fear of abandonment, but any sense of security, love, or safety achieved by surrendering control is tenuous and fleeting. A relationship built on this kind of boundary-less control can't produce anything remotely like genuine love, respect, or trust. In many cases it progresses to abusive control and even domestic violence. Trying to hold on to relationships that depend upon our complete lack of boundaries attracts the wrong kinds of people.

When I was an ER doctor, I used to see women (sometimes men) coming in to have their injuries treated after suffering assault at the hands of their "lover" or spouse. Many such women were coming in repeatedly, and every time they would insist that *this* time they were putting an end to the abuse, *this* time they were going to file a police report, *this* time they were going to leave their abusive partner. And they were often accompanied by a friend who insisted that they would make sure of it. However, I kept seeing the same victims over and over again, sometimes only a few weeks later. When abuse occurs the only correct boundary is to terminate the relationship and get out; expecting the other person to change or things to be different *next* time amounts to insanity. "Wait and see" never works.

*

Setting boundaries becomes meaningless if they're not upheld and enforced with consistency. This is especially true of active addicts, who will seek cracks in our personal space and exploit them to enable their substance use. Allowing unacceptable behavior rewards it, which means that it will be repeated. When we don't speak up when a boundary has been crossed, it gives the impression that it's OK. When a boundary is crossed, we should show that it's not OK.

Enforcing boundaries doesn't mean that we always have to make a threat, or that we must have a consequence in our back pocket that we can unleash on the perpetrator. Consequences don't always have to be a threat of some kind, an "or else" statement, or an inflicted punishment. However, some boundaries lend themselves to statements of consequences. For example:

- If you continue _____, I will leave the room (or leave the house),
- If you continue _____, I will ask you to leave the house,
- If you _____ even one more time, you will no longer be able to stay at this house,
- If you continue _____, there will be a serious change in our relationship, and
- Up to this point, I've gone out of my way to help you, but if you ever speak to me like that again, I'm not going to be involved anymore.

Consequences don't always have to be included as we assert our boundaries. For example: *I'm not going to do that for you. I love you, but you need to take responsibility for yourself.* That's an excellent boundary, and no threat or consequence was needed. In many cases our only recourse is to remove ourselves from a situation when our boundaries are being pushed or violated, thereby ending the interaction. That stops the boundary violation, and sends a message to the violator that we're not tolerating their behavior.

Boundary violations that threaten or harm anyone's safety must be acted upon immediately. This is especially true of physical (including sexual) violence. However, it may be unwise or unsafe to make your action plan known to the violent person ahead of time.

Anyone who's in immediate danger should call 911 (in North America), or the police emergency number if 911 service isn't available. The police are trained in dealing with domestic violence and other violations of physical or sexual boundaries. They can help victims to get a peace bond, and put them in touch with victim services. Victim services can help with getting a non-criminal protection order, and with finding a safe place for victims and their children to stay, if necessary.

Anyone who's in a dangerous situation but not in immediate danger can call a local community services organization, victim services, shelter, health center, help line, or the police for help in figuring out what to do next. Other resources include a doctor, social worker, public health nurse, counselor, legal aid, or member of the clergy. They can help and they keep the interaction confidential (unless abuse of a minor is involved, in which case they are legally obliged to report the concern). They're often able to provide a list of emergency numbers and instructions in a disguised format – such as in a lipstick tube – that can be carried at all times.

The important thing is that individuals who're subjected to abuse not keep it a secret and tolerate the behavior. If it's difficult calling for help, then telling a neighbor or trusted friend about it and asking for help is a good idea. When I was an ER doctor, just about every person I saw who had been beat up in a domestic abuse crime was brought in by a friend. Friends care and want to help.

I won't say anything more about abuse except to say that these situations are best handled with an action plan made in advance with professionals who're trained in these matters. It's better to get out of an abusive situation early, rather than wait for a crisis or tragedy to occur. I suggest checking to see what resources are available in your area if you fear you may be at risk. Now is the time to lean on family, friends, and community resources.

*

It may be wise to simply walk away from a boundary-crosser when they're intoxicated, and address the matter the next day when they're sober. One of my absolute boundaries is that I won't talk to people when they're intoxicated. I give my cell phone number out to a lot of people with addictions, and I frequently get calls when they're intoxicated. I've also been confronted by intoxicated people face-to-face. Usually they're asking for help, often in tears, but during intoxication isn't the right time for them to ask, nor is it the right time to help, other than perhaps seeing to their immediate safety. I tell them that I don't talk to people when they're drunk or high, and then I end the conversation. Trying to have a conversation with an intoxicated individual is pretty much useless.

Trying to defend our boundaries when an intoxicated individual crosses them is similarly an exercise in futility. Better to remove ourselves from the situation and deal with it when they're sober. If an intoxicated addict offended me, I'll contact them the next day to tell them that they offended me when they were high/drunk, and that it was unacceptable. I assert my boundaries with sober people, because it's useless to try when they're drunk or high.

As you know, when anybody – addict or not – is in an intoxicated state they can be uninhibited, aggressive, and even psychotic. They may also have volcanically labile moods. Therefore, their behavior can be unpredictable and dangerous. As such, I advise avoiding any interaction with anyone who's intoxicated, especially if it involves confrontation or conflict. Besides, it's highly unlikely you could accomplish anything when someone's in that state anyway. It's not the time for boundary setting or enforcing, unless it's an immediate safety issue.

*

Some people will easily accept a boundary and others will continue to challenge and escalate their pushing. There are people who won't respect our boundaries no matter what we do. This often happens with people who're narcissistic, have self-esteem issues and are compensating with an inflated pride/ego, and – you guessed it – addicts. In such cases, the best approach may be to practice "detachment." This involves moving away from trying to change these people or force them to respect our boundaries. Instead, we remove ourselves from the toxic situation as best we can. That means:

- Walking away from conversations or interactions where our boundaries are violated,
- Understanding that the other person is the one with issues, rather than taking their disrespect personally,
- Not giving the other individual the reaction they're looking for; in other words, not responding in anger, or allowing ourselves to be drawn into an argument,
- Declining invitations to spend time with them,
- Not offering our advice or our opinion,
- Allowing them to make their own decisions and face the consequences on their own, and
- Ultimately, it may mean changing our relationship, such as no longer living together, limiting our contact, or ceasing our contact.

Detachment doesn't mean that we no longer love or care about the individual. In fact, some psychologists refer to it as "loving detachment."

Rather, detachment is about choosing to no longer participate in a disrespectful, dysfunctional situation that someone else is trying to force on us. Detachment is a natural and reasonable consequence that we can respond with when someone refuses to respect our boundaries, despite being given clear opportunities to do so.

Al-anon – acknowledged experts in establishing boundaries with addicts – suggests detachment as a way of protecting ourselves from repeated boundary violations from an addict. From their pamphlet "Detachment" (available for free from al-anon.org): *detachment is neither kind nor unkind. It does not imply judgment or condemnation of the person or situation from which we are detaching. Separating ourself from the adverse effects of another person's [substance use] can be a means of detaching: this does not necessarily require physical separation. Detachment can help us look at our situations realistically and objectively.*

In previous chapters, we've framed addiction as a disease. People have an addiction because they have a disease, not because they're unkind, selfish, or immoral. Their addiction doesn't define them. I've seen this first-hand many hundreds of times, where people who once engaged in awful behaviors and treated other people horribly were returned to thoughtful, loving, caring people once they were in recovery and had taken care to undergo the healing that comes from proper addiction treatment. So, detachment isn't about detaching from the person, it's about detaching from the disease and the chaos, dysfunction, and horrible behaviors that it entails. Detachment isn't about coldly distancing ourselves from the addict; it's about correcting a dysfunctional relationship with someone we love.

We've discussed in previous chapters that the key to stopping being an enabler and instead becoming part of the solution lies in backing off from the addict and the situation a bit – in other words, exercising some detachment. We're not doing this detachment because we're done with the addict; rather, we do it in order to better help them. Remember the Chinese finger trap? Not every problem is solved by pulling harder; many problems require us to draw back and let up the pressure. Detachment isn't being cold; as I've mentioned, many psychologists refer to it as "loving detachment." As such, detachment has nothing to do with ceasing to love or care about the person with the addiction, it's about making choices about how we go about interacting with that person. We use our new attitude about the situation to approach the problem of our loved one's addiction in a way that's healthier for us, and which is more likely to help the addict. Detachment isn't about building walls; it's about putting in place healthy boundaries.

Practicing detachment takes some time and practice, and the addict will likely try to provoke you while you try to establish your boundaries. The addict – an expert manipulator – will assault your boundaries by trying to guilt you, draw you into arguments, or engage in attention-seeking behaviors. They like having people in their circle of chaos; misery loves company. However, as with all boundaries, detachment requires sticking to your guns to work. I've seen many mothers heartbroken because their 20 year-old addict son or daughter wound up in jail, but I've seen many of them refuse to allow it to live in their head rent-free. With proper detachment, they allow the addict to deal with the consequences of their actions, and the parent carries on with their own life, refusing to surrender their own happiness, time, or plans because of the addict's behavior. They aren't going to enable the addiction by taking care of the consequences for the addict. They're taking back and protecting their happiness, peace of mind, and sanity through the proper use of boundaries and loving detachment.

*

When addicts have completed treatment and are in recovery, things change in their relationships with family and friends. Many people are relieved to see their loved one's old personality shining through again, and many are surprised to see that their loved one is better at interacting respectfully with others; indeed, they're often easier to get along with than they were before the addiction occurred. This is especially so if the addicts have completed the Twelve Steps, which are heavily focused on putting right past wrongs and finding new ways to connect with people so as to have quality relationships. As such, addicts in recovery begin to earn trust again.

Boundaries can be a double-edged sword. While they're important for allowing us to protect ourselves from toxic behaviors, when overly done they can cause us to place barriers that keep well-meaning people out. This can happen when we interact with a loved one in recovery. After all, we've been burned by the addict: we've been hurt, lied to, manipulated, and even abused for so long, trust can be slow to come. After all, the addict has had periods of abstinence in the past and said all the right things, and then ended up going right back to the substance use. So, we often justifiably continue to detach from the addict loved one in early recovery.

However, when addicts in recovery show us that they mean business – *showing* us through their actions rather than *telling* us with their words – with time the trust will rightfully return. People do relapse, but people do recover, too. With trust comes opportunity to get to know our loved one again, and to enjoy their second lease on life. When that occurs, at some point old detachments can become obsolete barriers to re-establishing a healthy relationship with a recovering addict loved one. I suggest that people consider this, and be wary of overly-rigid barriers and detachment when circumstances warrant allowing one's guard down, even if only slowly.

In the next chapter, we'll discuss healing from the traumatic effects of someone else's substance use. Once friends and families of addicts have an attitude change about addiction, addicts, and their role in helping an addict, and once they have appropriate boundaries in place with addicts (and other people, for that matter), then they're ready to heal from the insanity of being caught up in someone else's addiction. This can happen no matter what the addict in their life is up to – whether the addict is still actively involved in substance use, in recovery, or even removed from their life due to death, divorce, or separation. You don't have to wait until your loved one is in recovery to heal, and you shouldn't. So, let's talk about healing... *your* healing.

14

Recovering Your Peace of Mind and Happiness

Folks are usually about as happy as they make their minds up to be.

– Abraham Lincoln

So far we've talked about re-orienting our attitude about addiction, about addicts, and about our role in helping an addict. This allows us to understand and help an addict in a way that's smart and science-based, rather than by desperately throwing our whole self at the problem, trying to "straighten out" the addict. Addiction is one of those problems that requires brains instead of brawn. Helping an addict is best done by pushing less and working smart, just like when we try to get our fingers out of a Chinese finger trap. This allows us to be much more effective in our goal of helping the addict, but it also allows us to step back and stop being a part of the addiction and participating in the chaos.

We've also talked about boundaries, which is how we keep ourselves outside the addict's circle of chaos. Our attitude change allows us to see that we have choices; we can choose to no longer participate in the action-reaction cycle with the addict, because that doesn't help the addict, and it doesn't help us. This protects our ability to live our life and take care of ourselves and our own responsibilities without taking upon ourselves responsibility for the consequences of the addict's substance use – a responsibility that's not rightfully ours to take up.

We also talked about detachment – or "loving detachment," as the psychologists call it – whereby we make a decision to no longer allow our happiness and peace of mind to depend upon the addict's behaviors. Our attitude change shows us that we can choose to stop surrendering our happiness, peace of mind, and sanity to the addict. That's too much power to hand over to anyone, especially an addict.

So, now we have in place an approach to the problem that's more likely to help the addict, and allows us to keep our sanity. However, our past dealings with the addict amount to a traumatic experience that can leave even the strongest among us with serious mental, physical, emotional, financial, social, and vocational scars. In the past all the focus was on what's wrong with the addict, and how to help the addict. Now, we'll look at *you* and your "recovery" and healing from the experience of someone else's addiction.

Remember: your recovery and healing from the effects of someone else's addiction doesn't have to wait until the addict is in recovery, nor should it. Once we have the proper attitude, boundaries, and loving detachment in place, we're able to stop the ongoing trauma and begin healing from the experiences of the past.

In this chapter, we'll examine the effects of dealing with the chaos of someone else's substance use in the framework of how it may have been a traumatic experience for you, and how you can identify and address the effects of the trauma on your happiness, peace of mind, and ability to function. Then, we'll talk about self-care, something that's likely more challenging than you may be inclined to think. You've been so focused on someone else for so long, you may feel uneasy or even guilty about focusing on yourself for once. But you're no use to anyone – including the addict and other people in your life – unless you're healthy and happy.

Let's start out by talking about the stress of dealing with a loved one's addiction and how it affects our capacity for handling other stressors in life.

*

I liken the mind's ability to handle stress to a glass of water, where the glass represents the mind's capacity for stress, and the water represents stress. If our glass is nearly empty, we can add lots of water before it overflows and makes a mess. However, if the glass is filled nearly to the top, even adding a little bit of water will overflow and cause a mess. So it is with our mind and stress. If our mind is filled with lots of unresolved stress, even adding a little bit more stress will create a mess: we'll blow up with anger and rage at what would otherwise be a minor stressor. All that compressed, unresolved stress with no outlet seeps out of every pore until we just explode when that extra stress puts us over the top – overfilling the glass.

However, we don't have to have a stress-free life in order to keep our glass low or empty so that we have a great capacity to absorb more stress without creating a mess. In fact, many people who undergo a great deal of stress have their stress-glass nearly empty all the time, while other people with low-stress lives have their glass constantly full and ready to overflow. The trick lies in reducing the amount of water in our glass by draining out the water periodically, before the glass has a chance to get too full. The way we keep our stress-glass low is through healthy stress coping skills.

A lot of people who deal with an addict have a pretty full stress-glass most of the time, and with good reason. Watching a loved one engage in dangerous behaviors while they ruin their life is stressful enough. When we add in the lies, the theft, the empty promises, the invasion of our space and belongings, the constant detective-work, the pointless arguments with the know-it-all addict, and the effort required to hide the "family problem" from others to avoid embarrassment and unsolicited advice, the stress levels reach traumatic proportions. Feelings that a loved one's chance of recovery decreases with each relapse only further complicates the grief experience. Even when the addict is in recovery, the stress from an addict loved one can be significant: constant worry about relapse, trying to make sure the addict is doing their recovery work, and walking on eggshells around them.

When our mind is full of unresolved stress, we have difficulty with other functions of the mind. We tend to be unhappy, and our mind is filled with conflict and worry rather than peace. It's hard to concentrate on anything else than the problems that have taken over our mind. Learning to keep that stress-glass low or empty is an important skill for being happy and at peace of mind regardless of what's going on in our life. After all, we all live better, happier lives when we have resilience – the ability to maintain our serenity and "roll with the punches" regardless of what's going on around us.

Even when we're no longer dealing with an active addict – because they're in recovery, or because of separation, or death – the stress-glass can remain full for a long time, until such time as the stress has been drained from the glass. Whether we're dealing with an active addict now on an ongoing basis, or we have an addict in our past, we'll talk in this chapter about how to drain the stress-glass and keep it low, so that our capacity for handling regular life stressors doesn't result in every stressor becoming a happiness-killing crisis.

*

In the previous two chapters we discussed two of the most important tools for insulating ourselves from unhappiness, anxiety, and a negative mindset when dealing with an addict. This involved changing our attitude about addiction, addicts, and our role in helping an addict (chapter 12), and using barriers and detachment (chapter 13) to remove ourselves from the chaos of someone else's substance use. These tools help us to stop an addict from filling up our glass on an ongoing basis, but we still need to deal with all the excess water (stress) that's in our glass from past chaos and insanity from dealing with an addict.

People who've been caught up in the chaos of dealing with a loved one with addiction should recognize that they've been through trauma. There's no way to quantify how an adverse experience will affect someone. Some people are traumatized by events that others would view as relatively minor, while others endure horrible traumatic events but suffer no ill after-effects. A person doesn't have to have post-traumatic stress disorder (PTSD) in order to suffer ongoing ill effects and mental symptoms from past troubles. Lots of people are haunted by past memories, left over emotions, and even unwanted invasive thoughts from past events but don't meet the criteria for PTSD.

To be traumatic, experiences don't necessarily have to be as awful as having been sexually or physically abused, or having witnessed a death. Past trauma may not even be from one specific event; it can also be the result of having lived through a prolonged period of accumulated adverse conditions, such as poor treatment in the workplace, bullying during the school years, or a childhood scarred by uncaring and neglectful parents. As well, the effect of past happenings is based on the person's perception of events and memories. Events that may be traumatic for one person may be easily shaken off by another. Certainly, the emotional roller-coaster of trying to help a loved one who's self-destructing through substance use and trying their best to drag everyone else into their misery can traumatize even the strongest among us. It can be a miserable and prolonged experience, a struggle of a lifetime.

For some who've lived through a loved one's addiction, the trauma may be especially deep, such as those who've lost a loved one due to separation or death, those who've had a loved one end up in prison, or those who've had to watch a loved one resort to prostitution, to name only a few examples. Those who've experienced other bothersome ordeals in their past may find that the addiction experience adds to their psychological wounds and causes them to relive troubling memories and feelings.

In my practice, I've found that a lot of people who seek counseling for self-esteem issues, problems with relationships, anger and stress problems, and other psychological hang-ups often don't even recognize that their problems grew from unresolved past traumatic experiences. People who're focused on caring for someone else – such as when they're trying to help an addict – may be so focused on the person they're helping that they fail to see their own sicknesses. Often they feel guilty about thinking about their own distress when someone else is needy.

For once, those who've experienced the chaos of someone else's addiction should step back and turn the focus away from the addict for a moment, and focus on themselves. They can apply their attitude change about addiction – the part that tells us that addiction is a family disease – and examine the effects that this family disease has had on them. It may be difficult to cut through the mess of feelings and emotions, especially if they've never taken the time to sit back and sift through their own thoughts and feelings. When the emotions are separated and sorted, there may be a wide variety of opposing emotions, such as pity and love for the addict, versus anger and resentment toward the addict. Feelings of pity and love are good, those are not undesirable emotions, and they help us to treat the addict with compassion and dignity. Anger and resentment, however, are not. Those emotions are like a cancer that eats away at the mind and, if they go unresolved, can become a reliable source of daily pain. Likewise, the sorrow and grief that may have followed from someone else's addiction may have to be confronted in order to "get over" the trauma.

I'm always concerned by the latent anger that I see in people who're trying to help an addict loved one. Trying to help someone who doesn't want to be helped, the constant cycle of hope followed by let-down with every new promise, being lied to, stolen from, and used, and the feeling that they're alone and not loved all cumulate into significant frustration and anger. Even though their anger is certainly justified, anger is truly a toxic emotion and it does them no good to keep it around. Being filled with anger over one issue spills out into other aspects of daily life. It makes people into impatient and angry drivers, it makes them difficult to get along with in the workplace or at home, it affects their relationships, and it gnaws away at the psyche. People take out their anger on whoever or whatever happens to be unfortunate enough to be standing in front of them. Black emotions beget black emotions. It's not a nice way to live, whether the anger is justified or not.

Letting go of latent anger and resentment is a deeply therapeutic remedy for impatience, intolerance, aggressiveness, and being short-tempered. It's hard to be happy and at peace when one is an angry person. For people who've been victims of trauma – such as crime, abuse, disease, or disaster – letting go of a resentment may seem an impossible task. That's especially so when the trauma was deliberate, at the hands of another, and the resentment is justified. Suffering abuse and mistreatment at the hands of an addict loved one is a form of victimization as well. Victims have every right to be angry. However, by carrying around anger and resentment they're allowing themselves to be re-victimized every day. This is true whether they were victimized by some past abuse or tragedy, or from more recent mistreatment at the hands of an addict. Just like we make a conscious decision to stop allowing another person's substance use determine whether or not we're happy and at peace, so we can make a conscious decision to let go of resentment's power over us. It doesn't necessarily mean that we forgive or forget, because those things may not be possible. This process may take time, may need to occur in baby-steps, and may benefit from outside help from a counselor or even a trusted friend who's a good listener. Even getting to the point of talking about the resentment may take time. Journaling or simply listing resentments is a helpful way to get started. We should be patient and take all the time we need. However, regardless of how long it takes, we must always hold onto the goal that we will rid ourselves of the power that our resentments hold over us. We must never allow ourselves to become comfortable with anger and resentment; the price can be true happiness and peace of mind. Resentments do us no good; what benefit do we gain from allowing past events boil inside of us day after day, month after month, year after year? You're reading this book because you want to be happy and at peace despite having a person in your life with addiction. Well, anger and resentments are a major barrier to that peace of mind and happiness. So, let's now talk about "getting over" past traumas – including the trauma of dealing with an addict – and the anger and resentments that they leave us with.

When we have serious, justified resentments in our past, it's important to have a proper understanding of what we can expect when we address past traumas and resentments. I've found that when it comes to grief, trauma, and loss people tend to have unreasonable expectations. People often believe that "getting over it" means that the offending experience is forgotten and no longer bothersome. That's not a realistic expectation, but many will cling to this forlorn hope for a lifetime. Realistically, "dealing with" a traumatic event, grief, or loss means arriving at a point where we can get through our days without the event dominating our thoughts and dictating our actions. For those who've suffered serious traumatic events, the memory will always be there; what we can expect and should be striving for is that the memory be put in its proper place. We can expect that the memory no longer sits in the forefront of our mind, no longer crushes our self-esteem, no longer causes fear and anxiety, and no longer generates the constant anger and resentment that it has in the past. In other words, "dealing with it" means that these events no longer "own" us. We decide that other people's actions and events – no matter how horrible – will no longer live in our head rent-free.

The amount of pain and dysfunction that result from being a victim of sexual or physical abuse, serious illness, crime, disaster, or mistreatment at the hands of another can leave people with profound legitimate resentments, grief, and pain. However, I've seen many people find relief from these soul-crushing emotions, and this has clearly greatly relieved the pain and dysfunction that they suffer from their past. However, I don't kid myself. I've been involved in the care of many such people as a physician and as a therapist, and I know very well that it doesn't just all go away, especially for people with deep psychological scars. Again, we must have realistic expectations. "Getting over it" doesn't mean that all is forgotten and forgiven; rather, it means that these experiences no longer dominate our thoughts and behaviors, and no longer ruin our days.

Let's now discuss three ways to "get over" the painful emotions and memories of past traumas, such as those that we experience when we suffer the ill effects of another person's substance use. These ill effects include grief, sorrow, anger, and resentment.

*

The first approach to coming to terms with painful experiences – for those who're carrying anger and resentment – is to try to understand the offender, the object of the resentment. A very important part of recovery and healing from addiction is that addicts must identify and cast away their considerable anger and resentments, as those ugly emotions are largely responsible for the negative psychology that underpins addiction. So it is with people in recovery from the effects of someone else's addiction. Anger and resentment are a rock in our shoe, whether we're an addict or not.

Letting go of a resentment begins by trying to understand the person who caused our resentment. This isn't the same as forgiving them, and it certainly doesn't mean we forget what happened; that memory will always be a part of us. Rather, understanding people that we resent is about taking an empathetic look at why they may have wronged us. In most cases they've wronged us because they were sick and haunted by demons. When we've been wronged by an addict, we can use our knowledge about addiction to try to understand that our loved one was afflicted with a disease, and the horrible behaviors were symptoms of that disease, brought on by the effects of toxic substances on their brain. This doesn't excuse the behavior; rather, it allows us to put the behavior into context.

One of my long-standing resentments that I had to let go of when I wanted to overcome my addiction was my resentment toward my father. His behavior toward me and my mother and then his abandonment of us when I was young left us to suffer many hardships and affected me deeply well into adulthood. It also saddened me to see how it affected my mother. My resentments toward my father were longstanding and deep, even though he had passed away some years ago. In recovery, I needed to let go of that resentment, so I sought to understand my father. I never knew him well, so I researched him a bit. He was an alcoholic and his behaviors were consistent with the behaviors of people who're sick with addiction. I also learned that he had been abused as a child by a step-father, and ended up living in an orphanage because his mother gave him up to appease her husband. I could easily imagine how he would've had anger, resentments, insecurities, and self-esteem issues of his own from those traumatic experiences. Understanding that my father was mentally and spiritually sick didn't excuse his behavior, and it didn't necessarily mean I forgave him, but it helped me to understand him and his behavior. His behavior toward me was about him, not me.

People have an unfortunate tendency to internalize the experience when they've been mistreated by someone else. They look inside themselves for the cause and may even conclude that they were mistreated or victimized because they're unlovable, or undeserving of respect, or perhaps were even deserving of the mistreatment. Many even somehow blame themselves for the experience. The impact on self-esteem is profound, and can spill over into other aspects of their life, besides just making them unhappy. Their self-blame and feelings of unworthiness may render them unable to set boundaries, and this may make them targets for further victimization. They may struggle with finding the confidence they need to undertake projects, speak their mind, or otherwise assert themselves in the home and workplace. Coming to understand the individual who mistreated or victimized them allows them to focus the blame for the mistreatment where it belongs – on the individual who mistreated them – rather than on themselves.

If we've been traumatized and hurt by an addict, our knowledge about addiction and the effects of substance use on the brain and behavior may help us understand the experience, to put the addict's behavior into context. Again, it doesn't excuse the behavior, nor does it absolve the addict of responsibility for it. However, it helps us to see that the words and deeds were not based on our own merits or value as a person, but were based on demons haunting someone else's substance-soaked mind. It's on them, not on us.

Understanding that those who've wronged us may have been sick with their own demons helps us to detach ourselves from the horrible actions of someone else. Although their actions were deeply hurtful to us, these actions weren't about us; they were about someone else's struggles with sickness.

*

If you harbor anger and resentments toward the addict in your life, I'm going to ask you to consider forgiveness. Even if the addict in your life has done unforgiveable things to you and those you love, and even if they're still drinking or using and doing awful things, I'm going to ask you to consider forgiveness.

Forgiveness isn't something we do for someone else. Sure, it might make the other person feel better to know that we've forgiven them – IF they're repentant – otherwise they probably don't care. Even if the other person doesn't deserve forgiveness, we the victims deserve the positive effects that forgiveness gives us. In fact, there's no real reason to even communicate our forgiveness to the other person unless they come to us seeking to right past wrongs. No, because forgiveness is for us; it's the key to letting go of the hold that past traumas – including the trauma of dealing with an addict – have over us. Al-Anon – the experts at recovering from the effects of someone else's addiction – tells us: *forgiveness is no favor. We do it for no one but ourself* (*How Al-Anon Works*, p. 86). Forgiveness is how we stop allowing another person and their actions to live in our head rent-free. It's our path to happiness and peace of mind. So, I'm going to ask you to consider forgiveness.

Forgiveness may be something that takes time, but that's OK. When it comes to very deep traumatic resentments, outside help in the form of trauma counseling may be advisable. I suggest that every person, no matter how bad the event that caused the resentment, should aim for forgiveness, even if it takes a long time. And that forgiveness must be unconditional. It must not require that the other person show remorse, or ask for our forgiveness. If we wait for that to happen we're handing power back to the offender. And forgiveness doesn't need to be offered to the other person. In many cases having contact with the other person would not be helpful, especially if that person isn't repentant.

If the thought of forgiving someone who did you wrong is repulsive to you, and you feel that they don't deserve it, then think again. When people say: *she doesn't deserve my forgiveness*, I say: *OK, but you do*. Forgiveness is not for the benefit of the other person; rather, it's for *our* benefit. It's the ultimate release from the power that past traumas hold over us. Anger and resentments are physically and mentally toxic to us, and a major barrier to serenity and peace of mind. Indeed, research has shown that forgiveness improves our physical and mental health. Keep an open mind about forgiveness if you carry deep-seated or justified resentments; it should be your goal.

I don't wish to diminish or belittle the significance of negative feelings that some among us may have, whether it's related to the trauma of dealing with someone's addiction or other past traumas. As such, our discussion here is certainly not intended to be a cure-all and fix-it solution for difficulties that haunt the psyche. Rather it's meant as a primer for an attitude change that reveals choices that we have when it comes to enduring serenity-killing emotions and feelings. I would suggest that anyone who struggles with such issues consider seeing a professional counselor or therapist who's experienced in dealing with such matters. Those who struggle with anger and resentments specifically related to dealing with someone else's substance use may wish to consider checking out Al-Anon. They're the experts at getting together people with such backgrounds so that they can express their feelings in a safe and understanding place, share their experiences, and help each other heal. Al-Anon is a Twelve Step program, so it takes advantage of the wonderfully therapeutic power of the Twelve Steps. Al-anon isn't about the addict; it's about those who've been affected by an addict.

*

Acceptance is another tool for healing from past traumas. You may notice that acceptance is a recurring theme in this book, and that's because it's such a powerful tool for positive psychology and overall happiness. When it comes to past events, we have no choice but to accept them. Those events have happened, and there's nothing we or anybody else can do about it. For that reason, it makes sense to make an effort to accept past events – even terrible events – as something we can't change. What we *can* change is how we respond to such events now. We'll talk more about that shortly, when I tell you the incredible story of Dr. Viktor Frankl and what his experiences tell us about horrible trauma and the power of acceptance and choosing how we respond to trauma.

Another effective way at putting anger and resentments and other harmful emotions to rest involves coming out of our shell and opening up about our feelings and our past experiences. People who help others often feel guilty when they turn attention to their own needs, and expressing their pain and unmet needs to another person may make them feel like they're being selfish. Again, an attitude change is in order for people who feel that way. As we discussed in the last chapter, if we don't look after ourselves, nobody will. As a therapist, I've noticed that many individuals go through their whole life living with frustration and unmet needs because they keep waiting for someone else to take care of them. And self-care is far from selfish; if we're not healthy and whole we're not much use to anyone else. In fact, our unaddressed negative feelings may make us difficult to be around. By adopting the attitude that self-care is not a selfish act, and is a necessary part of our health and well-being, we give ourselves permission to turn attention to our own needs. This is especially important if we're hurting inside.

Coming out of our shell and getting our hardships and struggles off our chest can be especially difficult, because we may be embarrassed or uncomfortable talking about it. It may feel like ripping a band-aid off an old wound. When people have an addict in their life, it often becomes the "family secret," and they put on an outward show that all's well whenever they're around someone else. The same may apply when we carry other emotional burdens, such as a past history of abuse. However, getting such things off our chest is so overwhelmingly therapeutic that it's worth making the effort to overcome the barriers. There are many options: a trusted friend, a doctor or therapist, a member of the clergy, a family member. Writing our thoughts and feelings in a letter to ourselves and then burning the letter may help us become ready to open up. Maybe even sitting in the garden and telling our story to a big oak tree can help us to screw up the courage to open up.

The Twelve Step program recognizes very well the toxic effect that negative feelings and emotions have on our life, how they sour our dealings with other people, and how they impede our happiness and peace of mind. When helping people to overcome anger and resentments, the Twelve Step program employs a very effective process of putting their anger and resentments down on paper, and sharing them with someone else. Whether you're involved in a Twelve Step program or not, getting these emotions off your chest by explaining them to an understanding listener is a wonderful way to become ready to release their grip from your psyche. We'll further discuss the importance of opening up with others and not bearing burdens alone a little later in this chapter.

Once we've told our story and gotten things off our chest, we can cast off anger and resentments. Some may find it a relief to leave their burdens with God, or some other higher power, or to simply throw their burdens up in the air, to release themselves from their pain. Healing is a process, and such actions can really help to move that process along.

*

Past trauma can leave us with more than just anger and resentment. When past events have left us mourning, grief-stricken, and sorrowful, letting go of the dominance of those emotions can be especially difficult. Some people feel guilty when they try to let go of grief; they may feel that by doing so they no longer honor the memory of the person they've lost or have seen come into great hardship. However, it's important to remember that "getting over grief" doesn't mean forgetting someone or something, or that our loss no longer matters to us. Rather, it means that we're able to release ourselves from ruminating on our loss at the expense of our ability to function properly. In many ways, one of the best ways that we can honor someone we're mourning is to be the best, most effective person we can be. We can honor and mourn our loved one in meaningful ways, rather than by sitting around moping and allowing our life to stop. This is what 18th century Scottish poet Thomas Campbell meant when he wrote: *to live in hearts we leave behind is not to die.*

One of my favorite writers, Victorian-era novelist George Eliot, illustrates my point in his masterpiece novel *Middlemarch*. I like this book because it's all about the consequences of the past and how people allow the past to shape their future, an area of interest to any psychologist. Late in the story we're introduced to a scene where grief-stricken Dorothea spends a sleepless night of: *loud-whispered cries and moans* and *helpless sobs*. After she finally cries herself to sleep: *in the chill hours of the morning twilight, when all was dim around her, she awoke – not with any amazed wondering where she was or what had happened, but with the clearest consciousness that she was looking into the eyes of sorrow*. Dorothea had finally recognized and acknowledged her grief – "with the clearest consciousness" – which allowed her to free herself from suffering its ongoing unkind effects on her behavior: *the fire of Dorothea's anger was not easily spent, and it flamed out in fitful returns of spurning reproach*. Dorothea's unacknowledged and suppressed grief was causing her: *to sit in the narrow cell of her calamity, in the besotted misery of a consciousness that only sees another's lot as an accident of its own*. Her sorrow and grief were not forgotten or abandoned, but put into their proper place in her mind so that she could resume living her life as she should: *she was no longer wrestling with her grief, but could sit down with it as a lasting companion and make it a sharer in her thoughts*. Eliot is telling us that coming to terms with grief – in other words, choosing to stop allowing unrequited grief to dominate our thoughts and actions – isn't about abandoning sorrow or hardening oneself to tragedy. It's about giving it its proper place in our mind, where it is a "sharer of thoughts." There are times in life when it's time to remember and honor past loss and hardship, and there are times in life when it's time to take care of living.

Let's talk about grief and a loved one's addiction for a moment. In my practice I've observed that people with an addict loved one often experience grief that they haven't recognized or acknowledged. If a loved one dies from addiction, there's a defined focus of grief, and the deceased addict's loved ones recognize their grief and have a chance to acknowledge and take care of it. However, unlike grieving a death, where there's a single terminal event, people who watch the gradual decline of a loved one to the insidious process of addiction face a prolonged painful event, often marked by milestones that provoke another new event to grieve (such as a mother seeing her addict child in jail). It's like they're watching the slow death of the person they once knew.

When people watch the person they once knew slowly slip away into addiction, they experience emotions that go well beyond the usual expression of grief that comes with a sudden loss. They're subjected to an emotional roller coaster of emotions – hope followed by disappointment, love and concern followed by anger, as well as being the recipient of rejection, insults, and ire – that would predispose anyone to an emotional breaking point. This is often compounded by self-blame and guilt, as they question why they couldn't help their loved one "just stop" the substance use. They don't even see to their own pain because they're laser-focused on helping the addict. The tangle of emotions is dark, but can be summed up by one term: unrecognized and unaddressed grief.

Caring for and taking on extra responsibilities for an addict is a tremendous burden. Most people do so largely in secret, because they're embarrassed by the "family secret," and they know others won't understand what they're going through. They don't want to be judged or blamed for not being able to help the addict, and they're tired of getting useless advice from people who don't know what it's like. As such, many caregivers of addicts receive little or no respite, and must sacrifice other aspects of their life to care for their loved one: such as time with their children or spouse, career, leisure time, and sleep. As the addiction progresses and their loved one further alienates themself from family and friends it becomes more like looking after a stranger. The increasingly intense care requirements become less and less personal, and more of a thankless handicap. This is totally different from what happens when a death occurs and friends circle around, acknowledge the grief, and offer their support and help.

The end result is that those who care about an addict loved one are overburdened with self-imposed obligations to pick up the addict's dropped responsibilities, cover for the addict, and desperate attempts at helping the addict. They have no time or emotional capacity to grieve in a healthy way. They might not even recognize their own need to grieve, and others may not recognize it either. The litany of emotions related to their feelings of loss over seeing their loved one increasingly consumed by substance use becomes a stagnant emotional cesspool.

I suggest that those among us who're dealing with a loved one in active addiction take some time to look inside and examine their sense of loss and their grief over the awful experience of this family disease. When unresolved grief becomes our companion, a significant emotional toll follows. For anyone to reclaim their happiness and peace of mind, they may need to acknowledge and confront their grief. This can only happen when the grief is recognized.

One study examined the effects of a child's death on parental grief; the study looked at the effects suffered by parents following losing a child to death from substance use and/or suicide, and compared them to the effects of losing a child to an accident or a natural cause. The study found that the parents who lost a child to suicide or substance use were significantly more troubled by grief and mental health problems than those with natural or accidental deaths (i.e. non-drug-related). The study authors concluded that the intense and powerful societal stigma around substance use, mental illness, and suicide impaired healing due to the lack of compassionate responses from others; including the public at large as well as close family members. The study authors described those who're grieving the loss of a loved one to addiction as: *a greatly neglected bereavement population* (Fiegelman et al., p. 291). This study tells us that seeking an understanding and compassionate support system when mourning a loved one who died or suffered other calamity from addiction is a crucial necessity for grieving in a healthy way.

When an addict dies, people gather around and support the grieving family and friends, and this can make talking about and confronting the grief much easier. For those who're dealing with an active addict, that just doesn't happen. However, there are lots of salutary resources out there for those who wish to address their grief around a loved one in active addiction. Counselors with experience in trauma and addiction, members of the clergy, and support groups for those affected by someone else's addiction are all wonderful ways to commit to moving forward in life without the unnecessary troublesome baggage of unresolved grief and trauma. Again, I highly recommend Al-Anon. There's no cost involved, and Al-Anon allows individuals to meet other people who've had similar experiences. Many Al-Anon members have loved ones still in active addiction, while others have lost family members to addiction through death or separation, and others have a loved one who's been in recovery for decades. It doesn't matter what type of substance was involved – it doesn't have to be alcohol – Al-Anon is a fantastic resource for anyone. Their excellent book *How Al-Anon Works* is available from their website for $6, and is available at meetings at cost. Good stuff. Advice columnist and novelist Cheryl Strayed nailed it when she said: *the healing power of even the most microscopic exchange with someone who knows in a flash precisely what you're talking about because [they] experienced that thing too cannot be overestimated* (from her book *Tiny Beautiful Things*).

*

So far we've discussed a couple of serenity-defeating effects of the trauma of dealing with an addict: anger and resentment, and grief. However, there are other self-defeating emotions that commonly arise from trauma: such as guilt, insecurity, and mistrust. Some people beat themselves up mercilessly with self-imposed guilt over an adverse experience; even victims of sexual assault may do this. Indeed, the traumatized human mind seems to have a penchant for blaming itself for just about anything. Guilt seems to be especially prevalent among those who've had to deal with someone else's addiction. Blaming themselves for their loved one's addiction, or suicide, or imprisonment is a terrible, toxic mindset that accomplishes nothing but deepening the trauma. It seems that this guilt is often due to a belief that the individual caused their loved one's addiction, or worsened it, or could have and should have done more to stop the addiction.

I hope that by this point in your reading, with your knowledge of addiction and the attitude changes we've discussed, you're able to free yourself from such nonsensical guilt if you're beating yourself up with it. If not, repeat the following to yourself several times a day until you finally let go of the guilt and get on with using your brainpower for more productive purposes: *addiction is caused by a disease, not by me... I am not responsible for someone else's substance use... I am not responsible for the consequences of someone else's substance use... addicts are responsible for their own recovery.*

Sometimes the guilt is due to a psychological phenomenon known as *survivor's guilt*, where people believe they've done something wrong by surviving when someone else died, or because they survived a life-threatening situation, such as an assault. Survivor guilt can even occur when someone else didn't die, and an individual blames themself for avoiding some kind of harm that befell others. This can happen in situations where people blame themselves for someone else's addiction, or they feel guilt because they believe subconsciously that they should have been the one to go through addiction rather than their loved one. Parents are particularly vulnerable to this effect, because they tend to wish that they could be the one suffering, rather than their child. Survivor's guilt can be so powerful that it may even cause PTSD.

Carrying guilt about a traumatic event – including survivor's guilt – may be something that some individuals want to seek professional counseling for. However, there are things that people can do to address this terrible symptom. Research has shown that survivor's guilt tends to fade with time, and about one third of affected individuals will recover within one year without any sort of treatment. Time sometimes heals emotional wounds, something doctors refer to as "the tincture of time."

Understanding the experience can also help people overcome survivor's guilt. This type of guilt is usually driven by false, unreasonable, and irrational beliefs, such as a belief that the individual could have somehow predicted and avoided the event, or that they played a role in the unfortunate outcome. Even when people did have some kind of negative interaction or involvement that may have been partly responsible for the traumatic event, they may fail to put it into the correct context. They exaggerate their role, and they take too much of the responsibility upon themselves. Even when people *are* responsible for a tragedy – such as a drunk driver who killed other people – they must come to terms with their guilt and put things right in the best way they can. They can either live their life in depression and isolation, or they can do their best to do good things for others and somehow make the world a better place, even if only in some small way. While doing good things for others can help people who are to blame for tragedy, it's also useful for those who suffer from survivor's guilt, or from grief over a loss, or anger and resentment over being victimized, or from haunting memories due to past events.

Many survivors of trauma – especially deliberate trauma at the hands of others – live life with a deep sense of insecurity and mistrust because of their past experiences. They don't view the world as a safe place, and they put up walls that prevent closeness with other people. Getting close to anyone is unthinkable to some of these people. Research has shown that easing into doing good deeds, especially volunteer work directed at people who've been through similar traumatic experiences, can be a therapeutic way to begin to allow the outside world back in again. In fact, helping others has proven to be an excellent way to recover from many of the adverse psychological effects of trauma.

Clinical investigations have identified brain changes that occur following trauma. It turns out that specific neural pathways result from traumatic experiences and cause the dysfunctional thought processes, behaviors, and emotions that make up survivor's guilt and the self-punishment that people put themselves through following trauma. However, further research has shown that selflessness, altruism, and social support all help to reroute those disrupted brain connection networks back to their normal state. Specific studies have clearly demonstrated these simple measures as effective at helping people to let go of the intrusive thoughts and persisting anger, resentment, sorrow, grief, and guilt that often follow adverse events and mistreatment by others. That may be one of the reasons that support groups for loved ones of addicts – such as Al-Anon – work so well. They give individuals the chance to connect with and help others who've also suffered from someone else's substance use.

*

Mental health problems, especially depression, can easily occur in those who're engaged in the deeply frustrating endeavor of trying to help an addict. The personal nature of the stress, chronicity of the chaos, the grief involved, the ups and downs, and feelings of hopelessness and loss can contribute to a depressed mood. There's a fine line between the sorrow and grief that naturally occurs when watching the downfall of a loved one, and pathological depression. The difference lies primarily in its duration and effects on function. For example, when grieving becomes an ongoing impairment, where the individual doesn't want to get out of bed or participate in any activities, and is unable to concentrate on important activities, then depression may be factor. The DSM 5 (the standard diagnostic manual for psychological problems) recognizes that the normal response to loss may resemble depression, and suggests that treating depressive symptoms during grieving may be beneficial, particularly in the presence of feelings of worthlessness, suicidal thoughts, and impairment of function. In my practice, I generally offered grieving people a mild sedative to help with sleep, because disrupted sleep can magnify grief and dysfunction. I also advised them to be watchful for any symptoms that they felt went beyond the normal grief response, so that we could discuss possible treatment if necessary.

The grief associated with the death of a loved one is a definable point of trauma, but the grief associated with the gradual, ongoing decline and loss of attachment with a loved one can be especially difficult because of its chronicity, and the lack of recognition it receives as a definable point of grief. As well, the social stigma, lack of understanding by the general public, and judgmental attitudes of would-be supporters make the grief of dealing with addiction especially prone to not being recognized or acknowledged. The result is that many individuals don't acknowledge their own grief, or they deal with it in social isolation. The research literature refers to this kind of bereavement as *disenfranchised grief*, meaning that it's grief that's associated with a loss that isn't or can't be openly acknowledged, socially supported, or publicly mourned. It's a recipe for unhappiness and mental anguish, and should be addressed.

*

A number of research studies of the effects of addiction on the family – most involving the parents of adolescent or adult children with addiction – document some of the traumatic difficulties of dealing with a loved one's addiction. In many cases in these studies, the addicts moved in and out of their family's life, just as they moved in and out of sobriety, jails, and institutional care and custody. Other cases turned out better, where the addict had succeeded in treatment and recovery. Some died or disappeared. Five themes emerged from the study participants' experiences:

- **Stigma** – the family members felt stigmatized by society in general, but also by their friends and family. It's well known that addicts are subjected to considerable negative stigma by society, but these studies show that the addict's family can be stigmatized as well. One mother reported that it took years just for her to be able to say: *my daughter is an addict* (Zucker et al., p.764),
- **Regret** – by "regret" they meant feelings of guilt, self-blame, and depression. These feelings tended to alternate between self-imposed guilt over their child's addiction and understanding that the addiction was not caused by parental actions or shortcomings. One mother said: *as a parent you have to forgive yourself because your behavior could*

have very well contributed to your child's behavior and there is not anything you can do about it now (Zucker et al., p.764).

Depression was a significant factor, with one mother at one point contemplating suicide due to the stress of the constant ups and downs. One mother also found that she was using alcohol to cope, which she was (fortunately) able to recognize and stop before it became a problem. Many family members report crying daily, due to the discovery of the addiction and from the ongoing stress,

- **Disrupted lives** – the addicts would come and go from their family's life, causing chaos and confusion in the family unit. When an addict child was incarcerated the parents once again played the role of caring parent, filled with hope that the addict would stay in recovery after jail. However, often the parent wouldn't hear at all from the addict again after release until the next incarceration.

  Familial disruption also occurred because the family dynamic with the addict affects how other family members interact with each other. Often there are conflicts between family members on how to deal with the addict, the stereotypical situation being the where one parent wants to throw the addict out while the other doesn't. Other conflicts arose due to short tempers among family members due to the stress of caring about an addict who doesn't care about themself. One study clearly demonstrated that higher levels of grief were associated with lower levels of family cohesiveness,

- **Loss of support** – there was considerable frustration due to not finding adequate supports in the community and within the medical system. One study found that families in England seeking help for an addicted family member felt condescended to or actively excluded by services.

  Finding an understanding, safe, and non-judgmental support system was universally found to be one of the most effective ways at coping and reducing the problems associated with the stress of a loved one's addiction. One parent found a "parents of addicted children" support group, which she described as being: *like a miracle and I finally stopped suffering on my own* (Zucker et al., p.764), and

- **Loss of quality of life** – this was most affected by having to quit jobs due to the time it took to help the addict, money spent on various recovery programs, and money and time spent on visiting and caring for the addict. Parents felt they had to rearrange their day around the addict, and felt they: *have to go and put the safety net up and make sure I am going to catch her [the addict] today* (Zucker et al., p.764).

The study participants described gratitude, self-fulfilling activities, social networking, and doing things for other people as their most effective coping mechanisms. Said one: *I cope by being... very thankful for my life, because I have a good life. I have lots of positive things in my life... when I start feeling badly, something that works very well for me is to do something for someone else... I like stuff that makes me happy: making jewelry, knitting...* (Zucker et al., p.765).

We discussed earlier how research studies have clearly shown that these same activities (helping others, and self-fulfilling activities) help people overcome the effects of traumatic experience and grief on the brain, and to recover their ability to function. Let's look at these measures in more detail and how to use them as effective coping strategies, starting with helping others.

*

Altruism – giving to others and expecting nothing in return – and past trauma have a kind of a reciprocal relationship. Psychological research has demonstrated that people who've been through traumatic experiences are more likely to empathize for others who've had similar experiences and they're also more likely to wish to reach out to help those they empathize with. They can understand what others are going through, and are better equipped to reach out to them. People are best equipped to help those they can identify with, and this trauma-specific altruism helps them to heal. Some survivors of trauma internalize their pain, but others are driven to try to address their trauma by helping others who've suffered the same adversities that they themselves have experienced. In psychology, this is known as a *survivor mission*, where the individual derives healing benefits from giving meaning to their personal trauma by transforming it into positive social action. This phenomenon, where people who are themselves survivors of trauma are driven to find healing by helping others is known as *altruism born of suffering*. Altruism born of suffering is deeply therapeutic, and anyone who struggles with any kind of pain left over from past events may wish to avail themself of this rich source of healing.

Therapists try to facilitate altruism in their trauma patients because the healing it provides prevents a repeating cycle of trauma, where the anger, rage, resentments, sorrow, and guilt can lead to a cycle of perpetual unhappiness, negative psychology, substance use, and even violence. Studies have shown that altruism is most effective for healing from trauma when it's mentored, done within the context of a support system, and with some healing already accomplished. This implies that the optimal effects of volunteer work or other acts of altruism may be best achieved if the altruism is done while undergoing trauma counseling, or within the context of a support group that offers mentoring, such as Al-Anon. In fact, Al-Anon incorporates altruism into its program of healing, as part of the Twelve Steps.

Studies have demonstrated that voluntarily helping others results in improvements in life satisfaction, sense of well-being, happiness, self-esteem, and hopefulness. Further, altruism reduces symptoms of depression, anxiety, and the physical symptoms of mental health disorders. In fact, giving help was found to be significantly more beneficial for mental health symptoms than was receiving help.

The interpersonal benefits of altruism are obvious, but have been confirmed by studies in the social sciences. Helping others is associated with enhanced social integration, better connectedness with others, enhanced meaningfulness in life, and an improved perception of one's own self-efficacy and competence. It just plain makes people feel good about themselves and their place in the world. It also reduces psychological pain from past negative experiences.

Surprisingly, helping others also impacts our physical health. One large study that followed people over a period of thirty years to study what factors determined their health found that those who voluntarily helped others were significantly less likely to develop serious illness. Other studies have demonstrated that volunteering and helping others is associated with longer life. Helping others has also been found to be linked to other important physical parameters, such as improved energy levels, reduced fatigue, and self-reported good health.

Interestingly, studies into the effects of altruism have shown that helping others reduces negative emotions, many of which are the same negative emotions that plague people who've been through adversity: fear, anxiety, depression, sadness, anger, and hostility. Says one researcher: *it is difficult to be angry, resentful, or fearful when one is showing unselfish love toward another person* (Post, 2005). Researchers theorize that the positive effects of altruism stem from enabling people to emerge from preoccupation with the self, which gets people outside of the negative thoughts that inhabit their mind.

Researchers have, however, identified one landmine that can turn helping others into a negative: becoming too involved, or allowing ourselves to become too emotionally engaged in our efforts at altruism can be harmful to us. As with all things, when we're helping others we must strive to find a balance. So where does that balance lay?

Altruistic behavior is linked to health and well-being benefits when it's not experienced as overwhelming. When we become overwhelmed by helping tasks that are chronic and unchanging, like being a caretaker for a family member with addiction, we may be at greater risk for depression. This doesn't mean that we shouldn't care for a loved one, it just means that we should recognize when it's time to ask for help or take a step back. Altruism does us harm if our emotional and physical health diminish as a result of our altruistic activities. However, when helping is voluntary, not experienced as a burden, not enduring and repetitive, there are numerous mental and physical benefits. The key to keeping a balance – especially for chronic tasks such as caring for a sick family member – is to ensure that we take time and space for self-care. Once again, it's about boundaries and self-care.

Altruistic acts don't necessarily have to be some kind of organized effort, like volunteering at a sexual assault trauma center. We can also derive great benefit from going out of our way to help others in smaller ways when opportunities arise. Helping an elderly person load his groceries at the market, shoveling the snow from the neighbor's sidewalk, and dropping food off at the food bank are small but significant acts that can help us to heal, and make the world a better place. Likewise, by being courteous, patient, and tolerant with others, we are helping other people. Even a smile can help change someone's day in a meaningful way.

Helping others provides a new healthy coping mechanism to help us attenuate the effects of past trauma, whatever those effects may be. Helping others is known to release endorphins, those feel-good chemicals that improve our mood, motivate us, and give us energy. We get a feeling of satisfaction that distracts us from our own problems and helps us to feel grateful for what we have, rather than indulging in self-pity for our problems. They are spiritual acts that take us outside ourselves, which is known to improve our self-confidence and outlook on life.

Recently, a physician friend of mine – who is not an addict or a victim of trauma – told me she was struggling with feeling down about life and wallowing in self-pity. I suggested that she try volunteering at a soup kitchen in order to get outside herself, develop a sense of gratitude, give her some deeper meaning in life, and to boost her humility. She found the exercise to be so therapeutic that she now does it weekly to keep her mind in the positive. So it is that altruism can help anyone who finds that life is getting under their skin; a good dose of altruism may be exactly what they need.

*

Some kinds of pain never fully heal, especially those caused by deep trauma. I have a suggestion for people who live with that kind of pain, over and above the suggestions we've already been discussing in this chapter – such as self-care, altruism, and social connectedness. To lessen the grip of past traumatic events on our psyche, I suggest finding meaning in the pain and suffering. That may sound strange, "finding meaning" in pain, but let's talk about what that means.

One of my all-time favorite reads is Viktor Frankl's 1959 book *Man's Search for Meaning*. Many people have never heard of this book, but it has sold more than 12 million copies, and is still in print. The New York Times has called Frankl's book one of the most important books of the 20th century. Among psychologists it's an iconic work that has had a profound impact on trauma counseling, but the beauty of the book is that you don't have to be a psychologist to read it and find personal enrichment in it. It's a very short book, but a beautiful read for anyone who wishes to have a healthy and invigorating attitude change about life.

Viktor Frankl was an Austrian psychiatrist of the Jewish faith. As an Austrian Jew during the Nazi era, he and his wife and kids were dragged from their home, completely dispossessed, and sent to the Auschwitz death camp in Poland. All that was left of their worldly possessions was a suitcase of items they were permitted to bring with them, and even that was stripped from them at the camp. Upon arrival, Frankl's wife and two children were immediately murdered: gassed and cremated. The only thing Frankl had left in the world – the clothes he was wearing – were taken from him and he was given the ragged striped camp uniform so that he looked just like everyone else. Even his identity was taken: his head was shaved to make him look nondescript, and he was no longer permitted to use his name. He was now officially known only by the number tattooed on his left arm. In a matter of a few days, Frankl went from being a respected physician with a thriving practice, with a beautiful home and family and all the trimmings, to having nothing. He didn't even have the ashes of his wife and children or a grave to visit. There was nothing left of his life but a shell. Frankl could easily be forgiven for feeling like a victim, and holding deep seething resentments for his situation.

It must be remembered that concentration camps like Auschwitz were not simply a prison for Jewish people. The Jews who were not sent to the gas chambers on arrival were sent to work, but the purpose was to work them to death. Historical studies have produced ample evidence that the productivity of the Jews' work was secondary to their demise; in fact they were often given heavy work with no purpose whatsoever except to wear them down, such as carrying sacks of cement across a field and then moving them right back again. The Nazis thought it to be some kind of ironic justice to work these people to death. As a consequence, only 1 in 28 Jewish people who went to concentration camps survived.

Many among us would view Frankl's life in the concentration camp as life not worth living. He and his fellow prisoners were given a 400 Calorie a day diet of poor-quality food – usually watery nettle soup once a day (I don't know what nettle soup is, but the sound of it doesn't exactly make my mouth water) – well below a starvation diet, and were worked mercilessly 18 hours a day. They were very poorly clothed with wooden clogs and only one set of clothes. They endured sub-zero temperatures in the winter without warm clothing. They suffered random clubbings and killings. Worse, they knew that the intention was for them to die, and that there was no hope of release.

As such, Frankl could've been forgiven for losing all hope in life, and wanting to die. Many of his fellow prisoners did; it was commonplace for prisoners to throw themselves on the high voltage electrified fence or just not get out of their bunk in the morning and perish at the hands of the enraged camp guards. Frankl observed that most prisoners who didn't give up and die became degraded to behaving like animals, acting only out of pure instinctual self-interest to survive the day. They abandoned all human civility and became willing to steal from and even kill their fellows just to survive. Frankl was determined not to allow himself to become degraded like that.

Despite having literally nothing left to live for, Frankl found hope within himself and spread that hope to others, saving a number of lives by doing so.

He found hope by finding purpose – meaning – in his suffering. This is not to be confused with the philosophical search for the meaning *of* life, the reason life exists. To a psychologist, the search for the meaning *of* life is irrelevant to our happiness and health. To me, the search for the meaning *of* life is futile, unanswerable, and a waste of time; finding meaning *in* life, however, is what makes life worth living, even in difficult times. Having meaning *in* life is a fundamental need for humans, and lacking meaning in life leads to hopelessness and a negative outlook. Loss of meaning in life is one of the underlying causes of a negative mindset.

Frankl could have become like the others. He could have felt sorry for himself, he could have filled his soul with anger and resentment, he could have raged with blame for others, he could have ruminated on what *should* have been. But, no; Frankl decided that he wasn't going to be a victim of circumstances beyond his control. He wasn't going to be consumed by pessimism, hate, anger, resentment, selfishness, sorrow, and self-pity. Rather, he was going to endure the suffering, maintain his principles, and not allow his circumstances to "own" him, no matter how grave they were. He was going to find meaning in his suffering. But how did he do that?

*

Frankl frequently cites the German philosopher Friedrich Nietzsche: *he who has a why to live can bear almost any how*. That "why" is meaning in life; a person who has meaning in life can endure anything. Frankl's experience in the concentration camp proved that Nietzsche was absolutely correct. Frankl found meaning in life and that carried him through the experience and enabled him to help others to likewise endure the experience and find a reason to survive. Amazingly, even though Frankl didn't resort to his fellow prisoners' tactics of stealing food and clothing from each other (he even gave his own meager food to others on occasions), he ended up being one of the 3% of Jewish people who survived the camp. Frankl found meaning in life – even his bare, naked existence – in three ways: loving and caring for someone, leaving a legacy, and work that's meaningful.

Frankl's wife and children had been murdered at the camp, and he didn't know what had become of any of his extended family. There was no one he knew in the camp. So, instead of finding meaning in loving and caring for family and friends, he decided he would reach out and help as many of his fellow inmates as he could. While most other inmates were doing anything they could to survive, even if it meant doing harm to others, Frankl helped others survive by helping them find food, evade murderous work, and stay mentally strong. His focus on others took his mind outside of his own situation, his own suffering.

Frankl found meaning in his work, even while at the concentration camp. Prior to being rounded up by the Gestapo he had been working on a book about psychiatry. When he left for the concentration camp one of the few belongings that he took with him was his precious manuscript, which was promptly ripped up by one of the German guards when Frankl arrived at the camp. To Frankl, finishing his manuscript was deeply important to him, so he began to collect scraps of paper and jot down notes for re-writing his manuscript. The idea of one day finishing his manuscript and publishing his book gave Frankl meaning, a reason to endure and survive the adversity. (By the by, after the war, when Frankl was liberated from the concentration camp, he had managed to keep those scraps of paper and ended up finishing and publishing his book.)

The other way that Frankl found meaning in what was left of his life was by finding meaning in his suffering. That may sound strange, but to him, his suffering became meaningful by exercising his freedom to choose how he endured that suffering. Many of his fellow prisoners understandably degenerated to near-animals, displaying extreme selfishness, theft, and even violence in their drive to survive. Instead, Frankl found meaning in maintaining his principles and dignity in the face of his suffering. Not only did he not give in to his instincts to survive at any cost, but he even reached out to help others, putting concern for others above his own welfare. He found meaning in his suffering by choosing to *act on* the suffering in a positive and uplifting way, rather than *reacting to* the suffering by allowing his mind to be dominated and his actions determined by his situation. In other words, he had an attitude change that made him see that he had choices other than simply reacting on emotion and instinct, much like we are doing in our interactions with the addict in our life.

*

What can we learn from Dr. Frankl? He was subjected to the extremes of trauma: the murder of his entire family, the loss of everything he owned, wrongful imprisonment, repeated vicious physical and mental abuse, and the trauma was ongoing with no end in sight. Yet, he found that focusing on meaningful activities kept him from obsessing and ruminating on his deplorable traumatic past and present. He was able to free himself of the mental torment of the anger, resentments, sorrow, grief, self-pity, and "what-ifs" that would otherwise naturally come with focusing on the injustice of his situation. Unlike most of his fellow prisoners, he was able to maintain his principles and dignity, maintain his hope and outlook, and survive the camp.

So, too, can those who're haunted by memories and thoughts of past traumas free themselves from mental torment by focusing on activities that give meaning to life. This doesn't mean that terrible past experiences will be forgotten or even forgiven; rather, like Dr. Frankl, it's about preventing ourselves from becoming a product of our past traumas, dominated by their presence in our mind. It's about not allowing ourselves to be defined by our past experiences.

Frankl found meaning in loving and helping others. We, too, can find life-affirming meaning in loving and helping others, and they don't necessarily have to be family or friends. As we previously discussed, mental health research has shown that survivors of trauma find significant relief in altruism directed toward people who've suffered similar trauma. For example, sexual assault survivors were able to find significant relief from the enduring mental effects of the assault by doing volunteer work to help other sexual assault victims. This same principle can be applied to those who have trouble letting go of resentments, especially justified resentments. Placing our attention and care on others turns our mind away from a brooding inward-focus.

As well, Frankl found that meaningful work is a powerful way to prevent a self-pitying inward-focus. This isn't necessarily work in the sense of our job. If we find meaning in our job, that's great, but work that's most meaningful to us usually involves something outside of our employment. Frankl found meaning in the book he was writing, and a determination to survive the camp and finish his book was a strong motivator for him to never give up. Meaningful work tends to be something that helps others, makes a difference, and leaves our mark on the world. My mother has endured a lot of hardship in her life, and she finds great joy in her work as a volunteer. She knits mittens and warm hats for underprivileged children, she visits lonely elderly people in nursing homes, and has taken – on her own initiative – responsibility for keeping a stretch of a nearby street clean of garbage. For her, these activities are meaningful work that helps others, makes a difference, and leaves her mark on the world. This work gets her outside herself and stops her from feeling sorry for herself or focusing on her woes. Meaningful work doesn't necessarily have to be focused on others. For example, some people find that taking courses online and working toward a degree is meaningful, giving them a reason to look forward to the future, and allows them to leave their mark on the world. Others may find something like learning to grow their own vegetables meaningful. Joining a committee, getting involved in a community project, starting a blog; there are countless ways that any person can find meaningful work. Seeking out meaningful work is a terrific therapeutic measure for those who suffer lingering effects from past traumas. Such things allow us to focus on the here and now and the future, rather than the past.

Dr. Frankl also sought to find meaning in his suffering, and we can do the same when we're suffering from painful memories. Frankl decided that he would maintain his human principles and dignity despite his suffering and the strong natural tendency to abandon those principles in order to survive. Likewise, we, too, can maintain our principles in our suffering, by not hating people who've done hateful things to us, by striving to forgive the unforgiveable, by being happy in unhappy circumstances, by being positive in the face of a negative situation, and by taking the high road when we've been wronged in the lowest of manners. This may take a major change in attitude and thinking for some of us, and this won't happen overnight. I suggest starting by making a commitment to uphold your principles and dignity in the face of suffering from someone else's past wrongdoings. Then, pursue that commitment. Talking with a counselor who specializes in trauma may be helpful for some individuals.

*

One of the most important lessons in Dr. Frankl's remarkable experience is acceptance. We cannot expect nor should we seek a life devoid of pain and suffering. Our situation is what it is; we can't go back in time and change it. Rather, we should find some meaning in how we bear that pain, and exercise our freedom to choose how we let it affect our attitude and behavior.

Frankl could have railed and obsessed over his unjust situation, and no one would blame him for it. But he would've driven himself crazy and accomplished nothing but his own mental torment. Rather, he accepted what he couldn't change – his situation – and instead changed what he could – how he behaved in the face of his situation. Says Frankl in his book:

> *We must never forget that we may also find meaning in life even when confronted with a hopeless situation, when facing a fate that cannot be changed. For what then matters is to bear witness to the uniquely human potential at its best, which is to transform a personal tragedy into a triumph, to turn one's predicament into a human achievement. When we are no longer able to change a situation... we are challenged to change ourself.*

Acceptance is a key component of letting go of the power that past events hold over us. Things that have happened to us in the past have happened; we can't change that fact. So, we have no choice but to accept them... or do we? Unfortunately, we do have a choice, and many people refuse to accept the past and to do their best to let it go. Instead, they choose to ruminate and obsess about it, running over "what-ifs" and the injustice of their situation in their mind day in and day out. Acceptance doesn't mean we concede that what has happened to us in the past was OK. Acceptance doesn't mean that those things will go away and stop being painful for us; many people have had some really terrible things happen to them. Rather, acceptance is about making a decision about whether or not we allow these things to "own" us, to dominate our thoughts, to make us angry, to rob us of any chance of having peace and tranquility of mind, and to continue being a reliable source of daily unhappiness.

It might sound like I'm being idealistic, but let me tell you about some people who know something about acceptance. In my medical practice, I've always been amazed by people who've lived with disabilities for a long time. These people schooled me on what acceptance means. I'm talking about people who've been blind since birth or childhood, or confined to a

The human mind is remarkably susceptible to variations in interpretations of our world. The amazing thing is that our mere interpretation of things in the world can totally control the quality of our life. Two different people can be in the exact same situation, and one person will be happy and content while the other is miserable. The difference is on how each person perceives their situation; in other words the person's perspective.

Changing our attitude about our situation – our perspective – can, in fact, have a robust effect on our happiness in life. One man in recovery from substance use puts it this way: *when I focus on what's good today, I have a good day, and when I focus on what's bad, I have a bad day. If I focus on a problem, the problem increases; if I focus on the answer, the answer increases* (Alcoholics Anonymous, page 419). We've already been working on changing our attitude about certain things in order to give ourselves choices about how we think and act, so changing our perspective should come easy to us. It's a free way to have better days!

The key to a perspective that leads to happiness is gratitude. It's human nature to take what we have for granted, and to covet what we don't have. When we receive something we wanted we're soon focused on obtaining the next thing. There's even a certain dissatisfaction that sets in when we get what we want. It's healthy to want things and to set realistic goals and work toward achieving what we want – that helps us succeed in life. However, when wanting something becomes a focus of envy, anger, jealousy, resentment, and self-pity, we're hurting ourselves. The antidote to always feeling like we don't have enough is gratitude.

Gratitude is an issue of perspective. A little exercise in empathy helps to illustrate this. The next time you see someone who has less than you, imagine yourself in their shoes looking at you and what you have. Maybe it's a homeless person, or someone dying of cancer, or someone who's blind or in a wheelchair, or afflicted with birth defects, such as being born without arms or without eyes. What amazes me is that even when we're specifically discussing their disability, I never hear them express anger or resentment about it. And these are people who have every right to shout out: *why me???* and be resentful, sorrowful, and self-pitying. They have every right to ruminate about what they cannot do. But that's not what I see from them. These are people who've long ago realized that the price of carrying resentments over something you cannot change is very high, and they've gotten on with life through acceptance. Rather, I find these people to be hugely resilient, and focused on what they can do, or what they plan to do. It's about perspective: they choose to look at and challenge what they can do, rather than ruminate about what they can't. They choose to stop obsessing over the tragedy of their unfortunate situation, and instead get on with living. Now, let's talk about perspective.

*

wheelchair. Try seeing yourself from their perspective, and how they could be envious or jealous of you because of what you have. Maybe also resent you for it. Now, does what you have suddenly seem a little more fulfilling? Do you think the person in the wheelchair will be able to walk again or be happier in life by burning in resentful envy over you and your ability to walk? These people with glaring deficits in their life have long ago learned to be grateful for what they do have so that they don't spend their lives chained to the green-eyed monster and his good buddies anger, resentment, and self-pity. We can do the same if we have an attitude change.

Gratitude is a therapeutic emotion. I always say that it's impossible to be unhappy while you're holding a bunch of balloons; likewise, it's impossible to feel gratitude and self-pity at the same time. So, if you find yourself wallowing in self-pity, replace it with gratitude; it'll push that feeling of being life's victim right out of your head. Probably the most effective way to do that is to write a gratitude list.

Having gratitude means having an awareness of what's good in our life, as well as an appreciation for our life. It's the difference between having a day filled with regret and envy or a day filled with contentedness and appreciation. Anyone who hasn't tried it should do a "gratitude list." This simple exercise – sitting with pen and paper and listing what in life we're grateful for – always has a healing impact. A lot of people don't do well with their list until they've had a chance to be exposed to people less fortunate than themselves. That's one way that giving of our time to help others helps us: it makes gratitude come a lot easier when we need it to chase away the self-pity monster. Many people do a gratitude list every time they're feeling down on themselves and experiencing the "poor-me's." I go through a list of the things I'm grateful for in my mind a couple times a week, usually when I'm driving or walking. It keeps me grateful and contributes to my happiness and peace of mind. No matter what's got me down, running through a gratitude list in my mind always makes me feel better.

Doing a gratitude list helps us to focus on what we do have in life, and to beat the human tendency to focus on and envy what we don't have. It's so much better to go through life with an awareness of what we have to be grateful for than to go through life burning over all the things we don't have. The difference is living in happiness, or living in frustration.

Some of the most content people I know are people in recovery who have glaringly little in terms of material treasures. This is likely because they participate in the Twelve Step program, where they learn the value of gratitude and perspective about their situation. Their peace of mind comes from acceptance, and gratitude fills them with appreciation. Their perspective is that they're a success today if they don't drink or use today, so they feel like a success every day. They've chosen to rid themselves of the unhappy yoke of unsatisfiable envy. Let me tell you about one guy in particular, a guy named Lucas.

I was fortunate in that before my drinking and using misadventures I was able to put together a life: get myself educated, surround myself with wonderful family and friends, and put together a good work history. Lucas was not so lucky. His drug and alcohol use started while he was a teen, so he never finished high school, never got an education or a trade, never built up any kind of positive work history, and never developed any meaningful relationships. When he finally got sober, he was nearly 60 and basically had the same employability as a teenager who hasn't finished high school. As a result, he does minimum wage manual labor jobs, barely survives paycheck to paycheck, and lives a very simple life. He does without a lot of things that some of us take for granted. However, he's by far one of the most grateful people I've ever met, and that's the basis of his happiness. If he began comparing himself to others who have more possessions, or a better life situation, or a better job, his happiness and peace of mind would quickly evaporate. However, Lucas does volunteer work with people on the street who're struggling with addiction, and I'm sure that helps him to keep his perspective healthy. He's so wonderfully grateful for life, his sobriety, and the few material things he does have that I find him to be an inspiration, especially when human nature gets the better of me and self-pity creeps in.

*

Taking care of our own well-being is something many individuals have a real difficulty with, especially if they're involved in the care of someone else, such as an addict who has become an irresponsible source of anxiety. As we've discussed, people who care about someone in active addiction – or even in early recovery – often feel obliged to pick up on the addict's dodged responsibilities, and become their protector from the consequences of the substance use. It's a full-time job.

Besides taking on too much of other people's responsibilities, I've noticed in my medical practice that there are other reasons that people neglect self-care. Some are shy and reluctant or afraid to speak up for themselves, and are constantly waiting for someone else to perceive and look after their needs. This is often the case with people who lack boundaries, or who live in an abusive or domineering relationship, or who grew up in a home where their opinion was not valued or validated. They wait for someone else to sense and take care of their needs, which seldom happens.

Others are uncomfortable giving themselves attention, or spending money on themselves, because they're always putting other people's needs first. They may even feel guilty about taking care of their own needs. While this kind of selflessness is admirable, it's dysfunctional and in the long run it's detrimental to all involved, including the beneficiaries of their selflessness. Some such people have been taught right from childhood that other people's needs always come first, and they never really learned to take care of themselves properly.

By this point in your reading, you're probably well used to attitude changes, so let's look at adopting another attitude: *we are all responsible for our own self-care*. If we don't uphold our responsibility to take basic care of ourselves, then we will fail those we take care of. We're most useful to other people when we're healthy, happy, well adjusted, and our needs are met. Self-care is hardly a selfish act.

Passengers on an airline flight are instructed that in the case of depressurization and loss of oxygen in the cabin, each individual must put on their own mask before helping anyone else with theirs. This isn't because the airline believes that your life is more important than your eight year-old daughter's in the seat next to you; rather, it's because they know that you'll be unable to properly help your daughter unless you're able to breath. This is analogous to life in general. There are times when other people's needs and wants will have to wait as we take a time-out for some self-care. This isn't selfishness; this is simply the maintenance we require to keep ourselves operating well for our benefit as well as the benefit of those who need us. We're essentially taking the time to put on our own oxygen mask before we help someone else put on theirs. A car would be more useful if it was constantly used to transport people around all the time. However, without stopping for necessary maintenance, it wouldn't be long until the car became totally unreliable and not able to give anybody a ride. Therefore, we take time to ensure the car's maintenance is looked after, so that it can be useful to all who need it. So it is with us when it comes to basic self-care.

In an ideal world, other people would recognize and take care of our needs. However, that's an unrealistic expectation, and people who don't speak up for themselves and ensure their needs are looked after end up as disappointed, angry, frustrated, resentful people, with unmet needs. It falls on us to take care of our own needs, and to speak up if we feel someone else is interfering with our self-care.

The human body needs proper nutrition, adequate sleep, and at least a minimum of physical activity. That's common sense, right? Well, as much as it's obvious, it's amazing how many people forego those three basic necessities, especially if they're busy with life commitments, and especially if those life commitments involve taking care of someone else. Indeed, I've observed in my medical practice that when people become placed in a caregiver role, the first thing that disappears is self-care. The result is early caregiver burnout, which helps no one.

Worry can be an especially potent impediment to taking care of our basic needs. Worry and anxiety can take away our appetite, make sleep seem impossible, and exercise of any kind becomes the furthest thing from our mind. This is a situation that's often experienced by people with a loved one in active addiction, as worry about their addicted loved one becomes a constant companion.

The worry and work associated with caring for a loved one who can't properly care for themself – such as an addict – is referred to as *caregiver stress*. Research has shown that caregiver stress takes a heavy toll on the physical, mental, and spiritual health of the caregiver. Compared to the general population, stressed and worried caregivers have poorer physical health, higher levels of sickness, and more illness-related symptoms. As well, caregiver stress often worsens existing health problems that caregivers may have. Caregiver stress is also known to cause suppression of the immune system, fatigue, sleep disturbances, feelings of hopelessness, feelings of anger, and reduced overall well-being. These adverse effects of caregiver stress are largely because the time commitment to take on the extra responsibilities, and the stress itself lead caregivers to neglect their own health. However, many of the adverse effects of caregiver stress are also due to the constant release of cortisol – the "stress hormone" – that becomes quite toxic to our health.

Caregiver overload – often referred to as *caregiver burnout* or *compassion fatigue* – is a serious problem among people who try to help an addict. This is where we take on more responsibilities than we have the capacity to handle. The result is that our own responsibilities and needs are sacrificed in order to take on someone else's responsibilities and needs. This is one of the reasons that the attitude changes we discussed in chapter 12 and the boundaries we discussed in chapter 13 are healthy for everyone involved. When people become too involved in an addict's circle of chaos, the reality of the amount of work, sacrifice, frustration, and thanklessness of the job quickly makes it a major life stressor for the caregiver. The ups and downs (mostly downs) involve a set of emotions that predispose to compassion fatigue, burnout, and even lashing out in trying moments. These same negative emotions can cause individuals to be intolerant of stress, and render them difficult to be around in the home or workplace.

The extra work and worry – often resulting in sleepless nights and non-restorative sleep – can cause fatigue and tiredness that are physically and mentally penetrative. Although the words "fatigue" and "tiredness" are often used interchangeably, they're different entities. Tiredness is a tendency to fall asleep, whereas fatigue is an overwhelming sense of tiredness, lack of energy, and impaired physical and cognitive functioning. Fatigue is caused by more than just lack of quality sleep; it's also caused by stress, work demand, and compassion fatigue, and it persists even after periods of rest.

Stress in general can be very bad for our overall health. It's normal to feel stress in a moment of emergency, such as if we were to trip and almost fall down the stairs. In such situations, the body's stress response provides a burst of energy so that we can act fast and deal with the problem by grabbing on to something and preventing disaster by falling down the stairs. Our heart beats faster, our blood pressure spikes, we breath faster, and we have heightened awareness, all so that we can react fast and save ourselves from danger. However, as soon as the danger passes, the stress response stands down and everything in our body goes back to normal.

When we're chronically stressed, however, the stress response continues to work, sometimes all day and all night. This even happens with chronic low-level stress. The hormones that create the stress response – such as epinephrine (also known as adrenaline), and cortisol (known as the stress hormone) – continue to be released and don't back down. So, our body and mind end up being like a car engine idling dangerously fast with a stuck gas pedal.

The stress hormone cortisol causes lots of detrimental effects to our physical and mental health when it's released on a continuing basis. It causes blood sugar to elevate, and promotes the build-up of body fat. Together, these can lead to the development of obesity and diabetes. Cortisol also impairs the immune system, making individuals more likely to get sick and stay sick. Epinephrine, which is also continually released in chronic stress situations, results in elevated blood pressure and rapid heart rate, both of which can damage the heart and blood vessels and elevate the risk of heart attack and stroke. The stress-related hormones together also disrupt sleep and impair memory and concentration. These factors can make people less able to handle the stress they're facing; in other words, the continual release of stress hormones makes people less able to handle stress. You can see how a vicious cycle develops when we're over-stressed.

Sorrow and grief are also potent impediments to basic self-care. It's ironic that worry, sorrow, and grieving prevent people from getting adequate nutrition, sleep, and physical activity, because all three of those things make people feel much better when they're hurting. Studies have shown – and common sense tells us – that self-care activities improve our ability to tolerate the stress of caring for and worrying about someone else, decrease the health-defeating effects of stress and worry, and improve our ability to function. These "health promotion activities" aren't time consuming, expensive, fancy interventions; we're talking about eating nutritionally balanced meals, getting restorative sleep, and engaging in even minimal physical activity.

The point here is that if you're experiencing a lot of stress over someone else's substance use and related behaviors – whether that stress is by worrying a lot, carrying anger and resentment, experiencing grief and sorrow, taking the addict's responsibilities upon yourself, or failing to properly take care of your own needs – then it's probably costing your health and well-being a lot more than you think. Even if your stress is level is relatively low, the effects of chronic stress are harmful. So, probably the single best self-care decision we can make is to disengage ourselves from the chronic stress created by someone else's substance use. As well, we can take some simple – and enjoyable – measures to reduce our stress levels and the effects of stress on our health. Let's talk about how to do that.

In the two previous chapters, we talked about having an attitude change about certain things, including our role in helping an addict. The idea of these attitude changes was so that we could see that we have choices, that we don't have to throw our whole self entirely at a loved one's addiction. It doesn't really help the addict anyway, and it just draws us into the addict's circle of chaos, where we participate in the addiction. In chapter 13 we talked about healthy boundaries and creating "loving detachment" so that we can protect ourselves and make sure that we no longer assign the addict (or anybody else) the power to control whether or not we're happy and at peace. These two measures – boundaries and detachment – are about making choices that allow us to more effectively help the addict while also keeping our life separate from the chaos, and these two measures alone will significantly cut our stress level when dealing with an addict.

However, we're talking about addiction, a horrible disease that's ripping apart our loved one. So, of course we're not able to be bullet-proof, completely without worry, concern, or some kind of extra responsibilities when we're dealing with an addict. So, we must accept that there will be some ongoing stress involved. Fortunately, there's much we can do to mediate the how the stress affects us. In other words, we can make sure that our stress-glass remains nearly empty, regardless of what's going on around us. We can accomplish this by using healthy coping mechanisms that have been validated by an overwhelming volume of research.

The first thing we can do to mediate stress's effects on us and to improve our resilience to stress is by doing what we've already talked about: very basic self-care. Just those three simple things: getting regular nutritional meals, restorative sleep, and a little physical activity. Those three basic things alone have a powerful effect on stress tolerance, and overall health.

I've heard many people say: *there just aren't enough hours in the day for me to eat properly, or to get exercise*. Fair enough. But let me tell you this: when I was in medical school, I was also running my own martial arts and boxing gym and volunteering in the community. My schedule was insane. I could easily have said: *there aren't enough hours in the day for me to eat properly and get exercise*. But I knew that if I didn't take proper care of myself my whole schedule would fall apart and I wouldn't be able to handle all the irons I had in the fire. So, I made time – every day – for some sort of physical activity. I would teach a boxing class, or I would park my car further away from the hospital and take a brisk walk before and after my shift, or I would pedal my stationary bike while watching a TV show before bed. These are all things I enjoy doing, and I really enjoyed their relaxing effect on my body and mind. I found that if a day passed where I didn't get some kind of physical activity I didn't feel right, and I usually didn't sleep as well.

When it comes to physical activity, I find that most people go about it wrong. They think getting exercise means they have to join a gym, or do some kind of intense and painful workout. No way. If an exercise habit is to be sustainable it has to be something that we enjoy. For many people, that's a half hour walk through the neighborhood, or following a yoga video from YouTube in their living room, or twenty minutes of brisk housework, or whatever. It also doesn't have to be prolonged. A twenty-minute bout is plenty. I'm never too busy to find twenty minutes to keep myself healthy and well. In fact, one of my personal boundaries is that I never allow life to rob me of my opportunity to get some sort of exercise every day. I'd rather fall short on a responsibility than fall short in my most basic self-care. That's my attitude.

When it comes to eating regular meals, I also have an issue when people say they don't have time. When I worked as an ER doc, I used to do 14 hours shifts with an insane work pace. There was great pressure to work faster and keep wait-times down, and there were lots of emergencies that required immediate attention. There was no lunch break. However, I never went through a shift without eating properly. I became a master at finding little pre-packaged healthy snacks and meals, many of which don't even require microwaving. I always kept a bunch of these on hand, and I'd grab what I needed for the day before leaving for my shift. In medical school I used to pick one evening a week where I'd take an hour to watch a show I liked and cook up my own pre-packaged meals for the week, and I'd just put them in the freezer. Even if you have to eat at your desk or while commuting, there's always time for proper nutrition. Always.

When it comes to sleep, it may be a bit tougher to get right. Some people need very little sleep, some need more. When I was in my 20s, I felt well rested with five or six hours of sleep a night; now, a little further on in life, I need a good eight hours. And then there's the matter of sleep quality. When we're stressed, we tend not to sleep well, and the sleep we get may not be restorative. If we're wracked with worry about a loved one, we can spend many sleepless or restless nights, leaving us feeling unrested in the morning. Sleep is *so* important to health and function that I place great emphasis on it. When I was in general medical practice, I used to prescribe brief courses of mild sedatives for people who weren't sleeping well, just to get them on track and through a stressful time. There are non-addictive sleep-aids that – when used properly – can be a temporary expedient to finally getting some restful nights. As well, there are lots of non-medication ways to improve sleep. Many people get lots of sleep but don't feel rested in the morning. Often it's due to a simple problem such as sleep apnea, or iron deficiency, vitamin B_{12} deficiency, or some other easily treated issue. I suggest talking it over with your doctor if sleep quality is an ongoing problem for you.

So, that's basic self-care and its role in stress reduction and health. Now let's talk about another way to improve your resilience to stress: "brain hygiene."

*

Brain hygiene is a pretty cool concept. It's where we use the brain's "plasticity" (or *neuroplasticity*) to enhance its performance for improved physical, mental, emotional, social, and spiritual well-being. As you may recall, the term "plasticity" refers to the body's ability to adapt to change, and the brain is one of the most plastic tissues in the body. Just like our muscles benefit from exercise, so too does our brain. Sitting around on our butt doesn't do much for our muscles, and they'll soon become deconditioned and weak if we don't challenge them through some physical activity. Likewise, sitting around with an inactive brain staring at the TV doesn't do much for the brain. However, if we use our brain and challenge it, it will grow in capacity and ability. Neuroplasticity means that our brain will adjust according to what we need it to do. If all we need it to do is to sit around and vegetate, it will adjust and become weak and vegetative. Like well-exercised muscles, a well-used brain will be strong, robust, and healthy.

Brain hygiene is about more than just exercising the brain; it's also about keeping the brain healthy. Healthy bodies house healthy brains, which in turn provide the necessary environment for healthy minds. Regular physical exercise, yoga, deep breathing, sound sleep, relaxation, socialization, positive thinking, hobbies, a healthy diet, sports, listening to music, meditation, reading, and mindfulness are very enhancing activities for the brain and mind – brain hygiene. Good brain hygiene helps us to better tolerate stress, and to think our way through adversity.

One especially potent form of brain hygiene is meditation. Some people may see meditation as a wonky new-age thing that takes lots of practice, but that's not the case at all. Meditation takes surprisingly little time and effort to make a huge difference in anyone's life. Good thing for me, because I definitely have attention deficit disorder, so no way am I going to sit there meditating for hours on end like some cloistered monk. It takes me ten minutes to teach someone basic meditation. Once people learn some basic concepts and skills, they can totally personalize meditation, and meditate in a way that makes sense to them and works for them.

Another really cool thing about meditation is that the sky's the limit; you can use it in its very basic form to help you cope with a stressful day or a stressful event, or you can take your skills as far as you want to go with them. Meditation is a tool with much depth, and – if you wish – you can keep learning about it and improving your skills and doing new things with it, making it a fulfilling hobby in its own right. There are many people who've become expert meditators and really enjoy it as a relaxing and enjoyable pursuit.

The medical and scientific communities have long recognized the positive effects of meditation, and there has been much empirical study into the effects of meditation on health and well-being. Research studies have shown meditative practice to be particularly effective for reducing stress hormone levels and improving a number of domains of health and wellness. When we have an addict in our life driving up our stress hormone levels, meditation is a great way to get them back down; it's a great way to keep our stress-glass empty. But it does much more for us than just helping us to cope with stress.

One interesting study found that a short program of meditation improved immune function (as measured by response to a flu vaccine), as well as baseline brain activity. Meditation has also been shown to be an effective approach to reducing physical pain. One clinical trial published in *The Journal of Neuroscience* looked at how meditation affects our perception of pain. The researchers used a special type of functional magnetic resonance imaging (fMRI) to assess the neural mechanisms by which meditation influences perception of pain. After some basic meditation training, the test subjects were exposed to pain-inducing stimuli (I don't know how they suckered people into participating in this study!). Meditation reduced pain perception by 57% and pain-intensity ratings by 40% when compared to rest. The brain scans showed that meditation worked on multiple brain sites involved in pain perception processing. Meditation helps reduce how much pain we feel. Other research has shown that meditation works in a manner different from any existing pain medications, which means that it can be used to enhance pain reduction in people who're already using medications.

We know that mental stress is a major cause of disease exacerbation for virtually any kind of not only mental, but also physical illness, especially inflammatory diseases like arthritis (joint inflammation), gastritis (stomach upset and pain), and Crohn's Disease (bowel inflammation). Given that meditation is focused on relaxation and stress-reduction, the natural question to ask is if this stress reduction affects the severity of physical diseases. Indeed it does. For example, in one study, meditation was used for stress-reduction, and then post-stress inflammatory responses were compared to participants who underwent a non-meditation stress-reduction program. The results showed that stress-reduction in general reduced inflammation, but meditation was significantly more effective than other stress-reduction programs.

A number of studies have suggested that meditation is an effective way to reduce high blood pressure – the "silent killer" – which is hardly surprising given the well-known association between stress and high blood pressure. Speaking of killers, meditation has also proven effective in smoking-cessation trials.

It has been well established by numerous studies that meditation reduces depression, anxiety, stress, and feelings of loneliness. Meditation increases social connection, emotional stability, self-control, and compassion. Physically, it increases brain size and density in areas involving concentration, higher brain functions, attention span, multi-tasking, and creativity.

Meditation also has innumerable positive effects on our body's physical function, such as improvements in hormone levels (especially via reduction of the stress hormone cortisol), improved regulation of digestive functions, as well as improvements in blood pressure, heart rate, immunological, respiratory, and neuroplastic function. I'm not going to dwell on the effects of meditation on physical and mental health, because there are innumerable research studies that have established support for meditation. Rather, my purpose here is to make a point: meditation can have far-reaching positive effects for our physical and mental health. It is indeed a powerful tool for health and well-being, and a great tool for stressed-out families and friends of addicts.

There's a strong body of research evidence that clearly upholds meditation as a powerful healthy coping mechanism to replace destructive coping mechanisms, such as substance use or other escape behaviors. For this reason, meditation is used extensively in addiction treatment programs, and it's part of the Twelve Steps (Step eleven). Further, meditation is known to enhance the ability to maintain self-insight and an awareness of our vulnerabilities and destructive thought processes, and to challenge these processes before they take over our behaviors. Separate studies have confirmed the positive effects of meditation on promoting healthier function of the brain's mechanisms for emotional regulation and stress reduction. These are things that can benefit all of us, not just recovering addicts.

What's more, meditation is a low-cost and enjoyable approach to reducing the effects of stress – so enjoyable that it has been referred to as a "positive addiction." It's not a time-consuming endeavor. I've been practicing meditation for close to thirty years, and I find that brief three-to five-minute meditations have a significant impact on my mindset and how I feel. In fact, I even use "walking meditation," which can be practiced while driving, out for a walk, or sitting at a desk. If you're interested in learning about meditation, I've included as an appendix at the back of the book a primer on meditation that can help you get started. Check it out: it's excellent brain hygiene.

*

Another type of brain hygiene that's known to be an impressive counter to stress is prayer. Before those who are not religious recoil at the suggestion of prayer, hear me out on this. Prayer is a powerful tool for everyone, not just the religious or those who believe in God. The word prayer has become inescapably saddled with a religious connotation, but it's used by many people who're not at all religious. If we keep an open mind about it, and look at it differently than its usual association with religion, we can open up a new avenue of brain hygiene and stress coping. Prayer is simply a form of meditation that involves conveying what we wish to say, rather than simply using mind-focus. Prayer doesn't have to be directed at God, or anyone else. In other words, it's a specific type of meditation that happens to have become associated with religion.

Who prays? Lots of us do. More than half (55%) of Americans say they pray every day, according to a Pew Research Center study, while a further 21% say they pray weekly or monthly. Even 20% of those who don't belong to any religion pray daily. About 12% of atheists say they pray (yes, *atheists*). Prayer seems to hold an appeal for a lot of people, and a lot of well-designed medical and scientific research studies over the last forty years tell us why.

The benefits go well beyond the spiritual, and there are many known measurable physical and mental benefits.

Psychological research supports the use of prayer as an effective healthy coping mechanism, particularly with severe stressors, and has demonstrated that the use of prayer during difficult times is not at all a passive response to problems. As well, research has shown that prayer is an effective release for anger and aggression, and improves self-control. What's especially interesting and is that the beneficial effects of prayer have been shown to exist even among atheists when they pray. Taken together, the research on prayer suggests that – in the context of someone who's dealing with an addict loved one – prayer is useful for calming down, not reacting to the addict's provocative behaviors with emotional outbursts, and coping with the stress… whether one is religious or not.

Addiction treatment programs and the Twelve Step program teach prayer as one of the tools of recovery in the context of "no robes, no rituals" – in other words, in a way that's open to all people of any belief (or non-belief) system. There's very convincing research that demonstrates the value of prayer – in any context – in addiction recovery and relapse prevention. Interestingly, one particularly illuminating clinical study of people who had been taught prayer as a tool for recovery found that not one of the randomly selected people involved in the study disparaged prayer, including the atheists and agnostics.

Let me recount a story that illustrates the value of prayer for stress coping, self-control, and well-being. A guy I know from A.A. meetings – his name is Tyler – was deep into a life of addiction to crystal methamphetamine when he started coming to A.A., desperate to stop his substance use. He was a low-bottom addict, and was homeless when he first walked through the doors of A.A. Happily, he made it – he got clean and sober. Last time I saw him it was coming up on three years since his last substance use, and he had put a very nice life together, with a good job that he liked, a steady girlfriend, and his own apartment. He was happy and healthy, and he looked fantastic; a far cry from the pathetic meth addict that I saw come through the doors three years prior.

I always like to interview people like Tyler, because that's how I collect data for my research, and I find their stories to be interesting and illuminating. Tyler was a guy who had tried many times to stop his drug use on his own, and had failed each time, so he was very impressed with what the Twelve Step program had enabled him to do. When I asked him what he found most useful about the program, the first thing he listed was prayer. I found this surprising, because I remembered that when he first started coming around to meetings he recoiled when prayer was suggested to him: *sorry, I can't do that, I'm an atheist and I won't do prayer*. I asked him how he – a card-carrying atheist – was able to come to terms with prayer; he replied: *when I'm stressed, or I start thinking about using, or I'm angry, or just not feeling right, I say a quick prayer. I don't know who or what it goes to; I just throw it up in the air and let it go. I always feel better after*. Well, it seems to work for Tyler, the atheist. His go-to coping mechanism was once injecting meth into a vein, now it involves healthy coping strategies, including prayer.

For anyone who's interested in trying out prayer to add to their arsenal of healthy coping strategies, I've included at the end of the meditation primer in the appendix a primer on prayer. For those who're already pray-ers, I've included suggestions about how to optimize prayer as a tool for better mental health and well-being.

*

Another excellent and firmly proven coping strategy to de-stress from the effects of someone else's substance use is social contact. We've already talked about how altruism – helping others – is therapeutic for people who struggle with negative and depressive emotions and mindset, but now we'll look at straight-up social contact.

People who try to help an addict often do it alone, especially if it's a family member. Addiction carries a crushing social stigma, so family members often try to hide the "family secret" from others. They're embarrassed by it, and they may fear that others will judge them and their family: *she must be a bad parent*, or: *they must have a really bad marriage*, or: *he's a drug addict, you know*. Much better to keep it a secret from everyone, right? Being alone becomes our "safe" place. We isolate ourselves, and shun help or caring. It's just easier that way.

It can be surprising how much relief we feel when we finally let go of our secrets; the more painful the secret, the better it feels to get it off our chest. We've talked in previous chapters about how addicts in recovery must stop keeping secrets, because their secrets make them sick. Well, the same can be applied to people who struggle with an addict in their life. They tend to hide their loved one's substance use, and put on an outward appearance that all is well in the home. That's fine, nobody wants to advertise their troubles or air their dirty laundry for all to see. However, one of the keys to letting go of someone else's addiction's dominance over our life is to open up and let go of the secrets. Bottling up emotions, frustrations, and pain is never healthy.

The trick is to share our worries, fears, and frustrations with the right person. Few people understand what it's really like to deal with an addict unless they've been through it themselves, or they're a trained counselor. Opening up with someone who has shared the same experience and really gets it can be quite therapeutic, and a way to release ourselves from the cold grip of the secrets. However, even some friends who don't understand are just good listeners, and they won't judge, jump to conclusions, or offer impractical and idealistic platitudes as advice. Certainly, there are people out there who've never been through the addiction experience, but are worthy of trust and open-minded enough to listen and learn.

The problem is that addiction is such an illogical and baffling problem that talking to someone who hasn't been through the experience may prove frustrating. *How could someone else understand this horrible experience, when I don't understand it myself? How could I explain what it's like?* In such cases, it may be best to reach out to talk to someone else who understands because they've been through it themself. When we're hurting, we need to tell our stories, to explain our experiences to someone who understands, a sympathetic ear. For anyone who's in the situation where they're keeping their secrets to themself and don't have someone they feel comfortable talking to, there are options. Talking to a counselor who's experienced in trauma and addictions is a safe option. Contacting Al-Anon is another option. Al-Anon is a group of individuals who've been through the trauma of someone else's addiction, who get together to share their experiences and to support each other through a program of discovery and healing. They don't talk about the addict or addiction, other than how it affects them. Their sole focus is on their healing and their family's healing. They use the remarkable Twelve Step program as the basis of their healing.

Socially isolating and keeping secrets isn't healthy for any of us, and it propagates the effects of the trauma. Humans are social beings, and cues for social interaction are built right into our genes. To wit, we actually need social contact to develop and thrive. Humans rely on interaction with others, and we cannot properly develop without it. Interpersonal interaction is critical for the survival and development of babies. Infants are born to learn, but their developing brain circuits rely entirely on input from social interactions. Our brain's higher functions (cognition) will not develop properly or even at all without this interaction. Interactions with people and things outside of ourselves are a primal human need, not just a nicety.

Our ancient ancestors were only able to survive by banding together. They needed each other for protection, gathering food, hunting, and for propagating the species. Those who formed close connections with others were more likely to survive, especially when faced with adversity or danger. Nowadays, that need for connection continues, deeply embedded in our DNA and our most basic instincts. Connection with others makes us feel empowered and less anxious. Connection, especially transcendent connection (i.e. to something larger than ourselves), is an antidote to stress and hardship. If you ever observe people who've just experienced a traumatic event, they're hugging each other and seeking connection; they sense that they need connection to feel better and to not feel anxious or out of control. It's part of our survival instinct to seek connection and to want to attach when we feel stress or danger.

Humans have always been tribal creatures, surviving by hunting and protecting each other from danger, and we were never meant to be alone. This instinct remains, so that when we feel isolated our anxiety goes up and we feel more vulnerable to danger. The alarms start going off in our brain when we feel isolated. Certainly, we don't feel comfortable, at ease, or well.

Humans were especially not meant to be alone under hardship. Being alone may feel like a safe place, but it's not a healthy or a healing place. Stress and adversity are much easier to cope with when we aren't isolated. Isolation runs counter to our natural primal need for connections and provides an additional layer of psychological stress. We need to re-establish meaningful connections outside ourselves to break the cycle of trauma and to heal.

The effect that we get from connections with others can be strengthened by connection with a power greater than ourselves. Those who have a faith or belong to a religious group may find availing themselves of these connections to be an excellent coping mechanism. The higher power attachment stays with us, and we can draw on that association anytime, anywhere, even if we're alone. An awareness of this connection helps us to stay focused as we face stressful situations. This helps stave off the alarms that go off in our mind when we face danger or adversity alone. Many people enjoy some kind of an awareness or a connection with a higher power who's not named "God." Nature, the cosmos, fate, or any meaningful thing that's greater than ourselves works. Some people don't even know what it is, they just know that they're not the most powerful thing in the universe. Feeling a bond to something larger than ourselves overrides our immediate panicky, emotional, and selfish reactions. This helps us to switch from the "toddler" brain (our primitive emotional, reflexive reactions) to the "adult" brain (our advanced cognitive functions in the pre-frontal cortex), and we think and act better. Connection with a higher power enhances this powerful effect that comes with connections outside ourselves. Thus, a need for spiritual ties is a deep-rooted human need, and restoring and improving these connections is of great therapeutic value when we've lost these bonds.

The absence of social connection is a cruelty. Social isolation is used as a form of punishment, and even torture for prisoners of war. Social isolation drives people crazy, literally. The effects of social connections on mental and physical health are very well documented, and people who're socially connected are healthier and live longer than those who are not. In fact, it was proven in the 1980s and confirmed by numerous clinical studies since, that social isolation is as bad a risk factor for physical illness and premature death as are the very worst physical risk factors: smoking, obesity, sedentary lifestyle, and high blood pressure. Given that these are the things that kill the vast majority of people in the world, that makes social connectedness a pretty crucial aspect of good health and function, not just a simple nice-to-have. For people who need to escape the powerful grasp of intolerable stress and past trauma it's an absolute must-have.

Social isolation, loneliness, or a lack of quality, supportive, and meaningful interpersonal relationships have well known effects on brain function and mental health. For example, social isolation is associated with declining higher brain (cognitive) functions, such as planning, problem-solving, memory, learning, etc., and is associated with an increased risk of Alzheimer's disease. It's also associated with depression and other mental illness.

Promoting social connectedness has been shown to be an effective treatment for mental health in general, and is even used as part of the treatment strategy for many serious mental illnesses, such as schizophrenia.

Surprisingly, social isolation affects much more than our mental health. We know that a lack of social connectedness adversely affects our hormonal and nervous systems (it creates increased sympathetic tone and hypothalamic-pituitary-adrenal activation – our stress activation systems), and negatively impacts the immune system (specifically: decreased inflammatory control, reduced lymphocyte proliferation, higher basal cortisol, increased oxidative stress, glucocorticoid resistance, and altered glucocorticoid gene expression). As such, insufficient connectedness outside ourselves can have serious physical health consequences.

However, if you're not the type of social butterfly who can juggle hundreds of close friends, fear not! Studies have shown that the health benefits of social connectedness depend on our *perceived* social connectedness. So, if we're fulfilled with a few good friends and have quality, supportive, and meaningful contact with them, our health is just as safe as it is for the social butterflies. The risk for mental, cognitive, and physical problems lies with those who feel isolated and lack quality interpersonal attachments.

It has been demonstrated in clinical studies that our body is driven by physical and mental cues to seek social connection when we're isolated; again this demonstrates that we are, by our very nature, social and spiritual animals. As I've previously mentioned, neuroimaging investigations have identified the brain changes that occur following trauma, involving specific neural pathways that result from traumatic events and cause the dysfunctional thought processes, invasive thoughts, behaviors, and emotions that often follow traumatic experiences. Further research has shown that selflessness, altruism, and social support all help to reroute those disrupted brain connection networks back to their normal state. Our social interactions with others are deeply therapeutic when we've been through difficult times; so much more so when we make meaningful connections with people who allow us to tell our story and be heard and understood.

So, we've talked about "brain hygiene" and other ways to cope with difficult experiences and to keep our stress-glass empty. Now, let's look at some tools for dealing with life's stressors on a day-to-day basis.

*

Dealing with stressors and life in general on a day-to-day basis can be helped along by another of our attitude changes. Once we've found peace of mind and happiness, we can adopt an attitude that our happiness and peace of mind are so precious to us that we will not allow anybody or anything to take it away from us. When we adopt this attitude we can view life and the world around us as just stuff that we need to deal with, but refuse to allow it to penetrate our serenity. With this attitude, we can see that we can choose to no longer allow the world – including the addict in our life – to decide if we're happy or not.

One of the reasons that some people get so stressed when complications arise is because they have unreal expectations of life. The human mind is often preoccupied with fears of things going wrong, problems arising, and things not turning out well for us. But those fears are based in unreasonable expectations that everything must go just right for us and that we must get what we want for life to be good. But life is never going to go just right and be problem-free for anybody, no matter who they are. We must accept that not everything in life is going to go our way. Yes, it's disappointing when things don't go well, but we can either drive ourselves crazy worrying and fretting over it, or we can decide to be happy within ourselves rather than allow our happiness to be determined by what's going on in our life at that particular moment. Again, our attitude change reveals to us that we have a choice.

The point is that we will be OK no matter how things go in life. Happiness and peace of mind derive from living life on life's terms, come what may. As we learn to live life on life's terms, we learn to accept that things are not always going to go just right for us all the time, but we know that we'll be OK regardless of how things turn out. The human animal has the capacity for great resilience when armed with a positive mind-set, even in the face of great adversity. People – all people – are capable of great things when fortified with the proper attitude. Think of our friend, Dr. Frankl.

There are things in life that will go wrong and we have no control over them. What we do have control over is how we respond to them. Like we learned from Dr. Frankl, we can derive meaning from adverse experiences by how we handle adversity. If we fall apart and give in to whining and the poor-me's, then we're allowing external events to control us. If we maintain our composure and dignity, and respond in an admirable way – accepting things that are beyond our control rather than whining about them, and helping others rather than feeling sorry for ourselves and taking from others to make ourselves feel better – then we're choosing not to allow external events to control us. If Viktor Frankl was able to accomplish that in a Nazi concentration camp, then surely we, too, can do so in our everyday life, come what may.

It's completely unreasonable to expect life to go smoothly without any hiccups. We're setting ourselves up for failure and disappointment when we entertain such an expectation. Unfortunately, such unrealistic expectations come naturally to us, and the inevitable failures and disappointments that occasionally happen as part of life can bring out the worst in us, if we allow them to rob us of happiness and peace of mind. Some people turn to drugs and alcohol in such circumstances. When we allow our happiness to depend upon whether or not everything goes our way in life, we're setting ourselves up to be frustrated, unhappy people.

Rather than expecting that everything will always go just fine, we can choose to adopt a different mind-set, an attitude about life and its inevitable ups and downs. Life is not about never *facing* hardship; rather, it's about how we *endure* hardship. When times are tough, it helps to remember a few simple mantras: *this, too, shall pass*, and: *the sun sets on every day*. Meaning comes from handling hardships by acceptance, fortitude, using our strength to help others through the ordeal, and maintaining our integrity. Contrast that to enduring hardship by complaining and engaging in selfishness and self-pity.

Acceptance is not something that comes naturally to humans. Strangely, we like to feel and act like victims, we like other people's pity, we like to complain and get angry, and we loathe accepting things that aren't how we want them to be. Acceptance is definitely an acquired trait, and one that takes some practice and presence of mind. We should accept the things we can't change. The choice is to burn with rage over our perception of unfair treatment from the world, or to be happy and grateful for what we do have. Most people go through their entire life with very poor levels of acceptance, and spend their life *reacting* to everything that happens to them. They don't seem to understand that they have a choice, because that choice comes with a changed attitude about life, an attitude of acceptance, gratitude, and determination to remain happy and at peace of mind regardless of what life dishes out.

For addicts, this kind of perspective, attitude change, and approach to life's stressors is a matter of life and death. Addicts are people who react to stress by reaching for the bottle or needle, so they need a better way to handle life on life's terms. The Twelve Step program isn't at all about not drinking or using; rather, it's about handling life on life's terms, and using healthy coping strategies, so that the need to drink or use falls away. It really is as simple as that. Thanks to my recovery work, I've known a peace and happiness such I had never previously known in my life. What's more, it has imbued me with a resilience and hardiness to all of life's stressors. My peace and serenity is so hard-won and so valuable to me that I cherish it and refuse to allow people or things to penetrate it and take it from me. It's a great way to live, and it all began with an attitude change: I refuse to allow other people or things get under my skin and take my happiness and peace of mind from me. If other people had a similar attitude change, we'd have a lot fewer angry and unhappy people in the world.

Peace of mind and happiness may not be a matter of life and death for you like it is for addicts, but it's definitely a matter of health and quality of life for anyone and everyone. Making up your mind to protect your happiness and peace of mind from stress – psychologists refer to this as stress resilience – is up to you.

*

Another technique for maintaining happiness and peace of mind involves protecting ourselves from being overwhelmed by life and its challenges.

When we have an addict in our life, the extra stress may make life's other demands seem overwhelming. When we feel overwhelmed, we have a tendency to succumb to stress and just shut down, or to sacrifice self-care in order to try to handle everything. But, let me ask you a question: *how do you eat an elephant?* The answer: *one bite at a time!* When stress mounts because we have too much on our plate, it's helpful to break down problems and tasks that seem overwhelming. In other words, to take life, tasks, and problems one bite at a time. Psychologists refer to this as "chunking."

Chunking involves breaking down otherwise overwhelming problems and tasks into bite-sized chunks, rather than looking at the problem as a whole. This helps us to avoid becoming overwhelmed by information overload, or by the size of the task or problem. For example, if a person needed to buy a car and the car cost $20,000, paying that amount all at once up front may be an overwhelming and impossible endeavor. However, a financing option would allow the person to buy the car and make manageable monthly payments so that the cost of the car is no longer overwhelming. Over time, the small loan payments add up to large sums, and the car gets paid off. Similarly, we can break down our problems and tasks into manageable chunks and focus on taking care of one chunk at a time. When we focus on the bite-sized chunk we have before us, we can let go of worry about the rest of the task, safe in the knowledge that we'll take care of each chunk as it comes, one at a time.

Chunking is a widely recognized technique for self-motivation and for avoiding feeling overwhelmed. Chunking is supported by considerable research and is even used by the U.S. Navy SEALs as a tool for facing the most daunting tasks. The Navy SEALs – famous for their mental toughness and ability to endure any kind of hardship – employ chunking as a mental technique to help them get through physically or mentally demanding situations. For example, during their BUD/S training (considered to be the most grueling military training in the world), Navy SEALs trainees don't focus on completing the six months of hell that they must endure, or they would feel overwhelmed and fearful and may doubt their ability to get through it. Rather, they focus on getting through the particular task that they're confronted with *right now*. If they're facing their notoriously punishing obstacle course, they focus on getting through that and giving their very best effort. They forget about everything else, they just focus all their resources on that particular task. If even that seems overwhelming, they break it into further chunks, such as each individual obstacle, one obstacle at a time.

The Twelve Step program employs chunking very effectively with its focus on staying sober "one day at a time." Rather than becoming overwhelmed by the thought of having to stay clean and sober for months or years, addiction treatment teaches addicts to break down sobriety into bite-sized chunks – one day at a time. If the day is tough, they can break it down into one hour at a time. The program also uses the same concept for helping addicts in recovery cope with life when they feel overwhelmed. Rather than focusing on dealing with all their problems, they break their problems down to what they can do to help their problems *today*, and let go of worrying about the rest. Like the U.S. Navy SEALs, recovering addicts use chunking to get through sobriety's difficulties and life's challenges. We, too, can use the same concept for dealing with our problems and challenges.

The human mind tends to scare itself by projecting problems into the future. This generates fear because we have a tendency to blow things out of proportion, to think the worst, and to be pessimistic. Some people go through life ruminating about things that will never happen, which creates fear and anxiety. They worry, dread, and fear what hasn't happened and what probably never will, thereby putting themselves through torture for naught. Often they'll lay awake at night and allow themselves to be consumed by anxieties of the future. In the dark of night, the mind can dream up terrible things, anticipating the cruellest of evils. They suffer intense fear from their imagination, rather than anything real. These are fears about things that aren't even present, or don't even exist, something psychologists refer to as *anticipatory anxiety*. In short, people are afraid because they imagine what *might* happen.

Anyone who finds themselves worrying about problems and how they may play out may wish to try the "one day at a time" attitude. The idea is that every morning we get up and resolve to do what we can do on that day to help our problems, and we let tomorrow take care of itself. We can plan for the future, but it's counter-productive to plan the outcome, wasting brain-power on the "what-if's" about tomorrow. Projecting our problems and worries into the future is counter-productive, wasted brain-power, and self-manufactured artificial stress. Don't sell your hard-earned serenity and peace of mind for cheap!

*

It's poetic irony that many of the same tools that addicts are taught in treatment for stress reduction, coping with life, and establishing and maintaining a happy and peaceful mindset are the same tools that can be applied to people who're "in recovery" from dealing with an addict. But, these are well proven life skills that all people – addict or not – can use to improve the quality of their life.

Just as the biopsychosocial model is applied to treating addiction, so it can be applied to those who've had to deal with someone else's addiction. Self-care is most effective when we nurture all our basic needs: our biological needs – especially nutrition, sleep, and physical activity – our psychological needs – such as learning to handle life and its stressors better – and our social needs – the need for closeness, social contact, and not handling everything by ourselves.

Addiction is considered to be a family disease, and fighting this horrible disease often ends up being a family battle. Millions of people have successfully overcome addiction, and healed from the brutal effects of the obsessive substance use. However, we seldom hear about how their families and friends are doing, and whether or not any care has been given to helping them recover from the effects of dealing with someone else's addiction. As usual, the focus remains on the addict.

Unfortunately, not every addiction story turns out well, far from it. Just the other day a 19 year-old boy from my neighborhood lost his battle with addiction and died from an overdose. I had never met him, but by all accounts he was a delightful and bright young man. He was living with his parents, and I can only imagine what they and the rest of his family and friends are going through. I hope they recognize – despite all the focus having been placed on the addict – that they, too, are victims of addiction and have mental, emotional, and physical scars that require healing. In a very real way, they are in recovery from addiction.

May your experience with addiction turn out better than theirs.

Appendix – A Primer on Meditation

Meditation is like a gym in which you develop the powerful mental muscles of calm and insight.

– Ajahn Brahm

If you think meditation is just some kind of a new-age pursuit... think again. It's a practical coping mechanism backed by extensive research, with far-reaching benefits for physical, mental, social, and vocational health.

The way I first came to know meditation was definitely not because of some new-age pursuit. Believe it or not, I was first introduced to it as a young man as part of my training in martial arts. I had no desire to learn meditation; I was just doing it because it was a requirement for my belt promotions. Its benefits were never really explained to me, I just went through the motions of learning how to do it and I practiced it. I discovered the remarkable benefits of meditation by accident on my own as meditation increasingly became a part of my life. Soon I was doing meditation because I enjoyed it and liked what it was doing for me, not because I had to do it to get my martial arts belts.

The basic premise of meditation is that the human mind is inherently weak, and it wanders off on its own wherever it wants to go. That's why we tend to get distracted so easily. I refer to the "wandering" mind as an "undisciplined" mind, and I compare it to a child sitting in class staring out the window at the soccer game going on outside rather than listening to the lesson. The teacher keeps rebuking the child, drawing his attention back to the blackboard, but the child is soon focused on the soccer game outside again. Our "undisciplined," wandering mind can cause us quite a bit of dysfunction when it comes to times of stress. Rather than think our way through a stressful situation, our undisciplined mind will – on its own initiative – focus on anger, fear, or other primal emotions that distract us from thinking through the situation and responding logically.

In psychological terms, meditation is about establishing "top-down" control of our actions and behaviors over "bottom-up" control. "Top-down" control is when we use our higher brain functions to think our way through a situation, rather than allowing "bottom-up" instinctual, unthinking reactions to prevail. Think of how many times in life that you reacted to a situation out of spite and later regretted your action. That's what happens when we allow our "bottom-up" primitive reactions to decide how we react to situations.

In fact, the undisciplined mind will react to distractions really quickly, reflexively, without first consulting our brain's higher thought processes and decision-making functions. These instantaneous reactions remove our higher mind functions – such as reasoning, planning, and thinking – from determining our actions. Then our primitive instincts – such as lashing out in anger – take over. That works well when we touch a hot stove and reflexively jerk our hand away, but it doesn't work so well when someone offends us in our day-to-day life. The hot stove is a stimulus where our knee-jerk reaction saves us from harm, but a knee-jerk reaction to a stimulus involving a daily stressor, such as someone bumping into us, can land us in trouble. Better we think about it a second and smile and say "excuse me" than to lash out and insult and push the person who bumped us.

Meditation is about learning to keep our mind from darting off on its own. It's about stopping the undisciplined mind from making its own snap decisions without consulting our higher reasoning faculties as we face various situations in our day-to-day life. Through meditation we can teach our mind to be disciplined, more under the control of our higher, intelligent brain functions and less under the control of our primitive, instinctual reactions. In other words, meditation allows us to assert "top-down" processing rather than instinctual "bottom-up" reactions. Then, when we run into stressful events through the day we're able to give measured, thought-out responses rather than lashing out unthinkingly. It allows us to *act*, rather than *react*. Think back to all those times in life when you wish you could take back something you said or did out of haste, and you'll see the value of having better control over the undisciplined mind's tendency to react unthinkingly.

*

It may sound strange that the peaceful practice of meditation is required learning for martial arts, but the reason for it illustrates perfectly what meditation can do for us in everyday life. Meditation, as I learned it, was intended to help a fighter who takes an injury to focus on finishing the fight rather than focusing only on the pain of his injury. Let's use an example to illustrate. A person is assaulted, punched on the nose. Getting punched on the nose produces a blinding, debilitating pain that only someone who has experienced it can truly understand. The undisciplined mind will immediately focus only on that pain and forget everything else, and the person will therefore double over, turn away from the assailant, and cover their nose. This will result in a defenseless posture against a further, more thorough, beating. However, the mind that's well trained in meditation can maintain focus on the assailant, ignoring the pain for the moment, and deal with the attack by fighting back, or escaping, or whatever it takes to prevent further injury. Once the danger is over, then the focused mind can deal with finding help for the pain. The person with meditation skills is able to maintain their mind on proper thought and decision-making, rather than allowing the mind to run off wherever it wants to go, in this case on the distracting stimulus, the pain from being hit on the nose.

However, as I came to learn, the true value of meditation for martial arts lies in its power to help us to avoid a fight, rather than winning a fight. Therein lies its usefulness for us in everyday life. The undisciplined human mind has impulse control problems; when we feel slighted we usually respond with a burst of angry emotion that, if we act on it, could make us do something we ordinarily wouldn't do or that we might later regret. The undisciplined mind acts out of impulse, rather than first letting the thought filter through our higher brain processes and consider our options and the ramifications. Thus, the disciplined mind can avoid lashing out in situations that might lead to conflict or a fight. The experienced meditator can head off ill-advised impulses by not letting the naturally weak mind go where it wants to in an uncontrolled fashion.

*

Meditation isn't some kind of arcane ancient ritual, and it's not mystical. You don't have to belong to a secret society to learn how to do it. It's not some kind of otherworldly hypnosis. It's a very practical thing, and it's easy to get started at doing it. You don't even have to be good at it to start feeling its benefits.

A few things that meditation is not: time consuming, sitting in weird positions, chanting, religious, or otherworldly. In fact, it's about being comfortable, takes only a few minutes or can be done momentarily on the fly through the day, involves an active mind, and it's very real and practical: I did it to get my black belt in martial arts, and the United States Marine Corps teaches it to their soldiers. U.S. Navy SEALs rely heavily on meditation for their famous mental strength and resilience training.

To start out a meditation, you should find a comfortable position that suits you. Sitting on the couch or floor, cross-legged or not, with your posture as you like to sit. Some people like to meditate lying down, but I don't. You'll be surprised by how incredibly relaxed your mind becomes as you meditate, and I have a tendency to drift off to sleep when I meditate lying down. In fact, on nights that I find myself unable to sleep I start meditating on something pleasant and it always helps me get to sleep.

I recommend closing your eyes, as it's much easier to concentrate and focus the mind with the eyes closed. Meditating with eyes open can be a part of more advanced meditation, but to start out it's usually best to have eyes closed, shutting out the outside world. Even though eyes open can be an advanced meditation technique, I've been meditating a long time and I still prefer keeping my eyes closed.

Breathing is very important for starting out, because we want to send a burst of fresh oxygen to our brain to kick-start the lazy thing into action. Even though our brain makes up only 2% of our body, it uses 25% of our entire oxygen intake. Our brain needs to breathe, especially during a brain hygiene workout like meditation. While we meditate, we breathe in through the nose and out through the mouth. If we keep our back straight and erect it gives our diaphragm – the big breathing muscle between our chest and abdomen – more room to do its job as it contracts to draw fresh air into our lungs.

Once you're comfortable, start with three deep breaths in through the nose and out through the mouth, but no more than three big ones. You don't want to make yourself dizzy. Some people call these three initial deep breaths "cleansing breaths." As you meditate, continue breathing in through the nose and out through the mouth, but otherwise just breathe normally. As people get good at meditation, their breathing rate, pulse, and blood pressure all decrease, indicating deep physical and mental relaxation. Sometimes your breathing is barely perceptible when you're in a good meditation.

After your cleansing breaths, focus your mind and all your thoughts, with eyes closed, on a dark, empty space. Blackness. Nothing. Every time your mind starts thinking about something, including what you're doing, guide it back to focusing solely on the nothingness. This can be done for increasingly longer periods of time. It's important to keep your mind focused, not allowing it to wander. You will notice your mind wandering: to some problem you've been dealing with, something someone said to you, something you forgot to do, what to have for supper, some big task coming up, and so on. That's your challenge: to not allow your mind to go wherever it wants to. Quite often, you'll find yourself thinking about something during meditation and you don't even realize it initially, until after you've been thinking on it for a while. If you feel your mind wandering, snap it back in focus. Try doing this exercise for a few minutes at a time initially, and as you get better at it begin increasing the time. With practice, you'll get better and better at keeping your mind on task.

*

Once you've done this initial meditation a few times, and you've gotten a bit used to guiding your mind away from distraction and back onto the darkness, let's try a little meditation mind relaxation exercise. Now, when you breathe imagine breathing in cool, blue air, always through the nose. Imagine the cool air actually being blue in color, cool, very fresh, and clean. The blue air you're inhaling is cool and calm. When you exhale, imagine hot, red, bad, toxic air going out through the mouth. It's actually red in color; hot, dirty, angry air. This red air is turbulent and poisonous. Imagine your lungs are filled with it. Continue breathing in this cool blue air, in through the nose, and exhaling this hot red air, out through the mouth. Visualize the cool blue air going deep down inside you and swirling around your lungs, and pushing out the hot red air, which rushes out through your mouth and dissipates into the sky.

As you continue breathing in and out, visualize the cool blue air gradually replacing the hot red air down deep in your lungs. Visualize how, with each breath, there becomes progressively more blue air deep down in your lungs, and less and less red air as it gets pushed out by the cool, fresh, blue air. Gradually, there's less and less red air, and more and more blue air, until finally there's just blue air; blue air coming in when you breathe in – your lungs full of cool blue air – and cool blue air coming out through your mouth when you exhale. There's nothing but cool, blue, calm, clean, smooth air in and out. At this point, your mind is relaxed. You'll probably be unaware of your body at this point, and without any thoughts beyond your breathing. If your mind tries wandering off, snap it right back to the cool, blue air going in and out.

The cool blue air represents peace, serenity, confidence, love, goodwill, cleanliness, health, and positivity. The red air represents anger, hatred, conflict, fear, and resentment. Now, imagine the cool blue air filtering through your entire body, as it leaves your lungs and circulates in your blood, diffusing throughout your body. Feel the cool, peaceful, serene, confident, loving, positive effects of the cool blue air throughout your body, and feel it tingling as it reaches the tips of your fingers and toes. Keep visualizing this and let it affect your mood. For the rest of your meditation just keep your mind focused on the clean, cool blue air coming in and out, reaching every part of your body.

This exercise is an excellent way to practice relaxing and focusing your mind. Once you've practiced this visualization a few times, you can use it to focus your mind and center your mood at the start of a meditation, or you can use it as the entire meditation for its calming, centering effects.

*

After a while, when you feel you're good at doing this and it's effortless to keep focused on the breathing for your entire meditation session, you can try moving from visualizing your breathing to visualizing an object. I suggest a plain white candle burning in a dark, black space. Start with your comfortable position, eyes closed, cleansing breath, and your cool blue air relaxation exercise. Then, visualize the candle, the texture of the wax, with the streaks of melted wax trailing down its sides. Notice every detail, even the barely perceptible sound of the flame burning and melting the wax. Visualize the flame, sometimes still, sometimes flickering. See the soft orange flame surrounding the black wick, with a halo of blue flame around the orange, tapering up to the hot white tip of the flame, with a thin wisp of black smoke rising straight up from the tip. Continue breathing in through your nose and out through your mouth while you're doing this visualization. If your mind wanders away from the candle flame, bring it right back into focus. Some people enjoy enhancing the candle flame meditation by using an actual candle in a dark room; feel free to try that as well. The point is to focus your mind on every small detail of the candle and flame (without hurting your eyes) and snapping your mind back on task every time it attempts to wander off.

Practice this mind-focusing until it becomes easier and easier, with less and less interruption by the weak mind trying to go where it wants to go. Meditation is like any other skill or form of exercise: the more you practice the better and stronger you get at it and the easier it becomes. Remember: because of neuroplasticity your brain will rise to the challenges that you set for it, kind of like lifting weights for the brain. You don't need to meditate for long periods of time. Even just 3-5 minutes initially is fine. Meditation is not a skill that requires a lot of time commitment. As you get better and better at it, and as you have more and more things you wish to meditate on, you may start spending more time at it. It becomes something to look forward to, a reward at the end of a long day. The relaxation helps center us and purge our mind of all the turmoil of the day.

When you're finished meditating, simply open your eyes, slowly allow your mind to come back to reality, get up, and you're done your session. Congrats: you now have some basic meditation skills!

*

Thus far, we've done some basic meditation that helps us – with practice – to accomplish two things: 1) to relax our mind and body, and 2) to discipline our mind by keeping it focused and not allowing it to wander off on its own. The more we practice these basic skills, the better we get at those two important goals. When you feel ready, we can take the next step and introduce some focused meditation.

We've already gone through two different ways of focusing our meditation: the blue and red breathing and the candle flame visualization. Focusing our meditation can do two things for us. First, it gives us something to center our mind on so that we can practice keeping our mind focused. Second, we can choose a specific meditation focus to help us address specific concerns or problems we're facing, including conflicts, stressors, or emotions. We can choose any meditation focus we wish, based on our current needs, goals, or interests. So far we've used darkness, our breathing, and a candle flame as the focus of our meditation, but our focus of meditation can be anything we want.

If you've had a rough day and just want to wind down, or if you're dealing with anger you want to purge, or if your mind is too active for sleep, you may want to simply meditate on something pleasant and soothing. Again, we get set up, do our breathing, get our mind cleared and centered, and then allow our mind to fill with a beautiful scene, or a fun event, or some other thing that's really nice for us. Every time our mind tries to slip off our beautiful scene and back onto our anger, or our finances, or when is garbage day this week, or otherwise become overactive and jump around, we bring it back to our pleasant scene. Once our mind has stopped trying to get off topic and surrenders to enjoying our pleasant meditation, it's a safe bet that we'll be more relaxed and better able to sleep when we finish our meditation. And our mind is that much more disciplined.

The more we meditate, the better we become at it, and the more disciplined our mind becomes. The goal is an awareness of what the mind is doing, and an ability to pull it back when it tries to go off on its own. After a while, this ability begins to show itself all day long, not just when we're actively meditating. Psychologists refer to this as *trait mindfulness*, and there's considerable evidence linking trait mindfulness to self-control, and numerous measures of health and happiness. So, when someone does something that would anger us, and our mind darts to thoughts of retaliation or harsh words or worse, we immediately recognize that our mind is operating on its own, and we pull it back and use our higher brain functions to assess the situation and our response to it. In other words, our trait mindfulness allows us to assert top-down brain control. Eventually, with practice in meditation, this occurs spontaneously, as our mind becomes accustomed to staying centered, including in times of stress. Rather than having anger carry us away, our higher brain functions determine our actions. Our mind is disciplined.

A disciplined mind is a huge life asset that many people will never possess unless they learn to meditate. Psychologists recognize this mental discipline – trait mindfulness – as a valuable life skill that allows people to function optimally in all life situations. If everybody had strong trait mindfulness, psychological therapists would go broke.

*

There are many ways we can focus our meditation. Sometimes we may wish to choose a problem-and-solution-based meditation focus. Here we meditate on a specific problem we're facing, and work through the problem and come at it from different perspectives and angles. We keep our mind from going to the emotions that surround the problem, and we instead focus on a detached, objective view of the problem and potential solutions. This may be the only time we'll consider all possible approaches to the problem and we may even realize some aspects of the problem or repercussions from it that we hadn't previously considered. You may be surprised at how much clarity and perspective that you get from meditating on a problem. However, when focusing on a problem we must be mindful to keep our mind on task, rather than allowing it to wander off and generate anger, resentment, fear, or self-pity because of the problem we're considering. That kind of negative psychology must not be allowed to invade our meditation.

If we become mindful of feeling down, or we find ourself indulging in self-pity, or feeling short-changed in life, it's therapeutic to meditate on gratefulness. This centers us, and moves our psychology away from the negative. We focus our meditation on all the things in life that we are – or should be – grateful for and what life would be like without these things. I find myself smiling when I come out of my gratefulness meditations. I do these gratefulness meditations a couple of times a week and whenever I need a boost. They really help me a lot. Sometimes it really helps defeat the human tendency to do the self-pity thing when we include in our gratefulness meditation an appreciation for some of the terrible things that we *don't* have in our lives, and which we take for granted. For example, I think of people who're falsely incarcerated, or who live in a dangerous country, or in a war zone, or who're dying, and so on, and then I think of how grateful that I am that I'm not facing those kinds of challenges.

Focused meditation is a powerful way to "psyche ourself up" for something that's creating fear or worry for us. I'll use a boxing match as an example. Prior to getting in the ring with another fighter, a boxer will have trained for years as a boxer, and for months specifically for that particular fight. The constant fear is of failure: losing the fight, performing poorly, getting knocked out on the canvas. Imagine any of those things happening in front of a large crowd of people and maybe even on TV. Just imagine the fear of getting knocked out in front of all those people. So how does a boxer even work up the nerve to get in the ring? How does a boxer heading to the ring in front of a huge crowd not become suddenly unnerved by anxiety over the possibility of being beat and humiliated in front of all those people? The same situation applies to a professional baseball player stepping up to the plate during the World Series. Or an Olympic gymnast about to perform on the parallel bars. How do they not suddenly become choked up over fear of failure? It's about being psyched up. For that, boxers and other athletes use visualization by meditation. We can use the same meditation technique prior to an important interview, or some other life event that's raising our anxiety levels.

Using visualization as a focus of meditation helps us to "psyche ourself up" for a difficult task, including working up the courage to face the task, but it also helps us to prepare and plan for the task. Even if you don't have a boxing match, or a World Series game, or an Olympic performance coming up, you can use the same technique to overcome performance anxiety for a job interview, public speaking, or any other task that's causing you anxiety. Our focus of meditation here is the visualization of ourself doing the task, and playing it through to the end. As we do so, we're able to foresee potential problems we'll face so that we're mentally prepared for them, and this enables us to develop our plan of action. We should not abandon this line of meditation until we've worked through a viable, workable approach to our task and a plan of action for any problems that we may foresee cropping up. The undisciplined mind will – on its own initiative – visualize failure, and that's what creates fear. This fear is exaggerated, because the undisciplined mind has a penchant for blowing things out of proportion, and the fear is dysfunctional because it doesn't protect us from failure, but can actually make us more likely to stumble. This fear can cripple us, and become a self-fulfilling prophecy. Some people freeze up or shut down from this fear, the so-called "performance anxiety." Meditating on success, or gracious acceptance if things don't go the way we would want them to helps alleviate that fear, and gives us a much better chance of success. Preventing the mind from wandering off and creating dysfunctional and exaggerated fear is a goal of meditating prior to a stressful task. That same mental discipline allows us to keep our mind from scaring us and paralyzing us with fear by visualizing failure at the time we do our task. This is exactly what the high-priced sports psychologists train professional athletes to do to avoid performance anxiety.

It really is an odd thing that it's in the nature of the mind to visualize and anticipate failure, because this in itself can be a cause of failure, becoming a self-fulfilling prophecy. For some reason, our mind loves to stew on things that worry us, to dream up worst-case scenarios, and then to blow those out of proportion. It gets worse at night, when all is quiet and our undisciplined imagination outruns us, and even outruns reality. Before we know it, we can't sleep and we're so shaken that we can't even face what's bothering us. "Getting psyched up" is about defeating that process, which can only be done by reining in our weak mind when it tries to do this self-destructive exercise in futility. Meditation is exactly how we do this. A practiced meditator has a disciplined mind, which is not allowed to wander off and visualize failure and create anxiety. Rather, through meditation we can guide the mind into projecting a more realistic outcome, and then a pathway to success and an outcome that's very positive for us. Not false hope, but a realistic positive outcome that's within reach of our abilities. We can back up our meditation by taking action to support a positive outcome, filled with our confidence that we have the ability to complete our task.

Properly psyching ourself up usually doesn't happen with just one meditation session. We may have to revisit the meditation to keep our mind focused and on task, especially if the task we're psyching ourself up for is a big one. Each time we meditate on the task, we can consider things that hadn't previously occurred to us, and strengthen our mind's purchase of reality. The more we've meditated in our preparation for the stressful event, the less likely it is that our mind will be able to run away from us and smother us with fear at the time of the challenge.

*

It's a really nice thing to spotlight our meditation on a specific person sometimes, and this can be part of our gratitude meditation. On Mothers' Day – for example – it's a great gift and tribute to mom to meditate on how much we love her, how much she does for us, and to reflect back on all the things she has done for us from earliest childhood. Also, it helps our gratitude to meditate on how it would affect us if she suddenly disappeared from our life. If mother is deceased, this same meditation will fill us with warm feelings and provide a worthy tribute to her life on Mother's Day, the anniversary of her death, or her birthday. Any particular day where we miss our mother the most and are most reminded of and saddened by her death is a good day to do such a meditation.

Perhaps your experiences with your mother weren't good. If you still harbor anger or resentment, meditation around Mothers' Day may be a good time to use your meditation skills and your attitude change to unburden yourself of these negative feelings, using the same tools that we discussed in chapter 14. Meditating on mom's past experiences to understand that she was sick may help us to let go. We can also meditate on how useless and harmful it is for us to allow these negative emotions to live in our head rent-free. This, too, may help us to let go. When we're in a relaxed and positive state of mind during meditation, we're more likely to let go of the negative.

If we've been fighting with our spouse or partner lately, the relationship is strained, or there are hard feelings, it will almost certainly help us to find peace in our home if we meditate on our partner. We do this in a similar way to our "meditation for mom" example. We can meditate on what our partner means to us, the good times we've had, and how we would feel if they suddenly passed away (hopefully this would be sad). This helps our relationship and us. Gratitude for another person in our life makes us much more likely to have positive interactions with that person.

One type of meditation that's particularly uplifting is a focus on togetherness. The power of "we" is potent and salubrious, if we allow it to be. We talked in chapter 14 about the many health and wellness benefits of answering our need for connections with others, and meditations on these connections may enhance this effect. Meditating on togetherness – on our connections with people outside ourself – fills us with strength, warmth, and hope. It helps us to realize that we're not alone, to value people in our life, and to reciprocate to those who add meaning to our life.

*

It can be very relaxing and calming to allow our senses to be the focus of a meditation. Meditating in a beautiful place, whether in nature – such as overlooking a lake set in the trees – or something man-made – such as overlooking the majestic architecture of a bustling city, is one way we can do this. Meditating on something specifically made for contemplation – such as a painting or a sculpture or while listening to an inspiring piece of music – is a natural way to relax. Here we focus our mind on our senses and examine these senses. We use our sight to contemplate every minute detail – especially the ones we ordinarily wouldn't notice as we go about our busy life. We focus on the smells and the freshness of the air if we're in nature, we allow our mind to lose itself in the sounds – this is especially nice if we're meditating with music. Listen to rain falling. Pick out every sound, especially the ones you usually don't notice or divert your attention to. Our touch is a fantastic focus as part of our meditation. Pick up a leaf and hold it with eyes closed, feeling its texture, its details, its softness. Run rich soil through your hand. Feel the fresh air as it touches your whole body. Taste the air, taste the smells, or put something of flavor in your mouth and focus on breaking it down. Think of how you would put that flavor into words or emotions.

Now let's carry that memory of these sensual meditations with us, so that we can revisit them mentally when we need some spiritual and mental relaxation. During the day when the stress is adding up we can lean back and close our eyes and revisit the place we meditated, or the music, or whichever sensation-focused meditation appeals to us at the time. At the end of a stressful day we can do a proper meditation where we again focus on this meditation. We can visualize the place we meditated without even being there, by focusing our mind on the memory.

A particularly useful application of revisiting our sensation-based meditation is when we're laying in bed at night unable to sleep, when our thoughts are keeping us up, or our problems and challenges are cycling through our mind. In times of stress many of us project our problems into the future, making issues worse in our mind, and we face a long night of sleeplessness. Instead, as we lay there, we can close our eyes and meditate on one of our relaxation sensual meditations. Next thing we know we're asleep. It works for me, it may work for you.

*

Earlier, I used the term "walking meditation." What, exactly, is walking meditation? That's a term I use for brief mini-meditations where we center our mind and pull it in when it's doing something it shouldn't be doing as we go about our day. When we become practiced at meditation and used to snapping our mind back on track when it wanders off during meditation, that skill begins to appear in our day-to-day life. This is the "trait mindfulness" that psychologists so revere.

When our mind wanders off, trait mindfulness allows us take notice and snap it back in place when we need to. This is important because it helps keep us from reacting out of emotion and letting our "bottom-up" primitive brain take over when something stressful happens. If someone bumps into us or does something we don't like and our mind goes instinctually to an anger reaction and tells us to lash out, trait mindfulness allows us to recognize our errant mind and snap it back into place, often without even thinking about it.

When our mind gets really angry an experienced meditator can pause and consciously bring it back on track. A lot of people who struggle with "road rage" find this very helpful because they otherwise find it difficult to curb their anger and stop themselves from lashing out at other drivers during their commute. That's an important benefit to meditation and a disciplined mind, because road rage is a very un-nice thing and can get us in trouble. It really puts on a bad show for other people, especially anyone who's unfortunate enough to be in the car with us. Besides, it's a terrible thing to show up at work every day already edgy and in a bad mood from the commute. I've done therapy for a number of patients who're really nice people but suffer terribly from road rage and uncontrollable anger when they drive. Always, I teach them some basic meditation skills, and it always works.

Sometimes (when we're not driving) we can even sit back for a moment as we go about our day and do a very brief mini-meditation where we close our eyes, detach ourself from a stressful situation, and center our mind. For the experienced meditator, this takes but a moment. We can do this, too, while driving, but with our eyes open. When we center our mind and snap it back from an emotion-driven reaction to a stressor we're allowing our higher brain functions take over rather than allowing instinct and emotion to drive our actions. I'm sure we've all had times in our life when we wished we could have a do-over for some unfortunate and not thought-out reaction to a stressor.

Our improved behavior as we're confronted by stressors in our daily routine doesn't go unnoticed. People react to our response much better when our reaction is measured and appropriate. If we lash out at them they're likely to do the same in kind. When we respond to anger with patience, understanding, and restraint it has a calming effect on the other person and the situation. Difficult situations diffuse away rather than escalate. We become known as rational, measured people who handle stressors well. People start respecting us, maybe even wanting to be like us. Life becomes easier, and we come home at the end of the day with much less frustration and anger than we once did. Not only do other people like us better, but we like ourself better. We're handling life in a better way.

*

Some people find it helpful to repeat a useful phrase to calm themselves in times of stress. In meditation lingo, this phrase that we repeat in stressful times is known as a mantra. Personally, I find some of the Twelve Step program slogans to be calming mantras, such as: *easy does it*, and: *one day at a time*. Each of us should have a few of these in our back pocket for use in stressful times. For example, when I become angry, impatient, or intolerant of some person or situation, repeating: *easy does it* to myself really helps me center myself, and gives me something to focus my mind on other than my anger.

Some other mantras that I find useful are: *this, too, shall pass*, and: *I'm not selling my peace of mind and happiness cheap,* and: *I'm taking the high road,* and, best of all: *it ain't worth it.* Everyone can find some catch-phrases that are meaningful to them and are helpful mantras to stave off emotional reactions to stressors.

*

There are various techniques or disciplines or styles of meditation, such as Vipassana meditation, Zen meditation, mantra meditation, transcendental meditation, Buddhism, and mindfulness meditation. I don't get hung up on different dogmatic meditation styles, but some people may enjoy exploring some of these for themselves. What's important is just finding what makes sense for you and works for you. What's nice is that nowadays you no longer have to climb the Himalayas to consult a guru to sample different meditation styles; rather, you can check them out by using YouTube videos, making it really easy to do. The various types of meditation and advanced meditation techniques are beyond the scope of our discussion here, but I encourage anyone who enjoys meditation and wishes to explore it further to do so. Joining a meditation class, attending a retreat, or even watching YouTube videos on meditation are great ways to learn more and try new things. Some of the guided meditations available on YouTube are quite nice.

This primer on meditation provides the basics, enough to get you started and for you to give meditation a try to see if it fits as a healthy coping mechanism for you. If you're interested in pursuing meditation further, I strongly encourage you to do so. It's a rewarding pastime, and a potent way to improve our ability to thrive in life. The sky's the limit when it comes to meditation; I've been practicing meditation for a long time, and I'm still learning and improving. Personally, I don't buy into any of the specific meditation doctrines. I just look for what works for me and what feels right, and I do it.

Now, let's look at a specific type of meditation: prayer.

A Primer on Prayer

Although prayer is strongly associated with religion, I regard prayer as a specific form of meditation that's open to everybody, religion or no religion. As I pointed out in chapter 14, a Pew Research poll showed that even atheists pray. I personally know quite a few atheists and agnostics who pray. Prayer is simply a type of meditation where we engage in communicating thoughts and sentiments, rather than passive or active thought. Who or what that communication is directed to is up to you. As I pointed out in my story about Lucas in chapter 14, some people just say their prayer and "throw it up in the air" without any idea where it goes, because it makes them feel better.

Scientific research has – as we will discuss – upheld prayer as a therapeutic type of meditation. So, I suggest starting out by changing our way of thinking of prayer: sure, it's something used by religions, but it's also something that can be used by those who are not religious.

*

There's a tremendous body of research evidence supporting prayer as an immensely effective way of coping with life's problems, which is central to our happiness and peace of mind. The scientific evidence has consistently shown an association between prayer and an improved sense of well-being, sense of purpose in life, self-esteem, and satisfaction with life.

There's also a great deal of evidence from well-designed clinical trials that shows that prayer has many benefits for our physical health. As one researcher puts it: *prayer, like meditation, influences our state of mind, which, in turn, influences our state of body* (Koenig, para. 71). Perhaps most notable for us is that prayer has been shown to reduce cortisol levels in our blood, with a significant impact on our health and how we feel. Cortisol is known as the "stress hormone," and it causes a lot of detrimental effects to our physical and mental health; cortisol is the main reason that stress is so harmful to our health. As such, by reducing cortisol levels, prayer exerts a very real contribution to our resilience to life's stressors, both physically and mentally.

Prayer reduces the experience of anxiety, elevates a depressed mood, lowers blood pressure, stabilizes sleep patterns, and impacts autonomic functions like digestion and breathing. Further, in influencing our state of body-mind, prayer and meditation also influence our thinking. This prompts a shift in the habits of the mind, and, subsequently, patterns of behavior. These changes, in turn and over time, induce changes in the brain, further influencing our subjective and objective experience of the world and how we participate in it. Speaking in medical terms, prayer is a potent catalyst for positive neuroplasticity.

So, prayer by any name – whatever label you wish to put on it – can do a lot for us. However, how people pray may determine how effective it is as a coping strategy. One of the most common approaches to prayer may actually be detrimental. Let me explain.

Some people allow their prayers to become like a "Christmas wish list." They pray for all the things they want to go right in their life. They pray that they'll get that job they applied for, that their health will be good, maybe even that they'll win the lottery. This can be psychologically destructive, because they double their disappointment when some things don't go their way. We can't all have everything go our way every time. Instead, I suggest that people pray for other people rather than themselves, and that instead of asking in prayer for a certain situation to go their way, they should ask for the strength to do their very best and to get through the situation, whichever way it goes.

It's tempting to turn our prayers into our wish list for life, asking for good things to happen to us. However, such a selfish and inward-looking mind-set isn't healthy, and can lead us to focus on things we don't have rather than increasing our gratitude for what we do have. Besides, we're setting ourself up for psychological disaster, because when something in life doesn't go our way – as is bound to happen from time to time – after we've prayed and prayed for it to go just right for us, we can become disappointed, angry, and resentful. Remember: expectations are the prelude to resentments, and putting expectations upon prayer is no exception. Rather than asking for everything to go our way as we face a stressful event, we should ask for the strength to do our best and to get through the stressful event and still uphold our principles, regardless of how events turn out. When we're facing a life crisis, we should pray for the strength and courage to accept the situation and to get through the experience, not for it to just go away.

*

So, what should we pray for? Well, I'm no expert on prayer, but from a psychological perspective, it's healthy for us to avoid selfishness in our prayer. As we pray, we should pray for those in need. We can name specific people who're in need of specific help, or we can be more general: we can pray generically for those who're hungry or thirsty, those who're tired, those who're in trouble or despair, those who're lost, those who're afraid, those who're in the throes of addiction, those who're alone or lonely, those who're poor or destitute, those who're in danger, and those who need help.

I don't participate in organized religion, but I was intrigued to see what the clergy would say about the selfless approach to prayer. I spoke to a number of members of the clergy from several religions, and found that they agree very much with the concept of selfless prayer. The reason behind it is that – according to these clergy members – God has a plan for all of us, our "destiny," as it were. Just because we pray to God every night that we want this to happen or that to happen isn't going to change God's plan for us. In fact, it just makes us come across as selfish and a little greedy. We're asking God to make things go our way instead of according to God's will. By praying for the ability to be helpful and useful to others, and praying for knowledge of God's will and the power to carry that out we're showing a willingness to accept God's plan. This is what was explained to me by clergy members.

Science, too, has something to say about praying for others. It has been well established by research that praying for others reduces anger and aggression, even directly after a provocation. The research demonstrates that praying for a stranger who just angered us reduces our anger and aggression more than simply thinking about them in a positive way. We can become victims of our own anger and resentments, and selfless prayer is a helpful way to defeat these terrible demons. Prayer that isn't focused on ourself has also been shown to improve our sense of well-being, including: self-esteem, optimism, meaning in life, and satisfaction with life.

So, praying for *others* is good for *us*. It's easy to pray for the people we love and care about; however, a difficult aspect of praying for others involves praying for those we don't like. Believe it or not, doing so helps us too. Let's look at that now.

*

The suggestion to pray for someone we don't like may seem like a big ask, but it's a very therapeutic exercise. Taking the high road is always calming to the soul, even if not at the time. It may go against every fiber of our being in the moment, but it always feels good later on, and we're better for it. When someone wrongs us, it's our primitive instincts that make us brew up in anger, vengeful thoughts, and aggression. The dark corner of our heart wants a piano to fall on the person in question and the thought of praying for them may be repulsive to us. However, these are exactly the primitive thoughts that lead to the anger and resentment that kill our peace of mind and happiness, and this is the kind of self-destructive thinking that we're trying to overcome with our meditation-disciplined mind. Praying for the well-being of someone who wronged us is a potent way to accomplish exactly that.

Our willfulness wants to indulge our impulsive thoughts of lashing out and getting revenge on those who've wronged us, or secretly wishing for their demise, but those kinds of ugly thoughts can destroy our peace of mind. We have our hard-earned peace of mind and serenity and we don't want to lose it because of new or ongoing anger and resentments. Praying for those we don't like helps us to do that. Besides, anybody can pray for someone they like, but it's a true test of a strong and virtuous character to pray for someone we don't like.

It's key to our serenity and peace of mind that we re-frame how we think about those we don't like. We can't control how other people behave toward us. However, we can control how we react and behave toward them. Therefore, we can choose to stop criticizing how the other person is behaving and instead examine our own role in the conflict and reflect on how we can set these things straight. Often our anger and instinctual need to blame others makes us completely lose sight that maybe we played a role in the conflict, and makes us completely unable to see things from the other person's perspective. When we use our newfound meditation skills to calm ourself and think through our dislike for the other person we can prevail in our efforts to keep our stress-glass from filling up with anger and resentment.

If we pray for a person who wronged us or whom we don't like, then we're taking action to show our commitment to personal growth. Psychologically, when we do an action our mind will get behind that action and adopt the reasoning behind it, because the mind likes our actions and our beliefs to be congruent. That's where we get the expression: *it's easier to act yourself into thinking than it is to think yourself into acting.*

To help us prepare to swallow what might seem a bitter pill of praying for someone who probably doesn't deserve it, some meditation may be in order. We can try focusing our meditation on our new role as a pray-er for others, including people we don't like or care for, and on our new attitude where we view other people's unsavory behavior as being simply symptoms of a sickness, some kind of demon that they struggle with that drives their selfish and antisocial behavior.

*

While I am an experienced meditator, my prayer skills are not so insightful. However, as a therapist I can't ignore the powerful evidence-based effects of prayer on health and well-being. As such I encourage anyone who wishes to pursue prayer to learn more about it.

Works Cited and Consulted

Acton, G.J. Health-promoting self-care in family caregivers. (2002). *Western Journal of Nursing Research, 24(1)*, 73-86.

Adler, N., Glymour, M., & Fielding, J. (2016). Addressing social determinants of health and health inequalities. *JAMA, 316(16)*, 1641-1642. https://cdn.ymaws.com/hpaapta.site-ym.com/resource/resmgr/Resource/social_Determinants_Adler_20.pdf

Ajzen, I. (1985). From intentions to actions: A theory of planned behavior. In J. Kuhl & J. Beckmann (Eds.), *Action control: From cognition to behavior* (pp. 11-39). Springer-Verlag.

Ajzen, I. (1991). The theory of planned behavior. *Organizational Behavior and Human Decision Processes, 50*, 179-211.

Alavi, H.R. (2011). The role of self-esteem in tendency towards drugs, theft, and prostitution. *Addiction & Health, 3(3-4)*, 119-124.

Albrecht, Karl. (2015). The paradoxical power of humility [Web log post]. *Psychology Today.* www.psychologytoday.com/blog/brainsnacks/201501/the-paradoxical-power-humility

Alcoholics Anonymous World Services. (1939/2001). *Alcoholics Anonymous: the story of how many thousands of men and women have recovered from alcoholism* (4th ed.). Author.

Alcoholics Anonymous World Services. (2014/1975). *Living sober.* Author.

Alcoholics Anonymous World Services. (1953/2014). *Twelve steps and twelve traditions* (80th ed.). Author.

Alden, L.E., & Trew, J.L. (2013). If it makes you happy: Engaging in kind acts increases positive affect in socially anxious individuals. *Emotion, 13(1)*, 64–75. https://doi.org/10.1037/a0027761

Alderson-Day, B., & Fernyhough, C. (2015). Inner speech: Development, cognitive functions, phenomenology, and neurobiology. *Psychological Bulletin, 141(5)*, 931–965. https://doi.org/10.1037/bul0000021

Alfonso, J., Caracuel, A., Delgado-Pastor, L., & Verdejo-García, A. (2011). Combined goal management training and mindfulness meditation improve executive functions and decision-making performance in abstinent polysubstance abusers. *Drug and Alcohol Dependence, 117(1),* 78–81. doi:10.1016/j.drugalcdep.2010.12.025

American Psychiatric Association (APA). (2013). *Diagnostic and statistical manual of mental disorders* (5th ed.). Author.

American Psychological Association. (2012). *What you need to know about willpower: The psychological science of self-control.* http://www.apa.org/helpcenter/willpower

American Society of Addiction Medicine (ASAM). (2015). *National practice guideline for the use of medications in the treatment of addiction involving opioid use.* https://www.asam.org/docs/default-source/practice-support/guidelines-and-consensus-docs/asam-national-practice-guideline-supplement.pdf

Amodeo, J. (2015). Why pride is nothing to be proud of [Web log post]. *Psychology Today.* https://www.psychologytoday.com/ca/blog/intimacy-path-toward-spirituality/201506/why-pride-is-nothing-be-proud

Anderson, B. (2016). What is abnormal about addiction-related attentional biases? *Drug and Alcohol Dependence, 167,* 8-14. http://dx.doi.org/10.1016/j.drugalcdep.2016.08.002

Andersson, H.W., Wenass, M., & Nordfjærn, T. (2019). Relapse after inpatient substance use treatment: A prospective cohort study among users of illicit substances. *Addictive Behaviors, 90,* 222-228. https://doi.org/10.1016/j.addbeh.2018.11.008

Antonio, T., Childers, S., Rothman, R., Dersch, C.M., King, C., Kuehne, M., et al. (2013). Effect of iboga alkaloids on µ-opioid receptor-coupled G protein activation. *Plos One.* https://doi.org/10.1371/journal.pone.0077262

Arigo, D., Suls, J., & Smyth, J.M. (2012). Social comparisons and chronic illness: Research synthesis and clinical implications. *Health Psychology Review, 8(2),* 154-214. DOI: 10.1080/17437199.2011.634572

Armitage, C.J., Harris, P.R, & Arden, M.A. (2011). Evidence that self-affirmation reduces alcohol consumption: Randomized exploratory trial with a new, brief means of self-affirming. *Health Psychology, 30(5),* 633-641. DOI: 10.1037/a0023738

Aronson, E., Wilson, T.D., Fehr, B., & Akert, R.M. (2013). *Social psychology* (5th Canadian ed.). Pearson.

Arts, N.J., Walvoort, S.J., & Kessels, R.P. (2017). Korsakoff's syndrome: A critical review. *Neuropsychiatric Disease and Treatment, 13,* 2875–2890. https://doi.org/10.2147/NDT.S130078

Ashim, K., & Tridip, C. (2017). Stress and its vulnerability to addiction. *Global Journal of Intellectual & Developmental Disabilities, 3(5).* DOI: 10.19080/ GJIDD.2017.03.555623

Ashwini, U.R., & Indumathy, J. (2018). Altruism and general well-being among adults. *International Journal of Research in Social Sciences, 8(4),* 528-540.

Aspinwall, L.G. & Tedeschi, R.G. (2010). The value of positive psychology for health psychology: Progress and pitfalls in examining the relation of positive phenomena to health. *Annals of Behavioral Medicine, 39,* 4-12.

Aten, J. (2019). Humility and resilience [Web log post]. *Psychology Today.* https://www.psychologytoday.com/intl/blog/heal-and-carry/201901/resilience-and-humility

Atkinson, R.C., & Shiffrin, R.M. (1968). Human memory: A proposed system and its control processes. In K.W. Spence & J.T. Spence (Eds.). *The psychology of learning and motivation* (pp. 89–195). Academic Press.

Austin, Michael W. (2012). Humility [Web log post]. *Psychology Today.* www.psychologytoday.com/blog/ethics-everyone/201206/humility

Baler, R., & Volkow, N. (2006). Drug addiction: The neurobiology of disrupted self-control. *Trends in Molecular Medicine, 12(12),* 559–66. doi: 10.1016/j.molmed.2006.10.005

Balhara, Y.P., Kuppili, P.P., Gupta, R. (2017). Neurobiology of comorbid substance use disorders and psychiatric disorders. *Journal of Addictions Nursing. 28(1),* 11-26. doi: 10.1097/JAN.0000000000000155

Bandura, A. (1994). Self-efficacy. In V. S. Ramachaudran (Ed.), *Encyclopedia of human behavior* (Vol. 4) (pp. 71-81). Academic Press. (Reprinted in H.

Friedman [Ed.]. (1998). *Encyclopedia of mental health*. Academic Press).

Bandura A. (1977a). Self-efficacy: Toward a unifying theory of behavioral change. *Psychological Review, 84(2)*, 191–215. https://doi.org/10.1037/0033-295X.84.2.191

Bandura, A., & Locke, E.A. (2003). Negative self-efficacy and goal effects revisited. *Journal of Applied Psychology, 88(1)*, 87–99. DOI: 10.1037/0021-9010.88.1.87

Banks, S., Eddy, K., Angstadt, M., Nathan, P., & Phan, K. (2007). Amygdala-frontal connectivity during emotion regulation. *Social Cognitive and Affective Neuroscience, 2(4)*, 303–312. https://doi.org/10.1093/scan/nsm029

Baranowski, T. (1990). Reciprocal determinism at the stages of behavior change: An Integration of community, personal and behavioral perspectives. *International Quarterly of Community Health Education, 10(4)*, 297–327. https://doi.org/10.2190/NKBY-UVD6-K542-1QVR

Bartone, P., Hystad, S., Eid, J., & Brevik, J. (2012). Psychological hardiness and coping style as risk/resilience factors for alcohol abuse. *Military Medicine, 177(5)*, 517-524. https://watermark.silverchair.com/milmed-d-11-00200.pdf

Baskin-Sommers, A., & Sommers, I. (2006). The co-occurrence of substance use and high-risk behaviors. *The Journal of Adolescent Health*, *38*(5), 609–611. https://doi.org/10.1016/j.jadohealth.2005.07.010

Batho, D. (2017). Addiction as powerlessness? Choice, compulsion, and 12-Step programmes green paper (November 2017). *University of Essex*. Doi: 10.13140/RG.2.2.20695.16809. p.12.

Baumeister, R.F. (1982). Self-esteem, self-presentation, and future interaction: A dilemma of reputation. *Journal of Personality, 50(1)*, 29-45.

Bayer, R., & Spitzer, R.L. (1982). Edited correspondence on the status of homosexuality in DSM-III. *Journal of the History of Behavioral Science, 18(1)*, 32–52.

Bechara, A. (2005). Decision making, impulse control and loss of willpower to resist drugs: A neurocognitive perspective. *Nature Neuroscience, 8*, 1458-1463. https://doi.org/10.1038/nn1584

Bechara, A. (2004). Disturbances of emotion regulation after focal brain lesions. *International Review of Neurobiology, 62*, 159-193. https://books.google.ca/books?hl=en&lr=&id=mT2_OVo9ugoC&oi=fnd&pg=PA159&ots=Jio9CXYW4p&sig=scwIbDvGhgr5XIyVCjEIxRqDTdI&redir_esc=y#v=onepage&q&f=false

Bechara, A., Nader, K., & van der Kooy, D. (1998). A two-separate-motivational systems hypothesis of opioid addiction. *Pharmacology, Biochemistry, and Behavior, 59(1)*, 1–17. doi: 10.1016/S0091-3057(97)00047-6

Becker-Phelps, L. (2010). The secret of success: Lower your expectations [Web log post]. *Psychology Today.* https://www.psychologytoday.com/ca/blog/making-change/201007/the-secret-success-lower-your-expectations

Bem, D.J. (1972). Self-perception theory. *Advances in Experimental Psychology, 6*, 1-62.

Bergland, C. (2012). The neurochemicals of happiness. *Psychology Today.* https://www.psychologytoday.com/ca/blog/the-athletes-way/201211/the-neurochemicals-happiness

Berman, M., Misic, B., Buschkuehl, M., Kross, E., Deldin, P., Peltier, S., et al. (2014). Does resting-state connectivity reflect depressive rumination? A tale of two analyses. *NeuroImage, 103*, 267–279. doi: 10.1016/J.NEUROIMAGE.2014.09.027

Bernhard, J. (2016). A sure-fire way to silence your inner critic [Web log post]. *Psychology Today.* https://www.psychologytoday.com/ca/blog/turning-straw-gold/201604/sure-fire-way-silence-your-inner-critic

Bevilacqua, L., & Goldman, D. (2009). Genes and addictions. *Clinical Pharmacology and Therapeutics, 85(4)*, 359–361. https://doi.org/10.1038/clpt.2009.6

Bhat, P.S., Ryali, V., Srivastava, K., Kumar, S. R., Prakash, J., & Singal, A. (2012). Alcoholic hallucinosis. *Industrial Psychiatry Journal, 21(2)*, 155–157. https://doi.org/10.4103/0972-6748.119646

Bigler, M., Neimeyer, G.J., & Brown, E. (2001). The divided self revisited: Effects of self-concept clarity and self-concept differentiation on psychological adjustment. *Journal of Social and Clinical Psychology, 20(3),* 396-415.

Bishop, S. (2009). Trait anxiety and impoverished prefrontal control of attention. *Nature Neuroscience, 12,* 92-98. doi: 10.1038/nn.2242

Bishop, S.R., Lau, M., Shapiro, S., Carlson, L., Anderson, N.D., Carmody, J., et al. (2004). Mindfulness: A proposed operational definition. *Clinical Psychology: Science and Practice, 11(3),* 230-241. doi:10.1093/clipsy.bph077

Black, J. & Enns, G. (1997). *Better boundaries: Owning and treasuring your life.* Raincoast Books.

Blanchard, M., & Farber, B. (2015). Lying in psychotherapy: Why and what clients don't tell their therapist about therapy and their relationship. *Counselling Psychology Quarterly, 29(1),* 90-112. https://doi.org/10.1080/09515070.2015.1085365

Bliss, T.V., & Collingridge, G.L. (1993). A synaptic model of memory: Long-term potentiation in the hippocampus. *Nature, 361,* 31-39. doi:10.1038/361031a0. PMID 8421494.

Blum, D. (2010, Feb 19). The chemist's war. *Slate Medical Examiner.* http://www.slate.com/articles/health_and_science/medical_examiner/2010/02/the_chemists_war.single.html

Bluth, K., & Neff, K. (2018). New frontiers in understanding the benefits of self-compassion. *Self and Identity, 17(6),* 605-608. https://doi.org/10.1080/15298868.2018.1508494

Boening J. A. (2001). Neurobiology of an addiction memory. *Journal of Neural Transmission, 108(6),* 755–765. https://doi.org/10.1007/s007020170050

Bogenschutz, M.P., Tonigan, J.S., & Miller, W.R. (2006). Examining the effects of alcoholism typology and AA attendance on self-efficacy as a mechanism of change.
Journal of Studies on Alcohol, 67(4), 562-567.
https://doi.org/10.15288/jsa.2006.67.562

Bollinger, R.A., & Hill, P.C. (2012). Humility. In T.G. Plante (Ed.), *Religion, spirituality, and positive psychology: Understanding the psychological fruits of faith* (pp. 31–48). Praeger.

Boney-McCoy, S., Gibbons, F.X., & Gerrard, M. (1999). Self-esteem, compensatory self-enhancement, and the consideration of health risk. *Personality And Social Psychology Bulletin, 25(8),* 954-965.

Bourg-Carter, S. (2014). Helper's high: The benefits (and risks) of altruism [Web log Post]. *Psychology Today.* www.psychologytoday.com/blog/high-octane-women/201409/helpers-high-the-benefits-and-risks-altruism

Bowler, J., Bowler, M., & James, L. (2011). The cognitive underpinnings of addiction. *Substance Use and Misuse, 46,* 1060-1071. DOI: 10.3109/10826084.2011.552934

Bremner, R.H., Koole, S.L., & Bushman, B.J. (2011). "Pray for those who mistreat you:" Effects of prayer on anger and aggression. *Personality and Social Psychology Bulletin, 20(10),* 1-8. DOI: 10.1177/0146167211402215

Brewer, C., Streel, E., & Skinner, M. (2017). Supervised disulfiram's superior effectiveness in alcoholism treatment: Ethical, methodological, and psychological aspects. *Alcohol and Alcoholism, 52(2),* 213–219. https://doi.org/10.1093/alcalc/agw093

Brown, A. (1987). Metacognition, executive control, self-regulation and other more mysterious mechanisms. In F. Weinert, & R. Kluwe (Eds.). *Metacognition, motivation, and understanding* (pp. 65– 116). Erlbaum.

Brown, T.K. & Alper, K. (2018). Treatment of opioid use disorder with ibogaine: Detoxification and drug use outcomes. *The American Journal of Drug and Alcohol Abuse, 44(1),* 24-36. DOI: 10.1080/00952990.2017.1320802

Brown, G.W., Bifulco, A.T., & Andrews, B. (1990). Self-esteem and depression: III. Aetiological issues. *Social Psychiatry and Psychiatric Epidemiology: The International Journal for Research in Social and Genetic Epidemiology and Mental Health Services, 25(5),* 235–243. https://doi.org/10.1007/BF00788644

Brown, S.L., Brown, R.M., House, J.S. & Smith, D.M. (2008). Coping with spousal loss: Potential buffering effects of self-reported helping behavior. *Personality and Social Psychological Bulletin, 34(6)*, 849–861. DOI: 10.1177/0146167208314972

Brown, S.L., Nesse, R.M., Vinokur, A.D. & Smith, D.M. (2003). Providing social support may be more beneficial than receiving it: Results from a prospective study of mortality. *Psychological Science, 14(4)*, 320–327.

Buchanan, K.E., & Bardi, A. (2010). Acts of kindness and acts of novelty affect life satisfaction. *The Journal of Social Psychology, 150*(3), 235–237. https://doi.org/10.1080/00224540903365554

Buri, J. R. (1988). The nature of humankind, authoritarianism, and self-esteem. *Journal of Psychology and Christianity, 7*, 32–38.

Burkhouse, K., Jacobs, R., Peters, A., Ajilore, O., Watkins, E., & Langenecker, S. (2017). Neural correlates of rumination in adolescents with remitted major depressive disorder and healthy controls. *Cognitive, Affective, & Behavioral Neuroscience, 17*, 394–405. doi: 10.3758/s13415-016-0486-4

Buss, D. (Ed.). (2016). *Handbook of evolutionary psychology* (2nd ed.). John Wiley & Sons.

Butler R. & Bauld L. (2005) The parents' experience: Coping with drug use in the family. *Drugs, Education, Prevention and Policy, 12(1)*, 35–45.

Buunk, B.P., & Ybema, J.F. (1997). Social comparison and occupational stress: The identification-contrast model. In B.P. Buunk, & F.X. Gibbons (Eds.). *Health, coping, and well-being: Perspectives from social comparison theory* (pp. 359-388). Erlbaum.

Cacioppo, J., Reis, H., & Zautra, A. (2011). Social resilience: The value of social fitness with an application to the military. *American Psychologist, 66(1)*, 43-51. http://dx.doi.org/10.1037/a0021419

Campbell, J.D. (1990). Self-esteem and clarity of the self-concept. *Journal of Personality and Social Psychology, 59(3)*, 538-49.

Campbell, J.D., Chew, B., & Scratchley, L.S. (1991). Cognitive and emotional reactions to daily events: The effects of self-esteem and self-complexity. *Journal of Personality, 59(3)*, 473–505. https://doi.org/10.1111/j.1467-6494.1991.tb00257.x

Campbell, J.D., Trapnell, P.D., Heine, S.J., Katz, I.M., Lavallee, L.F., & Lehman, D.R. (1996). Self-concept clarity: Measurement, personality correlates, and cultural boundaries. *Journal of Personality and Social Psychology, 70(1),* 141–156. https://doi.org/10.1037/0022-3514.70.1.141

Canadian Nurses Association (CNA). (2010). *Nurse fatigue and patient safety.* https://www.cna-aiic.ca/-/media/cna/page-content/pdf-en/fatigue_safety_2010_report_e.pdf?la=en&hash=AB24ABDD277F83524AA6F7083298FC3B35221070

Cardinal, R.N., Parkinson, J.A., Hall, J., & Everitt, B.J. (2002). Emotion and motivation: The role of the amygdala, ventral striatum, and prefrontal cortex. *Neuroscience and Biobehavioral Reviews, 26,* 321-352

Carlson, B., & Larkin, H. (2009). Meditation as a coping intervention for treatment of addiction. *Journal of Religion & Spirituality in Social Work, 28,* 379-392. DOI: 10.1080/15426430903263260

Carmody, J., Reed, G., Kristeller, J., & Merriam, P. (2008). Mindfulness, spirituality, and health-related symptoms. *Journal of Psychosomatic Research, 64(4),* 393-403. https://doi.org/10.1016/j.jpsychores.2007.06.015

Cartwright-Hatton, S., & Wells, A. (1997). Beliefs about worry and intrusions: The meta-cognitions questionnaire and its correlates. *Journal of Anxiety Disorders, 11(3),* 279-96. DOI:10.1016/s0887-6185(97)00011-x

Carver, C.S., & Johnson, S.L. (2010). Authentic and hubristic pride: Differential relations to aspects of goal regulation, affect, and self-control. *Journal of Research in Personality, 44(6),* 698–703. https://doi.org/10.1016/j.jrp.2010.09.004

Caselli, G., Bortolai, C., Leoni, M., Rovetto, F., & Spada, M.M. (2008). Rumination in problem drinkers. *Addiction Research & Theory, 16(6),* 564-571. https://doi.org/10.1080/16066350802100822

Caselli, G., Ferretti, C., Leoni, M., Rebecchi, D., Rovetto, F., & Spada, M.M. (2010). Rumination as a predictor of drinking behaviour in alcohol abusers: A prospective study. *Addiction, 105,* 1041-1048. doi:10.1111/j.1360-0443.2010.02912.x

Caselli, G., Martino, F., Spada, M., & Wells, A. (2018). Metacognitive therapy for alcohol use disorder: A systematic case series. *Frontiers in Psychology.* https://doi.org/10.3389/fpsyg.2018.02619

Center for Substance Abuse Treatment. (2005). Substance-induced disorders. Substance Abuse Treatment for Persons With Co-Occurring Disorders. *Treatment Improvement Protocol (TIP) Series, No. 42.* https://www.ncbi.nlm.nih.gov/books/NBK64178/

Centers for Disease Control and Prevention (CDC). (2019). *2019 Annual surveillance report of drug-related risks and outcomes.* https://www.cdc.gov/drugoverdose/pdf/pubs/2019-cdc-drug-surveillance-report.pdf

Centers for Disease Control and Prevention (CDC). (2020). *CDC Drug Overdose Surveillance and Epidemiology (DOSE) System.* https://www.cdc.gov/drugoverdose/data/nonfatal/case.html

Centers for Disease Control and Prevention (CDC). (2020). *CDC WONDER.* https://wonder.cdc.gov/

Centers for Disease Control and Prevention (CDC). (2020). *Drug overdose deaths.* https://www.cdc.gov/drugoverdose/data/statedeaths.html

Centers for Disease Control and Prevention (CDC). (2019). *Prescribing practices.* https://www.cdc.gov/drugoverdose/data/prescribing/prescribing-practices.html

Centers for Disease Control and Prevention (CDC). (2020). *Synthetic opioid overdose deaths.* https://www.cdc.gov/drugoverdose/data/fentanyl.html

Centers for Disease Control and Prevention (CDC). (2020). *U.S. opioid prescribing rate maps.* https://www.cdc.gov/drugoverdose/maps/rxrate-maps.html

Centers for Disease Control and Prevention (CDC). (2017). Vital Signs: Changes in opioid prescribing in the United States, 2006–2015. *MMWR, 66(26),* 697-704. https://www.cdc.gov/mmwr/volumes/66/wr/mm6626a4.htm

Centers for Disease Control and Prevention (CDC). (2020). *Youth Risk Behavior Surveillance System (YRBSS).* https://www.cdc.gov/healthyyouth/data/yrbs/index.htm

Chartrand, T.L., & Bargh, J.A. (1999). The chameleon effect: The perception–behavior link and social interaction. *Journal of Personality and Social*

Psychology, 76(6), 893–910. https://doi.org/10.1037/0022-3514.76.6.893

Cheng, J.T., Tracy, J.L., & Henrich, J. (2010). Pride, personality, and the evolutionary foundations of human social status. *Evolution and Human Behavior, 31,* 334–347. doi:10.1016/j.evolhumbehav.2010.02.004

Ciccarone D. (2011). Stimulant abuse: Pharmacology, cocaine, methamphetamine, treatment, attempts at pharmacotherapy. *Primary care, 38(1),* 41–58. https://doi.org/10.1016/j.pop.2010.11.004

Cinoğlu, H., & Arıkan, Y. (2012). Self, identity and identity formation: From the perspectives of three major theories. *Journal of Human Sciences, 9(2),* 1114-1131. https://www.j-humansciences.com/ojs/index.php/IJHS/article/view/2429/972

Cicei, C.C. (2012). Examining the association between self-concept clarity and self-esteem on a sample of Romanian medical students. *Procedia – Social and Behavioral Sciences, 46,* 4345-4348. https://doi.org/10.1016/j.sbspro.2012.06.252

Collier, L. (2016). Growth after trauma. *American Psychological Association Monitor on Psychology, 47(10),* 48. https://www.apa.org/monitor/2016/11/growth-trauma

Cooke, S.F., & Bliss, T.V. (2006). Plasticity in the human central nervous system. *Brain, 129(7),* 1659–1673. doi:10.1093/brain/awl082

Cooney, R., Joormann, J., Eugène, F., Dennis, E., and Gotlib, I. (2010). Neural correlates of rumination in depression. *Cognitive, Affective, & Behavioral Neuroscience, 10,* 470–478. doi: 10.3758/CABN.10.4.470

Craig, A.D. (2009). How do you feel — now? The anterior insula and human awareness. *Nature Review Neuroscience, 10,* 59–70. https://doi.org/10.1038/nrn2555

Creswell, J.D., Welch, W., Taylor, S.E., Sherman, D.K., Gruenewald, T., & Mann, T. (2005). Affirmation of personal values buffers neuroendocrine and psychological stress responses. *Psychological Science, 16,* 846-851. DOI: 10.1111/j.1467-9280.2005.01624.x

Crews, F., & Vetreno, R. (2014). Neuroimmune basis of alcoholic brain damage. *International Review of Neurobiology, 118,* 315-57. doi: 10.1016/B978-0-12-801284-0.00010-5

Cristea, I., Kok, R., & Cuijpers, P. (2016). The effectiveness of cognitive bias modification interventions for substance addictions: A metaanalysis. *PLoS ONE 11(9)*, e0162226. doi:10.1371/ journal.pone.0162226

Crocker, J., Canevello, A., & Brown, A. (2016). Social motivation: Costs and benefits of selfishness and otherishness. *Annual Review of Psychology, 68,* 299-325. https://doi.org/10.1146/annurev-psych-010416-044145

Cui, C., Shurtleff, D., & Harris, R.A. (2014). Neuroimmune mechanisms of alcohol and drug addiction. *International Review of Neurobiology, 118,* 1–12. https://doi.org/10.1016/B978-0-12-801284-0.00001-4

Curry, O.S., Rowland, L.A., Van Lissa, C.J., Zlotowitz, S., McAlaney, J., & Whitehouse, H. (2018). Happy to help? A systematic review and meta-analysis of the effects of performing acts of kindness on the well-being of the actor. *Journal of Experimental Social Psychology, 76,* 320-329. https://doi.org/10.1016/j.jesp.2018.02.014

Cicero, T.J., Ellis, M.S., & Kasper, Z.A. (2020). Polysubstance use: A broader understanding of substance use during the opioid crisis. *American Journal of Public Health, 110,* 244-250. https://doi.org/10.2105/AJPH.2019.305412

Crummy, E.A., O'Neal, T.J., Baskin, B.M., & Ferguson, S.M. (2020). One is not enough: Understanding and modeling polysubstance use. *Frontiers in Neuroscience, 14,* 569. https://doi.org/10.3389/fnins.2020.00569

Culpepper, L. (2016). Positive psychology and spirituality. *Journal of Psychology and Clinical Psychiatry, 6(7),* 00407. DOI: 10.15406/jpcpy.2016.06.00407

Dale, S. (2015). Heuristics and biases: The science of decision-making. *Business Information Review, 32(2),* 93–99. DOI: 10.1177/0266382115592536

Daley, D.C., & Marlatt, G.A. (1997). *Managing your drug or alcohol problem: Therapist guide.* Oxford university Press.

Darke, S., Larney, S., and Farrell, M. (2017). Yes, people can die from opiate withdrawal. *Addiction, 112(2),* 199–200. doi: 10.1111/add.13512.

David, A.S. (1990). Insight and psychosis. *British Journal of Psychiatry, 156,* 798-808. DOI: 10.1192/bjp.156.6.798

David, V., Beracochea, D., & Walton, M. (2018). Editorial: Memory systems of the addicted brain: The underestimated role of cognitive biases in addiction and its treatment. *Frontiers in Psychology.* https://doi.org/10.3389/fpsyt.2018.00030

Davidson, R., Kabat-Zinn, J., Schumacher, J., Rosenkranz, M., Muller, D., Santorelli, S., et al. (2003). Alterations in brain and immune function produced by mindfulness meditation. *Psychosomatic Medicine, 65 (4),* 564–570. doi: 10.1097/01.PSY.0000077505.67574.E3).

Davis, D.E., Worthington, E.L., & Hook, J.N. (2010). Humility: Review of measurement strategies and conceptualization as personality judgment. *The Journal of Positive Psychology, 5(4),* 243–252. https://doi.org/10.1080/17439761003791672

Davison, G.C., & Best, J.L. (2003). Think-aloud techniques. In W. O'Donohue, J.E. Fisher, & S. Hayes (Eds.), *Cognitive behavioral therapy: Applying empirically supported techniques in your practice* (pp. 423-427). John Wiley & Sons.

Deci, E.L., Ryan, R.M., & Koestner, R. (1999). A meta-analytic review of experiments examining the effects of extrinsic rewards on intrinsic motivation. *Psychological Bulletin, 125(6),* 627-668.

Department of Justice, Government of Canada. (2019). *Get help with family violence.* https://www.justice.gc.ca/eng/cj-jp/fv-vf/help-aide.html

Diamond, S. (2008). The psychology of spirituality [Web log post]. *Psychology Today.* https://www.psychologytoday.com/blog/evil-deeds/200812/the-psychology-spirituality

Diaper, A.M., Law, F.D., & Melichar, J.K. (2014). Pharmacological strategies for detoxification. *British Journal of Clinical Pharmacology, 77(2),* 302–314. https://doi.org/10.1111/bcp.12245

Dillon, M.M. (2009). Is it good to do good? Altruism and health. *The University Dialogue, 48.* https://scholars.unh.edu/discovery_ud/48

Dolan, S.L., Martin, R.A., & Rohsenow, D.J. (2008). Self-efficacy for cocaine abstinence: Pretreatment correlates and relationship to outcomes. *Addictive Behaviors, 33(5),* 675–688. https://doi.org/10.1016/j.addbeh.2007.12.001

Domeier, M., Sachse, P., & Schafer, B. (2018). Motivational reasons for biased decisions: The sunk-cost effect's instrumental rationality. *Frontiers in Psychology.* https://doi.org/10.3389/fpsyg.2018.00815

Dominguez-Salas, S., Diaz-Batanero, C., Lozano-Rojas, O., & Verdejo-Garcia, A. (2016). Impact of general cognition and executive function deficits on addiction treatment outcomes: Systematic review and discussion of neurocognitive pathways. *Neuroscience & Biobehavioral Reviews, 71,* 772-801.

Dong, Y., Taylor, J.R., Wolf, M.E., & Shaham, Y. (2017). Circuit and synaptic plasticity mechanisms of drug relapse. *The Journal of Neuroscience, 37(45),* 10867–10876. https://doi.org/10.1523/JNEUROSCI.1821-17.2017

Donovan, D., Ingalsbe, M., Benbow, J., & Daley, D. (2013). 12-step interventions and mutual support programs for substance use disorders: An overview. *Social Work in Public Health, 28(3-4),* 313–332. doi:10.1080/19371918.2013.774663

dos Santos, J.C., Barros, S., & Huxley, P.J. (2018). Social inclusion of the people with mental health issues: Compare international results. *International Journal of Social Psychiatry 2018, 64(4),* 344–350. DOI: 10.1177/0020764018763941

Douaihy, A., Daley, D., Marlatt, A., & Donovan, D.M. (2016). Relapse prevention: Clinical models and intervention strategies. In R.K. Ries, D.A. Fiellin, S.C. Miller, & R. Saitz (Eds.). *The ASAM principles of addiction medicine* (5th ed.). Wolters Kluwer.

Dowling, G. (2011). *Advances in drug abuse and addiction research from NIDA: Implications for treatment* [Power point presentation]. https://www.bumc.bu.edu/care/files/2011/08/02-Keynote-CRIT-2011.pdf

Dugosh, K., Abraham, A., Seymour, B., McLoyd, K., Chalk, M., & Festinger, D. (2016). A systematic review on the use of psychosocial interventions in conjunction with medications for the treatment of opioid addiction. *Journal of Addiction Medicine, 10(2),* 93–103. https://doi.org/10.1097/ADM.0000000000000193

Duval, S., & Wicklund, R.A. (1972). *A theory of objective self awareness.* Academic Press.

Easterbrook, J. (1959). The effect of emotion on cue utilisation and the organisation of behavior. *Psychological review, 66,* 183-201. https://doi.org/10.1037/h0047707

Egevari, G., Ciccocioppo, R., Jentsch, J., & Hurd, Y. (2018). Shaping vulnerability to addiction – the contribution of behavior, neural circuits and molecular mechanisms. *Neuroscience & Behavioral Reviews, 85,* 117-125. https://doi.org/10.1016/j.neubiorev.2017.05.019

Ellemers, N., & Haslam, S.A. (2012). Social identity theory. In P.A.M. Van Lange, A.W. Kruglanski, & E.T. Higgins (Eds.), *Handbook of theories of social psychology* (p. 379–398). Sage Publications Ltd. https://doi.org/10.4135/9781446249222.n45

Elliott, K. (2006). Anthetic inner critic work as a method for relapse prevention. *Alcoholism Treatment Quarterly, 24(3),* 109-119. https://doi.org/10.1300/J020v24n03_07

Ehret, P.J., LaBrie, J.W., Santerre, C., & Sherman, D.K. (2015). Self-affirmation and motivational interviewing: Integrating perspectives to reduce resistance and increase efficacy of alcohol interventions, *Health Psychology Review, 9(1),* 83-102, DOI: 10.1080/17437199.2013.840953

Enright, R. (2017). Why resentment lasts – And how to defeat it [Web log post]. *Psychology Today.* https://www.psychologytoday.com/ca/blog/the-forgiving-life/201703/why-resentment-lasts-and-how-defeat-it

Epley, N., & Gilovich, T. (2016). The mechanics of motivated reasoning. *Journal of Economic Perspectives, 30(3),* 133-140. http://dx.doi.org/10.1257/jep.30.3.133

Epton, T., Harris, P.R., Kane, R., van Koningsbruggen, G.M., & Sheeran, P. (2015). The impact of self-affirmation on health-behavior change: A meta-analysis. *Health Psychology, 34(3),* 187-96. DOI:10.1037/hea0000116

Evans, J. (2008). Dual-processing accounts of reasoning, judgment, and social cognition. *Annual Review of Psychology, 59,* 255-78. 10.1146/annurev.psych.59.103006.093629

Ewald, D.R., Strack, R.W., & Orsini, M.M. (2019). Rethinking addiction. *Global Pediatric Health.* https://doi.org/10.1177/2333794X18821943

Exline, J.J., & Hill, P.C. (2012). Humility: A consistent and robust predictor of generosity. *The Journal of Positive Psychology, 7(3)*, 208–218. https://doi.org/10.1080/17439760.2012.671348

Evans, D.R. (1997). Health promotion, wellness programs, quality of life and the marketing of psychology. *Canadian Psychology, 38(1)*, 1–12. https://doi.org/10.1037/0708-5591.38.1.1

Feigelman, W., Jordan, J.R., & Gorman, B.S. (2011). Parental grief after a child's drug death compared to other death causes: Investigating a greatly neglected bereavement population. *Omega, 63(4)*, 291–316. doi:10.2190/OM.63.4.a

Feldman, R., & Dinardo, A. (2009). *Essentials of understanding psychology* (3rd Canadian ed.). McGraw-Hill.

Festinger, L. (1957). *A theory of cognitive dissonance.* Stanford University Press.

Festinger, L. (1957). A theory of social comparison processes. *Human Relations, 7(2)*, 117-140. https://doi.org/10.1177/001872675400700202

Festinger, L., & Carlsmith, J.M. (1959). Cognitive consequences of forced compliance. *The Journal of Abnormal and Social Psychology, 58(2)*, 203–210. https://doi.org/10.1037/h0041593

Field, M., Mogg, K., & Bradley, B. (2005). Craving and cognitive biases for alcohol cues in social drinkers. *Alcohol & Alcoholism, 40(6)*, 504–510. doi:10.1093/alcalc/agh213

Filkowski, M., Cochran, R., & Haas, B. (2016). Altruistic behavior: Mapping responses in the brain. *Neuroscience and Neuroeconomics, 5*, 65-75. https://doi.org/10.2147/NAN.S87718

Finney, J.W., Noyes, C.A., Coutts, A.I., & Moos, R.H. (1998). Evaluating substance abuse treatment process models: I. Changes on proximal outcome variables during 12-step and cognitive-behavioral treatment. *Journal of Studies on Alcohol, 59(4)*, 371–380. https://doi.org/10.15288/jsa.1998.59.371

Fischer, J. (2011). The Four Domains Model: Connecting spirituality, health and well-being. *Religions, 2*, 17-28; doi:10.3390/rel2010017

Fishbein, M. (1979). A theory of reasoned action: Some applications and implications. *Nebraska Symposium on Motivation, 27*, 65–116.

Fishbein, M. & Ajzen, I. (1975) *Belief, attitude, intention, and behavior: An introduction to theory and research.* Addison-Wesley.

Fishbein, M. & Ajzen, I. (2010). *Predicting and changing behavior: The Reasoned Action Approach.* Taylor & Francis.

Fleming, K., & Bartholow, B. (2014). Alcohol cues, approach bias, and inhibitory control: Applying a dual process model of addiction to alcohol sensitivity. *Psychology of Addictive Behaviors: Journal of the Society of Psychologists in Addictive Behaviors, 28(1),* 85–96. https://doi.org/10.1037/a0031565

Fontenelle, L.F., Oostermeijer, S., Harrison, B.J., Pantelis, C., & Yucel, M. (2011). Obsessive-compulsive disorder, impulse control disorders and drug addiction: Common features and potential treatments. *Drugs, 71(7),* 827-840. 827-40. DOI:10.2165/11591790-000000000-00000

Fox, K.C., Nijeboer, S., Dixon, M.L., Floman, J.L., Ellamil, M., Rumak, S.P., et al. (2014). Is meditation associated with altered brain structure? A systematic review and meta-analysis of morphometric neuroimaging in meditation practitioners. *Neuroscience & Biobehavioral Reviews, 43,* 48–73. DOI: 10.1016/j.neubiorev.2014.03.016

Fluyau, D., Revadigar, N., & Manobianco, B.E. (2018). Challenges of the pharmacological management of benzodiazepine withdrawal, dependence, and discontinuation. *Therapeutic Advances in Psychopharmacology, 8(5),* 147–168. https://doi.org/10.1177/2045125317753340

Franck, E., & De Raedt, R. (2007). Self-esteem reconsidered: Unstable self-esteem outperforms level of self-esteem as vulnerability marker for depression. *Behaviour Research and Therapy, 45(7),* 1531-1541.

Franken I.H. (2003). Drug craving and addiction: Integrating psychological and neuropsychopharmacological approaches. *Progress in Neuro-Psychopharmacology & Biological Psychiatry, 27(4),* 563–579. https://doi.org/10.1016/S0278-5846(03)00081-2

Frankl, V. (1959/2006). *Man's search for meaning.* Beacon Press.

French, M.T., McGeary, K.A., Chitwood, D.D., McCoy, C.B., Inciardi, J.A., & McBride, D. (2000). Chronic drug use and crime. *Substance*

Abuse, 21, 95–109 (2000). https://doi.org/10.1023/A:1007763129628

Friese, M., & Wänke, M. (2014). Personal prayer buffers self-control depletion. *Journal of Experimental Social Psychology, 51*, 56–59. https://doi.org/10.1016/j.jesp.2013.11.006

Furnham, A. & Cheng, H. (2000) Lay theories of happiness. *Journal of Happiness Studies, 1*, 227–246.

Galanter, M. (2007). Spirituality and recovery in 12-step programs: An empirical model. *Journal of Substance Abuse & Treatment, 33(3)*, 265–272. doi: 10.1016/j.jsat.2007.04.016. S0740-5472(07)00186-9

Galanter, M., Josipovic, Z., Dermatis, H., Weber, J., & Millard, M. (2017). An initial fMRI study on neural correlates of prayer in members of Alcoholics Anonymous. *The American Journal of Drug and Alcohol Abuse, 43(1)*, 44-54. DOI: 10.3109/00952990.2016.1141912

Garavan, H., & Stout, J. (2005). Neurocognitive insights into substance abuse. *Trends in Cognitive Sciences, 9(4)*, 194-201. doi:10.1016/j.tics.2005.02.008

Gardner, M., & Steinberg, L. (2005). Peer influence on risk taking, risk preference, and risky decision making in adolescence and adulthood: An experimental study. *Developmental Psychology, 41(4)*, 625–635. doi: 10.1037/0012-1649.41.4.625.

Garland E. (2011). Trait mindfulness predicts attentional and autonomic regulation of alcohol cue-reactivity. *Journal of Psychophysiology, 25(4)*, 180–189. https://doi.org/10.1027/0269-8803/a000060

Garland, E., Boettiger, C., Gaylord, S., Chanon, V., & Howard, M. (2012). Mindfulness is inversely associated with alcohol attentional bias among recovering alcohol-dependent adults. *Cognitive Therapy and Research, 36(5)*, 441–450. https://doi.org/10.1007/s10608-011-9378-7

Garland, E., Fredrickson, B., Kring, A., Johnson, D., Meyer, P., & Penn, D. (2010). Upward spirals of positive emotions counter downward spirals of negativity: Insights from the broaden-and-build theory and affective neuroscience on the treatment of emotion dysfunctions and deficits in psychopathology. *Clinical Psychology Review, 30*, 849–864. https://doi.org/10.1016/j.cpr.2010.03.002

Garland, E. , Froeliger, B., & Howard, M. (2013). Mindfulness training targets neurocognitive mechanisms of addiction at the attention-appraisal-emotion interface. *Frontiers in Psychiatry, 4*, 173. https://doi.org/10.3389/fpsyt.2013.00173

Garland, E., & Howard, M. (2018). Mindfulness-based treatment of addiction: Current state of the field and envisioning the next wave of research. *Addiction Science & Clinical Practice, 13(1)*, 14. doi:10.1186/s13722-018-0115-3

Gawronski, B. (2012). Back to the future of dissonance theory: Cognitive consistency as a core motive. *Social Cognition, 30(6)*, 652-668.

George, O., & Koob, G. (2010). Individual differences in prefrontal cortex function and the transition from drug use to drug dependence. *Neuroscience & Biobehavioral Review, 35(2)*, 232–47. doi: 10.1016/j.neubiorev.2010.05.002

Gibbons, F.X., Smith, T.W., Ingram, R.E., Pearce, K., Brehm, S.S., & Schroeder, D.J. (1985). Self-awareness and self-confrontation: Effects of self-focused attention on members of a clinical population. *Journal of Personality and Social Psychology, 48(3)*, 662-675. DOI:10.1037//0022-3514.48.3.662

Giovazolias, T., & Themeli, O. (2014). Social learning conceptualization for substance abuse: Implications for therapeutic interventions. *The European Journal of Counselling Psychology, 3(1)*, 69–88. doi:10.5964/ejcop.v3i1.23

Gipson, C.D., Kupchik, Y.M., & Kalivas, P.W. (2014). Rapid, transient synaptic plasticity in addiction. *Neuropharmacology, 76(Pt B - 0 0)*, 276–286. https://doi.org/10.1016/j.neuropharm.2013.04.032

Goldberg, S., Tucker, R., Greene, P., Davidson, R. , Wampold, B., Kearney, D., & Simpson, T. (2018). Mindfulness-based interventions for psychiatric disorders: A systematic review and meta-analysis. *Clinical Psychology Review, 59*, 52–60. https://doi.org/10.1016/j.cpr.2017.10.011

Golden, B. (2019). How self-criticism threatens you in mind and body [Web log post]. *Psychology Today.* https://www.psychologytoday.com/intl/blog/overcoming-destructive-anger/201901/how-self-criticism-threatens-you-in-mind-and-body

Goldhagen, D. (1996). *Hitler's willing executioners: Ordinary Germans and the Holocaust.* Random House.

Goldstein, R., Craig, A., Bechara, A., Garavan, H., Childress, A., Paulus, M., & Volkow, N. (2009). The neurocircuitry of impaired insight in drug addiction. *Trends in Cognitive Sciences, 13(9),* 372–380. https://doi.org/10.1016/j.tics.2009.06.004

Goldstein, R., & Volkow, N. (2011). Dysfunction of the prefrontal cortex in addiction: Neuroimaging findings and clinical implications. *Nature Reviews. Neuroscience, 12(11),* 652–669. https://doi.org/10.1038/nrn3119

Goodman, J., & Packard, M.G. (2016). Memory systems and the addicted brain. *Frontiers in Psychology, 7(24).* https://doi.org/10.3389/fpsyt.2016.00024

Gorski, T.T., & Miller, M. (1982). Counseling for relapse prevention. Herald House/Independence Press.

Grant, S., Colaiaco, B., Motala, A., Shanman, R., Booth, M., Sorbero, M., et al. (2017). Mindfulness-based relapse prevention for substance use disorders: A systematic review and meta-analysis. *Journal of Addiction Medicine, 11(5),* 386–396. https://doi.org/10.1097/ADM.0000000000000338

Grant, B.F., Goldstein, R.B., Saha, T.D., Chou, S.P., Jung, J., Zhang, H., et al. (2015). Epidemiology of DSM-5 Alcohol Use Disorder: Results From the National Epidemiologic Survey on Alcohol and Related Conditions III. *JAMA Psychiatry, 72(8),* 757–766. https://doi.org/10.1001/jamapsychiatry.2015.0584

Greenberg, J., Reiner, K., & Meiran, N. (2012). "Mind the trap:" Mindfulness practice reduces cognitive rigidity. *PloS One, 7(5),* e36206. https://doi.org/10.1371/journal.pone.0036206

Groome, D. (2014). *An introduction to cognitive psychology* (3rd ed.). Routledge.

Grueter, B.A., Rothwell, P.E., & Malenka, R.C. (2012). Integrating synaptic plasticity and striatal circuit function in addiction. *Current Opinion in Neurobiology, 22(3),* 545–551. https://doi.org/10.1016/j.conb.2011.09.009

Guenzel, N., & McChargue, D. (2020). Addiction relapse prevention. *StatPearls.* https://www.ncbi.nlm.nih.gov/books/NBK551500/

Grupe, D., & Nitschke, J. (2013). Uncertainty and anticipation in anxiety: An integrated neurobiological and psychological perspective. *Nature Reviews Neuroscience, 14(7),* 488–501. doi:10.1038/nrn3524

Gu, J., Strauss, C., Bond, R., & Cavanagh, K. (2015). How do mindfulness-based cognitive therapy and mindfulness-based stress reduction improve mental health and wellbeing? A systematic review and meta-analysis of mediation studies. *Clinical Psychology Review, 37,* 1–12. http://dx.doi.org/10.1016/j.cpr.2015.01.006

Guthrie, E.R. (1940). Association and the law of effect. *Psychological Review, 47(2),* 127-148.

Hall, J., & Fincham, F. (2005). Self-forgiveness: The stepchild of forgiveness. *Journal of Social and Clinical Psychology, 24(5),* 621-637. Retrieved from http://citeseerx.ist.psu.edu/viewdoc/download?doi=10.1.1.452.7231&rep=rep1&type=pdf

Hall, J., & Fincham, F. (2008). The temporal course of self-forgiveness. *Journal of Social and Clinical Psychology, 27(2),* 174–202. http://fincham.info/papers/jscp-The%20temporal%20course%20of%20self-forgiveness.pdf

Hallo De Wolf, A., & Toebes, B. (2016). Assessing private sector involvement in health care and universal health coverage in light of the right to health. *Health and Human Rights, 18(2),* 79–92.

Hammond, C. (2017). The 7 steps of accepting responsibility [Web log post]. *Psych Central.* https://pro.psychcentral.com/exhausted-woman/2016/05/the-7-steps-of-accepting-responsibility-for-wrongdoing/

Hamonniere, T., & Varescon, I. (2018). Metacognitive beliefs in addictive behaviours: A systematic review. *Addictive Behaviors, 85,* 51–63. https://doi.org/10.1016/j.addbeh.2018.05.018

Hardy, B. (2018). Why willpower makes things worse, not better [Web log post]. *Psychology Today.* https://www.psychologytoday.com/us/blog/quantum-leaps/201803/why-willpower-makes-things-worse-not-better

Hardy, J. (2006). Speaking clearly: A critical review of the self-talk literature. *Psychology of Sport and Exercise, 7,* 81-97. doi:10.1016/j.psychsport.2005.04.002

Harter, S. (1999). *The Construction of the Self. A Developmental Perspective.* Guilford Press.

Hartzler, B., & Fromme, K. (2003). Fragmentary and en bloc blackouts: Similarity and distinction among episodes of alcohol-induced memory loss. *Journal of Studies on Alcohol, 64(4),* 547–550. https://doi.org/10.15288/jsa.2003.64.547

Harvey, M.D., & Enzle, M.E. (1981). A cognitive model of social norms for understanding the transgression-helping effect. *Journal of Personality and Social Psychology, 41(5),* 866-875.

Harvey, P. & Martinko, M.J. Attribution theory and motivation. In N. Borkowski. (2016). *Organizational behavior, theory, and design in health care* (2nd ed.). Jones & Bartlett Learning.

Hasin, D.S., O'Brien, C.P., Auriacombe, M., Borges, G., Bucholz, K., Budney, A., et al. (2013). DSM-5 criteria for substance use disorders: Recommendations and rationale. *The American Journal of Psychiatry, 170(8),* 834–851. https://doi.org/10.1176/appi.ajp.2013.12060782

Harvard Medical School. (2020). Understanding the stress response. *Harvard Health Publishing.* https://www.health.harvard.edu/staying-healthy/understanding-the-stress-response

Hatzigiakoumis, D.S., Martinotti, G., Giannantonio, M.D., & Janiri, L. (2011). Anhedonia and substance dependence: Clinical correlates and treatment options. *Frontiers in Psychiatry, 2,* 10. http://doi.org/10.3389/fpsyt.2011.00010

Heavey, C.L., & Hurlburt, R.T. (2008). The phenomena of inner experience. *Consciousness and cognition, 17,* 798–810. doi:10.1016/j.concog.2007.12.006

Heilig, M., Egli, M., Crabbe, J.C., & Becker, H.C. (2010). Acute withdrawal, protracted abstinence and negative affect in alcoholism: Are they linked? *Addiction Biology, 15(2),* 169–184. https://doi.org/10.1111/j.1369-1600.2009.00194.x

Heinz, A., Löber, S., Georgi, A., Wrase, J., Hermann, D., Rey, E-R., et al. (2003). Reward craving and withdrawal relief craving: Assessment of different motivational pathways to alcohol intake. *Alcohol and Alcoholism, 38(1)*, 35-39. https://doi.org/10.1093/alcalc/agg005

Heylighen, F. (1992). Evolution, selfishness and cooperation. *Journal of Ideas, 2(4)*, 70-76. https://pdfs.semanticscholar.org/fc6d/93966c24f1ac8b6ded84d53de5d04cdc746f.pdf

Higgins, E.T. (1987). Self-discrepancy: A theory relating self and affect. *Psychological Review, 94(3)*, 319–340. https://doi.org/10.1037/0033-295X.94.3.319

Hogarth, L., Balleine, B.W., Corbit, L.H., & Killcross, S. (2013). Associative learning mechanisms underpinning the transition from recreational drug use to addiction. *Annals of the New York Academy of Sciences, 1282*, 12–24. https://doi.org/10.1111/j.1749-6632.2012.06768.x

Holland P.C. (2008). Cognitive versus stimulus-response theories of learning. *Learning & Behavior, 36(3)*, 227–241. https://doi.org/10.3758/lb.36.3.227

Hölzel, B.K., Lazar, S.W., Gard, T., Schuman-Olivier, Z., Vago, D.R., & Ott, U. (2011). How does mindfulness meditation work? Proposing mechanisms of action from a conceptual and neural perspective. *Perspectives on Psychological Science, 6(6)*, 537–559. https://doi.org/10.1177/1745691611419671

Hooker, S.A., Masters, K.S., & Park, C.L. (2018). A meaningful life is a healthy life: A conceptual model linking meaning and meaning salience to health. *Review of General Psychology, 22(1)*, 11–24. https://doi.org/10.1037/gpr0000115

Hsu S., Grow J., & Marlatt A. (2008). Mindfulness and addiction. In: L. Kaskutas & M. Galanter (eds.). *Recent developments in alcoholism*. Springer. https://doi.org/10.1007/978-0-387-77725-2_13

Human Rights Watch. (2016). *US: Disastrous toll of criminalizing drug use*. https://www.hrw.org/news/2016/10/12/us-disastrous-toll-criminalizing-drug-use

Hyman, S.E., Malenka, R.C., & Nestler, E.J. (2006). Neural mechanisms of addiction: The role of reward-related learning and memory. *Annual*

Review of Neuroscience, 29, 565-598. doi: 10.1146/annurev.neuro.29.051605.113009

Hynes, M. (Host). (2019, Sept 20). *Headlines and rejection: Interview with Dr. Steven Stosny* [Radio broadcast interview]. In Meyer, M., & Mahoney, S. (Producers), Tapestry. CBC Radio.

Ingram, R.E. (1990). Self-focused attention in clinical disorders: Review and a conceptual model. *Psychological Bulletin, 107*(2), 156–176. https://doi.org/10.1037/0033-2909.107.2.156

Irani, A. (2018). Positive altruism: Helping that benefits both the recipient and giver [Master's thesis]. *University of Pennsylvania.* https://repository.upenn.edu/mapp_capstone/152

Iversen, L. (2003). Cannabis and the brain. *Brain, 126(6),* 1252–1270. https://doi.org/10.1093/brain/awg143

Jacobsen, L.K., Southwick, S.M., & Kosten, T.R. (2001). Substance use disorders in patients with posttraumatic stress disorder: A review of the literature. *American Journal of Psychiatry, 158(8),* 1184-1190. https://doi.org/10.1176/appi.ajp.158.8.1184

Jankowski, P.J., Sandage, S.J., & Hill, P.C. (2013). Differentiation-based models of forgivingness, mental health and social justice commitment: Mediator effects for differentiation of self and humility. *The Journal of Positive Psychology, 8(5),* 412–424. https://doi.org/10.1080/17439760.2013.820337

Jeppsen, B., Pössel, P., Winkeljohn, S., Bjerg, A. & Wooldridge, D. (2015). Closeness and control: Exploring the relationship between prayer and mental health. *University of Louisville Counseling Psychology Commons.* https://ir.library.louisville.edu/cgi/viewcontent.cgi?article=1174&context=faculty

Jesse, S., Bråthen, G., Ferrara, M., Keindl, M., Ben-Menachem, E., Tanasescu, R., et al. (2017). Alcohol withdrawal syndrome: Mechanisms, manifestations, and management. *Acta Neurologica Scandinavica, 135(1),* 4–16. doi: 10.1111/ane.12671

Johnson, J. (2015). Good, neutral, and bad selfishness [Web log post]. *Psychology Today.* https://www.psychologytoday.com/ca/blog/cui-bono/201501/good-neutral-and-bad-selfishness

Johnson, M.H. (2001). Functional brain development in humans. *Neuroscience, 2,* 475-483. http://www-inst.eecs.berkeley.edu/~cs182/sp06/readings/Johnson%20-%202001.pdf

Jorgensen, C.H., & Pedersen, B. (2020). The efficacy of disulfiram for the treatment of alcohol use disorder. *Alcoholism Clinical and Experimental Research, 35(10),* 1749-58. DOI: 10.1111/j.1530-0277.2011.01523.x

Kabat-Zinn, J. (1990). *Full catastrophe living: Using the wisdom of your body and mind to face stress, pain and illness.* Delacorte.

Kadam, M., Sinha, A., Nimkar, S., Matcheswalla, Y., & De Sousa, A. (2017). A comparative study of factors associated with relapse in alcohol dependence and opioid dependence. *Indian Journal of Psychological Medicine, 39(5),* 627–633. https://doi.org/10.4103/IJPSYM.IJPSYM_356_17

Kadden, R.M., & Litt, M.D. (2011). The role of self-efficacy in the treatment of substance use disorders. *Addictive Behaviors, 36(12),* 1120–1126. https://doi.org/10.1016/j.addbeh.2011.07.032

Kang, D., Jo, H., Jung, W., Kim, S., Jung, Y., Choi, C., et al. (2013). The effect of meditation on brain structure: Cortical thickness mapping and diffusion tensor imaging. *Social, Cognitive, & Affective Neuroscience, 8,* 27–33. Doi:10.1093/scan/nss056

Karyadi, K., VanderVeen, J., & Cyders, M. (2014). A meta-analysis of the relationship between trait mindfulness and substance use behaviors. *Drug and Alcohol Dependence, 143,* 1–10. https://doi.org/10.1016/j.drugalcdep.2014.07.014

Kauer, J.A., & Malenka, R.C. (2007). Synaptic plasticity and addiction. *Nature Reviews: Neuroscience, 8(11),* 844–58. doi:10.1038/nrn2234

Kelley, A.E. (2004). Memory and addiction: Shared neural circuitry and molecular mechanisms. *Neuron, 44(1),* 161-179. https://doi.org/10.1016/j.neuron.2004.09.016

Kelly, T. M., & Daley, D. C. (2013). Integrated treatment of substance use and psychiatric disorders. *Social Work in Public Health, 28(3-4),* 388–406. https://doi.org/10.1080/19371918.2013.774673

Keng, S., Smoski, M., & Robins, C. (2011). Effects of mindfulness on psychological health: A review of empirical studies. *Clinical Psychology Review, 31(6),* 1041–1056. doi:10.1016/j.cpr.2011.04.006

Kiken, L.G., & Shook, N.J. (2011). Looking up: Mindfulness increases positive judgments and reduces negativity bias. *Social Psychological and Personality Science, 2(4),* 425–431. https://doi.org/10.1177/1948550610396585

Kleber H.D. (2007). Pharmacologic treatments for opioid dependence: Detoxification and maintenance options. *Dialogues in Clinical Neuroscience, 9(4),* 455–470. https://doi.org/10.31887/DCNS.2007.9.4/hkleber

Knowlton, B.J. (2014). Basal ganglia: Habit formation. In: D. Jaeger D & R. Jung (eds.). *Encyclopedia of Computational Neuroscience (pp.* 1–17). Springer.

Kobasa, S. C. (1979). Stressful life events, personality, and health: An inquiry into hardiness. *Journal of Personality and Social Psychology, 37(1),* 1-11. http://dx.doi.org/10.1037/0022-3514.37.1.1

Kober, H., Mende-Siedlecki, P., Kross, E. F., Weber, J., Mischel, W., Hart, C. L., & Ochsner, K. N. (2010). Prefrontal-striatal pathway underlies cognitive regulation of craving. *Proceedings of the National Academy of Sciences of the United States of America, 107(33),* 14811–14816. https://doi.org/10.1073/pnas.1007779107

Koenig, H. (2012). Religion, spirituality, and health: The research and clinical implications. *ISRN Psychiatry*, 278730. https://doi.org/10.5402/2012/278730.

Koncz, A., Demetrovics, Z., & Takacs, Z.K. (2020) Meditation interventions efficiently reduce cortisol levels of at-risk samples: A meta-analysis. *Health Psychology Review*. DOI: 10.1080/17437199.2020.1760727

Koob, G.F. (2020). Neurobiology of opioid addiction: Opponent process, hyperkatifeia, and negative reinforcement. *Biological Psychiatry, 87,* 44-53. https://doi.org/10.1016/j.biopsych.2019.05.023

Koob G.F. (2015). The dark side of emotion: The addiction perspective. *European Journal of Pharmacology, 753,* 73–87. https://doi.org/10.1016/j.ejphar.2014.11.044

Koob, G.F., & Le Moal, M. (2008). Review. Neurobiological mechanisms for opponent motivational processes in addiction. *Philosophical Transactions of the Royal Society of London. Series B, Biological Sciences, 363(1507)*, 3113–3123. https://doi.org/10.1098/rstb.2008.0094

Korteling, J., Brouwer, A., & Toet, A. (2018). A neural network framework for cognitive bias. *Frontiers in Psychology.* https://doi.org/10.3389/fpsyg.2018.01561

Kosten, T.R., & O'Connor, P.G. (2003). Drug and alcohol withdrawal. *New England Journal of Medicine, 348(18),* 1786-95. http://depts.washington.edu/psychres/wordpress/wp-content/uploads/2017/07/100-Papers-in-Clinical-Psychiatry-Substance-Use-and-Addiction-Psychiatry-Management-of-drug-and-alcohol-withdrawal..pdf

Kowalski, J., Wypych, M., Marchewka, A., & Dragan, M. (2019). Neural correlates of Cognitive-Attentional Syndrome: An fMRI study on repetitive negative thinking induction and resting state functional connectivity. *Frontiers in Psychology.* https://doi.org/10.3389/fpsyg.2019.00648

Kraft, B., Jonassen, R., Stiles, T., & Landro, N. (2017). Dysfunctional metacognitive beliefs are associated with decreased executive control. *Frontiers in Psychology.* https://doi.org/10.3389/fpsyg.2017.00593

Krause, N. (2012). Religious involvement, humility, and change in self-rated health over time. *Journal of Psychology and Theology, 40(3),* 199-210. https://doi.org/10.1177/009164711204000303

Krause, N., & Hayward, R. D. (2012). Humility, lifetime trauma, and change in religious doubt among older adults. *Journal of Religion and Health, 51(4),* 1002–1016. DOI: 10.1007/s10943-012-9576-y

Krause, N., & Hayward, R. (2013). Prayer beliefs and change in life satisfaction over time. *Journal of Religion and Health, 52(2),* 674–694. doi:10.1007/s10943-012-9638-1

Kress, L., & Aue, T. (2017). The link between optimism bias and attention bias: A neurocognitive perspective. *Neuroscience and Biobehavioral Reviews, 80,* 688-702. http://dx.doi.org/10.1016

Kus, R. (1995). Prayer and meditation in addiction recovery. *Journal of Chemical Dependency Treatment, 5(2)*, 101-115, DOI: 10.1300/J034v05n02_08

Lacroix, A. (2019). Glucocorticoid effects on the nervous system and behavior. *UpToDate.*

Lafaye, G., Karila, L., Blecha, L., & Benyamina, A. (2017). Cannabis, cannabinoids, and health. *Dialogues in Clinical Neuroscience, 19(3)*, 309–316.

Lambert, N., Fincham, F., LaVallee, D., & Brantley, C. (2012). Praying together and staying together: Couple prayer and trust. *Psychology of Religion and Spirituality, 4(1)*, 1-9. DOI: 10.1037/a0023060

Lambert, N., Fincham, F., Marks, L., & Stillman, T. (2010). Invocations and intoxication: Does prayer decrease alcohol consumption? *Psychology of Addictive Behaviors, 24(2)*, 209-219. DOI: 10.1037/a0018746

Lammers, S. M., Soe-Agnie, S. E., de Haan, H. A., Bakkum, G. A., Pomp, E. R., & Nijman, H. J. (2014). Middelengebruik en criminaliteit: ein overzicht [Substance use and criminality: A review]. *Tijdschrift Voor Psychiatrie, 56(1)*, 32–39.

Lanae, V., & Feinauer, L. (1993). Resilience factors associated with female survivors of childhood sexual abuse. *American Journal of Family Therapy, 2193*, 216-24.

Lander, L., Howsare, J., & Byrne, M. (2013). The impact of substance use disorders on families and children: From theory to practice. *Social Work in Public Health, 28(3-4)*, 194–205. https://doi.org/10.1080/19371918.2013.759005

Larimer, M.E., Palmer, R.S., & Marlatt, A. (1999). An overview of Marlatt's cognitive-behavioral model. *Alcohol Research & Health, 23(2)*, 151-160. https://pubs.niaaa.nih.gov/publications/arh23-2/151-160.pdf

Latt, N. & Dore, G. (2014). Thiamine in Wernicke's encephalopathy. *Internal Medicine Journal, 44*, 911-915. https://doi.org/10.1111/imj.12522

Laudet, A.B., Savage, R., & Mahmood, D. (2002). Pathways to long-term recovery: A preliminary investigation. *Journal of Psychoactive Drugs, 34(3)*, 305–311. https://doi.org/10.1080/02791072.2002.10399968

Law, B.M. (2005). Probing the depression-rumination cycle. *APA Monitor on Psychology, 36(10)*, 38.

Lazar, S., Kerr, C., Wasserman, R., Gray, J., Greve, D., Treadway, M., et al. (2005). Meditation experience is associated with increased cortical thickness. *Neuroreport, 16*, 1893–710. Doi:1097/01.wnr.0000186598.66243.19

Le Boutillier, C. & Croucher, A. (2010). Social Inclusion and mental health. *The British Journal of Occupational Therapy. 73(3)*, 136-139. 10.4276/030802210X12682330090578.

Lee, H., Roh, S., & Kim, D.J. (2009). Alcohol-induced blackout. *International Journal of Environmental Research and Public Health, 6(11)*, 2783–2792. https://doi.org/10.3390/ijerph6112783

Leipold, B., & Greve, W. (2009). Resilience: A conceptual bridge between coping and development. *European Psychologist, 14(1)*, 40-50. doi:10.1027/1016-9040.14.1.40

Leventhal, A., Kahler, C., Ray, L., Stone, K., Young, D., Chelminski, I., et al. (2008). Anhedonia and amotivation in psychiatric outpatients with fully remitted stimulant use disorder. *The American Journal on Addictions / American Academy of Psychiatrists in Alcoholism and Addictions*, *17*(3), 218–223. http://doi.org/10.1080/10550490802019774

Levinson, J. (2018, Apr 11). Americans going abroad for illegal heroin treatment. *BBC News*. https://www.bbc.com/news/world-us-canada-43420999

Levy, M.S. (2008). Listening to our clients: The prevention of relapse. *Journal of Psychoactive Drugs, 40(2)*, 167-172. DOI: 10.1080/02791072.2008.10400627

Li, W., Howard, M., Garland, E., McGovern, P., & Lazar, M. (2017). Mindfulness treatment for substance misuse: A systematic review and meta-analysis. *Journal of Substance Abuse Treatment, 75*, 62–96. http://dx.doi.org/10.1016/j.jsat.2017.01.008

Lightman, A. (2018). Fact and faith: Why science and spirituality are not incompatible. *Science Focus*. https://www.sciencefocus.com/the-human-body/fact-and-faith-why-science-and-spirituality-are-not-incompatible/

Linehan, M., & Dimidjian, S. (2003). Mindfulness practice. In W. O'Donohue, J.E. Fisher, & S. Hayes (Eds.), *Cognitive behavioral therapy: Applying empirically supported techniques in your practice* (pp. 229-237). John Wiley & Sons.

Lipka, M. (2016). 5 facts about prayer. *Pew Research Center.* http://www.pewresearch.org/fact-tank/2016/05/04/5-facts-about-prayer/

Lloyd, A. (2003). Urge surfing. In W. O'Donohue, J.E. Fisher, & S. Hayes (Eds.), *Cognitive behavioral therapy: Applying empirically supported techniques in your practice* (pp. 451-455). John Wiley & Sons.

Logel, C., & Cohen, G.L. (2012). The role of the self in physical health. *Psychological Science, 23(1),* 53–55. https://doi.org/10.1177/0956797611421936

Loke, A.Y., & Mak, Y.W. (2013). Family process and peer influences on substance use by adolescents. *International Journal of Environmental Research and Public Health, 10(9),* 3868–3885. https://doi.org/10.3390/ijerph10093868

Luciana, M., & Ewing, S.W. (2015). Introduction to the special issue: Substance use and the adolescent brain: Developmental impacts, interventions, and longitudinal outcomes. *Developmental Cognitive Neuroscience, 16,* 1-4. https://doi.org/10.1016/j.dcn.2015.10.005

Luders, E., Toga, A., Lepore, N., & Gaser, C. (2009). The underlying anatomical correlates of long-term meditation: Larger hippocampal and frontal volumes of gray matter. *Neuroimage, 45,* 672–810. Doi:1016/j.neuroimage.2008.12.061

Luks, A. (1988). Helper's high: Volunteering makes people feel good, physically and emotionally. *Psychology Today, 22(10),* 34-42.

Luscher, C., & Malenka, R.C. (2011). Drug-evoked synaptic plasticity in addiction: From molecular changes to circuit remodeling. *Neuron, 69,* 650–663.

Lyubomirsky, S., Kasri, F., & Zehm, K. Dysphoric rumination impairs concentration on academic task. *Cognitive Therapy and Research, 27(3),* 309-330. DOI: 10.1023/A:1023918517378

Lyubomirsky, S., & Nolen-Hoeksema, S. (1995). Effects of self-focused rumination on negative thinking and interpersonal problem solving. *Journal of Personality and Social Psychology, 69(1),* 176–90.

Lyubomirsky, S., & Nolen-Hoeksema, S. (1993). Self-perpetuating properties of dysphoric rumination. *Journal of Personality and Social Psychology, 65(2),* 339-349.

MacInnes D.L. (2006). Self-esteem and self-acceptance: An examination into their relationship and their effect on psychological health. *Journal of Psychiatric and Mental Health Nursing, 13,* 483–489.

Maier, S., & Seligman, M. (2016). Learned helplessness at fifty: Insights from neuroscience. *Psychological review, 123(4),* 349–367. doi:10.1037/rev0000033

Mann, M., Hosman, C.M.H., Schaalma, H.P., & De Vries, N. (2004). Self-esteem in a broad-spectrum approach for mental health promotion. *Health Education Research, 19(4),* 357-72. DOI: 10.1093/her/cyg041

Marcus, M.T., Fine, M., Moeller, F.G., Khan, M.M., Pitts, K., Swank, P.R., et al. (2003). Change in stress levels following mindfulness-based stress reduction in a therapeutic community. *Addictive Disorders & Their Treatment, 2(3),* 63–68. https://doi.org/10.1097/00132576-200302030-00001

Markou, A., Kosten, T., & Koob, G. (1998). Neurobiological similarities in depression and drug dependence: A self-medication hypothesis. *Neuropsycho-pharmacology, 18,* 135–174. Retrieved from https://www.ncbi.nlm.nih.gov/pubmed/9471114

Marlatt, G., & Chawla, N. (2007). Meditation and alcohol use. *Southern Medical Journal, 100(4),* 451.

Marlatt, G.A., & Gordon, J.R. (1985). *Relapse prevention: Maintenance strategies in the treatment of addictive behavior.* Guildford Press.

Martela, F., & Ryan, R.M. (2016). Prosocial behavior increases well-being and vitality even without contact with the beneficiary: Causal and behavioral evidence. *Motivation and Emotion, 40,* 351–357. https://doi.org/10.1007/s11031-016-9552-z

Martela, F., Ryan, R.M. & Steger, M.F. (2018). Meaningfulness as satisfaction of autonomy, competence, relatedness, and beneficence: Comparing the four satisfactions and positive affect as predictors of meaning in life. *Journal of Happiness Studies, 19*, 1261–1282. https://doi.org/10.1007/s10902-017-9869-7

Mash, D.C., Duque, L., Page, B., & Allen-Ferdinand, K. (2018). Ibogaine detoxification transitions opioid and cocaine abusers between dependence and abstinence: Clinical observations and treatment outcomes. *Frontiers in Pharmacology, 9*, 529. https://doi.org/10.3389/fphar.2018.00529

Maslow, A. (1954/1987). *Motivation and personality* (3rd ed.). Pearson Education.

Masters, K.S., & Spielmans, G.I. (2007). Prayer and health: Review, meta-analysis, and research agenda. *Journal of Behavioral Medicine, 30*, 329-338. DOI 10.1007/s10865-007-9106-7

Mathias, C. W., Duffing, T. M., Ashley, A., Charles, N. E., Lake, S. L., Ryan, S. R., Liang, Y., & Dougherty, D. M. (2015). Aggression as a predictor of early substance use initiation among youth with family histories of substance use disorders. *Addictive Disorders & Their Treatment, 14(4)*, 230–240. https://doi.org/10.1097/ADT.0000000000000068

Maynes, J. (2015). Critical thinking and cognitive bias. *Informal Logic, 35(2)*, 183-203.

Maze, I., & Nestler, E. J. (2011). The epigenetic landscape of addiction. *Annals of the New York Academy of Sciences, 1216*, 99–113. https://doi.org/10.1111/j.1749-6632.2010.05893.x

McCarthy-Jones S., & Fernyhough C. (2011). The varieties of inner speech: Links between quality of inner speech and psychopathological variables in a sample of young adults. *Consciousness and Cognition, 20*, 1586–1593. 10.1016/j.concog.2011.08.005

McCullough, M., Pedersen, E., Tabak, B., & Carter, E. (2014). Conciliatory gestures promote forgiveness and reduce anger in humans. *Proceedings of the National Academy of Sciences, 111(30)*, 11211-11216. doi:10.1073/pnas.1405072111

McCusker, C. (2001). Cognitive biases and addiction: An evolution in theory and method. *Addiction, 96*, 47-56. DOI: 10.1080/09652140020016950

McGee, M. (2008). Meditation and psychiatry. *Psychiatry, 5(1)*, 28–41.

McHugh, R.K., Hearon, B.A., & Otto, M.W. (2010). Cognitive behavioral therapy for substance use disorders. *The Psychiatric Clinics of North America, 33(3)*, 511–525. https://doi.org/10.1016/j.psc.2010.04.012

McKellar, J., Ilgen, M., Moos, B.S., & Moos, R. (2008). Predictors of changes in alcohol-related self-efficacy over 16 years. *Journal of Substance Abuse Treatment, 35(2)*, 148–155. doi:10.1016/j.jsat.2007.09.003

McQuaid, R.J., Jesseman, R., & Rush, B. (2018). Examining barriers as risk factors for relapse: A focus on the Canadian treatment and recovery system of care. *The Canadian Journal of Addiction, 9(3)*, 5-12. doi: 10.1097/CXA.0000000000000022

Means, J.R., Wilson, G.L., Sturm, C., Biron, J.E., & Bach, P.J. (1990). Humility as a psychotherapeutic formulation. *Counselling Psychology Quarterly, 3(2)*, 211–215. https://doi.org/10.1080/09515079008254249

Melemis S.M. (2015). Relapse prevention and the five rules of recovery. *The Yale Journal of Biology and Medicine, 88(3)*, 325–332. https://www.ncbi.nlm.nih.gov/pmc/articles/PMC4553654/

Midlarsky, E. (1991). Helping as coping. In M.S. Clark (Ed.), *Review of personality and social psychology, Vol. 1). Prosocial behavior* (pp. 238–264). Sage Publications, Inc.

Millar, M.G., Millar, K.U., & Tesser, A. (1988). The effects of helping and focus of attention on mood states. *Personality and Social Psychology Bulletin, 14*(3), 536–543. https://doi.org/10.1177/0146167288143012

Moeller, S.J., Hajcak, G., Parvaz, M.A., Dunning, J.P., Volkow, N.D., & Goldstein, R.Z. (2012). Psychophysiological prediction of choice: Relevance to insight and drug addiction. *Brain, 135(11)*, 3481–3494. https://doi.org/10.1093/brain/aws252

Mongrain, M., Chin, J.M., & Shapira, L.B. (2011). Practicing compassion increases happiness and self-esteem. *Journal of Happiness Studies, 12(6)*, 963-981. https://doi.org/10.1007/s10902-010-9239-1

Moos, R., & Timko, C. (2008). Outcome research on twelve-step and other self-help programs. In M. Galanter, & H. Kleber (Eds.), *Textbook of substance abuse treatment* (4th ed.) (pp. 511-521). American Psychiatric Press. https://www.mentalhealth.va.gov/providers/sud/selfhelp/docs/4_moos_timko_chapter.pdf

Morin, A. (2018). 7 ways to overcome toxic self-criticism [Web log post]. *Psychology Today*. https://www.psychologytoday.com/intl/blog/what-mentally-strong-people-dont-do/201801/7-ways-overcome-toxic-self-criticism

Morin, A. (2011a). Self-awareness part 1: Definition, measures, effects, functions, and antecedents. *Social and Personality Psychology Compass 5(10)*, 807-823. DOI: 10.1111/j.1751-9004.2011.00387.x

Morin, A. (2011b). Self-awareness part 2: Neuroanatomy and the importance of inner speech. *Social and Personality Psychology Compass, 5(12)*, 1004-1017. 10.1111/j.1751-9004.2011.00410.x

Morisano, D., Babor, T. F., & Robaina, K. A. (2014). Co-occurrence of substance use disorders with other psychiatric disorders: Implications for treatment services. *Nordic Studies on Alcohol and Drugs, 31(1)*, 5–25. https://doi.org/10.2478/nsad-2014-0002

Morse, E. (2017). Addiction is a chronic medical illness. *North Carolina Medical Journal, 79(3)*, 163-165. doi: 10.18043/ncm.79.3.163

Moynihan, R., Heath, I., & Henry, D. (2002). Selling sickness: The pharmaceutical industry and disease mongering. *British Medical Journal, 324(7342)*, 886–891. https://doi.org/10.1136/bmj.324.7342.886

Mruck, C. (2006). *Self-esteem research, theory, and practice: Toward a positive psychology of self-esteem* (3rd ed.). Springer.

Mughal, A.S. (2018). Reasons of relapse in hindrance or treatment in substance related addictive disorder: A qualitative study. *Journal of Alcoholism & Drug Dependence, 6(2)*. DOI: 10.4172/2329-6488.1000310

Muhuri, P.K., Gfoerer, J.C., & Davies, M.C. (2013). Associations of nonmedical pain reliever use and initiation of heroin use in the united states. *SAMHSA CBHSQ Data Review*. https://www.samhsa.gov/data/sites/default/files/DR006/DR006/nonmedical-pain-reliever-use-2013.htm

Murayama, K. (2018). The science of motivation. *American Psychological Association.* https://www.apa.org/science/about/psa/2018/06/motivation

Nasiry, Rodsari, A.B., & Nasiry, S. (2014). The prediction of tendency to substance abuse on the basis of self-esteem and components of emotional intelligence. *Research on Addiction Quarterly Journal of Drug Abuse, 8(31),* 103 – 111.

National Drug Early Warning System (NDEWS). (2020). *NDEWS.* http://ndews.org/

National Institute on Drug Abuse (NIDA). (2020). *Addiction and health.* https://www.drugabuse.gov/publications/drugs-brains-behavior-science-addiction/addiction-health

National Institute on Drug Abuse (NIDA). (2017). *"All scientific hands on deck" to end the opioid crisis.* https://www.drugabuse.gov/about-nida/noras-blog/2017/05/all-scientific-hands-deck-to-end-opioid-crisis

National Institute on Drug Abuse (NIDA). (2016). *Cocaine.* https://www.drugabuse.gov/publications/drugfacts/cocaine

National Institute on Drug Abuse (NIDA). (2020). *Drugs and the brain.* https://www.drugabuse.gov/publications/drugs-brains-behavior-science-addiction/drugs-brain

National Institute on Drug Abuse (NIDA). (2020). *Common comorbidities with substances use disorders research report.* https://www.drugabuse.gov/publications/research-reports/common-comorbidities-substance-use-disorders/introduction

National Institute on Drug Abuse (NIDA). (2020). *Commonly used drug charts.* https://www.drugabuse.gov/drug-topics/commonly-used-drugs-charts

National Institute on Drug Abuse (NIDA). (2010). Comorbidity: Addiction and other mental illnesses. *Research Report Series.* https://www.drugabuse.gov/sites/default/files/rrcomorbidity.pdf

National Institute on Drug Abuse (NIDA). (2020). *Drug misuse and addiction.* https://www.drugabuse.gov/publications/drugs-brains-behavior-science-addiction/drug-misuse-addiction

National Institute on Drug Abuse (NIDA). (n.d.). *Drug Topics.* https://www.drugabuse.gov/drug-topics

National Institute on Drug Abuse (NIDA). (2003). *Epidemiology.* https://archives.drugabuse.gov/publications/diagnosis-treatment-drug-abuse-in-family-practice-american-family-physician-monograph/epidemiology

National Institute on Drug Abuse (NIDA). (2019). Hallucinogens. *DrugFacts.* https://www.drugabuse.gov/publications/drugfacts/hallucinogens

National Institute on Drug Abuse (NIDA). (2014). Hallucinogens and dissociative drugs. *Research Report Series.* https://www.drugabuse.gov/sites/default/files/hallucinogensrrs.pdf

National Institute on Drug Abuse (NIDA). (2020). *How effective is drug addiction treatment?* https://www.drugabuse.gov/publications/principles-drug-addiction-treatment-research-based-guide-third-edition/frequently-asked-questions/how-effective-drug-addiction-treatment

National Institute on Drug Abuse (NIDA). (2020). *How is methamphetamine different from other stimulants, such as cocaine?* https://www.drugabuse.gov/publications/research-reports/methamphetamine/how-methamphetamine-different-other-stimulants-such-cocaine

National Institute on Drug Abuse (NIDA). (2020). *How is methamphetamine manufactured?* https://www.drugabuse.gov/publications/research-reports/methamphetamine/how-methamphetamine-manufactured

National Institute on Drug Abuse (NIDA). (2011). *Inhalants research report.* https://www.drugabuse.gov/publications/research-reports/inhalants/letter-director

National Institute on Drug Use (NIDA). (n.d.). *Infographics.* https://www.drugabuse.gov/drug-topics/trends-statistics/infographics

National Institute on Drug Use (NIDA). (2020). *Is there a link between marijuana use and psychiatric disorders?* https://www.drugabuse.gov/publications/research-reports/marijuana/there-link-between-marijuana-use-psychiatric-disorders

National Institute on Drug Abuse (NIDA). (2019). Marijuana. *DrugFacts.* https://www.drugabuse.gov/publications/drugfacts/marijuana

National Institute on Drug Use (NIDA). (2020). MDMA (ecstasy/molly). *DrugFacts.* https://www.drugabuse.gov/publications/drugfacts/mdma-ecstasymolly

National Institute on Drug Use (NIDA). (2020). *Monitoring the Future.* https://www.drugabuse.gov/drug-topics/trends-statistics/monitoring-future

National Institute on Drug Use (NIDA). (2018). *National Survey on Drug Use and Health (NSDUH).* https://www.drugabuse.gov/drug-topics/trends-statistics/national-survey-drug-use-health-nsduh

National Institutes on Drug Abuse (NIDA). (2020). *Opioid overdose crisis.* https://www.drugabuse.gov/drug-topics/opioids/opioid-overdose-crisis

National Institutes on Drug Abuse (NIDA). (2017). *Opioid prescribers can play a key role in stopping the opioid overdose epidemic.* https://www.drugabuse.gov/publications/improving-opioid-prescribing

National Institute on Drug Abuse (NIDA). (2020). *Part 1: The Connection Between Substance Use Disorders and Mental Illness.* https://www.drugabuse.gov/publications/research-reports/common-comorbidities-substance-use-disorders/part-1-connection-between-substance-use-disorders-mental-illness on 2020, June 19

National Institute on Drug Abuse (NIDA). (2018). *Prescription CNS depressant drug facts.* https://www.drugabuse.gov/publications/drugfacts/prescription-cns-depressants

National Institute on Drug Abuse (NIDA). (2018). *Principles of drug addiction treatment: A research-based guide* (3rd ed.). https://www.drugabuse.gov/publications/principles-drug-addiction-treatment-research-based-guide-third-edition

National Institute on Drug Abuse (NIDA). (2003). *Relationships matter: Impact of parental, peer factors on teen, young adult substance abuse.* https://archives.drugabuse.gov/news-events/nida-notes/2003/08/relationships-matter-impact-parental-peer-factors-teen-young-adult-substance-abuse

National Institute on Drug Abuse (NIDA). (2016). *Synthetic cathinones ("Bath Salts")*. https://www.drugabuse.gov/publications/drugfacts/synthetic-cathinones-bath-salts

National Institute on Drug Abuse (NIDA). (2019). Treatment Approaches for Drug Addiction *DrugFacts*. https://www.drugabuse.gov/publications/drugfacts/treatment-approaches-drug-addiction

National Institute on Drug Use (NIDA). (n.d.). *Trends & statistics*. https://www.drugabuse.gov/drug-topics/trends-statistics

National Institute on Drug Abuse (NIDA). (2018). *What is drug addiction?* https://www.drugabuse.gov/publications/drugs-brains-behavior-science-addiction/drug-misuse-addiction

National Institute on Drug Abuse (NIDA). (2020). *Why is there comorbidity between substance use disorders and mental illnesses?* https://www.drugabuse.gov/publications/research-reports/common-comorbidities-substance-use-disorders/why-there-comorbidity-between-substance-use-disorders-mental-illnesses

National Institutes of Health (NIH). (2015). *10 percent of US adults have drug use disorder at some point in their lives.* https://www.nih.gov/news-events/news-releases/10-percent-us-adults-have-drug-use-disorder-some-point-their-lives#:~:text=The%20study%2C%20funded%20by%20the,some%20time%20in%20their%20lives.

National Library of Medicine. (2020). Substance use disorder. *Medline Plus*. https://medlineplus.gov/ency/article/001522.htm

National Survey on Drug Use and Health (NSDUH). (2020). *What is NSDUH?* https://nsduhweb.rti.org/respweb/homepage.cfm

Nennig, S.E., & Schank, J.R. (2017). The Role of NFkB in drug addiction: Beyond inflammation. *Alcohol and Alcoholism, 52(2)*, 172–179. https://doi.org/10.1093/alcalc/agw098

Nordstrom, B.R., & Dackis, C.A. (2011). Drugs and crime. *The Journal of Psychiatry & Law, 39(4)*, 663–687. https://doi.org/10.1177/009318531103900407

Nestler E.J. (2013). Cellular basis of memory for addiction. *Dialogues in Clinical Neuroscience, 15(4),* 431–443. https://www.ncbi.nlm.nih.gov/pmc/articles/PMC3898681/

Nielsen, D.A., Utrankar, A., Reyes, J.A., Simons, D.D., & Kosten, T.R. (2012). Epigenetics of drug abuse: Predisposition or response. *Pharmacogenomics, 13(10),* 1149–1160. https://doi.org/10.2217/pgs.12.94

Nielsen, R. & Marrone, J. (2018). Humility: Our current understanding of the construct and its role in organizations. *International Journal of Management Reviews, 20*, 805-824. doi:10.1111/ijmr.12160

Noël, X., Bechara, A., Brevers, D., Verbanck, P., & Campanella, S. (2010). Alcoholism and the loss of willpower: A neurocognitive perspective. *Journal of Psychophysiology, 24(4),* 240–248. doi:10.1027/0269-8803/a000037

Nolen-Hoeksema, S., Stice, E., Wade, E., & Bohon, C. (2007). Reciprocal relations between rumination and bulimic, substance abuse. *Journal of Abnormal Psychology, 116(1),* 198–207. DOI:10.1037/0021-843X.116.1.198

Noller, G., Frampton, C., & Yazar-Klosinski, B. (2018). Ibogaine treatment outcomes for opioid dependence from a twelve-month follow-up observational study. *The American Journal of Drug and Alcohol Abuse, 44(1),* 37-46. DOI: 10.1080/00952990.2017.1310218

Nordfjærn, T. (2011) Relapse patterns among patients with substance use disorders. *Journal of Substance Use, 16(4),* 313-329. DOI: 10.3109/14659890903580482

O'Donnell, J., Gladden, R.M., Mattson, C.L., Hunter, C.T., & Davis, N.L. (2020). Vital signs: Characteristics of drug overdose deaths involving opioids and stimulants — 24 states and the District of Columbia, January–June 2019. *CDC Morbidity and Mortality Weekly Report, 69,* 1189–1197. DOI: http://dx.doi.org/10.15585/mmwr.mm6935a1

Okun, M.A., Yeung, E.W., & Brown, S. (2013). Volunteering by older adults and risk of mortality: A meta-analysis. *Psychology and Aging, 28(2),* 564–577. https://doi.org/10.1037/a0031519

Oregon Health and Science University. (2019). How a shrub may enable the "impossible" in treating addiction. *Proteomics & Metabolomics.*

https://www.technologynetworks.com/proteomics/news/how-a-shrub-may-enable-the-impossible-in-treating-addiction-318626

Oscar-Berman, M., & Marinković, K. (2007). Alcohol: Effects on neurobehavioral functions and the brain. *Neuropsychology Review, 17(3)*, 239–257. https://doi.org/10.1007/s11065-007-9038-6

Otake, K., Shimai, S., Tanaka-Matsumi, J., Otsui, K. & Fredrickson, B.L. (2006). Happy people become happier through kindness: A counting kindness intervention. *Journal of Happiness Studies, 7*, 361–375. DOI 10.1007/s10902-005-3650-z

Pagano, M.E., Friend, K.B., Tonigan, J.S., & Stout, R.L. (2004). Helping other alcoholics in alcoholics anonymous and drinking outcomes: Findings from project MATCH. *Journal of Studies on Alcohol, 65(6)*, 766–773. https://doi.org/10.15288/jsa.2004.65.766

Paine, D.R., Sandage, S.J., Rupert, D., Devor, N.G., & Bronstein, M. (2015). Humility as a psychotherapeutic virtue: Spiritual, philosophical, and psychological foundations. *Journal of Spirituality in Mental Health, 17*, 3–25. DOI: 10.1080/19349637.2015.957611

Palmgren, S.E. (2007). The efficacy of self-affirmation in debiasing defenses against continuation of substance abuse treatment. *Dissertation Abstracts International: Section B: The Sciences and Engineering, 67(11-B)*, 6744.

Pardini, D., Plante, T., Sherman, A., & Stump, J. (2000). Religious faith and spirituality in substance abuse recovery: Determining the mental health benefits. *Journal of Substance Abuse Treatment, 19*, 347-354. DOI: 10.1016/s0740-5472(00)00125-2

Pathan, H., & Williams, J. (2012). Basic opioid pharmacology: An update. *British Journal of Pain, 6(1)*, 11–16. https://doi.org/10.1177/2049463712438493

Penneback, J. (2016). Does confessing our secrets improve our mental health? *Scientific American Mind, 27(2)*, 71. doi:10.1038/scientificamericanmind0316-71a

Perkins, R. & Repper, J. (2018). Thinking about recovery and well-being in a social context. *Mental Health and Social Inclusion, 22(4)*, 161-166. https://doi.org/10.1108/MHSI-08-2018-058

Perlovsky, L. (2013). A challenge to human evolution-cognitive dissonance. *Frontiers in Psychology, 4*, 179. https://doi.org/10.3389/fpsyg.2013.00179

Pesut, B., Fowler, M., Taylor, E.J., Reimer-Kirkham, S. & Sawatzky, R. (2008). Conceptualising spirituality and religion for healthcare. *Journal of Clinical Nursing, 17,* 2803–2810. doi: 10.1111/j.1365-2702.2008.02344.x

Pew Research Center. (2014). Frequency of prayer. *Religious Landscape Study.* https://www.pewforum.org/religious-landscape-study/frequency-of-prayer/

Pew Research Center. (2015). *Religious practices and experiences.* https://www.pewforum.org/2015/11/03/chapter-2-religious-practices-and-experiences/#private-devotions

Post, S. (2005). Altruism, happiness, and health: It's good to be good. *International Journal of Behavioral Medicine, 12(2),* 66-77.

Post, S., Johnson, B., Lee, M., & Pagano, M. (2015). Positive psychology in Alcoholics Anonymous and the 12 Steps: Adolescent recovery in relation to humility. *The American Psychological Association Addictions Newsletter,* 18-20. http://www.helpingotherslivesober.org/documents/publications/Positive_Psychology_in_Alcoholics_Anonymous_and_the_12_steps_Adolescent_Recovery_in_Relation_to_Humility.pdf

Post, S., Pagano, M., Lee, M., & Johnson, B. (2016). Humility and 12-Step recovery: A prolegomenon for the empirical investigation of a cardinal virtue in alcoholics anonymous. *Alcoholism Treatment Quarterly, 34(3),* 262–273. doi:10.1080/07347324.2016.1182817

Priddy, S., Howard, M., Hanley, A., Riquino, M., Friberg-Felsted, K., & Garland, E. (2018). Mindfulness meditation in the treatment of substance use disorders and preventing future relapse: Neurocognitive mechanisms and clinical implications. *Substance Abuse and Rehabilitation, 9,* 103–114. doi:10.2147/SAR.S145201

Priester, P., Scherer, J., Steinfeldt, J., Jana-Masri, A., Jashinsky, T., Jones, J., et al. (2009). The frequency of prayer, meditation and holistic interventions in addictions treatment: A national survey. *Pastoral Psychology, 58,* 315. https://doi.org/10.1007/s11089-009-0196-8

Proulx, A. (2020). *A trip through the 12 steps with a doctor and therapist.* Recovery Folio.

Pruett, J., Nishimura, N. & Priest, R. (2007). The role of meditation in addiction recovery. *Counseling and Values, 52*, 71-84. doi:10.1002/j.2161-007X.2007.tb00088.x

Psychology Today. (2020). *Learned helplessness.* https://www.psychologytoday.com/ca/basics/learned-helplessness

Puchalski, C. M. (2001). The role of spirituality in health care. *Proceedings (Baylor University. Medical Center), 14(4)*, 352–357. https://www.ncbi.nlm.nih.gov/pmc/articles/PMC1305900/

Ramirez, R., Hinman, A., Sterling, S., Weisner, C., & Campbell, C. (2012). Peer influences on adolescent alcohol and other drug use outcomes. *Journal of Nursing Scholarship, 44(1)*, 36–44. https://doi.org/10.1111/j.1547-5069.2011.01437.x

Ramo, D. E., & Brown, S. A. (2008). Classes of substance abuse relapse situations: A comparison of adolescents and adults. *Psychology of Addictive Behaviors, 22(3)*, 372–379. https://doi.org/10.1037/0893-164X.22.3.372

Rasmussen N. (2008). America's first amphetamine epidemic 1929-1971: A quantitative and qualitative retrospective with implications for the present. *American Journal of Public Health, 98(6)*, 974–985. https://doi.org/10.2105/AJPH.2007.110593

Renthal, W., & Nestler, E. J. (2008). Epigenetic mechanisms in drug addiction. *Trends in Molecular Medicine, 14(8)*, 341–350. https://doi.org/10.1016/j.molmed.2008.06.004

Reese, S. (2014). Drug abuse among doctors: Easy, tempting, and not uncommon. *Medscape Business of Medicine.* https://www.medscape.com/viewarticle/819223

Rice, K.G., Ashby, J.S., & Slaney, R.B. (1998). Self-esteem as a mediator between perfectionism and depression: A structural equations analysis. *Journal of Counseling Psychology, 45(3)*, 304–314. https://doi.org/10.1037/0022-0167.45.3.304

Richardson, C.G., Kwon, J.Y., & Ratner, P.A. (2013). Self-esteem and the initiation of substance use among adolescents. *Canadian Journal of Public Health,104(1)*, e60-e63.

Rinn, W., Desai, N., Rosenblatt, H., & Gastfriend, D. (2002). Addiction denial and cognitive dysfunction: A preliminary investigation. *Journal of Neuropsychiatry and Clinical Neuroscience, 14(1)*, 52-57. https://neuro.psychiatryonline.org/doi/pdf/10.1176/jnp.14.1.52

Riso, L.P., du Toit, P.L., Blandino, J.A., Penna, S., Dacey, S., Duin J.S. et al. (2003). Cognitive aspects of chronic depression. *Journal of Abnormal Psychology, 112(1)*, 72–80.

Robinson, T., & Berridge, K. (2008). The incentive sensitization theory of addiction: Some current issues. *Philosophical Transactions of the Royal Society of London. Series B, Biological Sciences, 363(1507)*, 3137–3146. https://doi.org/10.1098/rstb.2008.0093

Robinson, T.E., & Berridge, K.C. (1993). The neural basis of drug craving: An incentive-sensitization theory of addiction. *Brain Research Review, 18*, 247–91. doi:10.1016/0165-0173(93)90013-P

Robison, A.J., & Nestler, E.J. (2011). Transcriptional and epigenetic mechanisms of addiction. *Nature Reviews: Neuroscience, 12(11)*, 623–637. https://doi.org/10.1038/nrn3111

Rogawski M.A. (2005). Update on the neurobiology of alcohol withdrawal seizures. *Epilepsy Currents, 5(6)*, 225–230. https://doi.org/10.1111/j.1535-7511.2005.00071.x

Rooke, S., Hine, D., & Thorsteinsson, E. (2008). Implicit cognition and substance use: A meta-analysis. *Addictive Behavior, 33*, 1314–1328.

Rosen, L.G., Sun, N., & Rushlow, W. (2015). Molecular and neuronal plasticity mechanisms in the amygdala-prefrontal cortical circuit: Implications for opiate addiction memory formation. *Frontiers in Neuroscience, 9(399)*. doi: 10.3389/fnins.2015.00399

Rosenkranz, M., Davidson, R., MacCoon, D., Sheridan, J., Kalin, N., & Lutz, A. (2013). A comparison of mindfulness-based stress reduction and an active control in modulation of neurogenic inflammation. *Brain, Behavior, and Immunity, 27*, 174–184. https://doi.org/10.1016/j.bbi.2012.10.013

Rösner, S., Hackl-Herrwerth, A., Leucht, S., Vecchi, S., Srisurapanont, M., & Soyka, M. (2010). Opioid antagonists for alcohol dependence. *Cochrane Database of Systematic Reviews, 12*, CD001867. DOI: 10.1002/14651858.CD001867.pub3

Ross, H., & Dolan, S. (2017). Forgiveness and its importance in substance use disorders. *Journal of Psychology and Christianity, 36(3),* 250-266. https://www.researchgate.net/publication/322339237_Forgiveness_and_Its_Importance_In_Substance_Use_Disorders

Ruiz, F., & Tanaka, K. (2001). The relationship between cognitive dissonance and helping behaviors. *Japanese Psychological Research, 43(2),* 55-62.

Russo, S. J., Dietz, D. M., Dumitriu, D., Morrison, J. H., Malenka, R. C., & Nestler, E. J. (2010). The addicted synapse: Mechanisms of synaptic and structural plasticity in nucleus accumbens. *Trends in Neurosciences, 33(6),* 267–276. https://doi.org/10.1016/j.tins.2010.02.002

Saavedra, J., Perez, E., Crawford, P., & Arias, S. (2018). Recovery and creative practices in people with severe mental illness: Evaluating well-being and social inclusion. *Disability And Rehabilitation, 40(8),* 905-911. http://dx.doi.org/10.1080/09638288.2017.1278797

Sachdeva, A., Choudhary, M., & Chandra, M. (2015). Alcohol withdrawal syndrome: Benzodiazepines and beyond. *Journal of Clinical and Diagnostic Research, 9(9),* VE01–VE07. https://doi.org/10.7860/JCDR/2015/13407.6538

Sack, D. (2012). Does willpower play a role in addiction recovery? [Web log post]. *Psychology Today.* https://www.psychologytoday.com/ca/blog/where-science-meets-the-steps/201211/does-willpower-play-role-in-addiction-recovery

Samek, D.R., & Hicks, B.M. (2014). Externalizing disorders and environmental risk: Mechanisms of gene-environment interplay and strategies for intervention. *Clinical Practice, 11(5),* 537–547. https://doi.org/10.2217/CPR.14.47

Sancho, M., De Gracia, M., Rodríguez, R., Mallorqui, N., Sanchez, J., Trujols, J., et al. (2018). Mindfulness-based interventions for the treatment of substance and behavioral addictions: A systematic review. *Frontiers in Psychiatry, 9,* 95. https://doi.org/10.3389/fpsyt.2018.00095

Sarvet, A.L., & Hasin, D. (2016). The natural history of substance use disorders. *Current Opinion in Psychiatry, 29(4),* 250–257. https://doi.org/10.1097/YCO.0000000000000257

Schacter, D. (1999). The seven sins of memory: Insights from psychology and cognitive neuroscience. *American Psychologist, 54(3)*, 182-203. https://www.researchgate.net/profile/Daniel_Schacter/publication/13099436_The_seven_sins_of_memory_-_Insights_from_psychology_and_cognitive_neuroscience/links/0c96052f3f81c5ece0000000.pdf

Schofield, T.J., Conger, R.D., & Robins, R.D. (2015). Early adolescent substance use in Mexican origin families: Peer selection, peer influence, and parental monitoring. *Drug and Alcohol Dependence, 157*, 129. DOI: 10.1016/j.drugalcdep.2015.10.020

Schuckit, M.A. (2014). Recognition and management of withdrawal delirium (delirium tremens). *The New England Journal of Medicine, 371(22)*, 2109-2113. DOI: 10.1056/NEJMra1407298

Schumann, K., & Dweck, C. (2014). Who accepts responsibility for their transgressions? *Personality an Social Psychology Bulletin, 40(12)*, 1598-1610. https://doi.org/10.1177/0146167214552789

Schunk, D.H. (2012). *Learning theories* (6th ed.). Pearson.

Schwabe, L., Dickinson, A., & Wolf, O.T. (2011). Stress, habits, and drug addiction: A psychoneuroendocrinological perspective. *Experimental and Clinical Psychopharmacology, 19(1)*, 53–63. doi:10.1037/a0022212

Schwabe, L., & Wolf, O.T. (2009). Stress prompts habit behavior in humans. *Journal of Neuroscience, 29(22)*, 7191–8. doi:10.1523/JNEUROSCI.0979-09.2009

Schwartz, C. (2007). Altruism and subjective well-being: Conceptual model and empirical support (Ch. 4). In S.G. Post: *Altruism and health: Perspectives from empirical research* (pp. 33-42). Oxford University Press.

Schwartz, C.E., Meisenhelder, J.B., Ma, Y. & Reed, G. 2003. (2003). Altruistic social interest behaviors are associated with better mental health. *Psychosomatic Medicine, 65*, 778–785. DOI: 10.1097/01.PSY.0000079378.39062.D4

Scully J. L. (2004). What is a disease? *EMBO Reports, 5(7)*, 650–653. https://doi.org/10.1038/sj.embor.7400195

Secades-Villa, R., Garcia-Rodríguez, O., Jin, C. J., Wang, S., & Blanco, C. (2015). Probability and predictors of the cannabis gateway effect: A national study. *The International Journal on Drug Policy, 26(2)*, 135–142. https://doi.org/10.1016/j.drugpo.2014.07.011

Seppälä, E. (2013). 20 Scientific reasons to start meditating today [Web log post]. *Psychology Today* https://www.psychologytoday.com/blog/feeling-it/201309/20-scientific-reasons-start-meditating-today

Setorg, S., Kazemi, H., & Raisi, Z. (2014). Effectiveness of meta-cognitive therapy on craving beliefs and substance-related beliefs in substance abuse disorder patients. *Journal of Research on Addiction, 7(28)*, 147-162. http://etiadpajohi.ir/article-1-285-en.html

Shah, M., & Huecker, M.R. (2020). Opioid withdrawal. *StatPearls.* https://www.ncbi.nlm.nih.gov/books/NBK526012/

Shahar, G. (2017). The hazards of self-criticism [Web log post]. *Psychology Today.* https://www.psychologytoday.com/ca/blog/stress-self-and-health/201708/the-hazards-self-criticism

Shahar, B., Britton, W., Sbarra, D., Figueredo, A., & Bootzin, R. (2010). Mechanisms of change in Mindfulness-Based Cognitive Therapy for depression: Preliminary evidence from a randomized controlled trial. *International Journal of Cognitive Therapy, 3(4)*, 402-418. https://doi.org/10.1521/ijct.2010.3.4.402

Shapero, B.G., Greenberg, J., Pedrelli, P., de Jong, M., & Desbordes, G. (2018). Mindfulness-based interventions in psychiatry. *Focus (American Psychiatric Publishing), 16(1)*, 32–39. https://doi.org/10.1176/appi.focus.20170039

Shapiro, S., Oman, D., Thoresen, C., Plante, T., & Flinders, T. (2008). Cultivating mindfulness: Effects on well-being. *Journal of Clinical Psychology, 64(7)*, 840-862. doi:10.1002/jclp.20491

Sharot, T. (2011). The optimism bias. *Current Biology, 21(23)*, R941-R945. https://doi.org/10.1016/j.cub.2011.10.030

Sharot, T., Guitart-Masip, M., Korn, C. W., Chowdhury, R., & Dolan, R. J. (2012). How dopamine enhances an optimism bias in humans. *Current Biology, 22(16)*, 1477–1481. https://doi.org/10.1016/j.cub.2012.05.053

Sharot, T., Korn, C. W., & Dolan, R. J. (2011). How unrealistic optimism is maintained in the face of reality. *Nature Neuroscience, 14*, 1475–1479. https://doi.org/10.1038/nn.2949

Sharot, T., Riccardi, A., Raio, C., & Phelps, E. (2007). Neural mechanisms mediating optimism bias. *Nature 450,* 102–105. https://doi.org/10.1038/nature06280

Sherman, D.K., & Cohen, G.L. (2006). The psychology of self-defense: Self-affirmation theory. In M.P. Zanna (Ed.) *Advances in Experimental Social Psychology* (Vol. 38) (pp. 183-242). Academic Press.

Shi, L., Zhang, D., Wang, L., Zhuang, J., Cook, R., & Chen, L. (2017). Meditation and blood pressure: A meta-analysis of randomized clinical trials. *Journal of Hypertension, 35(4),* 696-706. doi: 10.1097/HJH.0000000000001217

Shonin, E. & Van Gordon, W. (2016). The mechanisms of mindfulness in the treatment of mental illness and addiction. *International Journal of Mental Health & Addiction, 14,* 844. https://doi.org/10.1007/s11469-016-9653-7

Shpancer, N. (2015). How to stop worrying and get on with your life [Web log post]. *Psychology Today.* https://www.psychologytoday.com/ca/blog/insight-therapy/201501/how-stop-worrying-and-get-your-life?collection=168048

Shuler, P., Gelberg, L., & Brown, M. (1994). The effects of spiritual/religious practices on psychological well-being among inner city homeless women. *Nurse Practitioner Forum, 5(2),* 106-113.

Simão, T., Caldeira, S., & de Carvalho, E. (2016). The effect of prayer on patients' health: Systematic literature review. *Religions, 7(11).* doi:10.3390/rel7010011

Sin, N. L., & Lyubomirsky, S. (2009). Enhancing well-being and alleviating depressive symptoms with positive psychology interventions: A practice-friendly meta-analysis. *Journal of Clinical Psychology, 65(5),* 467–487. https://doi.org/10.1002/jclp.20593

Skinner, W. (2016). *A bio-psycho-social plus approach to addiction and recovery.* [Author's copy].

Skinner, M.D., Lahmek, P., Pham, H., & Aubin, H.J. (2014). Disulfiram efficacy in the treatment of alcohol dependence: A meta-analysis. *PloS One, 9(2)*, e87366. https://doi.org/10.1371/journal.pone.0087366

Slade, M., Rennick-Egglestone, S., Blackie, L., Lewellyn-Beardsley, J., Franklin, D., Thornicroft, G., et al. (2019). Post-traumatic growth in mental health recovery: Qualitative study of narratives. *British Medical Journal Open, 9*, e029342. doi:10.1136/bmjopen-2019-029342

Smith, R.H. (2000). *Handbook of social comparison.* Springer.

Smith, S. (2004). Exploring the interaction of trauma and spirituality. *Traumatology, 10(4)*, 231-243. https://doi.org/10.1177/153476560401000403

Smith, J.M., & Alloy, L.B. (2009). A roadmap to rumination: A review of the definition, assessment, and conceptualization of this multifaceted construct. *Clinical Psychology Review, 29(2)*, 116–128. https://doi.org/10.1016/j.cpr.2008.10.003

Snoek, A., Levy, N., & Kennett, J. (2016). Strong-willed but not successful: The importance of strategies in recovery from addiction. *Addictive Behaviors Review, 4,* 102-17. https://doi.org/10.1016/j.abrep.2016.09.002

Soleimani, M., Sharif, S., Zadeh, A., & Ong, F. (2016). Relationship between hardiness and addiction potential in medical students. *International Journal of Psychology & Behavioral Science, e6225.* DOI: 10.17795/ijpbs-6225

Solomon, R.L. & Corbit, J.D. (1974). An opponent-process theory of motivation: I. Temporal dynamics of affect. *Psychology Review, 81*, 119-145.

Spada, M., Caselli, G., Nikčević, A., & Wells, A. (2015). Metacognition in addictive behaviors. *Addictive Behaviors, 44,* 9–15. http://dx.doi.org/10.1016/j.addbeh.2014.08.002

Spada, M., Caselli, G., & Wells, A. (2013). A triphasic metacognitive formulation of problem drinking. *Clinical Psychology & Psychotherapy, 20(6)*, 494–500. https://doi.org/10.1002/cpp.1791

Spada, M., Caselli, G., & Wells, A. (2009). Metacognitions as a predictor of drinking status and level of alcohol use following CBT in problem drinkers: A prospective study. *Behaviour Research and Therapy, 47(10)*, 882–886. DOI:10.1016/j.brat.2009.06.010

Stacy, A, & Wiers, R.W., 2010. Implicit cognition and addiction: A tool for explaining paradoxical behavior. *Annual Review of Clinical Psychology, 6*, 551–575. https://doi.org/10.1146/annurev.clinpsy.121208.131444

Staub, E. (2011). Altruism born of suffering: The value of kindness [Web log post]. *Psychology Today.* https://www.psychologytoday.com/blog/in-the-garden-good-and-evil/201112/altruism-born-suffering

Staub, E., & Vollhardt, J. (2008). Altruism born of suffering: The roots of caring and helping after victimization and other trauma. *American Journal of Orthopsychiatry, 78(3)*, 267-80. doi: 10.1037/a0014223.

Stauffer, B. (2016). *Every 25 seconds: The human toll of criminalizing drug use in the United States.* https://www.hrw.org/report/2016/10/12/every-25-seconds/human-toll-criminalizing-drug-use-united-states

Steakley, L. (2013). How the brain processes trauma and why support, altruism can ease fear. *Stanford Medicine Scope.* https://scopeblog.stanford.edu/2013/04/16/how-the-brain-processes-trauma-and-why-support-altruism-can-ease-fear/

Steele, C. M. (1988). The psychology of self-affirmation: Sustaining the integrity of the self. In L. Berkowitz (Ed.), *Advances in experimental social psychology* (Vol. 21) (pp. 261-302). Academic Press.

Steele, C.M., & Liu, T.J. (1983). Dissonance processes as self-affirmation. *Journal of Personality and Social Psychology, 45(1)*, 5-19.

Stinckens, N., Lietaer, G., & Leijssen, M. (2013). Working with the inner critic: Process features and pathways to change. *Person-Centered & Experiential Psychotherapies, 12(1)*, 59-78, DOI: 10.1080/14779757.2013.767747

Stoeber, J. (2003). Self-pity: Exploring the links to personality, control beliefs, and anger. *Journal of Personality, 71(2)*, 183-220. https://doi.org/10.1111/1467-6494.7102004

Stoicea, N., Costa, A., Periel, L., Uribe, A., Weaver, T., & Bergese, S.D. (2019). Current perspectives on the opioid crisis in the US healthcare system. *Medicine, 98(20)*, e15425. doi: 10.1097/MD.0000000000015425

Substance Abuse and Mental Health Services Administration (SAMHSA). (1999). *Brief interventions and brief therapies for substance abuse.* Center for Substance Abuse Treatment. https://www.ncbi.nlm.nih.gov/books/NBK64947/

Substance Abuse and Mental Health Services Administration (SAMHSA). (2004). Chapter 2: Impact of substance abuse on families. *Treatment Improvement Protocol (TIP) Series, No. 39.* https://www.ncbi.nlm.nih.gov/books/NBK64258/

Substance Abuse and Mental Health Services Administration (SAMHSA). (2019). *Key substance use and mental health indicators in the United States: Results from the 2018 National Survey on Drug Use and Health.* https://www.samhsa.gov/data/sites/default/files/cbhsq-reports/NSDUHNationalFindingsReport2018/NSDUHNationalFindingsReport2018.pdf

Substance Abuse and Mental Health Services Administration (SAMHSA). (2009). Incorporating alcohol pharmacotherapies into medical practice Chapter 2 – acamprosate. *Treatment Improvement Protocol (TIP) Series, 49.* https://www.ncbi.nlm.nih.gov/books/NBK64035/

Substance Abuse and Mental Health Services Administration (SAMHSA) and National Institute on Alcohol Abuse (NIAA). (2015). *Medication for the treatment of alcohol use disorder: A brief guide.* HHS Publication No. (SMA) 15-4907. Rockville, MD: Substance Abuse and Mental Health Services Administration. https://store.samhsa.gov/sites/default/files/d7/priv/sma15-4907.pdf

Tang, S-H., & Hall, V.C. (1995). The overjustification effect: A meta-analysis. *Applied Cognitive Psychology, 9*, 365-404.

Tang, Y., Hölzel, B., & Posner, M. (2015). The neuroscience of mindfulness meditation. *Nature Reviews of Neuroscience, 16(4)*, 213–25. https://doi.org/10.1038/nrn3916

Tang, Y., & Leve, L. (2016). A translational neuroscience perspective on mindfulness meditation as a prevention strategy. *Translational Behavioral Medicine, 6(1)*, 63–72. https://doi.org/10.1007/s13142-015-0360-x

Tang, Y., Posner, M., Rothbart, M., & Volkow, N. (2015). Circuitry of self-control and its role in reducing addiction. *Trends in Cognitive Sciences, 19(8),* 439-444. https://doi.org/10.1016/j.tics.2015.06.007

Tang, Y., Tang, R., & Posner, M. (2013). Brief meditation induces smoking reduction. *Proceedings of the National Academy of Sciences, 110(34),* 13971-13975. DOI: 10.1073/pnas.1311887110

Tang, Y., Tang, R., & Posner, M. (2016). Mindfulness meditation improves emotion regulation and reduces drug abuse. *Drug and Alcohol Dependence, 163(Supp 1),* S13-S18. https://doi.org/10.1016/j.drugalcdep.2015.11.041

Tang, S-H., & Hall, V.C. (1995). The overjustification effect: A meta-analysis. *Applied Cognitive Psychology, 9,* 365-404.

Tanyi, R.A. (2002). Towards clarification of the meaning of spirituality. *Journal of Advanced Nursing, 39(5),* 500-509. https://doi.org/10.1046/j.1365-2648.2002.02315.x

Tartakovsky, M. (2018). Why ruminating is unhealthy and how to stop it [Web log post]. *PsychCentral.* https://psychcentral.com/blog/why-ruminating-is-unhealthy-and-how-to-stop/

Telles, S., Gerbarg, P., & Kozasa, E. (2015). Physiological effects of mind and body practices. *Biomedical Research International.* http://dx.doi.org/10.1155/2015/983086

Tesser, A. (2000). On the confluence of self-esteem maintenance mechanisms. *Personality and Social Psychology Review, 4(4),* 290-299.

The Self-Help Alliance (2010). *Building better boundaries.* https://www.ualberta.ca/anesthesiology-pain-medicine/media-library/documents/workbookbuilding-better-boundariesfeb2011.pdf

The Welland Tribune. (2019, Nov 18). Truck smashes through Wainfleet gas station in ATM heist. https://www.stcatharinesstandard.ca/news/crime/2019/11/18/truck-smashes-through-wainfleet-gas-station-in-atm-heist.html

Thoits, P.A., & Hewitt, L.N. (2001). Volunteer work and well-being. *Journal of Health and Social Behavior, 42(2),* 115–131. https://doi.org/10.2307/3090173

Thomsen, D.K. (2006). The association between rumination and negative affect: A review. *Cognition and Emotion, 20(8),* 1216-1235. DOI: 10.1080/02699930500473533

Tiffany, S.T., & Conklin, C.A. (2000). A cognitive processing model of alcohol craving and compulsive alcohol use. *Addiction, 95(8 Suppl 2),* 145-153. DOI:10.1080/09652140050111717

Toneatto, T. (1999). Metacognition and substance use. *Addictive Behaviors, 24(2),* 167–174.

Torregrossa, M.M., Corlett, P.R., & Taylor, J.R. (2011). Aberrant learning and memory in addiction. *Neurobiology of Learning and Memory, 96(4),* 609–623. https://doi.org/10.1016/j.nlm.2011.02.014

Trevisan, L.A., Boutros, N., Petrakis, I.L., & Krystal, J.H. (1998). Complications of alcohol withdrawal. *Pathophysiological Insights, 22(1),* 61-66.

Tsaousides, T. (2015). 7 things you need to know about fear [Web log post]. *Psychology Today.* https://www.psychologytoday.com/ca/blog/smashing-the-brainblocks/201511/7-things-you-need-know-about-fear

Tudor, K. (1996/2013). *Mental health promotion: Paradigms and practice.* Routledge.

Tuesta, L.M., & Zhang, Y. (2014). Epigenetic memory and addiction. *The Embo Journal, 33(10),* 1091-1103. DOI 10.1002/embj.201488106

Turrigiano, G.G. (1999). Homeostatic plasticity in neuronal networks: The more things change, the more they stay the same. *Trends in Neuroscience, 22,* 221–227.

Umberson, D., & Montez, J. K. (2010). Social relationships and health: A flashpoint for health policy. *Journal of Health and Social Behavior, 51(Suppl),* S54–S66. doi:10.1177/0022146510383501

United Nations International Narcotic Control Board (INCB). (2011). *Narcotic drugs: Estimated world requirements for 2012 and statistics for 2010.* https://www.incb.org/documents/Narcotic-Drugs/Technical-Publications/2011/Part_FOUR_Comments_NAR-Report-2011_English.pdf

U.S. Centers for Medicare & Medicaid Services (HealthCare.gov). (n.d.). *Mental health & substance abuse coverage.*

https://www.healthcare.gov/coverage/mental-health-substance-abuse-coverage/

U.S. Department of Health & Human Services. (2019). Mental health and substance use disorders. *MentalHealth.gov*. https://www.mentalhealth.gov/what-to-look-for/mental-health-substance-use-disorders

Vanderplasschen, W., Yates, R., & Miovský, M. (2017). Bridging the gap between research and practice in therapeutic communities (TCs) for addictions. *Journal of Groups in Addiction & Recovery, 12(2-3)*, 63-67. DOI: 10.1080/1556035X.2017.1331598

van der Schier, R., Roozekrans, M., van Velzen, M., Dahan, A., & Niesters, M. (2014). Opioid-induced respiratory depression: Reversal by non-opioid drugs. *F1000 Prime Reports, 6*, 79. https://doi.org/10.12703/P6-79

van Niekerk, B. (2018). Religion and spirituality: What are the fundamental differences? *HTS Theological Studies, 74(3)*, 1-11. https://dx.doi.org/10.4102/hts.v74i3.4933

van Osch, Y., Zeelenberg, M., & Breugelmans, S.M. (2018). The self and others in the experience of pride. *Cognition and Emotion, 32(2)*, 404-413. DOI: 10.1080/02699931.2017.1290586

Verdejo-García, A., Bechara, A., Recknor, E., & Pérez-García, M. (2006). Executive dysfunction in substance dependent individuals during drug use and abstinence: An examination of the behavioral, cognitive and emotional correlates of addiction. *Journal of the International Neuropsychological Society, 12*, 405–415. DOI: 10.10170S1355617706060486

Verdejo-García, A., & Perez-Garcia, M. (2008). Substance abusers' self-awareness of the neurobehavioral consequences of addiction. *Psychiatry Research, 158(2)*, 172-180. https://doi.org/10.1016/j.psychres.2006.08.001

Volkow, N.D., Baler, R.D., Compton, W.M., & Weiss, S.R. (2014). Adverse health effects of marijuana use. *The New England Journal of Medicine, 370(23)*, 2219–2227. https://doi.org/10.1056/NEJMra1402309

Volkow, N.D., & Koob, G. (2015). Brain disease model of addiction: Why is it so controversial? *The Lancet: Psychiatry, 2(8)*, 677–679. https://doi.org/10.1016/S2215-0366(15)00236-9

Vollhardt, J.R. (2009). Altruism born of suffering and prosocial behavior following adverse life events: A review and conceptualization. *Social Justice Research, 22(1)*, 53-97. doi:10.1007/s11211-009-0088-1

Vollhardt, J. R., & Staub, E. (2011). Inclusive altruism born of suffering: The relationship between adversity and prosocial attitudes and behavior toward disadvantaged outgroups. *American Journal of Orthopsychiatry, 81*(3), 307–315. https://doi.org/10.1111/j.1939-0025.2011.01099.x

von der Goltz, C., & Kiefer, F. (2009). Learning and memory in the aetiopathogenesis of addiction: Future implications for therapy? *European Archives of Psychiatry and Clinical Neuroscience, 259*, 183. https://doi.org/10.1007/s00406-009-0057-6

Voss, P., Thomas, M., Cisneros-Franco, J., & de Villers-Sidani, É. (2017). Dynamic brains and the changing rules of neuroplasticity: Implications for learning and recovery. *Frontiers in Psychology, 8*, 1657. https://doi.org/10.3389/fpsyg.2017.01657

Wakeman, S.E., Larochelle, M.R., Ameli, O., Chaisson, C.E., McPheeters, J.T., Crown, W.H., Azocar, F., et al. (2020). Comparative effectiveness of different treatment pathways for opioid use disorder. *Journal of the American Medical Association, 3(2)*, e1920622. doi:10.1001/jamanetworkopen.2019.20622

Walach, H., & Reich, K.H. (2005). Reconnecting science and spirituality: Toward overcoming a taboo. *Zygon, 40(2)*, 423-441.

Wang, S., Lilienfeld, S., & Rochat, P. (2019). Schadenfreude deconstructed and reconstructed: A tripartite motivational model. *New Ideas in Psychology, 52*, 1-11. DOI: 10.1016/j.newideapsych.2018.09.002

Warren, R. (2012). *The purpose driven life.* Zondervan.

Watson, P., de Wit, S., Hommel, B., & Wiers, R. (2012). Motivational mechanisms and outcome expectancies underlying the approach bias toward addictive substances. *Frontiers in Psychology.* https://doi.org/10.3389/fpsyg.2012.00440

Wegela, K. (2010). How to practice mindfulness meditation. *Psychology Today*. https://www.psychologytoday.com/ca/blog/the-courage-be-present/201001/how-practice-mindfulness-meditation

Weidman, A., Cheng, J., & Tracy, J. (2018). The psychological structure of humility. *Journal of Personality and Social Psychology, 114(1),* 153-178. http://dx.doi.org/10.1037/pspp0000112

Weiner, B. (1992). *Human Motivation: Metaphors, Theories and Research*. Sage Publications.

Weiner, B. (2000). Intrapersonal and interpersonal theories of motivation from an attributional perspective. *Educational Psychology Review, 12(1),* 1-14.

Weinstein, A., & Cox, W. (2006). Cognitive processing of drug-related stimuli: The role of memory and attention. *Journal of Psychopharmacology, 20(6),* 850–859. doi: 10.1177/0269881106061116

Weir, K. (2017). Forgiveness can improve mental and physical health. *American Psychological Association Continuing Education, 48(1),* 30. https://www.apa.org/monitor/2017/01/ce-corner

Weiss, H.M., & Knight, P.A. (1980). The utility of humility: Self-esteem, information search, and problem-solving efficiency. *Organizational Behavior & Human Performance, 25(2),* 216–223. https://doi.org/10.1016/0030-5073(80)90064-1

Wenk-Sormaz, H. (2005). Meditation can reduce habitual responding. *Alternative Therapies in Health and Medicine, 11,* 42–58. https://pdfs.semanticscholar.org/99f2/9a5f6f4277d98a582cc50e9b4490f7e2442b.pdf

Wheeler, S.B. (2010). Effects of self-esteem and academic performance on adolescent decision-making: An examination of early sexual intercourse and illegal substance use. *Journal of Adolescent Health, 47,* 582–590. doi:10.1016/j.jadohealth.2010.04.009

Whelan, P.J., & Remski, K. (2012). Buprenorphine vs. methadone treatment: A review of evidence in both developed and developing worlds. *Journal of Neurosciences in Rural Practice, 3(1),* 45–50. https://doi.org/10.4103/0976-3147.91934

White, N.M. (1996). Addictive drugs as reinforcers: Multiple partial actions on memory systems. *Addiction, 91(7)*, 921–950. doi: 10.1111/j.1360-0443.1996.tb03586.x

White, A.M., Signer, M.L., Kraus, C.L., & Swartzwelder, H.S. (2004). Experiential aspects of alcohol-induced blackouts among college students. *The American Journal of Drug and Alcohol Abuse, 30(1)*, 205–224. https://doi.org/10.1081/ADA-120029874

Whittington, B., & Scher, S. (2010). Prayer and subjective well-being: An examination of six different types of prayer. *The International Journal for the Psychology of Religion, 20*, 59-68. https://doi.org/10.1080/10508610903146316

Wiers, C., Gladwin, T., Ludwig, V., Gropper, S., Stuke, H., Gawron, C., et al. (2017). Comparing three cognitive biases for alcohol cues in alcohol dependence. *Alcohol and Alcoholism, 52(2)*, 242–248. doi: 10.1093/alcalc/agw063

Wild, L.G., Flisher, A.J., Bhana, A., & Lombard, C. (2004). Associations among adolescent risk behaviours and self-esteem in six domains. *Journal of Child Psychology and Psychiatry 45(8)*, 1454–1467. doi: 10.1111/j.1469-7610.2004.00330.x

Williams, K.M.B. (1985). Self-awareness theory and decision theory: A theoretical and empirical integration [Doctoral dissertation]. *Retrospective Theses and Dissertations*, 7895. https://lib.dr.iastate.edu/rtd/7895

Williams, L.A., & DeSteno, D. (2009). Pride: Adaptive social emotion or seventh sin? *Psychological Science, 20(3)*, 284–288. doi: 10.1111/j.1467-9280.2009.02292.x

Williams, L.A., & DeSteno, D. (2008). Pride and perseverance: The motivational function of pride. *Journal of Personality and Social Psychology. 94(6)*, 1007–1017. doi: 10.1037/0022-3514.94.6.1007.

Wilson, N., Kariisa, M., Seth, P., Smith, H., & Davis, N.L. (2020). Drug and opioid-involved overdose deaths — United States, 2017–2018. *MMWR Morbidity and Mortality Weekly Report, 69*, 290–297. DOI: http://dx.doi.org/10.15585/mmwr.mm6911a4external icon

Winch, G. (2014). The key difference between pride and arrogance [Web log post]. *Psychology Today.*

https://www.psychologytoday.com/ca/blog/the-squeaky-wheel/201407/the-key-difference-between-pride-and-arrogance

Winters, K.C., & Arria, A. (2011). Adolescent brain development and drugs. *The Prevention Researcher, 18(2)*, 21–24.

Winters, K.C., & Lee, C.Y. (2008). Likelihood of developing an alcohol and cannabis use disorder during youth: Association with recent use and age. *Drug and Alcohol Dependence, 92(1-3)*, 239–247. https://doi.org/10.1016/j.drugalcdep.2007.08.005

Wong, Y.I., Stanton, M.C., & Sands, R.D. (2014). Rethinking social inclusion: Experiences of persons in recovery from mental illness. *American Journal of Orthopsychiatry, 84(6)*, 685–695. http://dx.doi.org/10.1037/ort0000034

Woodward, C., & Joseph, S. (2003). Positive change processes and post-traumatic growth in people who have experienced childhood abuse: Understanding vehicles of change. *Psychology and Psychotherapy, 76*(Pt 3), 267–283. https://doi.org/10.1348/147608303322362497

World Health Organization (WHO). (1994). Assessment of fracture risk and its application to screening for postmenopausal osteoporosis: Report of a WHO study group. *WHO Technical Report Series, 843*, 1-129. https://pubmed.ncbi.nlm.nih.gov/7941614/

Wright, J.C., Nadelhoffer, T., Perini, T., Langville, T., Echols, M., & Venezia, K. (2017). The psychological significance of humility. *The Journal of Positive Psychology, 12(1)*, 3-12. doi: 10.1080/17439760.2016.1167940

Wubben, M.J., De Cremer, D., & van Dijk, E. (2012). Is pride a prosocial emotion? Interpersonal effects of authentic and hubristic pride. *Cognition & Emotions, 26(6)*, 1084-1097. doi:10.1080/02699931.2011.646956

Yang, C., Zhou, Y., Cao, Q., Xia, M., & An, J. (2019). The relationship between self-control and self-efficacy among patients with substance use disorders: Resilience and self-esteem as mediators. *Frontiers in Psychiatry, 10*, 388. doi: 10.3389/fpsyt.2019.00388

Young, M., DeLorenzi, L. & Cunningham, L. (2011). Using meditation in addiction counseling. *Journal of Addictions & Offender Counseling, 32*, 58-71. doi:10.1002/j.2161-1874.2011.tb00207.x

Zeidan, F., Martucci, K., Kraft, R., Gordon, N., McHaffie, J., & Coghill, R. (2011). Brain mechanisms supporting modulation of pain by mindfulness meditation. *The Journal of Neuroscience, 31(14)*, 5540–5548. http://doi.org/10.1523/JNEUROSCI.5791-10.2011

Zemore, S. (2007). A role for spiritual change in the benefits of 12-step involvement. *Alcoholism: Clinical & Experimental Research, 31(S3)*, 76S–79S. DOI: 10.1111/j.1530-0277.2007.00499.x

Zemore, S.E., & Pagano, M.E. (2008). Kickbacks from helping others: Health and recovery. *Recent Developments in Alcoholism, 18*, 141–166. https://doi.org/10.1007/978-0-387-77725-2_9

Zgierska, A., Rabago, D., Zuelsdorff, M., Coe, C., Miller, M., & Fleming, M. (2008). Mindfulness meditation for alcohol relapse prevention: A feasibility pilot study. *Journal of Addiction Medicine, 2(3)*, 165–173. doi: 10.1097/ADM.0b013e31816f8546.

Zhang, M., Ying, J., Wing, T., Song, G., Fung, D., & Smith, H. (2018b). Cognitive biases in cannabis, opioid, and stimulant disorders: A systematic review. *Frontiers in Psychology*. https://doi.org/10.3389/fpsyt.2018.00376

Zoellner, T., & Maercker, A. (2006). Posttraumatic growth in clinical psychology - a critical review and introduction of a two component model. *Clinical Psychology Review, 26(5)*, 626–653. https://doi.org/10.1016/j.cpr.2006.01.008

Zubaran, C., Fernandes, J.G., & Rodnight, R. (1997). Wernicke-Korsakoff syndrome. *British Medical Journal Postgraduate Medical Journal, 73*, 27-31. https://doi.org/10.1136/pgmj.73.855.27

Zucker, D.M., Dion, K., & McKeever, R.P. (2014). Concept clarification of grief in mothers of children with an addiction. *Journal of Advanced Nursing, 71(4)*, 751–767. doi: 10.1111/jan.12591